Hipparchia's Choice

HIPPARCHIA'S CHOICE

An Essay Concerning Women, Philosophy, etc.

MICHÈLE LE DŒUFF

translated by
TRISTA SELOUS

BLACKWELL
Oxford UK & Cambridge MA

Copyright © Les éditions du Seuil, 1989, 1990

First published in 1989 as *L'Etude et le rouet* by Les
Editions du Seuil
This edition published 1991

Basil Blackwell Ltd
108 Cowley Road, Oxford, OX4 1JF, UK

Basil Blackwell, Inc.
3 Cambridge Center
Cambridge, Massachusetts 02142, USA

British Library Cataloguing in Publication Data
A CIP catalogue record for this book is available from the British Library.

Library of Congress Cataloging in Publication Data
Le Dœuff, Michèle.
    [Etude et le rouet. English]
    Hipparchia's choice: an essay concerning women, philosophy, etc.
/ Michéle Le Dœuff: translated by Trista Selous.
        p.   cm.
    Translation of: L'étude et le rouet.
    Includes index.
    ISBN 0-631-17639-X (hardback) — ISBN 0-631-17641-1
(pbk.)
    1. Feminist theory.   2. Philosophy.   I. Title.
HO1208.L43   1991
305.42'01—dc20   90-9603
                                                                      CIP

The new translation of selected extracts from *Le Deuxième Sexe* by Simone de
Beauvoir appears by kind permission of the publishers, Jonathan Cape.

Typeset in 10½ on 12 pt Baskerville
by Graphicraft Typesetters Ltd, Hong Kong
Printed in Great Britain by T.J. Press Ltd, Padstow, Cornwall

Contents

Translator's Note   vii

Author's Note   xi

First Notebook   1

Second Notebook   55

Third Notebook   135

Fourth Notebook   211

Notes   317

Index   357

Translator's Note

This translation owes a great deal to the close involvement of the author, Michèle Le Dœuff. I am also indebted to Graeme Leonard and to Colin Gordon, whose translation of Michèle Le Dœuff's article 'The public employer' I have freely plundered for section 5 of the Fourth Notebook.

T.S.

A single sentence was enough for Hipparchia to sum up the situation of women in relation to philosophy: 'I have used for the getting of knowledge all the time which, because of my sex, I was supposed to waste at the loom.'

This was twenty-four centuries ago. Had she been asked to give an account of herself? The story is not so subtle. Some joker lost for an answer to an argument put forward by this Thracian philosopher thought it apposite to criticize her for neglecting the housework. To back up his critique, he even went so far as to lift her skirt. In his book Lives and Opinions of Eminent Philosophers, *Diogenes Laertius devotes a respectful passage to Hipparchia, praising the way she remained calm on this occasion.*

Author's Note

Discretion is obligatory when one slips into the room where a doctoral viva is being held. Indeed Sorbford University has inherited from its British past the conviction that such things should not be public at all. Its French past, on the other hand, has instilled into it the certainty that only silent witnesses lacking the faculty of memory may legitimately be present at this delicate moment in someone's life. Their role will be to give a friendly pat on the back afterwards to this small woman who is presently perched on a chair like a nervous bird and defending a thesis on Kant weighing several kilos. Opposite her on the platform is a long desk covered with a heavy-looking material, like brocade. Behind this desk sit five gentlemen all in a row; these are the panel of examiners. One of them is speaking at this moment and, indisputably, he can see her. Can she see him? Is she allowing herself to observe the shape of his chin, of his ears and hands? Has she even noticed the slightly odd tone of his voice, which is saying, 'Madame, in your bibliography you have omitted to cite Nabert! How, Madame, could you have forgotten Nabert? Nabert whose fine Kantian beard everyone remembers. And when I speak of Nabert's Kantian beard (pause), I do not mean "a fine beard like Kant's" (pause), for like everyone else I know that Kant was cleanshaven. I simply mean that all the great commentators on Kant have always worn fine patriarchal beards like Nabert's.'

Addressed to all, this book is particularly dedicated to those young women preparing to enter a world where it will be held against them that they do not belong to the side of the Almighty, and thus that they believe and spread the belief that intelligence lies elsewhere.

This first volume examines a few of the misadventures of this intelligence, such as the fact that, in the writings of a man philosopher, 'woman' may be no more nor less than a word for a foil whose role is to guarantee the philosopher's 'greatness' by contrast.

When sexism underpins the very method by which a system of thought is established (the example of existentialism will illustrate this hypothesis), how can we conceive of a method for a feminist philosophy, or for a philosophy which will allow men and women to come together in a common task? On the horizon of this inquiry lie a simple desire for a community of both sexes and a search for the practical and theoretical conditions which might make it possible to fulfil that hope. At the very least its intention is to identify some obstacles.

A second volume will compare the man-philosopher to Mr Everyman by noting their shared concern with the chastity of girls, the fidelity of wives and well-ordered fertility. Such concerns have also produced some great philosophical delusions, and there is no reason to believe that we have seen the last of these.

Without things having been really planned that way, the first volume has a lot to say about Simone de Beauvoir while the second aims to demonstrate the full importance of the thinking of Mary Wollstonecraft, the English philosopher of the French Revolution. Two women with two very different lives, two different frameworks of thought which are both equally important to us. Should we not ask them both to participate in the founding of Sorbford, Florheidelbridge and Amsterlona University in Saint-Denis? Since we are moving towards Europe in any case, intellectually as in other ways, it would be most unwise to leave our new-born community with nothing but godfathers who are more than happy to be all men together. Imagining what these heirs of Hegel (who describes women as the enemy within), of Tocqueville (who thinks it not such a bad thing for them to be sad), of Vivès (who approves of those who deprive women of shoes so that they have to stay at home) and of Samuel Johnson (who compares women who speak in public to dancing poodles) might be capable of doing with all of us, men and women, if we leave all the decision making to them is definitely a cause for serious anxiety.

'Europe? But weren't you supposed to be telling us about women and philosophy?'

'No philosophical thought is self-contained. Because it cannot stick to its programme, it proceeds by detours, lateral explorations and assorted digressions, including some related to contemporary life. There is no thinking which does not wander, and any serious work should have etc. in its title and honestly state that it will not stick to the topic. Saying what there is to say about women and philosophy requires discussions of many other issues. But any woman can take

Hipparchia's short cut and say that Time, of which we all have a meagre measure, is either wasted or pleasantly employed: whatever our sex, we can all be sure of that.'

As for those men and women whom I should like to thank, 'there are so many of you that it is impossible to name you all individually, and it would be shameful to leave anyone out', as Cicero said to those who brought him back from exile. I hope that in this book you will see the love of life with which you inspire me. A debt greater than words can say is sweet indeed. And then I could not write here what one so often reads elsewhere: 'Lastly, I should like to thank my wife, who typed the seven successive versions of my manuscript; who so graciously agreed that I should spend a great deal of my time abroad for my research; who helped me by reading a great number of general works for me, including some in the Bibliothèque Nationale; my dear wife, whose good humour has been my constant support; occasionally bringing me back to the level of daily life was not the least of her virtues and contributions to my work.'

As Virginia Woolf said, the truer the facts the better the fiction: I beg the reader to note that no similarity between the fruits of my imagination and real situations is accidental.

First Notebook

which makes a problem out of everything

which is scattered into different considerations in an attempt to assess the current state of things; which was nearly a preface; which is ultimately neither a foreword nor a methodological essay, but promises to shed some light on the difficulty, when one is a woman, a philosopher and a feminist, of speaking.

The desire to see philosophy continue: this is something that preoccupies us all. Yet have we thought ill enough of this discipline that we love? I do not exclude myself. On occasion I have maintained that this discourse which claims to understand everything better than any other is a mode of phantasmagorical hegemony; all the same, in it I saw my road to freedom.

Together we all complain, equally incoherently, that philosophy is in a state of stagnation, and yet we would find it very difficult to account for our regrets. What sort of philosophy, exactly, do we want to bring back? Which of today's issues that need urgent understanding can be dealt with only by philosophy? What object is waiting for our attention? What common hope can philosophy hold? We do not know how to answer these questions, but we are all sorry together, we who would no doubt become opponents tomorrow if a bit of philosophy were to be reborn and, with it, the beginnings of answers to these questions.

Given this, we might as well refuse to regard the various problems relating to the self-justification of philosophy as necessary preliminaries. Is there a desire to think philosophically which cannot explain itself? Let us take it as it is, partly in shadow. If this imposes a new limit on the project to 'understand everything', that limit can be accepted as such; if the limit is an old and indeed natural one, but one which has long gone unnoticed, accepting it is simply an act of lucidity. Philosophers have always claimed to know the source of their desire to think philosophically, or the desire for philosophical thought which passed through them. And at our school desks we repeated that philosophy *is* through its ability to account for itself and all the rest. If we now find ourselves unable to maintain a sufficiently self-grounding or specular discourse, let us leave such preoccupations to one side. We shall see what this decision will give rise to.

For if we knew exactly what hope philosophy held, today as yesterday, then everything would be simple. We would put it in the category of good things. And there is no reason – other than those of the tyrant – to exclude anyone from access to good things who has a taste for them. It would therefore be extremely unjust that women who might have had a penchant for philosophy have long been kept away from it. It would all be really simple. But since I cannot honestly maintain this general argument, all I can do is merely take note of this taste or whim that some men and women have for philosophical thinking. And it is a whim, in all cases, since no one today can justify their involvement in research whose very object escapes us.

If on the other hand we knew quite certainly that philosophy fell into the category of tyrannical discourses – a hypothesis which can never be ruled out in advance, in relation to any discourse – then we should merely need to invite everyone to scorn all those involved in it indiscriminately. Philosophy is like military life: either you think it is a good thing, and in that case you should be pleased to see women in West Point and the other military academies, or you think it despicable and support conscientious objectors.

1   On women, philosophy and feminism

In the preface to *The Phenomenology of Mind*, Hegel describes what he considers a preface to be: it is a text which begins 'by explaining the end an author had in mind, the circumstances which gave rise to the work, and the relation in which the writer takes it to stand to other treatises on the same subject.'[1] He adds that such an explanation is unsuited to philosophical work, for it merely leads to a stream of scattered propositions and gratuitous statements, which he considers deplorable from all points of view. On the subject in which I hope to interest my readers – women and philosophy – we shall have to follow the opposite principle, starting with scattered thoughts and proceeding by twists and turns. For the question is extremely difficult to broach and, when we go into it more deeply, obliges us to take account of widely differing factors.

One reason for this difficulty lies in the fact that whatever the 'woman question' may consist of (and the fact that we are obliged to speak of it so vaguely is already significant), it always presents itself to the conscious mind as the question-which-has-already-obviously-been-settled. If we wanted to start methodically, we should have to prove even before we began that the question has contemporary importance and is certainly important enough to make it worth a few hours of effort. I wonder if this would convince anyone who is not already convinced. For of course everyone is ready to agree that a short time ago (say the day before yesterday) women were unjustly kept away from a great number of interesting things, and everyone is quite amazed at the social system of that time, which imposed all sorts of vexations upon them – useless things like wearing a corset – and maintained forms of discrimination without rhyme or reason against them with an obstinacy which, looking back, seems disproportionate. How strange it is that for a century and a half the French Republic refused to allow our foremothers to benefit from the principles of the French Revolution, even though the *sans-culottes* wanted to export those principles to the whole world! Of course, from time to time over that century and a half, someone – an author, a little group of women who were activists or writers, or a political party – thought about this anomaly, sometimes as a challenge to a particular situation, sometimes with great determination, sometimes with little hope of being heard and sometimes out of pure opportunism.[2] After the First World War those who wanted to isolate the conservative right found it a fine question to raise in Parliament; but nothing ever came of it.[3] After the Liberation the matter was settled, and since there were no earthquakes as a result, we may indeed wonder why the Republic took so long to extend citizens' rights to women. Why such reluctance for so long? Still, since it has been sorted out now, there is no point ruminating on past wrongs.

Many women feel resentful whenever any question related to the 'position of women' is raised in their presence, as though they suspected they were being dragged down again. Might not this reopening of a problem which no longer exists be an attempt to put them back in the psychological position of inferiority suffered by earlier generations of women? At the very least might there not be an unintended risk that they will be weighed down by a past which should not be theirs and loaded with the mental blocks of a now outdated situation? And decent men (the others hardly count) also feel attacked, thinking that they are being reproached with the sins of their grandfathers. The particular question of women's position within the enterprise of philosophy gives rise to this kind of irritation, as does any raising of 'the woman question', especially because it is so particular.

Or perhaps, to convince people that the question is not at all settled, one should set out an array of shocking images and other horrors (they are easy to find), just as others begin their books by having the chill wind of the Gulag blow across the first page. My reasons for not adopting such an approach to my subject are not all moral or aesthetic: the immediate effect of intellectual terrorism is to block intelligence, starting with that of the writer. So there are also elementary intellectual reasons for doing without it.

'I have long hesitated to write a book on woman. The subject is irritating, especially to women, and it is not new. Enough ink has been spilled in quarrelling over feminism, and now the discussion is more or less closed. Let us say no more about it. It is still talked about, however, and the voluminous nonsense uttered during the last century does not seem to have cast much light on the problem. Besides, is there a problem? And if so, what is it?' wrote a perplexed author in 1949. These are the first lines of *The Second Sex*. Lines expressive of a deep confusion, for anyone who wants to listen to what they have to say, and that is what I propose to do.

For people are surprised, some forty years later. In 1949, problems abounded and were far from settled. Could one not go straight to the heart of the matter at that time? In those days there was no freedom of contraception or abortion, for, among other things, a certain French law, passed in 1920 and banning even publicity about contraception, was in force.[4] It still is, by the way. The state used it to raise the birthrate by making women's fertility its own property, leaving them no possibility of choice. This lack of freedom, which was scandalous in itself, gave rise to a great many real-life tragedies. Here was something that could and should have indicated that there was still an unacceptable problem somewhere. So why did she hesitate? Was it because the boundary was imperceptible between the heart of this matter, which had to be approached, and the howl of one who is wounded to the heart, which must always be held back if one is to write? But reciprocally, in forbidding oneself to complain and cry out, does one not always run the risk of failing to express what is most important?

Simone de Beauvoir's subjective position in writing those lines is real, and it corresponds to what we still feel – which will seem surprising in forty years' time. When it comes to writing, even on the limited topic I am dealing with – women in the theoretical enterprise – I feel a strange difficulty, which is doubtless of a psychological nature, but which also appears in a theoretical mode, so hard is it to pose the problem or problems at the outset, so hard is it not immediately to lose hold of all their complexity.

I have chosen to confront this discomfort and to give the reasons one might have for not writing this book, for writing a different one, or none at all and for stating that there is no problem. This method is an attempt to break down the obstacles as far as possible and to ensure that my thinking retains a certain element of doubt with regard to itself. This doubt could take us anywhere, but it will in all probability be to a more distant or a different place from the one we would be led to by a proclamation of the existence and importance of the subject under discussion.

The first intellectual obstacle relates to the idea I have already mentioned that there is a radical discontinuity between the past and the present, a discontinuity made greater by disproportion. If we consider the classical pantheon, the familiar band of 'great philosophers', we shall find that it is a masculine community, and quite crushingly so: it seems entirely masculine and, moreover, openly content to be such. It is only a small step from this observation to conclude that philosophical rationality is essentially masculine and some people, both men and women, have taken that step. On the other hand, if we look at the present time, we are within our rights to conclude that there is no longer a problem here. Nothing prevents a young woman from studying philosophy and then producing philosophical works. What is the point, therefore, in going over and over an outdated question and talking about what happened the day before yesterday? We could even propose a formal argument: reason is the most impersonal thing in the world; philosophical works are works of reason; could we not therefore now talk about something else? Particularly since by digging a bit one can find at least fifty women philosophers among the Greeks.[5]

The second block is also one of disproportion. Women's access to philosophy cannot be regarded as a high priority in the movement towards women's liberation; it only concerns or would only ever concern a very small number of people. Why should anyone be interested in so localized and indeed so marginal a problem, a plea for one's own cause, a strictly corporatist matter? However, when one considers the tense way in which so many men philosophers have taken care to see that no women entered the domain they regarded as theirs, how they still take care, when they can, to ensure that we feel we have no legitimate place there, that we have got in by accident, by mistake, by smashing the door down, thanks to patronage or as supernumeraries, in brief that we are not really there, when one sees how they have graciously provided and still provide the common ideology with themes or models representing the intellectual inferiority of women, how they have, at least apparently, grounded in reason the vocations that social life assigns to us anyway, or how they have theorized a solid basis for an entirely domestic life for the 'other sex', one is unavoidably driven to the conclusion that this is an enormity which has yet to be thought through and changed.

So the question seems insignificant and thus irritating; and yet, as soon as a woman thinks she is able to guarantee herself equal legitimacy in philosophical life, formidable resistances are deployed, often with unexpected crudity. This type of paradox is well known to anyone who has looked in any detail at any aspect of women's position. It's nothing, and yet . . . So little would be required to make life more pleasant, and yet one comes up against fierce opposition. It has all been over since about the day before yesterday, and yet I experienced it just this instant. But if you say that you experienced it just this instant, you will be told that you are making a lot of fuss about nothing. You will tell yourself that.

The situation of anyone who wants to write about such a subject can be described as a sort of double bind, or indeed as a scourge – a double agony – at any rate as far as the relevance of one's project is concerned, or the judgements one can make of one's own desires and will. Obviously I have always wanted to see women, of whom I am one, happily producing philosophical work. Does this mean I am sure that philosophy is something absolutely good, so that it is a pity – and most unjust – that it is refused to us? Does it mean that I can establish its value absolutely? No, and I have already admitted as much. In that case, why demand for oneself and others something whose intellectual and existential worth is not entirely certain?

Here one can begin to answer: it is precisely when philosophers undertake to give the value of their own efforts a theoretical basis that they start to drift off into myth. So we shall not lose much by leaving this question unanswered. Until now, self-justification has occupied a very great place in the preoccupations of my colleagues and has even tainted their freedom of thought, by rigidly keeping their thinking moving in a particular direction. What value can there be in philosophical thinking about politics, if it is understood from the outset that the conclusion will be that it is the vocation of philosophers to govern? How can one take thought about life, death and happiness seriously when the thinker has already got the good old concept of wisdom up his sleeve, in other words the idea that the practice of philosophy is enough to ensure a good life and to prevent fear of death? Everything can gradually become distorted by the corporatist imperative, which is often implicit but always categorical: think what you like, but in the end your words must once more reaffirm the value of philosophy. At least that of your own philosophy.

I cannot decide where I stand in relation to such a claim. After all, it is never certain that any thinking, even of a philosophical nature, has no pertinence. However, when I feel the difficulty of grasping, and then of conceptualizing the 'woman question', the question of women both in general and in philosophy, I have to conclude that this question cannot be integrated into our received frameworks of thinking, be it everyday thinking or that developed by philosophy. Such considerations lead me to wonder if all thinking might not be built on the rejection of a certain number of realities, of which that is one.

One can indeed advance the hypothesis that any intellectual construction proceeds from, among other things, a desire not to know about, understand or acknowledge forms of conflict, from an assumed indifference with regard to tragic situations, from an attempt to erect a wall of apathy. Reading Aristotle, we find support for such a notion: in the middle of his demonstration concerning happiness (a demonstration in which it is of course explained that theoretical activity is the most able to procure happiness), Aristotle indicates, as if in passing, that no one imagines that a slave can experience happiness, because in that case one would have to 'attribute a human existence to him too', something which is obviously impossible. According to Aristotle, the slave is an animated instrument and his life derives from that of his master. What are we to make of this philosophy which did not want to perceive slaves as human beings who were being made to suffer injustice? And what else did it refuse to perceive? And yet if every form of culture, be it popular or intellectual, undertakes to ignore anything that might cause it too many problems, what are we doing here? Retrospection is very disturbing: now that slavery has been abolished, here at least, we can see Aristotle's shocking blindness.[6] But there is no reason why we should think ourselves any wiser than he was, or should assume that we have any more direct a grasp of the difficulties than Simone de Beauvoir. Supposing today there were things as terrible as slavery that escaped our notice? As sinister as the thousands of unwanted pregnancies and the mass slaughter caused by backstreet abortions?[7]

On the threshold of my thinking about the relations between women and philosophy, I want to abandon the question of the value of theoretical work and to ask my reader to accept, at least as an experiment, a method whose rationality is limited or loose. Instead of wanting to justify our project at all costs, we can admit that an element of non-knowledge unavoidably inhabits any undertaking, including a philosophical one. Instead of always pushing questions as far as they will go, it is sometimes permissible to leave them halfway. Rather than trying to prove everything, we can allow beliefs, opinions and experiences to express themselves as such. However, the innovation of this lies less in the procedure than in the presentation: no philosophy has ever provided a theoretical basis for everything or proved everything it assumes, unless it be in appearance, and appearance has played more than one trick on theoretical work itself. So we might as well do away with false windows that lend symmetry and with illusory self-justifications.

I am convinced (there! she's started already!) that this recognition of the always incomplete and limited character of philosophical effort has advantages, if only that of the hope of finding a new way of thinking philosophically, a way which, unlike so many others, would not be hegemonic. Once we stop trying radically to justify a project from its roots to its ultimate effects, part-objects abound. I hope here to give a few examples of these. There are some questions on which philosophical discourse can become affirmative again, and others where it can return to the elation of a critical approach.

2   Riding my hobby horse: from fool to philosopher

Elation. There we are again, you will say to me. The self-justification of the project may not be a preliminary, but it comes along the way just the same. Inevitably, no doubt, but why should we seek asceticism and want desire to be fulfilled without pleasure? We can give up thinking about the value of philosophy, in advance and even in retrospect, without this meaning we must forbid ourselves to acknowledge something we know through ordinary or obscure experience, although not through any developed theory, in this case that the exercise of thought is sometimes a very joyful, or at least ordinarily pleasant activity. In any case, that is my position: the desire to philosophize imposed itself on me with unfailing clarity, without bringing promises of salvation; it has withstood all difficulties, and indeed sometimes in the form of disappointed love, for disappointment arises all the time. However, I have gained enough pleasure from it to think that making my living reading, teaching and writing philosophy is the finest job in the world, and I say this with all due naivety.

It is impossible to see how such a desire can be rationalized or deduced from an essence of philosophy of such great value that one would be conquered on first perceiving it and would decide to devote all one's energy to it. The origins of my taste are known to me only in the contingency of my autobiography. When I was still a child I developed a passion for Shakespeare, and especially for the characters of the fools. I wanted to be Feste, or the nameless Fool of King Lear when I grew up. Then I realized that life is not as well written as it would have been if Shakespeare had taken charge of it; it is very grey and there is no place in it for a fool. Besides, Shakespeare's fools are all men. This is a strange thing, in an author who often portrays women characters disguised as men. Viola passes for a page in this way, Portia for a lawyer and Rosalind for an older brother. They are all very 'wise' and often praised as such; none of them is a 'clown', that is to say, they are not 'corrupters of words', although Feste explains that foolery is an omnipresent thing that 'does walk about the orb like the sun, it shines everywhere.'[8] So Shakespeare played on sexual identity to the maximum, but he could not go so far as to imagine a certain form of comic utterance spoken by a female character. The two 'Merry Wives of Windsor' are certainly jokers, but they are not given the subversive speech of the Fool.[9]

I gave up my first vocation. Some years later I began to read philosophy; it seemed to me very close to the language of fools and, marvel of marvels, it was a way of speaking that existed on this earth: there are no longer any Fools in real life, but it would seem that there are still philosophers around. And women are not kept out of the business; indeed it is even a compulsory subject for all students in their last year at any French lycée, so I was about to be required to carry out my apprenticeship. Blessed obligation which removed all risk of being forbidden!

Looking back it seems to me that what had seduced me in the Shakespearian characters was already philosophy. With their sarcastic and corrosive utterances, their unseasonable taste for truth without pomposity, their corruption of words and their art of impertinence which forces authority, sometimes royal authority, to enter into their irony, my fools were the distant heirs of Socrates, of

Diogenes the Cynic, of Epictetus and many others. One day Aristippus of Cyrene was asked what benefits he had gained from philosophy. And he, whom they called 'the royal dog', replied: 'that of being able to speak freely to everyone'.[10] Shakespearian characters are certainly closer to the Greek philosophers than Auguste Comte ever was.

I should like, if I may, to note in passing that Aristippus taught his daughter Arete philosophy. She taught it in her turn, notably to her son, who was thus called 'the Metrodidact' (disciple of his mother); he followed her at the head of the Cyrenaic school. If Aristippus' proposition 'to speak freely to everyone' had not implied reciprocity (that everyone can also speak as freely and especially to Aristippus himself), it would have been the equivalent of a tyranny. Arete, who was schooled in and then taught this doctrine, provides the best proof of how serious Aristippus was in his anti-authoritarianism and his affirmation of freedom of speech. One day he threw himself at the feet of Denys of Syracuse, as was obligatory when addressing a tyrant. He seems to have done this for the pleasure of making a quip: 'tyrants' sense of hearing is located between their toes'. If he had inculcated into his daughter, or any other woman, the rule 'be prudish and keep quiet', we should have had to conclude that in making this quip he was guided entirely by a sense of competition between the power of speech and political power. When a philosopher calls himself a libertarian, his attitude towards women is the touchstone that indicates how serious he is.

When I was a fan of fools, I must have had accounts to settle with those in authority or power (who has not?), I loved to laugh and above all I wanted to find a coherent way of understanding life – no less! In literature classes the textbooks and teachers spoke to us of love and the human adventure in a way which seemed purely verbal.[11] On the other hand in mathematics and physics we worked in a rigorous and consistent way, but on subjects which had nothing to do with the interesting things of life. I thought philosophy the only good thing which had all the advantages of the other 'subjects' but not their faults. Foolery which could be integrated into reality and which women also had the right to embrace seemed to me in addition to be the best form of intellectual life imaginable. Later I was to discover academicism, respect for academic hierarchy and the great authors in place of Socrates' irreverence; I was to discover that even though a woman can study philosophy, and then make her living by teaching it, in her colleagues' eyes she is never completely credible in this role – and that 'understanding life' is often a question one puts off until later. However, since my vocation has withstood these various disappointments, I have to say that this is where I stand; 'this' being bound up with a philosophy which strictly speaking does not exist and which, far from being able to claim that it must be regarded as necessary, may well bear the stamp of individual contingency. I sense a big gap between the idea I had of philosophy before I started and its actual practice; many others are in the same situation. But there is no reason for us to conclude immediately that together we should propose this or that radical break. This would require us to be able to state that another mode of philosophical thought, the one we want, is possible and better than the current one. This has been done at least a dozen times since Pythagoras and the history of philosophy is one of constant reorientation. But so many people have announced such breaks with a great deal of fuss, without really bringing them about. I therefore prefer to start by playing a different game: that of abstention on the questions that are supposedly fundamental and whose answers nevertheless seem destined to remain forever imaginary. And also the game of immanence. Philosophy as it is practised here and now is academic and marked by the history of philosophy; for better or worse, it is from here that I grew. I might as well try to blossom here, hoping that this will mean, dialectically, outgrowing the pot. I am a woman, philosophy is my trade, chosen partly because I am a woman, and yet there is a tension between these two things. Let us set this tension to work, in particular in thinking about the history we have grown out of, and we shall see what openings it gives us, if it does.

3   The question of axiology

The abandonment of all attempts to establish the value of my own project, and ultimately that of philosophy itself, has for me gone hand in hand with a belief which can be stated as follows: if the value of philosophy cannot totally be put into thought, this is because in philosophical work essential values come first, before even thought itself. A set of values, which are simply assumed, structures the theoretical enterprise, providing at the least its governing rules and its meaning. We can call this set an axiology or a morality, giving the latter term the fairly wide meaning of a set of choices concerning that which is or is not 'done' in this enterprise, which it is important to

take into account, which means that the work of a particular predecessor is not worthy of the name philosophy; in other words a
whole series of theoretical orientations and also the trace left in the
theoretical language by people's practical and concrete interests.
Which people? That depends.

This deep axiology governs not only the writing but also the
reading of philosophy. And the ways one can experience one's reading give me a first element with which to approach the problem.
When, while reading the classics, I come upon words which are
malevolent, contemptuous or stupid with regard to women, I am
doubly shocked. Firstly because people should not write debasing
things about women, or about anyone, and secondly because when
philosophy allows itself to use the mode of insult it sinks beneath its
own validatory standards. Thus I am also doubly shocked when I
read, for example, Hegel's antisemitic remarks, etc.

'Reason is already of itself so confined and held within limits by
reason, that we have no need to call out the guard, with a view to
bringing the civil power to bear upon that party whose alarming
superiority may seem to us to be dangerous'; 'have no anxiety as to
[. . .] our practical interests, since in a merely speculative dispute
they are never in any way affected'.[12] We can grant this to Kant and
still note that, apart from a few treatises on logic perhaps, one rarely
comes across 'merely speculative' works. It is certainly exceptional to
see reason 'confined within limits by reason'. If philosophers' diver-
gences are insurmountable, this is because their disagreements touch
on principles that predate the speculative debate itself. This man-
ifests itself equally vigorously in the relationship between a work
and its reader: an author and a reader must have some practical
or theoretical values in common to be able to come together at
all.

Conversely, divergence can take many forms: 'Maine de Biran
sends me to sleep', 'I don't like Heidegger', or the other way round. A
moral reaction or an axiological rejection is doubtless the most
appropriate form, but even that must be built into some shape.
Indignation alone is useless, particularly in the case of old works. No
one is going to call out the guard against Auguste Comte; at the most
we may look askance at those of our contemporaries who are
charmed or comforted by Comte's sexism. When it comes to contemporary works, it seems useful to protest since, while there is hope that
we will never again see racist arguments developed in philosophical
texts (a law exists to prevent it, in France at least, and anti-racist
groups have a right to take cases to court), when it comes to sexist

'theories', women can count only on themselves and the art of convincing others with intellectual arguments.[13] It is, therefore, here that it is important to give irritation or anger some kind of shape.

But what method should we adopt? The one I intend to test out here will be to analyse stupid utterances made about women by people who, in principle, have no right to stupidity and, more precisely, to bring to light what is at stake in these utterances, by showing that they are pertinent at a level different from the one at which they appear to have meaning. It is possible to point out how they usually betray a theoretical weakness, a difficulty that the philosopher has been unable to overcome. This may sometimes invalidate the writer's entire system. It is therefore possible to provide these disagreeable scholars with hard-headed opponents and this is what I propose to do. Of course, when philosophy discusses women, women are not the real subject. But we can still have something to say about it and we do not have to agree to bear the brunt of problems which are nothing to do with us.

Can a philosophy be judged by its emblems, or its allusions to supposedly real figures? Lévinas calmly writes that the feminine can have no access to moral existence, in other words to what he regards as best, or almost best.[14] Adorno analyses the virile pose of the 'tough guy' as created by the cinema: dinner suit, whisky, cigar, leather, aftershave and haughty solitude.[15] Do such things influence our choice of reading? We cannot always choose what we read. But it is not pointless to think that there is a link between the images with which philosophical texts are studded, particularly those which describe a sexual status or a supposedly gendered attitude, and an author's 'fundamental thinking'; so that enjoying the caustic page Adorno devotes to the worldly macho means one is ready to think that this author's main work, *The Negative Dialectic*, is a great book. But anyone who thinks it a shame that this portrait ends by observing that, all things considered, the macho is feminine may tend to give Adorno's principle of dialectics itself a more qualified reading. So, on the basis of this position and without claiming that women's contribution to the domain of philosophy can save anything, we can outline a limited project, which on the one hand is related to the history of philosophy, since it involves analysing works, and on the other is philosophy pure and simple, since it involves criticism and objection or showing that the debate cannot really take place, for reasons that can be given. It is not simply a question of annoying those who annoy us (although that is a worthwhile aim in itself), but of bringing to light the fundamental reasons for our rejection.

4   Books I should like to read

Let me stress this point, for I have seen many young women turned
away from philosophy because it has sickened them; it contains too
many unpleasant things about us. To my way of thinking, this should
not lead us to reject philosophical work, but on the contrary to take
up its polemical and critical dimensions. When philosophy is a job,
we do not, of course, choose what we read, but we can go on reading
Emile despite the long passages that lambast poor Sophie; they also
give us food for thought. Two centuries ago, Mary Wollstonecraft
was already saying that what the Enlightenment philosophers, and
particularly Rousseau, had to say about 'woman' was a complete
contradiction of the very principles of Enlightenment philosophy.[16] If
this is true, and I think Mary Wollstonecraft was right, a host of
questions arise. We should review the principles in the light of this
contradiction, which gives us plenty to think about. From the point
of view of the history of philosophy, if we accept that Rousseau's
system has to include a contradiction in order to hold together, we
should review and reinterpret it. This might lead us to ask whether
the great works of philosophy are all that they claim to be, and are
believed to be. But, if these vast monumental totalities are riddled
with failure (which does not necessarily prevent them from existing,
nor from being products of thought), what should we conclude about
philosophical enterprises yet to be undertaken? Some theoretical
weaknesses cloak themselves in stupidities and these stupidities are
misogynist. Here too there is a good question which some women[17]
might like to look at: what are the likely consequences of misogynist
words – whether uttered by Jean-Jacques or General Bigeard? I have
no ready answer to this question, and I am only half sorry; I should
love to read a coherent essay on verbal violence, and it is good to
think that there is work enough for many still undone.

Far from giving way to disgust, women should know that the
sexism of philosophical discourse offers them a hold on that discourse
and that they can re-examine it in a way which has never been done
before. And that when they do so questions may emerge which will
be of interest to everyone. In the philosophical void of today, this
would be a river in the desert.

In recent years the forefront of the Parisian scene has been filled
with books full of grumbles. While level-headed people are happy to
chorus complaints at the erosion of philosophical thought that was
once so dynamic (but when, exactly?), others project our common
indigence on to other people and criticize each other for having not

performed their historic task. The students leave them to talk and read their classics – which have never been theirs to such an extent before – thus preparing to re-enact our nostalgia in ten years' time. Why are there no more people like Locke or Cleanthes around these days?

So what has happened in France and elsewhere for such exhaustion to have taken over, leaving behind it a desire for philosophical thinking which can no longer find an object and a practice of history of philosophy which is indeed serious and solid, which at the least has the merit of preventing the irreversible pervasion of culturelessness, but which painfully reminds us that this desire to think philosophically used to be able to find objects?

No discipline or fine art can control its own evolution or its periods of strength and decline. We are reduced to the observation of surface effects. Perhaps philosophy has not been able to bear the radical self-criticism it has undergone since no one quite knows when.[18] A ban has gradually been imposed: philosophy can no longer regard itself as having the right to speak on its own behalf. Readings of Marx, Nietzsche or Freud have given this ban (reinforced by cries of 'never again!') a content. Such disappointed self-love is, moreover paradoxical, since it often goes hand in hand with a tendency to attribute extreme historical importance to philosophy, which is seen as holding the key to the locks of various oppressions and thus being that which must be attacked first. Self-criticism is ultimately another hegemony, the simple negative of self-glorification. We would do better to turn our attention elsewhere.

5   The question of 'we'

Philosophers without a cause: perhaps this is what the future will call us; but women philosophers who place or will place their philosophical practice at the service of their liberation need not include themselves in this 'us' – women and, if there are any, men who would like to try to understand the strange socio-intellectual phenomenon of sexism with us. Who says philosophers have nothing more to say? We have, and we are philosophers; so it is incorrect to claim that philosophy no longer knows what to apply itself to. In the eighteenth century Montesquieu and a few others found fault with Negro slavery – to use the language of the time. Are there any theoretical grounds for abandoning this vein, when oppression still exists?

However, what emerges from some essays written so far is not the

figure of a committed philosopher, but rather that of a philosophy
which is trying to disengage itself and some other disciplines[19] from
the phallocentrism to which they are in thrall. Hoping at the same
time to make a contribution to a larger and more polymorphous
movement which has been appearing, disappearing and reappearing
for two centuries; a movement which, despite its polymorphism, can
be given the common name of feminism.

   In this movement, the writings of women philosophers have played
a role which certainly cannot be called preponderant, but which
there is no good reason to minimize either. The work of Mary
Wollstonecraft or Simone de Beauvoir, to name but two, has at least
had the merit of upholding the continuity of the discontinuous,
making a historical link which is particularly precious in the collective historical movement's periods of latency. During the French
Revolution, there were clubs of women revolutionaries, then they
were banned (20 October 1793);[20] one day the English suffragettes
stopped demonstrating at Epsom; today the Women's Liberation
Movement has stopped making the headlines.[21] Feminist books are
generally a prospective memory of a movement which constantly
needs to be taken up again; those of Mary Wollstonecraft and Simone
de Beauvoir are also excellent philosophy books and should be read
as such. Because books by women are all sectioned off under a special
heading (by women, about women, for women), half their potential
readers are deprived of solid reading matter. How hard it is too to get
someone who is 'not interested in feminism' to read Virginia Woolf's
A Room of One's Own, despite its being a fine discussion of writing and
of learning an art. Must we keep our best works to ourselves? In this
way we are turned into a 'we', separatists against our will.

   This is all the more discouraging because the audience targeted by
women philosophers who have been interested in feminism has precisely been a mixed one. Philosophy's fundamental task is not (at
least in principle) to address an audience restricted by any extra-
intellectual criterion. It is scandalous that many well known works
presuppose a 'we' (the author and reader) that is restricted: 'we
Europeans', 'we males', 'we Christians' or 'we free-thinkers'. This is
the usual practice, but should it be? Of course one type of descriptive
'we' is legitimate: the type that relates to a collective experience or
indicates a historical situation. But the 'we' specific to philosophy
should by rights be unplaceable and unidentifiable: the author and
the reader, who is unknown to the author. This does not mean that
any reader will agree with what is said and thus to be made part of
the 'we' the work proposes. There are two very different 'we's in the

work of Mary Wollstonecraft: that of reason, which (rightly or wrongly) assumes a logic common to both herself and the person who reads what she writes and, elsewhere, a descriptive 'we', that of the human group, which she talks about while placing herself within it. Sometimes it is humanity in general, sometimes women taken collectively. But whoever reads her can always slip out of this position or challenge it.

Moreover the feminism which thinks philosophically is precisely the form which seeks to address women and men together, 'general public' and legislators together, in the hope that by discussing matters in a poised and public way as decent people (since the others exclude themselves when the debate is open to all), we shall be able to eliminate many false problems and to reach agreement on making human relations a little better. I am no doubt exaggerating, and I can already hear some people shouting that I have fallen victim to the silliest possible illusion. But the postulate of an open debate, in which only reasonable people are likely to become involved, is something other than an illusion: it is the prerequesite for intellectual action.

For more than ten years, since the publication of 'Women in/and philosophy',[22] my inability to decide to play my part in continuing this tradition has been on my conscience. From time to time circumstances and friendship have wrung a short essay from me, never more.[23] This is because, despite everything, it is hard to gain a clear idea of the right way to speak as a feminist woman philosopher, except on some specific questions. On the other hand unfortunate ways of mixing the salt of philosophy with feminism are only too obvious. For the most common philosophical practice comes down to establishing that one is wrong to speak, whatever one says.

6   On philosophy's power of negation

The idea that philosophy undermines speech can be illustrated in many ways. One might choose to remember that scepticism first blossomed with the Greeks, or to stress that the viewpoint of 'critical critique' is the one which officially underlies state teaching of philosophy and that we are involved in it. This ironic notion is inherited from Marx and Engels's polemic against Bruno Bauer.[24] The latter regarded the mind's task as one of ceaseless negation, a perpetual criticism of what exists, because it exists, directed by a kind of empty jurisdiction, with no support in reality itself; an investigation carried out basically 'from nowhere', hence the sarcasm of the Marxist tradition. We have to acknowledge that the training we receive or dispense is impregnated with this kind of ideal: in so far as it is dispensed by the state, the teaching of philosophy is conceived of as something which should be absolutely neutral. And what could be more 'neutral' than an empty critical standpoint? We hear it constantly repeated that the point is not to 'indoctrinate' the students but to 'teach them to think', simply to think; no one ever says what about. Behind this conception of teaching, we find a dichotomy: on the one hand there are doctrines, in other words anything that states something, or has a content, including the canonical texts of the history of philosophy; on the other is the requirement not to become an adherent of any of these, to remain always on the outside and to challenge from any point of view anything that states a content. This project is often made explicit by quoting one of Kant's remarks, which has been adopted as a motto: 'No philosophy can be learnt; one can only learn to philosophize'. It would be pointless to try and invalidate (in turn) this configuration; I am simply trying to acknowledge, for myself, that when one is writing at the end of the twentieth century, in France and in some other countries, one has been bathed in this idea of philosophical practice; one is therefore likely to have been marked by the intellectual inhibitions it gives rise to. The (ultimately aesthetic) dichotomy between that which has substance (which makes it heavy) and philosophical negativity (which alone is fine and light) can be seen almost everywhere, and yes, even in the general introduction for a series of books from the French publishers Presses Universitaires: 'philosophy, which can only begin with the stupified astonishment that being simply is, can only continue through confrontation with an impasse [*aporia*], which welcomes it, and by pushing up against the unknown. It is only this that radically distinguishes philosophy from the sciences, which are located in being and sure of their method. The impasse does not prevent philosophy, it makes it possible, and philosophy dies when it forgets this'. I should like Jean-Luc Marion, who wrote these lines, to tell us where he has found these 'sure' sciences, when all of them that I have come across are pushing up against the unknown and always in the process of devising exploratory methods that nobody would present as 'sure'. Correlatively, there is such a thing as a dogmatism of the impasse, doubt or void, which is ultimately harder to root out than dogmatic conviction.

Rather than writing polemics against this univocal search for negativity (besides, how can one argue against a position that refuses to assert anything?) it might be better to expound the problem in a-theoretical terms, regarding it as a matter of mood. History shows us philosophical moods which differ greatly from each other.[25] Schematically speaking, we can identify two classic ones. The first is architechtonic and likes to construct systems or theoretical ensembles, while the second is corrosive, *pars destruens*, the exercise of polemical reason, and aims to demolish. There have been examples where these two forces have come together happily in the same enterprise. It could even be argued that only architectonics is really polemical and that affirmatory thought is the true critical force. However, it must be recognized that sometimes one of these two propensities dominates to the suffocation of the other. If we take the question as it is posed today (in a more cramped universe than that of the Greek quarrels, and indeed a more reduced one than that of the medieval arguments, since we often fight indirectly over readings of the old authors), we can say that perhaps affirmatory works or essays concerned with thinking something have recently been produced, but that the mood of the times is such that this aspect of philosophical production has gone unnoticed. All that has been recognized is the power to demolish which they also wield. One example should be enough: there is more than one idea in Foucault's thought, and the 'death of man' does not govern them all. And yet, if we look at the welcome his philosophy has received, from the immediate reactions to the publication of his first books, to the posthumous criticism, we shall find this theme stressed to such a degree that an association of ideas has been made and become dominant: Foucault equals anti-humanism.

The mood of a time hears what it wants to hear in what it is given. I already know something of this from personal experience, since my feminist works have on occasion received strange and contradictory praise. In the end I decided that all misunderstandings are possible and also that one misunderstanding can hide another. In itself this is quite banal and not worth lingering over, unless it helps to reveal the mood of the time and what that mood is seeking when it understands one thing rather than another in what it reads. Over the last twenty years interest seems to have been concentrated on the theoretical possibility of destroying language and undermining all speech. Having started as a theoretical phenomenon, this focus soon became social; it became integrated into everyday relations between intellectuals. We were begged not to use old words, all of which were suspected of bearing within them the sedimented residue of oppressive enemy thinking, either 'bourgeois' or 'metaphysical', depending on the preferences of the person you were talking to. Words were thought to be saturated with 'naiveties' (which were themselves complicit in an order which had to be broken) and were accused of surreptitiously leading back to theories which, it went without saying, we had all agreed to rid ourselves of. In a consensus on reciprocal censorship we have reduced each other to silence. This could well have made an empty space which could then be filled by an overt return to religion, whether in the name of post-modernity or in an unargued form. The strategy of the founder of a sect is first to remove people's points of reference and to invalidate all their previous ideas; when they are totally at a loss, the only beacon of light then becomes the guru and his words the only idea. Of course ordinary reference points can be criticized and commonly held ideas may be untoward. But it is one thing to discuss something step by step with another person, with his, her or our common liberty in view, and quite another to practise the intellectual terrorism which robs the other of speech.[26]

7   A difficult meeting

As a result of the publication of 'Women in/and philosophy' in England, I met a group of women philosophers for the first time in 1977. The simple existence of this group, one of the first of its kind, was a great encouragement to work on this subject. Moreover, as the anglophone philosophical context is very different from the one I had known until then, I was extremely curious to see how the relation between feminism and philosophy was thought of there. I was given some texts to read; in the pile I found a critical examination of the slogan 'A woman's right to choose', which was the watchword in the battle for free contraception and abortion. The critique said that the notion of right is bourgeois and metaphysical, and thus unusable by the revolutionary movement that feminism should be. The notion of choice was no better, since it was subject to all the pointless debates about free will. This was the first time I had heard such things, but not the last: whichever side of the Channel you are on, an aesthetics of radicalism can stifle the beginnings of speech.

While we are getting our breath back, we need to give a grateful thought to the rights we have and which we never think about precisely because we have them, such as free movement of persons. And if all choice involves blind-alley debates about free will, must we take this to extremes and state that it is impossible to decide between coffee and tea at breakfast every morning? It is hyperphilosophism to require that the philosophical problems posed by such a notion be re-examined before saying 'I want...' But let us leave mockery to one side, not to begin a strictly philosophical critique, but to ask an empirico-simplistic question: has anyone noticed that collective opinion almost never raises 'fundamental questions' or those supposed to be so, at random? When, in France, the Republic wanted to make children's schooling free, secular and compulsory, some bishops protested and set before the Assembly the thorny problem of the people's right not to be educated. The Republic went on regardless, without solving the metaphysical problem. Fortunately, you might say (if you think it was a good thing), since this problem can be solved philosophically only in a most approximative way: excellent arguments may be furbished, but intellectual honesty obliges one to say that there is always a fragment of possible doubt. When we are upset by the clitoridectomy practised on African girls, we are frequently told that we are 'eurocentric', or that we want to impose 'Western culture' on civilizations that are quite different. At best we are assured that such action cannot be envisaged until the very delicate problem of contact and exchange between different peoples is settled on the moral plane. On the other hand, the fact that a particular element of Western culture has long been installed in at least one Third World country (I am referring to the military applications of atomic physics, exported to India with no qualms) has given rise to no minute discussions of 'cultural identity' that must never be disturbed. In some cases 'it goes without saying', in others we first have to prove that bodily wholeness is more important than the anti-ethnocentric aesthetics of so-called enlightened opinion.

Having seen philosophy and its rigour being used to undermine a language of demands, despite the efficacy of that language where it was being used, I despaired of the meeting of philosophy and feminism and fled into classical studies on the Renaissance so that I could also go on being simply a feminist, on Saturday afternoon demonstrations for example, with no particular theory and without feeling the need for one. But the debate I had fled nevertheless continued in a corner of my head, accompanied by the belief that the theoretical situation was inextricable, to the point where it led to a sophist dialogue which was by definition interminable. Imagine that I defended the slogan 'A woman's right to choose' (or its French equivalent), saying that this was a case of language that was effective in making a demand: I knew in advance that women friends would then have been justified in criticizing the very notion of demand. For we have all heard Nietzscheo-Freudians explaining that this notion is bound up with hysteria and resentment and is thus unusable. If, driven back to my last bastions of defence, I had suggested that we should make a distinction between the radical tricks we know how to play in philosophy and political commitment which is in its own way equally radical, someone would certainly have had the intellectual agility to reply that the distinction between 'the philosophical' and 'the political' is itself part of a certain metaphysical conception which it would be naive to adopt. Such dogma can be refuted, but if the person you are discussing it with is tenacious, she or he will find more notions to criticize. Thus a phrase concerning 'every woman's right to choose' cannot be absolutely and unanswerably grounded in philosophical arguments.

We should be wrong to believe that this problem is unique. Antisthenes, that pupil of Socrates who otherwise has some claims on our affections[27] remarked, with all due cynical rigour, that the principle of non-contradiction should itself be demonstrated.[28] As this is not completely possible, Aristotle replied that 'it shows a lack of education not to know how to decide for which matters proof should be sought and for which such procedure is pointless'.[29] No doubt, but it is the greatest capitulation possible for a philosopher to refer to 'lack of education': it is an appeal to an inexpressible sense of distinction. I am not reproaching Aristotle with this capitulation, however: when intellectual agility leads to the paralysis of a tongue which has something to say, one is tempted, like Jankélévitch, to draw on 'a certain dullness of mind' so that Megarico-Eleatic quibbling does not stop us running. In any case, why single out the language of our own side as a target, when so much could be said about the woolly, badly reasoned and untenable character of the metaphysics of the so-called 'pro-life' movement and its various equivalents throughout the world? This choice betrays a doubt about the legitimacy of the struggle. It transposes alienation to the philosophical register: when a woman opens her mouth to say what she wants and others join in, something will always be found in the philosophical arsenal to silence this speech, since it is possible to find something to silence any and all speech, even that which says that you cannot state A and non-A at the same time.

It was a long time before I understood why women philosophers whose commitment to the cause of women's liberation was otherwise indisputable, should engage in this kind of pointless challenge. There is a classic philosophical trick at work in this business and I should have identified it earlier. This is the unfortunate mania for always and in every case dismissing both opponents, a necessary operation in order to remain 'above the fray'. From Pythagoras to Merleau-Ponty, the image of a philosopher perched on the terrace of a stadium watching the opponents wrestle is part of the idea that the profession has of itself. The women philosophers who were criticising the notions of 'right' and 'choice' certainly, but implicitly, agreed that the language of those who were (and still are) trying to ban contraception could be criticized. I do not think these women wanted to talk to those people, even to tell them they were wrong.

In other women's groups I have heard it said, a little too often for my liking, that rationality is a masculine thing, so that women trying to disengage themselves from the colonialist grip of the patriarchy should, urgently and once and for all, throw rationality into the bin. I made a few attempts to tell them how lucky they were to find the question so simple: there are so many different forms of rationality, depending on which fields one considers, that it is sometimes hard to make out a common core. If we cannot determine exactly where rationality begins, the notion suddenly seems boundless, which is no small subject for reflection. And then to maintain that rationality must be rejected by women because it is a masculine thing is an idea which is always advanced like a reasoned argument and is indeed trying to rationalize something, even if its premises are open to dispute. In reply I was told that I was once more proving that I was colonized to the marrow.

I therefore fled the arena where philosophy and feminism were so painfully meeting in the 1970s. And away from this arena, I found it possible to begin to form my own philosophical project: to prove that there is in philosophy an imaginary level which has not been imported from elsewhere but is specific to philosophy and sets the conditions of what can be constructed as rationality within it. To describe a flight is not however to justify it. Just as insoluble 'fundamental problems' are not raised purely at random, so no doubt my capitulation before the hyperphilosophism of some women and the irrationalist project of the others was not entirely a matter of chance. The question could be asked as to why I abandoned the issue to others and my flight can justifiably be interpreted in a highly critical way.

8 The void and its others

In any case, the socio-theoretical difficulty extends far beyond the possible area of intersection between philosophy and feminism: when one makes statements or advances something it either goes unnoticed (as though one were addressing deaf ears) or produces such savage reactions that the writer ends up by anticipating and internalizing them. As we have seen, Michel Foucault's audience attributed clear outlines to the theme of the 'death of man'. But sometimes in his work there appears the muffled style of a man who has rewritten his text many times, taking care not to expose himself to a particular objectification, since these days objections take the form of objectifications. Vigilance against running the risk of being classified, or put into a category, often seems to have flattened out contemporary thought, even that of Foucault. It is a collective phenomenon and the same concern in writers of lesser talent gives a nebulous, sluggish style, so that once you have finished reading the text you cannot give an account of what was said in it. Since opposing figures or discursive formations often co-exist, over the same period we have seen rough-hewn professions of faith and assertions employing categories so crude that they are not even worthy of philosophical discussion passing as philosophy.

This contrast between language rendered evanescent by prudence and the other of that language does not exist only between two types of production or two categories of writer. Sometimes it runs through a single work and notably distinguishes or delineates the very thing we are trying to talk about: the status of women in philosophy. For the same author may generally use language which exhausts itself in prolemogena to any discourse and wears itself out in caveats, while elsewhere devoting a chapter, paragraph or just a phrase to sexual difference, excuse me, to women, where all of a sudden there is a shift from the height of sophistication to a mode which has been somehow squared off and is at the same time so dogmatic that there is no place for mediation or dialectics.[30] Here we have a brutal return of thinking in categories and dualism. Despite questioning every concept and every play of opposites, the writer continues to know clearly what is 'masculine' and what is 'the feminine' – we hope we are being faithful to the language of the time in giving the linguistic mark of reification to the second term only. To the point where one whose words hitherto articulated only the inexorable absence of any free or meaningful speech proves dogmatically loquacious on the subject of what 'the feminine' is and more still on what this 'feminine' should not be, on pain of losing itself; by this we are to understand, the spaces which women should not try to occupy. Whether this is called 'the truth', 'the theoretical' or anything you like, it is of course philosophy, when it is said by a philosopher.[31]

So we are the exception in contemporary philosophy – if indeed we are what this is about. In a reciprocal way, philosophy has been called our exception by those philosophers who like us. Look at Condorcet or John Stuart Mill: both claimed to defend women and to support their liberation, yet these (self-proclaimed) defenders, while apparently pleading for the end of discrimination against women, upheld one exception: women could do everything, but they could not philosophize like the men.[32]

Philosophical discourse has lost its assertiveness and has almost been reduced to silence, but it has miraculously found a referent, the possibility of speaking of an essence. The good old question of 'what is' still has validity; philosophers ask themselves, 'what is a woman, or the feminine?' and they give their answer directly. Men philosophers have thus clung to the possibility of advancing dogmatic theses when talking about woman, and saying that she is an outsider to philosophy. On that basis, everything can be reconstructed.

For the thanatotic attitude which has predominated for the last twenty years or more can be analysed, at least in its superficial implications, as an avatar of philosophical narcissism. Traditionally philosophy has placed a very great value upon itself and sometimes may have accorded great worth to other forms of thought or discourse, but this worth is always derived, being assessed in relation to that of philosophy. A type of philosophy which has been self-critical but which remains caught up in the game of according worth necessarily ends up by trampling any attempt at speech. A satisfied narcissism could irradiate and thus validate geometry, music, some forms of politics, the formalist rationality of jurisconsults, art or religion; disappointed self-love tends to project aggressive melancholia on to all other forms of reflective thought or knowledge. Only ruins remain.

But everything can be reconstructed as though philosophy's self-criticism had never taken place once philosophical discourse, however exhausted its content, can retain its dogmatic approach to 'woman' or 'the feminine' as being outside the philosophical. When someone is placed outside, the existence of an inside is re-established by contrast, with no need even to take the trouble to prove the coherence of this inside. By affirming that 'woman' is incapable of philosophical thought and that it is no task for her, philosophers strengthen and reassure themselves with the idea that philosophy can do something and has a task, no need to state exactly what. The exclusion of someone maintains the structure, even if the structure is empty. That someone happens to be 'woman' but, taking the view that it is the exclusion that matters, we can assume the choice of who is excluded to be contingent: any group condemned to let others speak for it, with no right of reply, would do as well.[33] In any case, philosophy's self-criticism is a waste of time as long as it does not analyse its structure of exclusion and, since the excluded ones are at present women, as long as it has not analysed its own mysogyny. At any moment its vaunted scepticism is liable to collapse into its opposite, reinstating affirmations of the extreme worth of philosophy and its pre-eminence over all other discourses, be they scientific, legal, political or anything else one might care to imagine.[34]

There are two possible ways out of the current depression. One would be (will be, or already is) a brutal return to philosophism, by which I mean a philosophy which becomes one with its self-justification and in no way exceeds it. The other would be to refuse to play the game of theoretical domination, by recognizing that rational thought goes through a process of diversification and that the thing to do is to acknowledge this diversity, seriously and without according our own beloved discipline a greater worth than these other various modes of thought or postulating philosophy as the 'keystone' for some architectonics of the forms of rationality developed by the different scientific, legal, artistic or political fields. It is even possible to abandon thinking of the value of philosophical work as an absolute, without deciding that there is nothing of value in the discourses that abound in the public domain or in the goals that people set themselves between heaven and earth. Once the existence of these other discourses and goals is recognized, we might hope that philosophy will mingle with them and they with philosophy.

I have made my choice. For more than ten years I have been trying to explain that the desire to assert the extreme worth of philosophy gives rise to philosophers' sexist utterances. I should therefore like to work on the second branch of the alternative and invite others to work on it too. My ultimate hope would be to set the negative position women occupy in philosophy to work in a dialectical way, for of course being a woman and a philosopher has many everyday disadvantages in the social life of this 'philosophical community' which is not really a community. In one's most intrinsic relation to the discipline, it also represents an impossibility of accepting the phallocratic aspects of the philosophical project as it is ordinarily perceived and thus an impossibility of feeling directly 'at home' in philosophical work itself. However, that is not to say that one should reject everything – all that philosophy has to teach and everything it can make happen. Besides, women involved in philosophy (as teachers, readers, essayists or researchers) do not seem all to have jumped out of the boat. While it must be admitted that they and I are in a paradoxical situation – we are here, but not quite at home – we can see whether our ill-ease might not be creative and whether something could not be made from this precarious position, a way of seeing or thoughts which could rightfully be shared with anyone interested in philosophical problems. In this light it is out of the question to deny the uncomfortable nature of women philosophers' position; but let us not give way to simplistic groans. On the contrary, we must pay attention to paradoxes. Let me now try to give some idea of what this means.

9 In which the difficulty is outlined

When one looks at oneself through the eyes of others, being a woman and a philosopher is, among other things, a double loss: because you are a woman you will be thought less of a philosopher and because you are a philosopher, from time to time you will be given to understand that you are thought 'not quite a woman'. In *The Second Sex* Simone de Beauvoir stresses that there is a contradiction for a little girl or a woman between self-assertion and being seen as a little girl or a woman. In the first analysis, it seems that this general situation is particularly apparent in our own profession: since philosophical thinking is regarded as a practice linked to a certain self-assertion ('thinking for oneself'?), the difficulties we encounter may be seen as simply exacerbated versions of a more general phenomenon.

And we must see them as such in the first instance, and thus link the question of women in philosophy to a more global problem, considering it not as a local difficulty, but as a symptom to be investigated: what does the belief that there is a contradiction between being a woman and being a philosopher say about how women in general are thought of and what philosophy itself is thought to be? However, this basic question should not make us ignore more ordinary, everyday things, and first of all, the problem as it concretely presents itself to women who live and discover themselves in a world where this belief is patent or latent.

For the way others see us matters, as do their everyday attitudes. Their almost anecdotal reactions, a nasty smile, a word said in passing, to which you will be reprovingly told you have attached too much importance. Women coming to philosophy do not leave the ordinary world by doing so, but they enter a universe where a certain mode of trans-subjectivity exists through subtle nuances of reserve or irony. This can be simply described: these women often have to face people who do not believe that they can speak. The spring which keeps anyone thinking and writing is fragile and utterly vulnerable to a hostile environment or indeed to calm but firm incredulity which gives you to understand that your presence here is implausible.

Trans-subjectivity. I have chosen to invent a word rather than to use the common term of intersubjectivity, which means different things depending on the writer using it and does not necessarily refer to what I am trying to express. My referent is of a more rudimentary order and one that is also more charged with emotion, or with affects; it is conveyed by tone of voice or look, in the tiny delay before they answer you and in a thousand attitudes which communicate opinions, beliefs, refusals or invitations. All this may take place without being registered; however, it marks what I shall call, for want of something better, our drive to think, live and project ourselves into the future. And of course our drive to speak. From this point of view the philosophical republic is resolutely fraternal. Sometimes the brothers wrestle with each other, sometimes they fraternize, sometimes they fight over who can play at founding fathers, but in every case they are liable to exclude the sisters from their little games.

A woman who is slightly or perfectly bad tempered learns to get by reasonably well in this situation. But it took me twenty years to develop my temper; how can I now forget how hard I found it to confront the obstacle that still does not speak its name, when I was on the defensive and did not even understand why they were giving me a hard time? A woman involved in philosophy. So, where's the problem? In those days there was no third term to make it possible at least to pose the problem; when you are a woman and a philosopher, it is useful to be a feminist in order to understand what is happening to you. I use the term feminist here in its most basic sense of someone who knows that something is still not right in the relations between a woman and everybody else, in other words men, other women, the supposedly impersonal agents of institutions, and anyone else: some hitch that is strictly potential, of course, simply liable to manifest itself, but which you must learn to identify in everyday situations and conversations.

Considering the main aspects of the question, we can state that feminism is the term which makes it possible to integrate the other two – woman and philosopher – into a dialectic, without reducing them to nothing. Because first of all feminism is the simple knowledge that when one is a woman, that fact always matters in social situations and in relationships, including those where you might expect it least, where you would not think it was relevant. The reality of social relations is never what you might think, it is that which we still need to analyse. You might think there would be free or neutral zones, where the fact of being a man or a woman would not matter; when, for example, you are dealing with the transmission of knowledge which is supposed to be abstract, you might think that it was not important what your birth certificate says. And in one sense we should indeed continue to think this, knowing however that the facts will do much to undermine such a supposition. From this point of view to be a feminist is to integrate the fact of being a woman into dialectics: it is a way of knowing that sexualization matters and at the same time, but contradictorily, knowing that it would be possible for it not to matter and that the way in which it now matters is neither good nor legitimate. Whether one then goes on to think that the fact of being a woman should not matter at all, or that it should matter in a completely different way, is not very important and depends on personal choices or particular situations.

Being a feminist is also a way of integrating the fact of being a philosopher. Because for two centuries a feminist has been a woman who does not leave others to think for her, whether it be a question simply of thinking or, more particularly, thinking about the feminine condition or what it should be. If we make a link (at least as a hypothesis) between thinking philosophically and self-assertion through thought, or the individual withdrawal from generally held beliefs, then 'thinking philosophically' and 'being a feminist' appear as one and the same attitude: a desire to judge by and for oneself, which may manifest itself in relation to different questions. If philosophy particularly consists in questioning what happens in towns, houses and people's daily lives (and, according to Cicero, such is philosophy's task as seen by Socrates), then the issue of women's lives is necessarily on the agenda. But has it really been so, as an issue, in the twenty-five centuries of philosophy that we can observe? Too little or not in the right way, the feminist would say: so here we have an enquiry and a process to be taken further.

For the project of philosophy and that of feminist thinking have a fundamental structure in common, an art of fighting fire with fire and looks with looks, of objectifying and analysing surrounding thought, of regarding beliefs as objects that must be scrutinized, when the supposedly normal attitude is to submit to what social life erects as doctrine. Nothing goes without saying, including what people think about the roles which have come down to men and women.

More precisely still, philosophical criticism of what we can quickly call culture seeks to link a particular belief or thought to something outside itself and basically to say to the other person, 'Behind the thesis you're putting forward, I can see the reason why you're putting it forward.' Thus in Plato we find a phrase which will perhaps have the ring of a surrealist dictum in being taken out of context: 'You hold that self-advantage is what one ought to practise, Callicles, because you neglect geometry.'[35] Geometry tells us about 'geometrical' equality or proportion, which is the shape of justice itself. What interests me in this remark is the technique from which it proceeds, which is basically that of treating an opinion not as a simple opinion but as something whose tacit reason or cause can be drawn out and which may just as well be a lack or omission (as in the case of Callicles) as a full, efficient or final cause. This genealogical technique, which is formally very simple (you think that because...), is also typical of some feminist critiques. It is in this way, for example, that Mary Wollstonecraft deals with the widespread idea, which she finds scandalous, that women's 'innocence' should be 'protected' by maintaining them in the greatest possible ignorance. This, she says, is because you want to cultivate woman's blind obedience, so that you can make her into 'a sweeter companion to man', in other words 'a more alluring object of desire'.[36]

This method supposes a 'you' or a 'thou' with whom one is arguing, an interlocutor whose discourse is rooted in an interplay of interests and blindspots. And it is this interplay itself which is challenged, through the challenging of the other person's opinion, the opponent being regarded as the mouthpiece of those interests. Correlatively, philosophy can be seen as a way of arguing with a situation or a reality as if it were somebody's doctrine or thesis. Such a conception of philosophy explains the attachment one can feel for it: there are realities and situations I want to argue and take issue with. This also helps us understand the common desire not to see philosophy extinguished (despite all the faults we might find with it): there is a wish to preserve for the coming generations this possibility of arguing with what is or what will be, at least in this way. We imagine a world without philosophy as one where all opposition would be stifled. One notch more lucidity and we come to the realization that philosophical criticism is the minimal form of opposition.

If philosophy is a way of arguing with any concrete phenomenon, as though it were someone's 'theory', it must, in order to carry out its critique, first perform an operation by which the particular concrete phenomenon is transformed into a 'thesis' or discourse. This discourse will then be shown to have all possible logical defects and to refer to a reality which is itself inconsistent. The quintessence of this type of preliminary operation is to be found in the first book of Thomas More's *Utopia*. To open the debate on private property and its corollaries, the author creates characters who will be its apologists and a traveller who stubbornly argues against them. Mary Wollstonecraft often proceeds in this way. She seeks (and easily finds) texts which translate into words those attitudes and social practices which she wishes to challenge. In the chapter we have just mentioned, Rousseau and Milton play parts analogous to that of Callicles in the Gorgias, or that of the hero's interlocutors in More's *Utopia*. Milton describes an 'Eve with perfect beauty adorned' who says to Adam, 'God is thy law, thou mine; to know no more/Is woman's happiest knowledge'.[37] Mary comments on both the text and the social effectiveness of its meaning, thus taking Milton's lines as the mouthpiece of the social life she is criticizing, which combines a demand for perfect beauty with submission to man's law and the maintenance of women in a state of ignorance.

Thus we can say that the most lively philosophical attitude possible (I am not thinking of Nabert here) is in harmony with a certain feminist tradition; but in both cases words are all one can catch hold of at first. Philosophical criticism, that tiny seed of opposition obtained with a maximum of intellectual effort, does not reach silent social realities (if there are any), those that are so stable that they do not need words to legitimate them.

And yet, although we can argue that there is harmony between philosophy and feminism, although we can maintain that it is entirely in the interests of a woman philosopher that she be a feminist (as I intend to show), we must take the exposition of the difficulty further. We must recognize that to be a feminist and a philosopher may still generate a contradiction whose effect, at least in my case, was to produce a kind of long impossibility of speaking. The feminist seemed constantly to find objections to subjects that the philosopher might have chosen (these texts from the philosophical tradition contain too many dreadful things against women, I can't get enthusiastic about them), while the philosopher was always filled with reservations about the thousand and one theoretical discourses which intersected in the Women's Movement. How then are we to explain the fact that, while there is a kind of pre-established harmony between thinking philosophically and wanting independence for all women, to place oneself on the join between feminism and philosophy still leads to this kind of mutism?

This question, and my own part in this mutism, form one spring-board for my thinking. This core of silence allows me to orientate myself and to find my way between the philosophy we dream of and the one we practise, between a simple feminist will for change and the different theories upheld in the Women's Movement. For in the final analysis, abstention from speech, for a while at least, seems less damaging than the immediate constitution, whether as field or as a subject, of a 'feminist', 'feminine' or indeed 'femophile philosophy', or its opposite, which would be a philosophical rectrix of feminism. There is no need to try to establish such a thing theoretically in advance: some have already tried to do so, with results we can judge for ourselves. Here are two very different examples.

10   Where the impasse is shown in action in two bad examples

Janet Radcliffe Richards had her hour of glory in 1980, following the publication of *The Sceptical Feminist*. This book has the quite explicit aim of putting feminism in order philosophically, in which it concurs with the good old idea of philosophy as the referee in ideological or political conflicts.[38] Janet Radcliffe Richards sets about her task using a method which, apparently at least, fits with the received or popula-rized 'method' of analytic philosophy, which involves clarifying no-tions and identifying what is valid in them and what is not pertinent. Those looking for illustrations of the idea that any project describing itself as a simple exercise of clarification of burning issues is in fact coloured by values which the author keeps out of the discussion will find everything they could wish for in this type of work.

The book had considerable media success: of course, since it pro-posed to discipline feminists and bring them into line. And how the media relishes it when none of the notions current in feminist move-ments emerges unscathed from an analysis which confronts them with the basic data of common sense! In fact this work is fairly reactionary on more or less all the issues it deals with.[39] Philosophi-cally speaking, it is a disaster. Of course, this is always a difficult thing to establish, but I shall try to do so by analysing some extracts.

The author criticizes Irene Peslikis' remark that 'thinking that some women are smart and some women are dumb [. . .] prevents those women who think they're smart and those women who think they're dumb from talking to each other and uniting against a com-mon oppressor', on the grounds that it is an apology for 'irrationality'. Janet Radcliffe Richards considers this statement irrational because:

> if we are not allowed to regard some people as cleverer than others, it should have the consequence that we give equal weight to what they say, and regard all of them as equal in all discussion (which is of course [Irene Peslikis'] intention). Is that possible? If we notice that some women say what is obviously well judged and consistent, and that others make unsupported or contradictory assertions, how can we help noticing that there are differences in ability?[40]

Oh dear! And there was I thinking that once people engaged in a discussion were no longer all considered as equal, the discussion was distorted to such an extent that it was no longer a discussion at all! Of course this often happens, but that is no reason to transform the fact into a principle. I also foolishly thought that when we believe we have a sure criterion for distinguishing the 'well judged' from the 'unsupported', it becomes pointless to posit reified differences of ability between people: It matters little who said what, if such a criterion is operating in the debate. I naively believed that thinking philosophically meant laboriously producing agreement on this kind of criterion, through debate! Although of course I was aware that it was not always possible to succeed. In any case, why should a remark like Irene Peslikis' be called irrational when all it does is to describe imaginary obstacles to the beginnings of communication?

At this point, we begin to glimpse the reasons why we can call a book like Janet Radcliffe Richards' disastrous from a philosophical point of view. It does not assume a demanding reader. Richards has chosen to analyse an unpretentious remark, very honest in its clarity. Although claiming to examine it from a philosophical viewpoint, she in fact opposes to it a simple protestation, and quite a common one at that, to the effect that after all, we do still have the right to think some people cleverer than others! This protestation spirits away all possibility for philosophical discussion of an issue which is far from unimportant: what is it to talk to each other? Irene Peslikis asks this question from the viewpoint of political action and the building of alliances between individuals; but the problem and difficulties of debate or dialogue form an issue of particular importance for philosophy. If Socrates had agreed with Radcliffe Richards, instead of holding dialogues with various people and trying to establish what conditions make it possible to hold a debate where the aim is to discover the truth in the company of others, he would have settled for handing out good marks to his pupils and noting their different abilities. Of course, we must admit that, all things considered, the Socratic dialogues went further with some interlocutors than with others. But Socrates seems to have needed them all. Today, when we no longer write dialogues, we need to incorporate this structure into our writings, in other words to have imaginary interlocutors standing by our inkstands, people with whom it is not at first always easy to have an exchange. We need to imagine them sometimes as the recalcitrant champions of the most everyday ideology and sometimes as the most formidable connoisseurs of philosophical questions and extremely demanding. This is the wager of rationalism (if reason is primarily a search for meaning which can be tested by others). It is doubtless not absolutely tenable; there are no known examples of perfect success. Those who write must therefore know that they are bound by imperfection, which legitimates expression in a clumsy and personal voice. It allows us to go gropingly or to formulate beliefs. But, in recognizing this imperfection, we know that we are asking a great deal of the reader and that the author does not automatically have the last word in the imaginary dialogue.

Classically philosophical work is contrasted with the 'communiqué', that utterance to which there is no reply, which makes a statement in the first and last instance. This is the mode chosen by Radcliffe Richards. She does not assume the existence of thought either up or downstream of her own words. Upstream is the feminist discourse she assails, assuming from the outset that it is non-thought, that its ideas are guilty of non-sense, that it is an easy opponent with whom discussion is pointless; downstream, she assumes a docile, obliging reader who lets the teacher say whatever she likes. It is therefore hardly surprising that this whole book hums in unison with the most everyday ideology: readers will not accept all that is said to them unless they are told what they already fully believe. The extraordinary dogmatism of this book could only be maintained at the price of the greatest possible conformism.[41] I did not know that philosophy could take on the role of soothing the opinions of the majority by excising its own most precious questions, such as that of the conditions necessary for real debate. You live and learn.

In parentheses, all this worries me in relation to the very possibility of writing the present book. I shall be dealing with some real idiocies, uttered against women by the most eminent minds. By giving myself such an easy opponent, am I not stepping outside the rules of philosophy? My only hope is to take as my object of discussion, not the misogynist stupidities that appear in philosophical texts, but the gap between these howlers and the theoretical rigour required of the discourse in which they appear. By thinking about how not to proceed, one begins to see, by contrast, what it is worth trying to do. Let us now look a little more at examples that do not augur well.

The chapter Radcliffe Richards devotes to the question of freedom is pretty frightening, since it displays a total lack of either political or philosophical knowledge of the thing in question. It contains an exposition on the internment of Soviet dissidents in psychiatric hospitals. The author raises many issues in her reasoning on this example of deprivation of freedom, and in particular wonders if dissidents might not be cured and happier on their release, in which case, according to her, internment would be justified, so long as no one was forced into it. But she never even touches upon the question which, to naive minds, seems most important and which asks in what name is political dissidence persecuted and what does the disguising of this persecution as psychiatric 'help' signify? And what exactly is mental illness, if political opposition can so easily be assimilated into it?

My first fear is that in the twentieth century it seems possible to write philosophy in total ignorance of the most minimal meaning of what is at stake in politics. My second worry is that if I tackle such idiocies as these, I might slip into superficiality myself and become bogged down in an identical idiocy. My third anxiety is, why do we find this exposition in a book on women? The author generously says we should let the Soviet dissidents decide (for themselves) whether they would rather be happy or remain themselves. A parallel proposition is advanced: if happiness was all that mattered, there would be nothing intrinsically wrong with forcing women to swallow tranquillizers instead of doing something about their problems. Would anyone dare ask such questions, in such terms, other than in a book on women, in other words when attention is focused on a subject in relation to which the most repressive ideology always 'passes'?

From my point of view this exposition has an involuntary merit: it allows us to grasp the way in which our so-called liberal societies are not so far removed as it might seem from regimes regarded as totalitarian. One could argue in favour of the idea that there is an analogy between the attitude of both towards women and the attitude of the latter towards their own citizens, be they men or women. According to the usual doxa, women are dear creatures lacking in reason, who need looking after and must be locked away in their homes; if necessary they can also be put in a chemical straitjacket.

But if the parallel is valid, then we must draw from it a general methodological principle: in some of its aspects, the 'female condition' is not just the 'female condition': it reveals social structures which also weigh heavily on some men, in some situations. Thus a feminist study cannot always remain a strictly feminist study: there is no fence around the field of these investigations. If, starting from an analysis of the position of women, we climb up to the structure which creates this position, we need then to see if this structure does not also affect other human beings. The attempt to use this heuristic principle as often as possible offers us (among other things) a hope of escaping the doxa's categories. For received opinion suggests, as a self-evident fact, that the position of women is particular on all counts and feminism is seen as a specific struggle against the specific oppression of women. We can at least suspend judgement on this question, and freely examine individual cases and the various aspects of the problem.[42]

To finish with the worries raised by reading *The Sceptical Feminist*, here is a final sample: 'Freedom must be at least in part an internal thing. There certainly is no doubt that some such view is widespread in feminism' [is that so?] 'Perhaps the most striking indication of it is the use of the word "liberated" when applied to women. To the outsider as well as to the feminist a liberated woman is not one who is free to choose among a great many options, but one who makes certain kinds of choice.'[43] Here at least is something for us to get our theoretical teeth into! *The Critique of Practical Reason* and *Existentialism and Humanism* deal with nothing else. This is a classic subject for thought: does freedom lead to certain types of choices (or not), in other words can a necessity be deduced from it? And if so, in which spheres or which fields of action? As the book is subtitled a philosophical enquiry, we expect a theoretical digression. Unfortunately, without so much as a full stop, the text goes on 'she is not a woman with a tolerant and helpful husband who encourages her to achieve all her ambitions, but one who would not stand any nonsense from her husband if he tried any'.

If we were merely seeking to eliminate Janet Radcliffe Richards from the field, we could discuss this phrase. On what distant planet did she hear liberation talked of in such terms? But the problem lies not so much in the unintelligibility of the alternative she proposes as in her method. She does not make the theoretical digression we expected and in its place she gives us her personal vision and a summary projection of what she wants for herself and what she believes that others want. Before laughing at her, let us beware. In some cloudy region of our heads all of us humans have a fine collection of rudimentary ideas that we picked up here and there; these views are always ready to pour out in place of theoretical work, particularly when we are talking about things either closely or distantly related to our own experience or to psychological or social factors. If we acknowledge this phenomenon, we must suppose that I too am placing myself in the worst possible position, where I have the least chance of holding back my own stupid ideas. For, having assumed that values always dominate any theoretical undertaking, I am opening the door to immediate attributions of value, which may very well be idiosyncratic. In abandoning the idea of always taking all analyses to their extreme, I run the risk of giving even more room to these obscure beliefs. Personal experience and psychological, moral and social issues interest me. The subject I am dealing with requires that I concern myself with them, and in any case, if this type of issue is avoided, the only things left to philosophy are metaphysics, commentaries on the great texts and epistemology. These are the things to which philosophy was reduced in the nineteenth century, to the point that few now read Book III of Spinoza's *Ethics*, and even fewer read French moralists such as La Rochefoucault or Chamfort, at least among the ranks of philosophers. It is not so long ago that poor Vladimir Jankélévitch was verbally attacked by students who criticized him for a lack of concepts in his concern with the experiences of life. All the training they receive in schools turns young philosophers away from this sublunar world, which my colleagues have abandoned to the social sciences, those disciplines they so haughtily despise. But, if thinking about the way people live is, as it were, the repressed of contemporary philosophy, and if I am talking about it all the same, we must expect a pitiable return of the repressed. What, dear reader, have you not yet abandoned this book which claims to be wise by stating that it will in all likelihood be like the fool?[44] Let me try to prove you are not entirely wrong.

We began with a professor from the Sorbonne, soon we shall move on to publishers of philosophy and to Sartre, later we shall turn to Rousseau, to a highbrow literary journal, and it may be that the most eminent academics – say the philosophers of the College de France – will not all be spared. Our work may seem systematically to make digs at the finest institutions and the most reputable writers. This selection is part of our project, which is to show that where women are concerned the learned utter, and institutions let them utter, words which fall clearly below their own usual standards of validation. In other words, the fact that people play the game of being as theoretically exacting as possible, that they sharpen their concepts and test out their words in the most rigorous circles does not prevent them from coming out with some prize twaddle.[45] Once one realizes that no methodological or institutional precautions can offer full protection against ridicule, one feels free to say what one pleases; it would be the last straw if Michèle le Doeuff did not have the right to be as naive as Jacques Le Goff![46] Wise men find wisdom bitter when it shows them that they will have the same fate as the foolish, whereas an ordinary woman relishes the wisdom which shows her that there is nothing to stop her from being as foolish as the greatest sage. We must then change our aesthetics where theory is concerned: since it is pointless to try and hold back the improper, let us not seek to corset what we say in the (vain) hope of rendering it free of absurdities. The gist of what Delacroix says is that great art is not art without faults. The only question is whether a particular instance of philosophical thinking explores or thinks something. As rigorously as possible of course.

We should not believe that the most strict institutions allow only men – and men who are already famous in other ways – to write rubbish on the question of women. I promised to give two examples of catastrophic philosophical treatments of 'the woman question'. Here is the second. In 1978, the worthy publishers Vrin brought out an opuscule by Edmée Mottini-Coulon. This was not a public event like Janet Radcliffe Richards' book, but still it did bear the label of one of the most prestigious and prestige-conferring academic publishing houses. The book is called *Pour une ontologie spécifiquement féminine*. You would think it was a hoax, if it wasn't from Vrin. Are these publishers so little interested in what anyone, woman or man, has to say about women that they could accept a text whose title in itself indicates a curious confusion? For if there is an 'ontology' specific to one human group or specific to another, the term ontology loses all meaning. The content of the work is in keeping with its title and a most surprising mode of discourse unfolds within it. The author behaves as if she were an 'ethnographer of herself' and it is in this respect that her book is of interest to us. When one assumes a specificity – 'of women' in this case, but it could be of any human group – and strives to set out the philosophical doctrine that that specific group must have, given that it is what it is, that doctrine is granted the status of a folklore, which is described from the outside, even if one swears that one belongs to the group concerned and one's signature as author seems to guarantee that membership. This approach results from the fact that one has internalized a way of seeing oneself through the eyes of a self-proclaimed universal other.[47] Ethnologists visiting Native American societies could decide to describe the religion, metaphysics and morals of those societies strictly as 'social facts' specific to the group under study. They did not discuss the principles of (for example) Hopi aesthetics, but simply (they thought) recorded them as intelligibly as possible. They certainly did not ask themselves if the Bororos' morality was moral: those people's practices constituted a system of beliefs, of ways of acting and of feeling which could be laid out and looked at as though one were dealing with the life of insects. My wise reader will already have realized that I am talking about yesterday's ethnology here and that what I say in no way applies to studies carried out since the end of colonialism.

Sometimes, of course, in research into the history of ideas, commentators will distance themselves from the system they are discussing and write about stoic metaphysics or Aristotelian logic as though they were fossils or simply factual beliefs, studied simply in order to draw out their inner coherence. However, such an attitude is extremely rare in the history of philosophy. Historians of science are the ones who tend to study obsolete scientific theories in this way.[48] And theories are obsolete or outdated when they have been supplanted by new ones. To undertake the ethnography of an intellectual system is always to assume that the locus of truth is elsewhere, even if that truth in turn may one day be undermined.

From this point of view Edmée Mottini-Coulon's undertaking appears as a perverse stunt for she locates truth outside herself and gives it back to its usual legitimate owners. This assessment is confirmed by the ending, where the author sets out some 'moral' considerations which are as unedifying as possible. In them she upholds the idea that a woman has the right to take her children with her into death, since this right is based on a 'fact': a woman cannot think of her children otherwise than as a continuation of her own body. The doctrine of the brahman husband in relation to his putative widow is here transposed into the relation between mother and child. The 'fact' is doubtful in itself and in any case, the author does not establish it. This may be a personal fantasy, or the idea that a man who is particularly jealous of the mother–child relationship might form of that relationship. It matters little. Since no fact has ever made a right (and everyone is supposed to know that), the effect of the text is to give credence to the view that 'feminine morality' is the exact opposite of morality and thus that women need to be controlled. I am sure that a misogynist was guiding Edmée Mottini-Coulon's pen, a misogynist and phallocrat.[49] For the idea of psychological fact constituting an absolute right reminds me of something: one often finds men in love making a formal complaint when they are refused a smile: 'I love you, so I am entitled to...'.

11   In which the impasse is further explored and then resolved

Sociologists, first Andrée Michel, then Colette Guillaumin, Christine Delphy and Liliane Kandel, have managed to construct a theoretical field of feminist studies. Historians have done so too, in particular Michèle Perrot.[50] In philosophy, the situation seems more complex. The project of producing a philosophy dealing with the question of women (whatever that question is), seems to lead to an impasse, for at least two reasons. The first is that philosophical reasoning must be allowed to follow theoretical digressions, so that it can never contain itself within the bounds of a 'subject'. Even a writer of treatises like Aristotle talks about mathematics, biology and the theory of language in a work on politics, Kant talks about morality in the *Critique of Pure Reason* and as for the Platonic dialogues, it is hard to tell exactly what is under discussion in each one. Philosophers constantly leave their topic behind, always assuming they claim to have one, which is not always the case. It is thus impossible for a philosophical exploration to set itself the task of containing itself within a field which has been well-defined in advance, to deal with one question and one question only. It is impossible, for example, for it to remain strictly within the field of feminist studies, dealing with the relations of women to philosophy and nothing else.

The second reason relates to the (in principle at least) universalist project which sets out the objects for philosophical discussion. This should not be confused with any pretensions this or that discourse may have to being universal and to offering itself for the approval of all; that type of universal, called *katholikos* in Greek, found a different application in the field of moral teaching (with the idea of rules which can be applied by all) and, as we know, in a religion, which first called itself Ecclesia Christi, but soon decided it could and should be taught to the people of all nations.[51] Philosophical universalism is something different, although philosophers of the Christian era have often merged it with the other type. It comes down to postulating that the things one is talking about have being, or at least that the ones that are worth talking about do. This does not mean that they 'really' exist, nor that language cannot talk about non-being, nor that they are radically independent of the thought that thinks about them. The postulate according to which the things one is talking about have being is more minimal than that. It is the idea that, even if 'the real' is a problematic issue, even if language says as much about non-being as being, even if the objects of thought vary, for example, throughout history, even if and even if, the simple fact that I posit something as the object of my thinking means that I postulate it as an object, that I throw it out towards you and that it is liable to have a consistency and coherence which is precisely what you and I are going to talk about. In technical vocabulary, this postulate of the being of the thing about which I am talking to you can be called a purely regulatory idea which has no content, constitutes nothing and prejudges nothing. Once this is accepted, you and I can begin to argue and this is moreover what has been happening for the last twenty-five centuries. But people have to argue about something, which is then a third term between the arguers. Socrates and Meno, in Plato's dialogue which bears the latter's name, completely disagree about what virtue is and yet they both assume that there is probably something which can be called virtue; they are arguing about its definition and description. Philosophical universalism is this entirely assumed independence of the object of the debate in relation to the particular people who are debating it. In what sense, then, can one speak of feminist philosophy? If it is a form of philosophy, its object is independent (or in any case postulated as such); but what independent object can reside in an empirically identifiable sociological 'place'? In the first analysis, this is a contradiction.

But for twenty-five years we have been learning to identify logical impasses and at the same stroke to resolve them. The first solution is by using a factual argument: here and there one reads essays setting out philosophical analyses which are important to feminism,[52] and then there is *The Second Sex* and, long before that, the *Vindication of the Rights of Women*. It seems that the thinking which circulates between feminism and philosophy has some chance of being able to raise possible disparate and limited issues based on an informed conceptual critique, effective questioning of received knowledge and a desire to change the position allotted to women. The existence of these works obliges us to ask ourselves about the theoretical conditions which made their production possible, as well as about the non-production or mutism mentioned above. We can also escape the impasse by showing that it contains something false.

The error concerns 'feminist studies', whether historical or sociological. Of course in practice few people other than feminists or those with particularly open minds show much interest in their objects of study (nineteenth-century women workers, the place of women in the general division of labour, and so on). But these objects of study are not a prolongation of some feminist essence; they are in themselves perfectly independent and thus, by rights, can be objects of research and thought for all. They are not elements in some feminist folklore, but perfectly universal instances; if they have been left out of a history which does not describe itself as particular, or a sociology which believes itself to be sociology pure and simple, it is this omission which can be criticized and reveals the particularism of these disciplines as they are. In other words, 'feminist studies' in some of the social sciences represent an element of the universal and reflect the basic task of the discipline concerned. On the other hand work which, while claiming to be exhaustive, forgets about women's existence and concerns itself only with the position of men should be described and considered as particularist. To give a name to this particularism which not only concerns itself exclusively with the history or social existence of men, but then redoubles this limitation with its assertions (they and their own point of view are the only ones that count), I have used the term masculinism. We shall clarify this term as we go along by putting it to use.

To say all this again even more simply: by rights the work of feminist historians and sociologists, or philosophers, could be done by men; this would need only an ideal state where men's relation to women was free of tyranny or contempt and where reciprocal recognition reigned supreme. Then a man historian might become fascinated by the past of all featherless bipeds. In practice, work 'on women' is progressing very slowly, gradually picking up an audience outside specifically feminist circles. Yet it still meets indifference, that formidable form of resistance, and almost as much from women as from men. For there are as many women as men, or almost as many, who think that the present or past concrete position of women is not worth bothering with. In the current state of affairs it has thus fallen to a few women to take up issues which should be of interest to everyone. And it is already saying a lot if they manage to get somebody interested in the results of their research.

In the course of the present work we shall instance a few 'pearls' from learned men who are philosophers or specialists in a given social science. This is not for the pleasure of revealing their murky depths, but to bring to light the obstacles which prevent many colleagues from thinking, or indeed from producing a mere 'right opinion', as soon as the topic turns to women. We must assume that these obstacles also stop them from hearing in a normal way or from understanding the things that women historians or sociologists have to say. Once again I am talking about women historians only because of the existing situation. By rights, a serious male historian should be able to hear, absorb and discuss in the normal way something that a woman colleague says, for example, about the convents of silk manufacturers in the Lyons area in the nineteenth century.[53] If he chooses to ignore this type of work, or to consider it as 'specialist' and of interest only to the equally specialized audience of women who are interested in the history of women workers, this betrays his own intellectual block. Just as surely as if he were expounding the idea that women are not part of history.

12   One last digression and then, at last, the question

Do we need to adopt Bachelard's notion of the 'psychoanalysis of objective knowledge'[54] to explain masculinist particularism in work regarded as intellectual? Bachelard maintains that rigorous knowledge can only be built by destroying what he calls 'opinion', by which he means ideas that preceded the intellectual effort. His view of opinion is that it 'thinks badly, or rather, does not think at all', but only translates needs into knowledge.[55] As one can never fully destroy this opinion, which keeps coming back in intellectual works, Bachelard believes a catharsis of scientific culture is required. Bergson before him said:

> the normal work of intelligence is far from being a disinterested work. We do not, in general, aim at knowing for the sake of knowing, but at knowing in order to take a stand, gain a profit, in fact to satisfy an interest. We try to find out up to what point the object to be known is *this* or *that*, into what genus it fits [...] To try a concept on an object is to ask of the object what we have to do with[56] it, what it can do for us.

Perhaps we should decide that Bergson and Bachelard have produced a theory which will simply explain the masculinism present in erudite culture as follows: because, until now, philosophers and other learned people have mostly been men, and men who only addressed other men, their opinions and interests could be interpolated without difficulty into the text of their work and even supported their efforts at knowledge, these same interests and opinions making them deaf to anything that did not translate their own needs or interests into knowledge.

Such reflexions could be at least tactically useful in constructing a theory of the a-theoretical element present in intellectual undertakings. However, we should note that their authors applied them not to philosophical discourse itself, but to 'knowledge', to the point where the psychological genesis of 'opinions' seems to affect all fields except their own. According to them, their domain is not a field of knowledge like any other, but a space of pure reflective thought. This means that we can no longer use Bachelard and Bergson directly. Moreover, although we might ratify the genetic principle itself, we have to ask ourselves whether psychological phenomena (needs, drives, desires, etc.) really constitute the origins, and the sole origins, of this unthought which hinders theoretical work by inhabiting it.

Besides, Bergson and Bachelard were neither the first nor the only ones to tackle the problem of the obstacles to thought represented by 'opinions': Roger Bacon, and then Francis, put forward a far broader theory of the genesis of blocks to intellectual investigation and knowledge.[57] Both suggested that these obstacles arise in part not from a reality external to the theory (such as psychological reality), but from an intention to present the theory as more finished than it actually is or could be. False windows are built out of a concern for symmetry. This happens in philosophy too. The question I want to deal with – that of sexism in philosophical texts – is crucial in this debate. What could be apparently more 'psychological' than sexism? And yet, analysis of the philosophical texts themselves reveals that it is not so simple.

The debate between Bergson and Bachelard on the one hand and the Bacons on the other forms one of the horizons of the present research, and perhaps an answer will be given later on. This is not certain. But I must confess that for me this debate provides the speculative interest of my 'subject': Where do the sexist images of men philosophers come from? From the depths of their drives? Or from their method itself? We shall see. At present we need only mention the critiques of the Bacons, Bergson and Bachelard as an introduction to the idea that no formed discipline can, in advance, be regarded as pure, in other words free of all specific interests, or apposite for understanding everything. There is ultimately nothing surprising in the fact that philosophy is not in some pre-established way an adequate mode of thought to analyse the oppression of women. On the contrary, behind it lies a long and weighty tradition of conniving with that oppression by either giving conceptual support to the alienation of women that it finds already constituted,[58] by proclaiming the exclusion of women from the ranks of the learned or by managing to kill two birds with one stone because, in kindly providing 'theoretical justifications' for the social status of women, it also finds a way of closing its doors to those women who may want to philosophize.

All the same, some women have wondered whether one particular form of philosophy might not be more appropriate than others for thinking about the liberation of women. This question should not be left aside. However, it has two disadvantages, the first being that it is too vague in its formulation and the second that it seeks a ready-made form of philosophy, which could be gratefully taken up and applied to the still shadowy question of women's condition. Inherent in this is the enormous risk of looking at that condition through the blinkers of the chosen form of philosophy and of wanting 'for women' that they should be whatever the doctrine wants them to be. It is wisest to leave this question hanging, particularly as we need to ask this other more radical one: must a form of philosophy be appropriate in advance to a project of investigating or theorizing something? Looking for such appropriateness is the same as regarding the form of philosophy in question, or all philosophy, as a tool which must, by definition, pre-exist the carrying out of a task. But surely to project this is immediately to leave the realm of philosophy.

The case of Simone de Beauvoir seems to me important in thinking about this issue, which is why it forms the centre of gravity of my investigation. In principle the theoretical presuppositions of *The Second Sex* and *Being and Nothingness* are the same. And yet what a distance there is between the conclusions each draws on the subject we are dealing with! Does this mean that the same conceptual framework can lead both to sexist observations and to an analysis of sexism? Or should we infer from this that the inappropriateness of a theoretical tool can ultimately be a positive thing? The 'Beauvoir-Sartre' case is exemplary from every point of view or, as we say in the jargon of the trade, it is paradigmatic. It allows us to perceive the link between these questions and to understand them. And it casts some light on the difficulty, when one is at once woman, philosopher and feminist, of speaking.

13 Being there

But in thinking about the complex relationship between Sartre's thought and that of Simone de Beauvoir, I have to ask myself what is the nature of the my undertaking and how do I think it relates to the two works I have mentioned? Is it a commentary or a work of history of philosophy? Such an undertaking is usually expected to remain neutral and the person carrying it out is supposed to take care to remain outside what is described. Any claim to such neutrality on my part would be a lie. It is because the issue of women's position interests me that I read Sartre in the way that I do and that certain problems are apparent to me which might well remain invisible to many other readers. But to state this at the outset amounts to too rapid a silencing of a problem which is only interesting because of its complexity. What does it mean to write about what one reads and to take up things that others have said?

My thoughts on Simone de Beauvoir and Sartre will be intercut with comments on this and other questions. Basically, I am not so much going to discuss a subject as to digress a great deal in trying to talk about it. For me, the issue of women's relation to philosophy offers a viewpoint which allows one to think about the destiny of philosophy itself and – at least this is one of the hopes that sustain me – to open up new perspectives on the position of women in general. No doubt to some readers this book will seem a labyrinth and they will be within their rights to ask if I have also provided a thread. But we are not dealing here in threads or labyrinths: any piece of work is basically a synthesis or reconciliation of evidence, interests and other considerations of heteroclite origins. Of course one can try to give these considerations a regular and finished shape. This is the usual aesthetic of treatises and *Summae*. But it is not the only possible aesthetic, even if the academic practice of philosophy tends to impose it to the point where we have lost our sensitivity to the mixing and burgeoning from which many living works of philosophy have grown. Allow me to imagine that there is a style of thinking that resembles a great port, where crews from all the four corners of the world meet, where words in different languages intermingle and where the people in the bars all know that all the world's ports communicate and that that is why there are ports. From this point of view the real Greek miracle was the ancestor of Piraeus, to which all the Mediterranean's questions came. Or better still, that country scattered between Ephesus, the islands, Delphi, Corinth and Paestum. Philosophers, even the Greeks, have often repudiated the sea and dreamed of closed intellectual and political spaces, sheltered from foreign influences which might produce change. In this – through a trick of dialectics which I shall take care not to judge – they were seeking the opposite of that which caused them to be.

The aim of an introduction is not to give a random stream of gratuitous statements and thoughts, while the main body of the text is shielded against a flood of heteroclite elements. Its only aim, I believe, is to make contact with whoever is going to read and to ask for that person's tolerance and goodwill, in other words for voluntary help. No argument can hold water completely without the finishing touch of the approval or ratification of the person on the receiving end of it – even mathematicians say they go through this strange waiting feeling when they present their research. Texts are written in anxious intersubjectivity. But if we accept that they can only stand up if the reader grants them something, we can infer, reciprocally, that readers must at all times have a grasp on the discourses presented to them. They may be in complete disagreement with what is said; but that matters little, for the essential thing is that a reader should be there, and this is not always guaranteed in advance.

Reciprocally, I have put myself here too, with my stated tastes, my political hopes, the values I wish to uphold and, quite simply, my biography. I had a little difficulty deciding to do this, if only because of the Baconian training I gave myself in former times, which is illustrated by a phrase from the preface to the *Instauratio Magna*: '*De nobis ipsis silemus; de re autem, quae agitur, petimus, ut homines eam non opinionem sed opus cogitent*'.[59] ('Of myself I say nothing; but in behalf of the business which is in hand I entreat men to believe that it is not an opinion to be held, but a work to be done.') It is now common practice to put oneself into parentheses as an empirical, individual person; but we can try to go beyond this practice.

A meeting helped me to take this decision and to try to overcome the forgetting of the self that modern philosophical work usually demands. In 1986, the Italian Communist Party asked me to lead a debate in Milan with Marisa Rodano on Simone de Beauvoir, in which Marisa was to say that *The Second Sex* is not a feminist book. I protested: of course, many misunderstandings of Simone de Beauvoir's work are possible, but that is just too much. Rodano explained herself later, saying that the book's method seems quite different from the one endorsed by feminism, which consists of starting from one's own personal experience. In *The Second Sex* at least, Beauvoir avoids talking about herself: she hardly even mentions herself. This exchange rattled around in my head for a long time. It would certainly be unhelpful for a woman to discuss the oppression of women without bringing herself into the picture – this would amount to positing herself as a 'third sex' and basically to saying: there are men, there are women and then there's me, off stage. But on the other hand it is even more unhelpful to fix on one method as the method of feminist thinking once and for all and particularly one that tends to restrict the method of feminist thinking to the genre of 'personal experience'. Defining the features of the feminist mode of thought inevitably means restricting it somewhere and, since 'all definition is a negation', we might ask ourselves what this mode prevents or checks, once it has become a norm. On this point philosophical thinking may be of great value to feminist thinking insofar as the former can try to identify limitations arising from the simple fact that the latter is now integrated into a historical tradition and sum of experiences. For whatever these limitations are, they create an obstacle to further investigations. Having rebelled (can't we sometimes choose to talk *about something* rather than always *from our own experience*!), I finally gave in to the idea that, although personal experience is not necessarily a good starting point – it is often limited and very obscure – it is however a good test if one can manage to integrate it into critical work; for the contrary is definitely a bad sign, not only where feminist thinking is concerned, but in any kind of philosophy. And particularly when one is seeking a form of philosophy which can grasp realities that need to be made appreciable, if only so that one can fight against them.

Involvement in the women's movement can then be seen as a precious experience which teaches one not to remain outside what one says. For feminism (whatever the content given to the term) draws on the idea of a pre-existent conflictual reality in relation to which we need to situate ourselves or which we need to get away from. One way or another, this reality passes through subjectivity, so that perception of it requires the opening of an intellectual debate within the subjectivity concerned with it. A rapid contrast with the profile of one of Foucault's works should allow us to clarify this a little.

Foucault's project to bring to light the modern episteme, which still provides the basis of our knowledge, can in itself be accepted as the general programme of any philosophical challenge to received knowledge. Since one of the great veins of our modern 'knowledges' is a certain division which is always postulated, often refined or embroidered, but never questioned – the one which guarantees that the difference between men and women is fundamental and basic – the bringing to light of this deep-seated episteme which governs our way of thinking could be perfectly integrated into the archaeological project. And Foucault's definition of his work as 'an inquiry whose aim is to rediscover on what basis knowledge and theory became possible'[60] is general enough to suit many philosophical projects, including my own.

And yet Foucault seems to hold the European *ratio* that he seeks to exhume at arm's length. He holds it as far as possible from himself and his reader, to such an extent that it is only mildly disturbing. It is not quite addressed to our own consciousness, which we must however assume to be caught in the episteme in question, as in the 'knowledges' which that episteme makes possible. Correlatively, such distance gives us to understand that, in the documents that the author has gone through in order to exhume the basis of received theories, nothing has hurt him. The text of *The Order of Things* always speaks of a 'disturbance' which must be reintroduced. But can we be sure that he has chosen to use the material most likely to disturb? The book discusses the 'social sciences' as they flourished in the early nineteenth century, observing that their object of study is 'man'. We should however note a curious omission: the inquiry does not tell us that the social sciences have not so much dealt with an object ('man'), as striven to underline all the possible differences, and thus all the hierarchies, in the general concept of humanity. They have particularly sought to produce a subordinating contrast between 'woman' (singular) and 'men' (plural). This contrast of woman with men can be seen as still structuring the social sciences and more or less anyone's everyday approach to any situation. An exhumation of the conditions in which a normative discourse of difference, positing a dissymmetrical difference, has become the rock on which academic (and popular) anthropology is founded would have held the power to challenge our vision of the human world. But to try and bring that discourse to light, it would have been necessary (at the minimum) to be irritated by the content of the social sciences, by Auguste Comte or by Proudhon, the ludicrous author of *The Pornocrat*.

I must confess that I always feel embarrassed to challenge *The Order of Things*, for I am assured that at the end of his life Foucault himself considered this book to be the most questionable of his own works. And his later ones are so different in tone. So let these remarks be taken purely as signposting a problem: when a particular slice of culture (for example, the social sciences in the nineteenth century, as they have come down to us) do not directly make a person suffer, nor cause that person distress nor produce that simple reaction which is described as 'hitting the roof', is it not likely that the research will remain more Olympian than it should? I think it is always a fine project to disturb a good conscience woven from received ideas or fallout from learned utterances whose historical origins we have forgotten. However, we need to avoid two obvious and symmetrical things. The first is thinking that, because philosophy has always surprised and disturbed, the philosopher is bound always to explore disturbance in its entirety, that this happens in some way by itself. The second, conversely, springs from a strict materialism and boils down to maintaining that only those who directly suffer from the effects of a given intellectual structure are able to communicate their suffering in the form of a theoretical challenge to that structure, and that they also cannot fail to do so. I think there is nothing more difficult to reach than the pole of disturbance in thought. One must make its conquest one's goal, in the knowledge that no one is predestined to occupy that place.

The revolutionary scholars of the Renaissance took the trouble to go and worry at commonsense assumptions on their own territory and, as well as the theoretical controversy suitable for such things, they also produced fictions which questioned these assumptions internalized by all – including themselves. I am particularly thinking of Kepler's *Dream*, a narrative which he long kept to himself and which he may have written for and against himself, trying to find a place on the imaginary level where it would be possible for him personally to experience the meaning of substituting heliocentrism for geocentrism. *De nobis ipsis petimus* – so let us find out where we are in what we think; or again, let us try to grasp the way in which what we think affects us. Even if all our academic training goes against such a project: this training at least has the immense merit of not leaving us ignorant of other times, other ways of thinking philosophically. And if the ancient can challenge the modern, we have some chance of finding there a sense of the anecdotal and of the familiar irony with which the philosophers of Antiquity or of the Renaissance implicated themselves in their thought, to the point where the daily weave of their subjectivity was involved in the adventure and could therefore by modified by it.

This work on subjectivity (my own or thine, benevolent reader) is my first aim here. I am not trying to discuss a topic, and my readers should not expect a treatise, exhaustive, serious and utterly theoretical, in brief a *Critique of Sexist Reason*. The exploration you have before you has addressees. Not just you, not just those who uphold some sexist nastiness in their scholarly way, but also myself. What kind of book would it be that did not speak to its author, as though she were, chronologically speaking, the first reader?

I am also looking for something else beyond the various thoughts presented here. I should like to suggest that rationality works in any case, in exile from itself and for better or worse. The worst will be illustrated by philosophers who, using nonsensical reasoning about women, have founded concepts which yet have all the formal appearance of philosophical productions. It will also be illustrated by those who, for reasons which are either obscure or too clear, exile women and some others outside philosophy, thus rooting the latter in an ad hoc masculine condition and conferring the status of internal exiles on those women who are part of the philosophical community. The best will be sought in the hope of a rationality considered in its movement towards decentring and its eccentric curves, a type of thought that acts on questions which it did not necessarily produce itself and which forgets all obsession with limits or carefully defined doctrinal bases built into an orthodoxy. A migrant rationality which never wants to understand itself absolutely, although this does not mean that it should not try to explain itself as best as possible. Such a project has its historical precedents, as does the idea that philosophical thought is not rooted in any kind of pre-given, personal way of being. We do not claim to introduce a totally new revolution into thought, nor to return to venerable sources and to a rediscovery of some original meaning. The precedents of philosophy are varied enough to allow anyone always to find what they want and to draw nourishment from it. For myself, I am seeking the greatest possibility of movement. Between different fields of knowledge, 'disciplines' or discursive formations, between different periods of thought and between supposedly different 'levels' of thought, from everyday opinions to the original metaphysical system. For I think we can call 'thought' only that which circulates between everything I have just mentioned and also, and above all, between people and groups who, however different they are before they make contact, have no reason to be indifferent to each other and can all take a little trouble to communicate and meet.

'Oh, lovely ignorance' says Rousseau of the future 'man's woman'.[61] To postulate and indeed love the principle of the other's ignorance always comes down to revealing or ignoring one's own stupidity, and 'lovers of wisdom' (in principle, philosophers) have too often been lovers of the other's non-wisdom. Poets, they tell us, do not know what they are saying, the sciences do not know their own objects of study, left to themselves politicians are asses, as for the

people, they are deprived of consciousness and women do not and
cannot think. In examining this last assertion I should like to invite
thinking on all the crude anathemas pronounced against philosophy's
various 'others'.

   Let us say it again: the idea that 'woman' does not think is not
strictly speaking the preserve of philosophers, even less of philosophers who have had some importance or are still known today.
Anyone brave enough to dive into the fourth basement of some vast
library would find dense and dusty piles of paperbound volumes,
often lacking a date or place of publication, telling her all about the
'congenital imbecility of woman'. This theme is like the psycho-
medical doublet of what the Napoleonic Code called the 'incapacity
of the married woman', in this case a legal incapacity. I promise that
I shall only recall the breadth of the phenomenon from time to time.

14   Envoi

'But, Your Honour, this woman is going to suggest that there is no
difference between a genius and a third-rate author, between one who
turned down the Nobel Prize and a literary lunatic, between Hegel
and Mgr Dupanloup!'
   'On some points, on some points.'
   'I cannot accept that a great philosopher, trained in the most
rigorous thought, the form which proceeds by concepts, should not
know what he is saying! One need not read the others.'
   'I shall answer you by saying that many concepts come from
buried and obscure inferences, called up by vague experiences. These
inferences spread to other perceptions, without one really knowing
which experience or inference established the concept in the first
place. We can call such concepts surreptitious. Many of them are in
part only a chimera, a hybrid of the imagination.[62] Today the idea
that the power of reason constitutes the great difference between men
and women is a stowaway carried by what has been said over the last
two centuries on the difference between the sexes and on the question
of reason.'
   'But experience. . .'
   'Experience is precisely what is lacking here. For if you need the
idea of reason to tell the difference between a woman and a man,
what conclusions are we to draw from that? And if you need sexual
difference to understand what reason is, I'm afraid this probably
means you give very little thought to reason.'

'It doesn't matter. When she speaks ill of great men she will shock me and when she cites mediocre ones to criticize them, she will bore me.'

'No one is forced to read a book.'

As long as we can use paraphrases of Kant or parodies of Bergson to make digs at the Rousseauphiles, the fans of Auguste Comte or philospholaters in general, we need not despair of philosophy. But if there is a dispute between philosophical reflective thinking and philosophical nonsense, we can be sure that the tribunal entitled to pronounce on this dispute cannot be 'philosophy' as a single entity. Even if I achieve nothing more than the establishment of that idea, I shall not have totally wasted my time in producing a book which I was not forced to write either.

Second Notebook

which is analytical

which deals in particular with the case of Sartre and Simone de Beauvoir;
which shows that the latter had a genius for the inappropriate, and
wonders whether she might not have stretched existentialism beyond and
above its means.

What a strange mixture *The Second Sex* is for a feminist reader of
today, or for anyone whose main motive for reading is to find elements of thought which could be used to support a practice or a
language which could become that of present or future debates. Such
a reader would feel tempted to approach it selectively. Of course,
there are countless observations, descriptions and analyses in the text
which, for my part, I can only endorse. For example, when Simone
de Beauvoir describes the repetitive nature of housework, when she
analyses the censorious treatment of aggressiveness in little girls,
when she cites and criticizes Stekel's conceptions of frigidity or when
she examines the prevailing conception of women's wages as *salaire
d'appoint* or 'supplementary income' and the sorrows of conjugal life,
she provides essential elements for a minutely detailed consciousness
of the oppression of women. And certainly the book's detailed nature
makes it very useful, because oppression always also exists where you
would not expect to find it, where it might go unnoticed.

Yet side by side with these valuable analyses exploring women's
condition, and indeed preceding them, we find a whole conceptual
apparatus which is now somewhat outdated and which makes the
book less accessible to more recent readers. What, for example, are
we to make of this:

> Every individual concerned to justify his existence experiences this
> existence as an indefinite need for self-transcendence. Now what marks

the specificity of woman's situation is that while she, like any other human being, is an autonomous freedom, she discovers and chooses herself in a world where men force her to assume herself as the Other: they claim to fix her as an object and to doom her to immanence, since her transcendence is to be perpetually transcended by another essential and sovereign consciousness.[1]

But is the problem really one of 'justifying one's existence?' Is it really necessary to use the concept of transcendence to bring the oppression of women to light? What happens if one refuses to give meaning to these categories? Is it not rash to hang a study of oppression on ideas like these?

What we chiefly sense in these lines is the aging of a philosophy which was in fashion in 1949. It must have been a factor in making the book more readable at the time, but it has since become a hindrance, now that we no longer speak fluent existentialist. This, and my vague perception that use of this language may have disadvantages, are the two reasons for the temptation I sometimes feel (and I do not think I am alone) to read this feminist *Summa* in a selective way. If many readers today skip those pages most imbued with existentialist doctrine and focus on the analyses of the 'world where men force her to', slipping over the transcended transcendences, they are giving *The Second Sex* an ordinary fate: *habent sua fata libri*, books have their own destiny and the most usual of these is to be fragmented – we'll take this and not that, says posterity.

However, it is fairer, and far more instructive, to read Simone de Beauvoir's essay as it is and to try to connect its two aspects, which seem heterogeneous, if only so that we can use it to ask one question that matters to us: in what respect, if any, is the choice of this or that philosophical frame of reference a crucial one for feminist studies? In the 1970s philosophist inflation also affected feminist theoretical productions, or 'women's books', by women who wanted to change things, but who rejected the label 'feminist'. The works of Luce Irigaray, for example, propound the idea that since philosophical discourse lays down the law to all other forms of discourse, it is the first that must be overthrown and disrupted, with the result that the 'main enemy' becomes 'idealist logic' or the 'metaphysical logos'.[2] I do not know myself whether philosophical discourse lays down the law to anything at all. At any rate, Simone de Beauvoir's book gives a very different impression: although her posing of the problems in no way seeks to overthrow a 'metaphysical logos', she still manages to highlight issues and put forward thoughts of which the least one can say is that they galvanized women's movements pretty well everywhere and helped them get going.

Or rather we should say that, for twenty years, *The Second Sex* was the movement before the movement. In the one-to-one dialogue of reading, thousands of women found what later they got from meeting in groups: reference points for understanding the situation given to all of them, a language to express feelings of unease and the sharing of this unease. In the 1960s, when I discovered this book, it helped me greatly in at least two ways. At the time, officially, women no longer had any problems. Even the extraordinary scandal of the difficulty of obtaining contraception was hidden. This meant that all the existential difficulties we experienced had become secret, and each of us thought them her own personal problem; each of us, surprised at feeling so bad in those heady days of expansion and the Beatles, could only wonder what was odd about herself. Reading *The Second Sex* taught us to objectify the question, to look at the social world with a critical eye, instead of looking within ourselves for some hidden cause of an existential incapacity. It taught us simply to situate some of our difficulties and thus to free ourselves from their internalization. It also helped each to discover that she was not a special case and that her situation was more or less that of all women.

In an interview with an American journalist in 1976, Simone de Beauvoir said that her book influenced only women who wanted to be influenced and helped the development of only those women who had already started to develop by themselves. In talking about influence and looking at her work only from the point of view of a possible 'radicalization' of her women readers, she is not doing herself justice. A book which puts an end to loneliness, which teaches people to see, has greater and more immediate importance than all the manifestos in the world. Manifestos can be judged against the standard of 'influence', if indeed this is something that can be measured. A real book offers something else: the possibility of meeting a voice, an intelligence and a particular kind of generosity. Simone de Beauvoir taught the young women that we were to trust ourselves and to send the ball back – we who were too often surrounded by cruel words and glances quick to censure.

1 Discordant harmony

My project is to show how the ethics of authenticity provided an appropriate and effective theoretical point of view for bringing the oppression of women to light. The philosophical substratum of Beauvoir's work cannot therefore be dissociated from its more empirical dimension, which I would however see as more contemporary than the conceptual framework she uses to undertake her feminist investigations.

But – and here's the paradox – although they cannot be separated, there is no pre-established harmony between this philosophical position and the results it leads to. I shall look for the negative proof of this in *Being and Nothingness*, where the 'same' problematics of authenticity gives quite opposite results. Beauvoir's text can thus be considered as a whole only in a dialectical fashion, as is also the case with that of Sartre.

We shall first briefly describe the conceptual framework on which *The Second Sex* is built. It is explicitly dualist and its notions are organized in pairs: immanence/transcendence, In-itself/For-itself, authentic/inauthentic, assumption/bad faith, subject and project/ object. It is an ethical ontology, for individuals are subjects and, when they assert themselves as such, they assume their freedom and transcendence in relation to the world: they live in the mode of authenticity. But they may also feel 'the temptation to avoid freedom and constitute themselves as a thing',[3] thus avoiding 'the anguish of authentically assumed existence'.[4] In this case the For-itself is degraded into an In-itself and freedom into facticity, in other words it is in bad faith. Lastly Beauvoir's problematics is a problematics of consciousness: 'the subject only posits itself in opposition. It aims to assert itself as essential and to constitute the other as inessential'.[5]

On this basis the fundamental thesis of the book is that all women are from the outset constituted as inessential. Because they are dominated, they have had to submit to an alien viewpoint. Hence the description of an oppression which arises from a power relation capable of producing the same effects as the moral fault: 'Every time transcendence falls back into immanence, there is a degradation of existence into the In-itself [...] This downfall represents a moral fault if the subject consents to it; if it is inflicted upon him, it [is an] oppression'.[6]

The analogy between fault and oppression seems destined to dramatize the latter and doubtless there is something to think about here concerning the writer's youth in 1949 and the oldest possible philosophical tradition. For it takes a real philosopher to wonder in what way oppression is damaging. Some philosophers have even gone so far as to maintain that suffering injustice is not really harmful (to the soul); the act of committing injustice alone causes a wound and very nasty scars – again to the soul, of course.[7] Later, when Simone de Beauvoir's commitment becomes more concrete and less isolated, first during the Algerian war and then side by side with other women, she no longer asks herself what is bad about oppression; it is not necessary to prove that a scandal is a scandal. This development of hers is important: seeking to justify oneself in fighting oppression means one is still caught in the ideology which sanctions that oppression. In stating that one is against the oppression of women because it puts them in a position where they commit a fault, is one not destined to remain indifferent to those aspects of oppression which do not resemble the fault of bad faith? In *The Second Sex* the aspects of oppression discussed are those and only those which would be moral faults in other circumstances.

The ethics underlying Beauvoir's thought are not hard to identify since she says herself that her point of view is that of existentialist morality. *The Second Sex* is also a labour of love, and as a wedding gift she brings a singular confirmation of the validity of Sartrism: your thought makes possible an understanding of women's condition, your philosophy sets me on the road to my emancipation – your truth will make me free.

Here we find a stereotype in philosophical liaisons. Since the days of Antiquity, women have been admitted into the field of philosophy chiefly when they took on the role of the loving admirer: we can call this the 'Heloise complex'. Perhaps the problem I mentioned above, and which preoccupies some women today, of seeking to discover which of the philosophies that are available is the most appropriate for thinking about the liberation of women, can be seen as the ultimate avatar of this configuration. In the French women's movement we have seen women advocating the view that Lacan's thought was the way to salvation. We have also seen Foucauldian or Nietzschean feminists. Worse, one is commonly asked whether one is a this man-ian or a that man-ian and, worse still, in an American collection Mr and Mrs Hintikka have together written an article which explains that, if Jaakko Hintikka's logic has not yet found the wide audience it deserves, this is because, being sympathetic to the way that little girls perceive relations between objects, it does not fit in with the masculine models which are, of course, dominant.[8] Thus denunciation of the oppression of half of humanity provides reinforcement to the glory of one master against his rivals. I have long been doing my best to show that it is time for women to stop being the devoted followers of one (and always only one) coryphaeus and that, once one becomes a whoeverian, that is the end of philosophy and of the desire for intellectual independence which should also be a characteristic of feminism.[9] There is much to be done here.

Simone de Beauvoir's gesture is commonplace, and infinitely recognizable. However, from a theoretical point of view, it does not go without saying. To convince ourselves of this we need only pinpoint two aspects of Sartre's theory available at the time: firstly, no oppression is thinkable in the existentialist system and that of women no more than any other; secondly, this theory offers a space for expressing a terror on the part of men in relation to women's bodies which provides the basis of an ontologico–carnal hierarchy between masculine and feminine. Simone de Beauvoir's use of the existentialist point of view thus appears as a tour de force which we must at least salute.

2   On the bad faith of the oppressed

In practice, the ethics of authenticity deny the efficacy of forms of social or historical determination in favour of what is basically a classic type of voluntarism: 'constraint could have [. . .] no grasp on a freedom' writes Sartre in *Being and Nothingness*.[10] Bad faith is the antithesis of this maxim, for it consists in refusing to recognize oneself as a free subject and claiming to be determined or hindered by external circumstances. Such a position has some pretty rich corollaries:

> It is therefore senseless to think of complaining since nothing foreign has decided what we feel, what we live, or what we are [. . .] What happens to me happens through me [. . .] everything which happens to me is mine. [. . .] Is it not I who decide the coefficient of adversity in things and even their unpredictability by deciding about myself?[11]

> Everything which happens to us can be seen as a chance (i.e., can appear to us a way of realizing this being which is in question in our being).[12]

A second consequence of this position is the view that revolutionaries are materialists, serious and in bad faith, for they assess the human situation on the basis of the world, to which they attribute a greater reality than that they attribute to themselves.[13] The main model for this type of bad faith is Marx, whom Sartre contrasts with Kierkegaard as a man who understood how play creates freedom and provides an escape from a nature made natural. A third consequence is that all feelings of inferiority arise from a free choice. The passage in *Being and Nothingness* concerning the failed artist and the modest craftsman is highly revealing of the way in which Sartre combines the social with 'phenomenological ontology' when the problem he is tackling obliges him to do so. 'Whatever our being may be, it is a choice; and it depends on us to choose ourselves as 'great' or 'noble' or 'base' and 'humiliated'.[14] Such an idea immediately runs up against some simple commonsense objections: being a Michelangelo, a shoemaker or a bad poet is certainly not a matter of free will. To these possible objections, Sartre replies in advance that to choose inferiority is to choose a type of work or a field of activities in which I shall be at the lowest level. The inferiority he is thinking of is that of mediocre artists, who have chosen to express themselves in art because they are inferior in that field, when in some other field they might without difficulty have been 'equal to the average'. In the same way, if I choose to be a modest artisan because in that field my talents permit me to be 'equal to the average', I am not providing an example of a masochistic choice of inferiority, but 'a simple example of the choice of finitude'.

This argument smacks unmistakeably of the student; it sounds as though Sartre is remembering La Fontaine's fable about an inept doctor ('be a mason instead') and that he understands inferiority, not in terms of the social hierarchy of tasks, but as a psychological perversion of the liberal model of successful career choice. It is moreover amusing to note that here the voluntarism of Sartre's philosophy indirectly finds its counterpoint: this entire analysis assumes the existence of congenital, or at least given, aptitudes. Everything that happens to me is my doing, except my IQ, except my talents. A former prizewinner can challenge everything except the idea that talents are unequal and that everyone should know their natural place and stay there. In any case, the example of the average craftsman who reasonably chooses the right finitude for himself speaks volumes: why should I not then choose to be 'a modest house-wife with an average gift for motherhood' if that finitude is right for me?

However, it is not in relation to the question of career choice that we find observations concerning women in *Being and Nothingness*; women are not mentioned in discussions of different jobs, but only when the topic is sexuality. Is this because women are 'the sex', as they used to say in the seventeenth century, the-sex-different-from-us, 'us' obviously being men? Or because they are beings-to-be-referred-to-by-their-sexual-existence-alone, because that is the only important thing about those beings?

3   Existentialism is definitely not a feminism

To the best of my knowledge, nowhere did Sartre put forward a
theory of woman's being or of sexual difference; but the examples he
uses for phenomenological analysis portray female characters and, on
the basis of these examples, we can discern the writer's presuppositions. In his philosophical writings I have nowhere come across a
female character involved in a historical situation (the war or the
Resistance, for example), nor even in a workplace scene (in the
fashion of, for example, the cafe waiter). Woman is always seen only
as a body, and a sexed body. In this Sartre's discourse rejoins a very
ancient tradition, which can be traced back at least as far as Philo of
Alexandria.[15]

But it was also written in the contemporary context of existentialist
doctrine, for the assimilation of woman to a sexed body relates to a
category in the system, namely what Sartre himself calls 'de facto
solipsism'.[16] This concept describes the position of a subject in situations where other people are reduced to their functions in relation to
that subject: thus 'the ticket collector is only the function of collecting
tickets; the café waiter is nothing but the function of serving the
patrons'. In the same way we could say that each of the women
described in the phenomenological examples 'is just' the function of
attracting the desire of a potential lover, but with the following
precision: she always disappoints this interest by evading it in a
dishonest way.

Thus the first female figure to appear in *Being and Nothingness* is that
of the 'frigid woman'. Then in the following chapter we are given an
account of a first date during which a woman pretends not to understand what a man wants of her; when he takes her hand, she leaves it
in his 'like a thing'. Both woman have the role of illustrating 'behaviour in bad faith'. Later, Sartre discusses the character of Alber-
tine who 'escapes Marcel' 'through her consciousness', even when he
'can see her and possess her at any hour of the day'.[17] And what pity
is expressed for poor Marcel that he should be so 'gnawed by anxiety', even though he has managed to 'make her completely dependent
on him economically'!

'Woman' is thus the name for a dysfunctioning of 'de facto solipsism', which sees others only 'according to their function for me'. She
is certainly defined by this solipsism, in this instance by the sexual
interest she arouses, but she is designated by the fact that she always
keeps something out of reach of this interest. Correlatively, and
strangely, when an actual sexual encounter is being discussed,

'woman' is conspicuously absent. Sartre discourses at length about 'my flesh' and 'the Other's flesh', and 'the joyful ease of flesh against flesh', but with practically no reference to sexual difference between flesh and flesh. His words are sufficiently general to be the phenomenological description of a relation which is that of neither a man and a woman nor two women nor two men, but which is the common denominator of all such relations, and of that between two teddy bears, or two partners who fall short of sexual difference.

What are the origins of a fantasy account of a sexual encounter which manages not to give the sexes of the protagonists? And is it a fantasy? If we adopted the perspective of Bergson, Bachelard or some disciple of Jung and assumed that such descriptions have a psychological origin and that a generically masculine mind is expressing itself in them, we should certainly admit that a woman (in this case, me; I am amazed) can make nothing of them, but we should also have to uphold the view that this product of the imagination is directly intelligible to any man. If this is not the case, we shall have to abandon the idea of a 'generic masculine' and emphasize the preciousness of the disconcerting character of this passage.

We live in an intellectual world where expressions such as 'masculine discourse' and also 'the Western tradition' have the force of clichés, which is great. One can cut these together ad infinitum and if, in my earlier discussion of 'de facto solipsism', I had expressed a few thoughts on 'the Western tradition dominated by the masculine psyche from ancient times at least until now', I should have been able to do so with impunity. But we should have thought nothing at all together. For the issue is not one of placing Sartre's philosophy in crude categories like that of masculine discourse, or the Western tradition and there is no reason to impute his presuppositions to all men. If we continue to regard them as psychologically motivated and personal, we have to see them as peculiar to him, related to the idiosyncrasy of Jean-Paul Sartre. This peculiarity would explain why they must be incomprehensible to many, both men and women. And the analysis stops there: it is because it was him.

Without invalidating this latter hypothesis, we can adopt a viewpoint which has nothing to do with psychology and say that some imaginary elements which appear in the theoretical texts may become analysable and comprehensible – and by rights to all – when it is possible to relate them to the discursive position of the writer and to socially determined situations. For, in both cases, we are dealing with elements accessible to all. We shall return to this, but here in any case is how we can account for this extraordinary asexual carnal

encounter: the description deals with those elements that all possible
erotic encounters have in common. It is thus placed at the highest
possible level of generality, as is moreover suggested by the use of a
term like 'flesh'. Nothing proves that we are dealing with a fantasy
here: a desire to 'be philosophical', using the greatest imaginable
abstraction, may lead to such a scenario, given that, for a philosopher
of the absolute freedom of the subject, to mention 'flesh' is already to
accept a fairly weighty adulteration.

4   Two female figures

So there are two important women in *Being and Nothingness*. The first,
who is frigid, is criticized for not acknowledging the pleasure her
husband gives her; the second, who lacks enthusiasm, for not acknowledging a man's desire for her. When I speak of 'sexism in
philosophical texts' I am not asking for any preliminary connivence
or requiring anyone to see what I am alluding to immediately; but I
do hope that gradually the reading of *Being and Nothingness* and of a
few other masterworks will give this notion a content. Here then are
two female figures who are reduced to their sexual existence, to two
modes of that existence assessed negatively and regarded as moral
faults. In both cases the fault comes down to this: the woman
portrayed does not acquiesce sufficiently to what her husband or the
man who flirts with her wants from her.

  The art of transforming a refusal into a scandalous fault is one of
the attitudes observable in any 'macho'. Here is a social factor which
makes these pages directly understandable and transparent, whether
in a conniving way or to a critical analysis. And yet we must also call
the sexism here philosophical, not so much because we find it in a
text which is itself called philosophical, but because it is used to give
a solid basis to a concept, that of 'bad faith'. We shall try to show
this in detail in relation to the first example.

  Sartre is careful not to mention any direct knowledge of frigidity.
He supports his words by referring to a book written by the Viennese
psychiatrist Steckel, *The Frigid Woman*, published in a French translation. But the words and thesis are strictly Sartrian: his aim is to
clarify the concept of bad faith, using the phenomenological analysis
of a 'case', in which it is shown that so-called frigid women suffer
from pathological bad faith. For there are no frigid women, but only
women who claim to be so, clinging 'fiercely' (sic) to a denial of their

pleasure. The proof of this is that 'frequently in fact the husband reveals to Steckel that his wife has given objective signs of pleasure', signs which 'the woman when questioned will fiercely deny'.[18]

How can anyone be so daft? Since the husband's account and the wife's (sorry, *his* wife's) are contradictory, Sartre decides the husband's version is an unshakeable truth, without even asking himself whether it might not be very much in the husband's interest to make the claims he makes, out of ordinary pride. And not only does he not believe the word of the person who says she is suffering, he charges her with a double crime: she lied when she claimed she was frigid and she is lying again when she is 'questioned' and 'fiercely' denies the evidence of the opposite side.

A deep-seated attitude is betraying itself here, a frightening but commonplace stupidity both on the political and the human planes. The text is presented as a courtroom drama, where the judge sums up by blaming the victim. Feminist lawyers who advise women who have been battered or raped are familiar with this phenomenon. It will be said that it is not Sartre who is speaking here, but Steckel, a psychiatrist, who is no doubt mentioned as a scientific guarantee. Nothing is less certain: we should note that Steckel is also cited by Beauvoir in *The Second Sex*, but in relation to ideas so different that one wonders if she and Sartre had read the same book.

Is this where the misunderstanding begins? Is it true that 'to read is to write' and to rewrite what one thinks one is reading? And if that is the case, does the 'same' book cease to be the same, depending on whether it is read by a man or a woman? But what allows us to say that a book's identity fades away because these two readings are by a man and a woman respectively? We should beware of false inductions. After all, when a book has the good fortune to give rise to a debate, fifteen different readers will speak of what might appear to be fifteen different books. And then, if a man and a woman read the same text in a radically different way, where will we find the angel who, having read *the* text, can understand this difference, and to whom will that angel explain it? Different periods have read Aristotle and Descartes differently, but this does not prevent a reader who has had some contact with historical and philosophical culture from understanding the different readings and putting them into perspective.

It is very likely that there are differences in the way that a man and a woman, and more so a feminist woman, approach the same work, particularly when the latter deals with a subject as highly charged with different emotions as that of frigidity. However, there is no need for us to make these differences into a radical and definitive difference, which would render all debate either impossible or pointless. Furthermore, when authors positively quote books in support of their own theses, we can see them as largely responsible for what they make the book in question say, without concluding from this that 'everything is relative' and depends on the reader or rewriter, so that all discussion of it becomes a waste of time. On the contrary, we would do better to assume that any way of using someone else's work can be analysed and should be examined. Schematically, we can explain the discrepancy between Beauvoir's Steckel and Sartre's in the following manner: she took up elements from this book because she was interested in the various manifestations of women's lives, one of which is frigidity while, when he wrote *Being and Nothingness*, Sartre was not interested in that issue, he simply needed an example to justify one of the fundamental concepts of his system. The aims underlying the two uses of another's thought are quite different. In *Being and Nothingness* Steckel's work has the status of 'reported speech', a classical mode which can be summed up in the phrase, 'it is so true that someone else said it', and which is currently used in philosophy to provide a fixed point, an absolute point of reference which allows thinking to be set in motion.[19] In *The Second Sex*, the same work has an exploratory value: because of his job, Steckel had access to a world which Beauvoir visits with him. Two different projects give two different readings. Whether I am right or wrong to understand the discrepancy in this way (the debate is still open), we can always heuristically put forward the following principle: what we ask of a culture is precisely that it should teach us to analyse what is said and notably to interpret the way in which people retransmit another's thought or thought which is not theirs. For the way something is said is largely formed of retransmissions (every book contains a library), which we also need to be able to read.

So what is Sartre saying here, under cover of another author? That there are objective signs, of pleasure in this case. The text is particularly insistent, since within it we also find the idea that these women (who are not frigid but seek to prove to themselves that they are) hide from themselves 'acts of conduct which are objectively discoverable'. This expression 'objective signs of pleasure' is a surprising one. Granted, the notion is probably current in the lexicon of psychologists of sexuality. If it turned up in a lover's language it would probably be a sign that it was time to leave him. But from the pen of a philosopher, the reference to the objectivity of a sign looks like a violent conceptual takeover. For a sign differs from a fact or a phenomenon insofar as it is a sign of something else, and it is only this through the presence of an interpreting consciousness or some agency of interpretation. However certain that consciousness may sometimes be in its interpretation, as long as it perceives the sign as a sign (something perceptible to the senses which alludes to something else) it cannot adopt a problematics of objectivity or of objectification, since it is the consciousness of the work of reading or decoding implied by the perception of a sign as a sign. The notion of objectivity on the other hand supposes that the fact or phenomenon that is described as objective does not refer back to something else which is its meaning; it also supposes that this fact or phenomenon is, even when no consciousness is there to perceive it. The expression 'objective sign' is thus as aberrant as that of 'square circle'. Above all, it contains a kind of violence of an authoritarian type, as though the issue was to forbid a possible deviation of interpretation: you have no right to suppose that the sign can mean anything other than what I say it means.

From Sartre's pen, the expression 'objective sign' is in addition completely unexpected, insofar as, according to him, the notion of objectivity – even of a phenomenon – is problematic. In the first pages of *Being and Nothingness* he has trouble distinguishing himself from Berkeley and he appears quite tempted by the famous phrase, 'to be is to be perceived or to perceive'. The phenomenon is finally defined as a relative absolute, relative insofar as 'appearance supposes in its essence that there is someone to whom it appears'. To whom, to whom indeed! Whom? This is the big question here. For there is no one phenomenon of pleasure or frigidity, since there is no true common measure between the proprioceptive perception of the woman and the external perception of the man. Unless we assume a fusion of subjectivities, but then we are stepping outside the framework of Sartre's thought.

This is not all: the expression 'objective signs' is a serious conceptual sliding, for in a Sartrian perspective, 'there are no signs in the world'; each event must be interpreted by freedom, which alone freely and constantly gives it meaning. *Existentialism and Humanism* is very clear on this question: even if we concede that an event may be a sign, 'it is I myself, in every case, who have to interpret the signs' and the individual thus 'bears the entire responsibility' 'for the decypherment'.[20] 'Man himself decyphers the sign as he pleases'. This is all cut and dried, but it may indiscreetly give us a key to understanding the remarks concerning frigid women: when the existence of a sign is posited, in the existentialist doctrine the existence of a

single subject – man – is also posited, a subject who has full latitude
to determine the meaning of that sign. Let us hold off the classic jokes
on the ambiguity of the word 'man' – the possibility of a debate
between two or many consciousnesses concerning the meaning of a
sign is clearly excluded by the idea of deciphering *ad libitum*.

Against all the general assumptions of his own doctrine, Sartre
thus draws on an 'objectivity of the sign' (and the objectivity of an
emotional state perceived by another person!). For us, this constitutes
the first illustration of the idea mentioned above: when philosophers
talk about women, their discourse unfolds without the usual theoretical requirements. There are no signs in the world, but women's
bodies provide signs which are objective.

5   Answers to a few objections [21]

But (people say to me) Sartre has a theory of precisely the immediate
readability of emotional manifestations, or of what he calls expressive
behaviour. According to him, such behaviour is immediately comprehensible because its meaning is its being: it refers to nothing beyond
itself and in no way indicates a hidden affection or one experienced in
secret by some psyche.

> These frowns, this redness, this stammering, this slight trembling of
> the hands, these downcast looks which seem at once timid and threat-
> ening – these do not express anger; they are the anger [. . .] In itself a
> clenched fist is nothing and means nothing. But also we never perceive
> a clenched fist. We perceive a man who in a certain situation clenches
> his fist.[22]

A hurried reading of *Being and Nothingness* may lead one to think that
the remarks on the objective signs of pleasure flow from the notion of
'meaningful act', which in this case has undergone at the most a
slight objectivist distortion. I think on the contrary that to speak of
an 'objective sign' and to speak of a 'meaningful act' is to speak of
two quite different ideas. Far from assuming that signs exist, the
theory of anger reminds us that they do not, since a clenched fist is
nothing and signifies nothing. What is significant is a meaningful act:
a man clenches his fist – he is the subject of his action here and the
other person perceives the intentionality of this subject in action. On
the other hand, the idea of 'giving objective signs' of whatever it may
be involves compartmentalization of the body and unintentionality –
for example, if a face betrays tiredness – whereas the portrait of the

angry man shows him whole and entirely involved in what he does. When Sartre talks of women's sexual pleasure in terms of 'objective signs' or 'acts of conduct which are objectively discoverable' that the woman 'cannot fail to register', he sees this pleasure as a passive bodily reaction of which the woman is merely the witness and a false witness in this case, since this woman in bad faith strives to distract her attention and to think about something else.

Even if we accept, for the sake of argument, that sexual pleasure can be a purely bodily reaction, a sort of neurophysiological state, without the woman being completely involved in that pleasure, Sartre's thesis remains untenable from the Sartrian perspective. For according to him, no bodily or neurological state can constrain consciousness, which always remains as free transcendence and choice, even when it has to deal with a migraine. This is an old old story: Epictetus said that a broken leg was no obstacle to the will and Pascal had terrible attacks of toothache, which he rose above. As for Sartre, he takes up Max Scheler's remarks on headaches: 'If I have a headache, I can discover an intentional affectivity within myself that is directed towards my pain, towards suffering it, accepting it with resignation or rejecting it, towards giving it value or fleeing it. Here, it is the intention itself which is affection, it is pure act and already a project'.[23] Here, no one is accused of or said to be in bad faith. On the contrary, in this example, as in that of the angry man, intentionality turns the event into an act on the part of the subject, who is entirely involved in his project. The expression 'cannot fail to register' can have no validity in a philosophy which assures us that consciousness does whatever it wants with bodily states and must know absolutely that it is doing what it wants.

'There's something dreadful about the way texts are read in philosophy. Words are taken absolutely literally, without the reader's wondering if they were not written quickly, on a cafe table corner. Sartre wrote "gives objective signs" and you get him into a corner over the literal sense of the phrase. But did he really mean that? Exactly that? Perhaps he wrote those words without really thinking. Then you measure the difference between meaningful acts and objective signs with the care of a subtle chemical analysis. Fine, but...'

The philosophical analysis of thought has never been anything other than an effort to discuss and reveal minute differences. A maximum of effort for a minimum effect. What we call philosophical rigour is just a greater degree of rigour and the obligation to be aware of differences which are not immediately apparent. For no one needs our help with the others. In our trade such niceties as wondering whether heliocentrism is a theory founded on physical proof or a simple convention which makes calculations easier, identifying several theses in heliocentrism or wondering how an argument is accorded the value of a proof are everyday practices. They do not stop the sun from rising every morning anyway and in most cases no one thinks of calling them 'niceties'. If we do not feel authorized to use the usual method to examine observations in a philosophical text in which 'women' are discussed, this comes down to saying that the problem is unimportant. Or that a thinker may say whatever he likes about 'women' (but not about physics). Or that we do not think we have the right to look critically at what is said about 'women'. Or all three things. What is irritating is that the usual standards of philosophical work are commonly abandoned by all writers once women are the topic. If you are discussing a theory of induction try to think technically, in other words in a way that is precise and rigorous, otherwise you are best advised to abstain. Why should it be any different when one is discussing, for example, the issue of women in philosophy?

6   On 'bad faith', considered as a speciality of inferior beings

We have seen that the observations on the 'frigid woman' cannot be validated in terms of Sartre's system and that the expression 'objective signs' must be regarded as impossible in itself. Yet however much we may criticize what is said about this example, it still has its uses: it has a function in the establishment of the Sartrian category of 'bad faith', described by the author as a 'lie to oneself'. Incorrectness thus serves the system.

This is because, in order for the idea of a 'lie to oneself' to be thinkable, one must assume first an absolute truth and then two consciousnesses, the one that lies to itself and the one which has the role of indisputable and sovereign elucidation. This is the structure of all the examples of 'bad faith' given: the lying consciousness is usually that of the person directly involved in or affected by the situation, the other is that of a third party who knows better than the person directly involved what is going on, who substitutes his own consciousness for that of the first person and reveals the lie to the self by contrast, by providing the true measure of the situation.

This revelation of the lie to oneself always comes about through a dramatization, with a distribution of parts which is far from neutral and refers back to social relations of domination, hierarchy or the great ascendancy of one character over another. The consciousness of the frigid woman is thus faulted by that of her husband, then by that of the psychiatrist, then by that of Sartre, where the argument alleges that the husband, the psychiatrist and Sartre all know what is really going on in women's consciousness (even though those women hide it from themselves) and this in the name of 'acts of conduct which are objectively discoverable, which they cannot fail to register at the moment when they perform them'.[24]

In *Existentialism and Humanism* a relation between teacher and student is set out: 'I will refer to the case of a pupil of mine...' This is the well-known story of a young man who is hesitating between staying with his mother and joining the Resistance and who believes, poor unfortunate, that he can base his decision on his feelings. According to Sartre basing one's decisions on feelings is a way of not facing 'abandonment', in other words the fact that nothing can 'show you what to do'. As this student is seeking ways to escape his freedom through feeling, his conduct comes into the category of bad faith as defined in this short work: 'Any man who takes refuge behind the excuse of his passions, or by inventing some deterministic doctrine, is a self-deceiver' and the text goes on, 'I define his self-deception as an error. Here, one cannot avoid pronouncing a judgement of truth'.[25]

Since it is another consciousness which has the task of substituting itself mentally for the consciousness which is slightly or seriously lying, to pronounce the indisputable truth in a judgement ex cathedra, we should not be surprised to see in Sartre's examples that the relation between the two consciousnesses is always grafted on to a hierarchy familiar to all. This is just the thing to guarantee the reader's semi-conscious 'understanding' or connivence. We need only change the characters participating in these little scenes, reversing their social status, and they become less convincing. For example, a man consults a psychiatrist because when he makes love he feels despair or disgust rather than pleasure. His wife reveals to the psychiatrist that her husband nevertheless gives objective signs of pleasure. Who on earth would build a philosophical system on the basis of such a tale? No reader would believe in it.

Sometimes, however, the reader's connivence is not so sure in advance, since the hierarchy between the two consciousnesses is not so apparent, except of course in the case of a reader who is already a disciple of existentialism. One case of this is when Sartre portrays Catholics or Christian trades unionists. In the author's taxonomy, such figures are always examples of human beings who do not reach

a full understanding of freedom. Sartre cannot be certain that everyone, all his readers whoever they may be, will immediately share this
classification. He must either accept a shrunken group of witness-
readers, or prepare the ground for his case: 'I made the acquaintance
of a somewhat remarkable man, a Jesuit'.[26] The text relates the way
that this man explained to himself the path that his life had taken
and then sharply criticizes his interpretation. But everything was
already there to be understood in the words 'somewhat remarkable'
which, of course, give a certain degree of worth to the character (we
do not find such precautions taken in relation to women and
students), but in which we should understand the 'somewhat' in
the sense of 'not as much as I am', I Sartre, who am the ultimate
acknowledger of abandonment, the absolute consciousness of freedom
(which provides the measure of all situations), I who am able to
judge in the final analysis, because of all this and also because I am
the one telling the story.

'What must be the being of man if he is to be capable of bad
faith? Take the example of a woman who...'.[27] I am not making
this up. These are the terms used to introduce the scene of the date,
where a woman pretends not to understand what a man wants of her.
The narrative ends, unsurprisingly, with the following comment: 'We
shall say that this woman is in bad faith.' Here, as in the other
playlets, there is a feeling of superiority in the air. After the husband's authority over his wife, which then appears in a slightly
different form in the authority of the psychiatrist over his female
patient, after the teacher's ascendency over his student (all the more
marked because the young man tried to discuss his decision with
Sartre), after the superiority with which the free thinker credits
himself in relation to the Christian, here is the classic authoritarianism of a man in relation to a woman he is trying to pick up, who is
always accused of knowing exactly what is wanted of her without the
man having said anything about it; the accusation creates the power
here, or reinforces the ascendency which generally exists. But added
to all this is the overview of the characters which the writer easily
grants himself, analysing their attitudes by making them transparent.
He knows all that is going on in this woman's head better than she
does herself, since he can portray her as knowing, but contriving not
to know, that the man has taken her hand. But, once again, this type
of scene would not be credible if the heroine was replaced by a
character with great authority in society, who, if his or her hand were
touched without permission, would certainly strike the face of the
importunate with that very hand. The heroine of this story had to be
a weak woman, of the well-known type.[28]

This superiority is necessary, because without the knowing-better of a consciousness absolutely connected to the truth, the very notion of bad faith would disappear in favour of a relativist doctrine. Since everyone is a consciousness which decides on the meaning of things and even on their coefficient of adversity, Sartre's thought could well have been orientated towards the legacy of Pirandello; for it is only a tiny step from the thesis according to which 'man deciphers signs himself and as he pleases' to the famous 'each to their own truth'.[29] On the other hand the doctrine of 'bad faith' reintroduces the idea that there is also a good faith – when one assumes one's freedom – to whose level existentialist morality invites us to raise ourselves. The indirect reminder of social hierarchies, portrayed as imaginary hierarchies of ethical lucidity in relation to a given situation, makes it possible to avoid relativism by restoring an idea which is come to that of no great interest, according to which someone has direct and full access to a truth so true that it can be called 'objective'. The philosophy of deciphering 'as I please' requires the subterranean support of rudimentary dogmatism.

What is it that permits us to regard the social relation between man and woman as having a particularly important place in the hierarchies mentioned? There are many possible answers to this question, starting with self-criticism. It may perhaps be an effect of my approach. It is because I am a woman that I feel attacked by these examples (particularly by the fact that Sartre considers the female characters to be transparent) and thus that I at least notice them. But once the potential bias of my reading is acknowledged, I can deduce from this that the book is not addressed to me, nor to any woman who is aware of being a woman. Nor to any revolutionaries either. In the same way one might say that *Existentialism and Humanism* is not addressed to Jesuits or to students or to some others. In this light Sartre's words appear to be written for a clique. Their implied audience is a small, strictly delineated group which constitutes the 'us' of the work in question. In one of Hume's texts we find a paragraph which contrasts animals, women and Indians with an 'us',[30] thus establishing an imaginary group of associates, who seem present on the page, by the author's side. We can be certain that this group was imaginary in Hume's case, since it was to his women readers, admirers and translators that he chiefly owed his reputation. *Being and Nothingness* sets up an 'us' which is equally clearly determined, and as imaginary, as that established by Hume's text. It is no surprise that I notice at once that I am not included.

However, were I merely the victim of an easily comprehensible partiality, attributing too much importance to the fact that Sartre gives women figures a hard time and, in his fantasy, addresses himself only to men, this (feminocentric?) mistake would be easy to rectify; for once the structure of one exclusion has been noticed and understood, the others become comically obvious and one need only quote them. 'Every purpose, even that of a Chinese, an Indian or a Negro, can be understood by a European.'[31] In this utterance, who is said to understand whom? And are there no European Negroes? The text repeats: 'the European of 1945 [...] may re-conceive in himself the purpose of the Chinese, of the Indian or the African [...] every purpose is comprehensible to every man [...] There is always some way of understanding an idiot, a child, a primitive man or a foreigner if one has sufficient information.'[32] If you are not laughing, I am wasting my time.

Paradoxically, this discussion of all sorts of 'other people' may allow us to explain why, in Sartre's philosophical imagination, the domination of men over women is used at greater length than, for example, the pre-eminence lent to Europeans over the Chinese. For woman is the other who is close enough for a man always to believe that he has 'sufficient information'. However, I hesitate to explain things in this way. Another question needs asking: when does an individual or group pride itself on having an immediate and total understanding of people in some other group? When the former has a statutory relation of domination over the individuals in the latter group. Colonials boast that they have a full and complete understanding of the colonized peoples. Teachers flatter themselves that they have a deep knowledge of who their students are, until reality gives the lie to their belief. The greater the domination, the more dogmatic and doctrinaire the 'knowledge' claimed, for the less it seeks information. In the same way, acknowledgement of the difficulty of understanding any 'other' is an elementary mode of respect, a mode which moreover must imperatively be combined with a question about the way that the other perceives me, in other words with a recognition of reciprocity.

As a result, the question of 'enough information' and the greater proximity of any given other (in this case women) is not pertinent to explain why the text 're-conceives' women's attitudes in itself more often than the purposes of Indians. We can simply say that a European man of 1945 was more certain of dominating the women around him than the Indians or Chinese, and for longer.

7   Excursus towards a philosophy yet to come

At its imaginary level, Sartre's philosophy rests on his social experience as a man, a European and a philosophy teacher which, taken as a whole, is an unequivocal experience of domination. But the philosophical critique with which I am trying to counter his work can also be linked to my everyday experience; for what I am seeking to challenge in Sartre's doctrine is an ordinary phenomenon which concerns me, or in this case, which particularly annoys me.

Of course, I have not experienced all possible forms of dependency. The women of my generation were born into a world where they were guaranteed citizens' rights. By earning my living from an early age and by not getting married I more or less avoided the most commonly noted modes of subordination. However, I always knew (long before feminist writings opened my eyes to serious problems) that there was something that was not quite right in my position as a woman. Not the forms of discrimination that the young ladies of my generation had to suffer, although these were quite patent, nor the abnormal legislation on contraception: I long remained blind to objective and politicizable data. But, very early, one aspect of relations between women and men frightened me and this was the non-reciprocity of looks and judgements, which I again encountered in Sartre's writing, but which I had already met elsewhere.

A friend of my youth lets his objectifying and standardizing gaze wander over the adolescent girls of his age and begins sententiously to explain how sad it is that some are like this and how necessary it is for girls to make an effort to be like that and how immoral it is that so many 'let themselves go' – 'just look!' And all of a sudden I look at him and I suddenly realize that he has probably not brushed his teeth since the beginning of the holidays and has perhaps not washed at all. He states his right to look at other people, while regarding himself as invisible. But I say nothing of this, sure in advance that I would not be understood.

I have interpreted this story, and many others of the same type, as relating to a situation marked by sexual difference: the division of roles was not contingent. It was a young man who turned his seemingly absolute look on his female contemporaries, at the same time blinding himself to his own visibility. A position of dominance alone can permit a belief such as: 'I see, I am not seen'. Parental and professorial authority give rise to similar attitudes: some power relations give people the right to look at others in an almost inquisitorial way and allow them to forbid those others to do the same to them.

Faced with this type of social relation, an adage scribbled in a collection of quotations which belonged to Francis Bacon seems to define the conditions in which a philosophy of the dominated might possibly emerge: 'A cat may look upon a king'; in other words, I do not need to be your equal to scrutinize you, I do not need to dominate in order to theorize.

I shall look at how he who looks, and sometimes looks at me, looks. In this way I shall prolong the look, or return it, but I shall also take the look as an object, since we can analyse the way in which someone 'sees', for example, women, but also politics, the rising sun or the human soul. Without forgetting that this game can go on and on. When I see someone else seeing, it does not make me invisible and the same can be done to me in a way that I cannot foresee. In my everyday experience, only a great naivety can make someone unaware that an onlooker is visible and that it is possible for looks to circulate. Such naivety must certainly result from forms of social dominance.

The idea that a point of view on something can in turn be taken as an object of study is a partial return to the classic philosophical project of meta-reflexivity. Whether one says that philosophy has no specific object but reworks different forms of knowledge in order to express their ultimate truth, or that it examines the great cultural models through which we apprehend the world, or that it criticizes the ordinary procedure of other disciplines, or that its task is, more modestly, to wonder how a given knowledge is possible, or again to make links between the different sciences, or to think about their foundations or to clarify their language, in every case philosophy is defined as a meta-activity whose task is to understand how people think in other intellectual or practical activities. The general idea that makes philosophy possible is that in any form of thought there is always something to rethink.

However, this idea has manifested itself in very different ways, which can be classified according to the degree of importance which philosophy attributes to itself or to its contribution. A maximalist conception of relations between the philosopher and the others was bequeathed to us by Plato, who says that the poet or the politician do not understand the truth of what they do, whereas the philosopher has the key to the truth of all the others and of himself. Ancient though it may be, this doctrine still impregnates philosophy as it is taught. What precedes allows us to split this idea into two different aspects.

For we can indeed validate the critical project which underlies this conception of philosophy and say that we must always consider the hypothesis that no form of thought is necessarily self-contained in all its aspects. Physics does not know everything about physics, for the historian of scientific institutions will always be able to explain how it has developed in a political context which can be explained and described. Sociology is not self-sufficient either and cannot produce a complete theory of itself (for example, linguistic analysis, has a grasp of the discourse in which it is set out and can reveal certain a priori at the root of sociological work). Furthermore, if we consider the edges of each field of knowledge, in other words its limits or the borders which separate it from another field, these areas can often only be dealt with by a third type of inquiry belonging to another, separate field of thought. For example, the distinction between ethnology and sociology was produced by extrascientific causes which can only be analysed by an interdisciplinary epistemology taking account of, in particular, the history of colonization. There is no need to list more examples. While we are waiting for someone to show us a single field of knowledge which can be said to hold the key to the entire truth about itself, we can adopt the following guiding principle: any form of thought is liable to be examined, continued, reworked or corrected by another form.

Thus insofar as Plato's legacy denies that any given form of knowledge or practice can have immanent self-sufficiency, we have no objections to it.[33] On the other hand, when this same tradition asserts that one form of knowledge, namely philosophy, is entirely self-contained, this statement is at odds with the former idea and shuts it off; in other words, it pronounces that the rethinking of thought does not go on forever. Today (at least today) we must object to this aspect of the doctrine on the grounds that other disciplines have a grasp on philosophical work. History examines the institutions which make philosophical thinking happen and cause a given form of philosophy to become dominant. Sociologists of knowledge reveal and comment on the fundamental values and categories of a given form of philosophical thought. A physicist has the right to regard what a particular philosophy has to say about knowledge as outdated and indeed archaic. A biologist may think the terms in which a philosopher speaks of living organisms to be totally lacking in meaning. Linguists are asking (but who is listening to them?) new questions of philosophical discourse.

This non-hierarchical entanglement of thoughts that various disciplines may propose about each other does not dissolve away philosophy's project, it defines philosophy as that which can circulate between different areas of knowledge, notably raising problems inherent in them. I believe that, thus defined, philosophical practice is suited to the idea of a mixed intellectual community in which men and women can come together. This community already exists, but still needs to be asserted.

Indeed we can say that any definition giving supremacy to philosophy maintains a kind of link with the masculinist or macho type of psychological position, if we agree that a 'macho' is a man who asserts his male superiority over both women and other men, a man who wants to be 'more of a man' than anyone else. This assertion of superiority is linked to virile metaphors and shows through fairly constantly in works of the philosophical tradition. I believe it to be the thing that ultimately distances women from that tradition, however interested they may be in the critical methods philosophy teaches. We observe that many women basically stop halfway on the path to becoming philosophers: something in the philosophical enterprise deters them and blocks their identification, although this was sufficiently strong to make them begin their initiation into the work. At a certain point along the way they undergo a process of de-identification. Some say that this is related to the masculine nature of the philosophical project. I must admit that, when intellectual life is in question, I do not know what it means to talk about an attitude that is masculine or feminine in absolute terms. For a long time too many women have wanted to take up philosophy and have gained something essential from their apprenticeship for us to be able to assume that this type of thought is marked through and through by 'masculinity'.

On the other hand, if we build up the concept of theoretical masculinism and regard it as merely an aspect of philosophy rather than encompassing philosophical thought as a whole, we can better understand what it is that distances women, preventing them from fully and entirely adhering to the philosophical project as it is and more still stopping them from wanting to take up the perpetuation of philosophical creation. By masculinism in general I mean the assertion of masculine dominance over the feminine and also the practice of taking this first 'superiority' as a point of reference to assert other forms of supremacy which apparently have nothing to do with the duality of the sexes. The masculinist attitude consists in disparaging both women in general, other men ('the common man', 'the man in the street', those involved in other forms of knowledge) and indeed other forms of discourse. When a Protestant author (Hobbes) refers to Catholic theology as a collection of 'old wives' tales', he is making a strong connection between two rejections and affirming a double superiority, or rather a superiority of man-plus-man which can be used twice, against 'old wives' and against 'papists'. The praise (or glorification) of 'theory' or the postulate of the pre-eminence of one form of theorization over another usually produces a position of this type, which deters not only women, but also many 'decent men'. In addition, nothing proves that it has ever been appropriate. In any case I hope gradually to show that it has no meaning, at least today. The relation between the man philosopher and 'Woman' cannot be completely separated from the relation that philosophy imagines it has to its various 'others'. This promises the reader a few more digressions. The fact remains that the impossibility of assuming this theoretical masculinism can be seen as splendid, even if it is the major obstacle preventing women and many men from identifying with the traditional form of philosophical thinking. Personally, if I did not stop halfway on the path to identification, it was because I thought I saw the possibility of a fork in the path ahead, and thus of throwing in my lot with a philosophical practice which was still to come.

8   From knowledge-rape to poisonous possessions

As we have seen, in its original Sartrian form, the philosophical doctrine borrowed by Beauvoir to describe women's oppression denies the importance of all forms of constraint and requires uncritical reference to structures of domination. But the most picturesque elements are yet to come. At the end of *Being and Nothingness* Sartre expounds a 'theory' of knowledge as appropriation which rests entirely on sexual metaphors, referring to an eroticism that is far from being among the most sympathetic; indeed it is quite chilling.

'Seeing is enjoying; to see is to *deflower*.'[34] 'Knowledge is at one and the same time *penetration* and a *superficial caress*.'[35] The description of this appropriative enjoyment, supposedly the pleasure of knowledge, wanders off into images which have nothing innocent or pertinent about them: 'The scientist is the hunter who surprises a white nudity and rapes it with his gaze.'[36] The reference to the 'smooth whiteness [?!] of a woman's body', a body on which possession leaves no trace (which seems to be very irritating), can be judged in two ways. We could simply say that, for Sartre, it is clear that the subject who knows is a man and the problem does not even arise. Faced with such a theory, 'the woman scientist' is unthinkable and Marie Curie did not exist. But there is another way to look at these pages: even in 1943 fantasies of this type could not in any case pass for serious epistemology. At this time the work of such as Gaston Bachelard had given a fair degree of currency to the idea that any process of knowledge is precisely a process and not just a look. This process requires the invention of complex mechanisms for making up questions, constructing experiments, correcting notions, formulating concepts and thinking about determining what it is to provide a proof. Any process of knowledge thus transforms reason, which must bend to rationalities that vary with the fields involved and are constructed by the conditions of a given knowledge at a given point in its history. One does not reason in the same way in physics, chemistry and biology; even within each discipline, differences can be found. Moreover, independently of Bachelard and long before his time, it was known that one cannot speak of the 'scientist' in such crude terms, far less in the singular. One might think that Sartre had taken his higher philosophy degree in a year when Bacon's *De Augmentis* was on the curriculum and that fifteen years later all he could remember from it was 'the hunt of Pan', a term on which he comments at length, having forgotten what it was about. In Bacon's work this term refers to a complex protocol of exploration which takes chance into account. Sartre retains only the metaphor (or not even the metaphor, the words) and does not hesitate to pass off this vague memory as though it were a theory of knowledge.

The definition of the 'relation between the knower and the known' as 'a kind of rape by sight' can be analysed as the way in which a highly qualified graduate hides his crass ignorance of even classical philosophy of science. But this conception of 'knowledge' as an act through which a mind tries desperately to 'appropriate' the thing is also an element in a diptych whose pendant is to be found at the very end of the book, where we find strange observations on sliminess and holes. These tell us that in knowledge the 'For-itself', which is the sole assimilating and creative power, appropriates the 'In-itself'. In a symmetrical way, sliminess reveals the converse possibility of a 'poisonous possession' of the For-itself by the In-itself.[37] 'There is a possibility that the In-itself might absorb the For-itself [...] the In-itself would draw the For-itself into its contingency, into its indifferent exteriority, into its foundationless existence. [...] Slime is the revenge of the In-itself. A sickly-sweet, feminine revenge...'[38] Here again, sexual metaphors abound. Slimy honey collapses in a manner comparable to the 'flattening out of the overripe breasts of a woman who is lying on her back.'[39] Slime draws me, it sucks at me [. . .] It is a soft, yielding action, a moist and feminine sucking [. . .] it draws me into it as the bottom of a precipice might draw me. There is something like a tactile fascination in the slimy. I am no longer master of halting the process of appropriation. It continues. In one sense it is like the supreme docility of the possessed, the fidelity of a dog that *gives* itself, and in another sense beneath this docility, it is a surreptitious appropriation of the possessor by the possessed.[40]

and so on.

The nightmare then moves on to the image of the hole, of which the female genitalia are a notable example. The hole 'originally appears as a nothingness to be filled with my own flesh', in a 'sacrifice of my body so that the plenitude of being may exist', in other words to 'preserve the totality of the In-itself'. 'A good part of our life is passed in plugging holes, in filling empty places, in realizing and symbolically establishing plenitude.' The 'tendency to fill' is 'one of the most fundamental tendencies of human reality.'[41] If Sartre kept to the observations on orality which illustrate this idea, we should not have much to say about this passage. At the most we might wonder whether the idea of a 'human nature' has not surreptitiously been reintroduced here through the reference to 'fundamental tendencies'. But the text goes on:

It is only from this standpoint that we can move on to sexuality. The obscenity of the feminine sex is that of every gaping thing. It is a call to being, as all holes are. In herself woman calls for foreign flesh which will transform her into plenitude of being through penetration and dilution.

The experience of the hole, when the child sees the reality, encompasses the ontological presentiment of sexual experience in general; it is with his flesh that the child stops up the hole and the hole, before any sexual specification, is an obscene waiting, a call for flesh.[42]

Here are words 'to be quoted with tweezers', to use an expression invented by Albert Lévy about one of Jean Cau's aphorisms.[43] We should note that here, as so often, only masculine adult experience is regarded as being continuous with the child's 'ontological presentiment of sexual experience in general'. The girl child will probably have to transform her 'ontological presentiment' and abandon the 'fundamental human tendency' to fill holes in order to become that which must be filled and thus to identify with the holey and engulfing

In-itself. The problem is not even posed. However, this phenomenology establishes an ontological hierarchy: in this light woman can be
assimilated to the In-itself and man to the For-itself, definitively and
forever. The masculine and feminine roles deduced from these woolly
theories make a non-subject of woman, who had already become an
object when the object of knowledge (or rather 'the thing') was
assimilated to 'the smooth whiteness of a woman's body'.

9   On woman as the last essence

In an example like the above, the incompatibility is obvious between
a metaphysicist delusion and an active political approach to a problem. Sartre tells us about the 'child' and recounts the latter's early
experience as a guaranteed and incontestable fact; on the basis of this
account two crude categories are set up, supposedly corresponding to
the masculine and the feminine, all outside the historical and social
spheres. And here are 'woman' as an entity and 'man' as a compulsion to bring about existence, established on an eternal stage or in a
heaven of essences and very far, as far as possible, from any potential
analyses of social relations. Many people probably have equally fixed
ideas in their heads and a representation of the duality of the sexes
which is as little connected to the diversity of historical reality.
Ordinary language assumes a substance called 'woman', which remains the same whatever the place, time or culture. This substance
has a particularity: one can say whatever one likes about it, without
proof, as though one ran no risk of being challenged. Even in everyday conversations, it is unusual to have available a subject in relation
to which one is never contradicted. Utter some commonplace about
the weather and you risk encountering people who will disagree, who
will maintain, for example, that despite appearances, seasons still
exist. Things can be said about women with a different kind of
assurance: that of the communiqué to which reply is impossible.

What is true for everyday gossip is true also of learned discussions.
If you are going to talk about the future of the tropical rainforests, it
is in your interests to be well informed; you will know that any error
will be picked up and any risky interpretation criticized. On the
other hand, you can freely say whatever you like about 'woman' or
anything else that you assimilate to the 'feminine'. If you are a man,
no one will think of contradicting you because they would feel they
were attacking you by challenging your phantasmagoria; if you are a
woman, whatever you say, dearest angel, about 'woman' as a nature

or substance will be taken as a manifestation of your serious concern with the problem of femininity; for a woman can give no greater proof of morality than by concerning herself primarily and permanently with cultivating her femininity, pondering and clarifying the ideal of femininity and further raising the standards of the feminine. I say this only in relation to the utterances of the substantialists, those who focus on the idea of an absolutely given feminine which is absolutely different from the multiple manifestations of masculinity. Of course it is not true of the utterances which have pulsed through the history of feminism. Those men and women who have said that 'women should be able to sit for higher degrees in mathematics' or that 'women should have the vote' or that 'women's bodies are their own' have met with disagreement. Not just because they were fighting oppression, but because these utterances bring about a change of level. They bring reference to 'woman' down from the eternal ontologico-insulting or mythico-eulogistic (in disparagement!) clouds to an earth where there are men, women and prosaic relations between them.

10   Questions of method

What have we found? A little horror – woman as the 'sugary death of the For-itself' – much conviction regarding superiority over women, an apparently self-evident and never questioned reduction of woman to the sexual interest she arouses but disappoints, the assimilation, also unquestioned, of the object to be known to the female body and, reciprocally, a relation to this body which is called 'appropriation' and 'rape'. Is it possible to be more exhaustive in expressions of sexism?[44] But, having itemized all this, we need to ask ourselves what to investigate in these bizarre considerations.

This question applies to any exposition of the same type: what should we do with it, to what type of analysis should this phantasmagoria be thrown? Three possibilities present themselves and they are not incompatible: firstly, whatever the theoretical reservations one might have concerning the psychoanalysis of texts, in the present case the author seems to have done all he could to turn his readers into wild Lacanians; secondly, as the text was printed (and oh so widely published), it also lends itself to a sociological investigation of intellectual life; lastly, since these wild imaginings appear in a work of metaphysics, it is simply ordinary philosophical work to wonder what they are doing there.

We must try to carry out these three analyses at once. Going through someone's secret fantasies with a fine toothcomb and examining consciouses and unconsciouses are procedures not terribly useful in themselves and somewhat lacking in taste. Of course, the French term *lisse* (smooth or sleek) which describes the woman's body, on which possession leaves no traces, can be heard as *lys* (lily), so that this phantasmagoria seems to speak of eternal virginity. But so what? The psychoanalytic investigation of a text is only of interest when it is combined with approaches informed by intellectual sociology and philosophical analysis. The fact that someone has bizarre ideas in itself concerns us only when that person writes a book giving expression to his anxiety, contempt and fantasies of a rapist faced with maddening virginity and then publicly acknowledges himself as the author, and all without producing any reaction. For this phantasmagoria long remained unnoticed.[45] If the publisher had blinked on receiving the manuscript, we should know it, so extensively did Sartre recount what went on behind the scenes of his work. Once the book was published, no critic described the considerations on holes and slime as outrageous. *Being and Nothingness* was to be read by millions of people who swallowed it all without a tremor and had been 'read and reread', alas, before anyone else, by Simone de Beauvoir, which gives us an idea of who she was a few years before she wrote *The Second Sex*.

We can describe these pages by saying that they relate to an anticipated experience of oneself in society. Granted we are dealing here with highly personal fantasies and thus with a 'self' structured at an imaginary level by the shoots of a fairly shattered libido. In making them public, the author is presuming on the part of his readers either a solid connivence or, at the least, the vague complicity which is born of indifference. His past experience of himself among other people must already have taught him that he could recount his reveries without having to face any form of censure, not even that which is expressed in the form of laughter. This experience is one that a woman almost never has. We are condemned to being much more reasonable, for any fragment of our personal myths uttered in public never fails to solicit censorious reactions or, at the least, derision: hence moreover the saying, *nous mourrons de n'être pas assez ridicules*, which some French feminists wore as a badge and which means, roughly, 'We do not dare to be ridiculous enough, and this may kill us'.[46]

First of all, *Being and Nothingness* gives us a measure of social tolerance in relation to a particular masculinist imagery, some of

whose elements are stereotypes, while others bear the mark of sing-
ularity. In this work a woman reader can never be anything but
adventitious and she has to deny herself in order to agree with the
remarks on the 'fundamental inclinations of sexuality', which are
limited to masculine eroticism. The phenomenological 'I' which
describes its relation to holes and to slime does not include her,
although, in principle, the phenomenological 'I' is 'anybody'. The
work is addressed to a strictly masculine group and unfolds in a 'men
only' atmosphere. Whether the woman reader ignores this or joins in
matters little: she does not count. This is fixed in advance by the text
which constructs her reading as superfluous.

But perhaps it is quite the opposite. If the writer's position is that
of the macho, what about the man reader? In *Situations II* the 'public'
is described in terms of its passivity and defined as an 'inert mass'. So
Sartre writes that the relation between author and reader is 'similar
to that of the male and female', for the author 'rapes and impregnates
an inert mass'.[47] Those who read these pages without taking them as
an affront to their dignity must have assumed that all readers were
other people: women, whom one has a right to 'rape and impregnate'
and men who are ultimately of the same type. 'Everyone is an inert
and feminine mass except me' is the usual theory of the man who
thinks himself the only man, 'a real man'; the masculine reader who
supports Sartre identifies with him, against women and most men.
Moreover, it is always the case that sexist insults or 'four-letter
words' are used indiscriminately to humiliate women and men in
subordinate positions.[48] Faced with texts like this, boycotts ('I'm not
buying this!') and analysis offer the woman reader ways of recovering
herself as a woman, by cutting herself off from something that denies
her existence. For a man they doubtless offer ways of recovering
himself as a 'decent man' who would like to live in a mixed world,
where anyone can speak and where culture is defined as that which
circulates between people who are different from each other.[49]

If we decline the text's invitation to cathect the proposed fantasies,
consigning it to its particularism and its limitations and regarding it
as characterized by a folklore which is not masculine but men-only,
we might wonder why public tolerance, whether 'scholarly' or not, is
so great for these pointless metaphors whose pretext is 'woman'. The
historian of philosophy might suggest the following answer to a
slightly different question: if in this century there are so many philosophical or scholarly delusions about 'the other term' of sexual difference, it is because where these delusions are concerned tolerance is
of a unique type. Once upon a time, a learned man could dream up

anything he wanted concerning matter or the origins of life and indeed could flirt with alchemy if he so chose. From the time of the Stoics until recently, stories about animals offered legendary support to metaphysical phantasmagoria. For a long time exotic peoples provided a blank screen on to which what were sometimes highly picturesque imaginings could be projected. Philosophers need to dream and for philosophical reasons – I am taking up the basic idea advanced by *The Philosophical Imaginary*. But today a whole set of reveries have ceased to be acceptable. We are more ascetic than our predecessors and anyone who fantasizes about anything other than 'woman' is very likely to be challenged. Look at the pitying smiles bestowed on Teilhard de Chardin or the scientific world's reservations about Michel Serres's visions; and everyone knows that those who fantasize about the Carib Indians will soon be discredited. Of course there are still children – except that psychoanalysis has appropriated those – and woman who, for her part, still belongs to everybody. If she is all that is left to lend support to imaginary productions, why should we be so surprised that so much is said about her? She is the last essence, and also the last permitted metaphor.

But, if we postulate that a maximum degree of social tolerance applies concerning what a man can say about women, there is no reason why we should not assume that what an author says really is the expression of his personal fantasies. When there is no risk of social censure, phantasmagoria has no need to conform to a code and we can see it as 'psychological' or 'psychoanalytic'. And yet even assuming that in these texts Sartre's personal dream production found a way of satisfying a need for self-expression, I do not think this is all we should see in the pages cited. This imaginary dimension, which combines with the concepts to form the text, provides indispensable links in the formation of the system.

We have already noted the strict symmetry of the metaphors concerning knowledge and the thoughts on slime. In the first case the For-itself tries desperately to appropriate the In-itself, for which the model is the smooth, white body of the woman; in the second case the text describes a sacrifice of the For-itself in favour of the In-itself and the fact that the For-itself is 'absorbed by the In-itself'. If Sartre's existentialism can be defined as a theorization of a megalomania of the subject ('nothing outside us has decided what we are'), we can then state that the term 'woman' appears in a contradictory way at decisive points where this megalomania is established and then contained.

It is established using the bad faith of women characters, which provides the necessary contrast to the position of authenticity as 'a self-recovery of being that was previously corrupted'.[50] Authenticity can be formulated using a scene that establishes a difference, where feminine sexuality is the best foil to highlight a superconsciousness which knows that 'I' decide who I am, even in the context of the unpredictability of things. So at once woman has a bit part in an argument which denies the influence of the external or the real. Her role is visibly the same in the theory of knowledge: here woman's body backs up the megalomania at a point where its case is very hard to plead. The subject who appropriates the object-woman's-body is once more an all-powerful figure. Of course as a theory such a theory of knowledge is quite simply crazy, but who will notice that, given that it is expressed in terms of virile metaphors whose effect is to put any man in the place of the knowing subject? As for slime or the In-itself-woman and the 'sweet and feminine revenge' on the For-itself, this seems to be the counterpart of the earlier remarks – but woman is playing the bit part here too: one way or another the megalomania had to be endowed with a weakness and the For-itself's achievements be undone, so that Sartre could say that 'man-in-the-world' can only make himself 'a failed God'.[51] Indeed the book concludes with observations on the perpetual failure of integration of the In-itself by the For-itself, 'an ideal which could be called God'. Megalomania tends to turn man into a God, so it is necessary that at the very end a counter-figure should undo the work of integration and persistently compromise the For-itself in order to ensure that this 'God' fails and thus that the For-itself's projects of conquest can continue indefinitely. An encounter with death (woman as the sugared death of the For-Itself) was necessary to guarantee the preservation of the For-Itself's identity, this being the condition which is absolutely necessary for the perpetual repetition of its destiny. Every morning 'man', the subject of the book, is a For-itself starting from scratch, who must construct his authenticity by differentiating himself from woman-decay who is assimilated to a thing. He works in a god-like way, trying to integrate the In-itself by means of free action and knowledge. But every evening his work is undone, the In-itself takes its revenge and everything has to be started over again. The very order in which the various metaphors are presented in the text outlines an odyssey. Moreover, anything which could not be given a theoretical foundation, but is necessary to make the system hold together and makes it possible to ground and reiterate the theory, is provided by sexism.

We thus find psychological, social and conceptual elements entangled: the experience of oneself in society is a factor in the constitution of the theory, through the mediation of imaginary elements which makes it possible to formulate pairs of opposites such as 'bad faith/ authenticity' or to carry out operations such as 'the integration of the In-itself by the For-itself', which are then rendered null and void by the revenge of the In-itself on the For-itself. All in all, a story of a failed God, contrasted with woman, who fails because of woman, or thanks to her, since his defeat allows him to start his conquests all over again.

11 Beauvoir's 'point of view'

If, therefore, we are not simply dealing with Monsieur Sartre's fantasies as importunate parasites on an abstract doctrine, if this imaginary production lies at the core of existentialism and if the latter is a system which seeks the connivence of masculinist ideology each time a case needs to be made for something unthinkable, then it was surely not enough for this theory to pass from a man's hands to those of a woman for it to change from the phallocratic discourse that it was into a proper theoretical tool for a feminist inquiry.

Before trying to see what transformations Simone de Beauvoir carried out on existentialism's formulation of the problems, we need to stress that these transformations were not thought out as such: nowhere does Beauvoir give a critique of Sartre's categories, nowhere does she state her intention to displace or modify them. Rather what we find is that they are remodelled 'in the heat of the moment'. We have said a great deal about the connivence that a reader must grant to Sartre in order to be carried along by the text and to accept what is said. It is highly possible that on Beauvoir's side this complicity was maintained by utter blindness. In the introduction to *The Second Sex* she quotes a phrase from Benda, without approving it of course, but regarding it as an exact photograph of the different situations experienced by men and women: 'Man can think of himself without woman. She cannot think of herself without man'.[52] To me, these words are only superficially true; if we look more closely, we realize that a man, Sartre for example, cannot think of himself, in other words that he cannot, alas, understand the humanity of man other than by postulating woman as a foil or as a protagonist, either annexed by conquest or used as a negative, terrifying figure. Since the eighteenth century philosophers have seldom failed to use this device, which we shall allow ourselves to regard as unpleasant, and which consists of regarding the active-and-free-human-being as masculine by means of a complex interplay of distinctions, assertions of dominance and the reduction of 'woman' to a single sexual dimension. Positive humanity is defined by contrast, through the production of an imago called woman.

This device is so firmly anchored in contemporary habits of thought that it is seldom noticed nowadays, except by one familiar with earlier philosophical works. And then, on some days, Descartes seems astounding: how did that man manage to define the human subject without using disgraceful contrasts, without saying anything unpleasant about women or Africans and indeed even including people who speak 'only Bas-Breton' among subjects able to think? The 'I' of his 'I think' thinks by itself without pejorative contrasts with anyone.[53]

We would suggest a very simple answer to this question: Descartes's subject in no way considers itself to be God, nor to be a relative or failed God. This subject thinks of itself as different from the divine, since the first thing it must recognize is its own finitude, in order to grasp that the idea of the infinite which it has within it was given to it, from elsewhere and higher up. As a hypothesis yet to be verified we suggest that in the work of all modern philosophers who exclude women, Jews, Indians, and so on from the most developed form of humanity one will find, even if only in a turn of phrase, that in one way or another man can be a God.[54]

The most obvious and no doubt most fundamental change operated by Beauvoir in the existentialist formulation of problems could well be this: she explicitly approaches her investigation from the perspective of existentialist morality. A *perspective* is a point of view or a chosen theoretical position which is applied to a particular area of experience assumed to exist before the investigation whose object it is. The task is to explore a section of social and intersubjective reality, not to build a system. Very briefly, we can say that when one builds a system, the things one discusses are present as examples, as supports for the argument, as links in the proof. The system itself produces those elements necessary to its functioning, including any little anecdotes which back up what it has to say. But the most effort goes into the formulation of a logic, of a structured group of concepts. It has often been noted that the 'objects' described by great philosophical architectonics – such as geometry, works of art, or war – can appear fictional because they are not discussed for themselves, but as cogs in a system. A method of thinking which claims only to be from a certain perspective is noticeably different. The 'point of view' is not supposed to create the object it is applied to; of course, it must construct questions and ways of analysing the section of reality that it is investigating so that its questions encounter data: we can then say only that it pro-duces things, in the sense that it is an art, and an action, to make something appear, to produce a piece of evidence, which is to be regarded as a document, to bring to light and put forward 'data' which sheer experience never gives as a gift.

From the point of view of the historian of ideas, this way of proceeding may seem derived. Simone de Beauvoir uses a conceptual framework which she did not create herself; she receives it ready made. But let us not immediately conclude that in theoretical work as in any other, women are always reflections. For her case is far from unique. Generations of epistemologists have been 'neo-Kantians', while in the early twentieth century some thought about politics 'from a Bergsonian point of view'. One could go on finding examples: it is a common thing to draw inspiration from models invented by a particular philosopher to try to understand a particular section of reality.

Furthermore, it should be emphasized that Simone de Beauvoir states that her inquiry will be carried out from the point of view of existentialist *morality*. What she takes from existentialism is thus not a collection of 'theoretical positions' which have been gathered together in a dogmatic approach, but values. Authenticity and free-dom form the ethical background to her work, and there is nothing ordinary about this. Thinking about the position of woman could slide towards other slopes such as the idea of happiness, or that of a nature to be fulfilled in the way that plants blossom, or again that of a questionable 'general interest': the view that women have to be a certain way because it is in everyone's interest, and too bad if it is not in theirs.

So Simone de Beauvoir's choice is first and foremost one of moral-ity. She thinks that once one has chosen a particular morality above all others, one has also chosen one's theoretical viewpoint: 'every so-called objective description is lifted from an ethical background'.[55] Thus in general a point of view can be defined as a set of values, which may be implicit or kept hidden but sometimes put on the table, in any case values with which one approaches and grasps concrete phenomena. This is stated, like a thesis, at the beginning of the book and Simone de Beauvoir's first merit is to have announced so explicitly this idea that values dictate descriptions, in other words that objectification is guided by something which is not of the order of the 'objective', as, for example, in anything said about sexual difference. And it is this that gives the book its philosophical cast: by making her own values explicit, Beauvoir makes it possible to read critically what she states; by stating that description 'is lifted from an ethical background', she even gives her readers a grasp on her own method. For they might reasonably ask her whether only ethical values exist, and whether those of existentialist morality (or of any other value system) are not liable to hide certain aspects of the reality they are seeking to reach.

We do not have to adhere in a servile way to any philosophical thesis. Of course the idea that a set of values always governs even a 'concrete' analysis of something is entirely plausible. Moreover, we should not forget that Simone de Beauvoir is going to discuss an object of study whose outlines and chief elements were in a vague state before her analysis: her work is to identify these outlines, in other words to change the object under consideration. It is also the case that this work does not change its object of study alone: in grappling with something, thought is itself transformed. And if the object of study is not constituted in advance, it is easy to understand that the effort required for its discovery is orientated by a particular will, which in this case is made explicit in the form of ethical principles. But we can also assume that in their details these principles are liable to be refined or to become part of a dialectic in the course of the work itself.

This would provide us with another notable difference between the 'point of view' or 'perspective' method and that of an attempt to set up a system. The project of a system is not so much to discuss something as to build a grammar in which great categories can be articulated and which makes it possible to conclude, for example, that 'the For-itself and the In-itself are linked by a synthetic connection which is nothing other than the For-itself itself'.[56] Two categories are defined, their type of relation is indicated, and so on: in the construction of a systematic whole, the most important thing is the grammar of the terms used and each term must be defined by the exact relations it has to the others. This primacy of the logical, or logicist, project means that in such a context any surreptitious slipping of a concept is a fault; if this happens in *Being and Nothingness* it is extremely regrettable. On the other hand, in a freer work like that of Simone de Beauvoir, where we see an investigation 'in progress', mutations may take place without necessarily endangering the consistency of thought, since the notions are made unsteady from the outset.

If we were to wonder how it is possible that existentialism led to sexist considerations in Sartre's thought but not in that of Simone de Beauvoir, we should first have to ask ourselves what mode of thought and what themes led the former to the unfortunate words noted above. We have suggested that the negative figure of woman as the 'sugary death of the For-itself' was invoked by Sartre's desire to build a closed system, in other words one which is always starting over again, like Sisyphus' task. Without such a project there is no need to maintain the figure of dissolution. *The Second Sex* is certainly not constructed to be closed and has nothing of *Being and Nothingness's* circular system. On the contrary, the relation of Simone de Beauvoir's work to time can be rapidly outlined as follows: we do not really know how women's oppression came into being, but we can see something of how it is maintained and how it causes suffering; at any rate, it is gradually ceasing, somewhat at least, and it must stop completely.

The evolution for which Beauvoir calls is one that must be irreversible and not repeatable. Moreover, by listening to the text carefully enough to hear in it the author's tastes and dislikes, we realize that the thing that she perhaps hates the most in women's position is the type of repetitive life associated with it. 'Bourgeois optimism promises the engaged girl [. . .] calm equilibrium in a life of immanence and repetition'.[57] This observation introduces the chapter on 'the married woman' and housework, work which makes a woman's life 'like the torture of Sisyphus, day after day'.[58] 'The housewife wears herself out going round and round in circles: she makes nothing, simply perpetuates the present in a struggle which starts afresh every day'.[59] Sartre is concerned with a subject which conquers its own authenticity and a power over things or over the external; but since the important thing is not to have conquered but to have a project of conquest and to throw oneself forward into a future (beware of the 'sucking of the past'!), it is a good thing that all is reduced to nothing and that everything has to be started over again. No destiny of repetition, no need for a 'sugary death' in Beauvoir's work.

12   Profound insignificance

We have seen that for Sartre the problem of 'bad fath' was always posed as 'the bad faith of the other': women, students, or Jesuits but most frequently women. In Beauvoir's work the notion of bad faith is merely on the horizon, as a kind of hollow mould of oppression, and it is noticeable that the category of 'the bad faith of the other' is never used, even when the context invites it. One has to admire the following words: 'many men will affirm *almost in good faith* [my emphasis] that women are the equals of man and that they [thus] have nothing to clamour for, while at the same time they will say that women can never be the equals of man and that their demands are in vain'.[60] At the level of morality, this sentence is spectacular in the degree of respect it shows for other people. With the concept of bad faith Sartre claimed to have access to the other's inner consciousness; Simone de Beauvoir is decent enough to examine only what people say. To speak of someone's 'bad faith' is to put that person's intentions on trial, since what is accused is an inner attitude. Men contradict themselves, but she credits them with being 'almost in good faith'. She might well have said that their reasoning is faulty and their thinking seems to break down here, but she does not do so and the approximation of good faith directs her comments on their contradiction towards an idea of naivety or candour which is excused from the outset. 'Forgive them Lord, for they know not what they say.'

The lady doth forgive too much, methink; but that is not the question. Sartre corrects everyone. Simone de Beauvoir excuses practically everybody. Could this be another effect of their respective experiences of themselves in society? Whatever the case, this change also has philosophical effects. Since no one is incriminated in *The Second Sex* and there is no one in the dock, all the evil is blamed on the situation, the set of harmful traditions and perverse ideologies, a nasty history without a Subject, formed of codes and oppressive institutions. And lies are not seen as 'lies to oneself' but as the 'lying ideals' of the language promoting untoward and unfortunate institutions. The kind of lie which must be fought is the social lie, such as the bourgeois optimism which sets an ideal of happiness sparkling in the young wife's eyes that is utterly unrelated to the reality she will encounter; at bottom, no one is the author of these lies.[61] 'Solid economic and social foundations' produce both 'masculine prestige' and the subordination of women.[62] The fact that some men are 'tyrants' or 'boors' is simply an effect of this situation.[63]

The fact that Beauvoir is not interested in the concept of bad faith saves her from the disgraceful arrogance of substituting her own consciousness for that of another – and of a socially dominated other. In harmony with this her position as a writer appears as different from that of Sartre. Sartre does not hesitate to call upon relations of dominance or pre-eminence, always identifying himself with the dominating element: he is man in relation to woman, teacher in relation to student, free thinker in relation to a Jesuit and white European in relation to all imaginable exotica. Thus he asserts the absolute overview of the writer, who holds the ultimate truth concerning all the characters who appear in his pages and, as we shall see later, outside them. For Beauvoir the writer's position seems more linked to the pursuit of a quite original project of understanding: in trying to understand what people say, she seeks to analyse the situation reflected in their speech and then to explain why this situation is not directly transparent to the people involved. Her approach is one of elucidation guided by indulgence, which is what being understanding is. Thus, having reported the contradictory things that have been said about equality, she writes: 'It is, in point of fact, a difficult matter for man to realize the extreme importance of social discriminations which seem outwardly insignificant but which produce in woman moral and intellectual effects so profound that they appear to spring from her original nature'.[64]

We should take the following guiding principle from this sentence: the object of a feminist inquiry can be defined by a paradox, since it brings to light a profound insignificance. The first correlate of this is a particular kind of subjective attitude in the writer, which requires a lot of nerve. Because the effect of discriminations is profound it is important to get to grips with them, although they may appear so trifling that your concern seems derisory. Simone de Beauvoir is aware of the theoretical difficulty of grasping this everyday unknown, this almost-nothing which does everything. She is also aware of the psychological difficulty of maintaining that things generally considered of no importance have such radical consequences that they are constituted into a nature. This is doubtless why she accuses no one, not even those who say contradictory things.

To tell the truth, I do find Simone de Beauvoir a little too good about this. She gives a fine example of the discretion with which, according to Gabrielle Suchon, women draw a veil over 'the weaknesses and failings of those who criticize them at every opportunity', a discretion which 'should make the latter speak better of them, as no doubt they would if they considered the usual moderation of women in contrast to their diatribes'.[65] Obviously moderation does not pay; but we should be able to find the golden mean between 'diatribes' and excessive kindness. I see this golden mean in logic: when there is a contradiction, no one need cover it up; it can be exposed without 'diatribes'. And if the various questions concerning equality or the integration of women in society are related to a 'profound insignificance', among the wealth of arguments fashioned by logicians there is one which is suited to the formulation of these questions: that of the dilemma. 'If it is insignificant, it costs nothing to grant us this thing that we want, so you can grant it to us. If it is something profound, then it is fundamentally important that you grant it to us and you can do so now.' Let us consider, for example, the third term of the motto of the French Republic, 'Liberty, Equality, Fraternity'. 'Fraternity' is an alliance between brothers and this word implies that the Republic is not a mixed state. It should long ago have been replaced by 'Solidarity'. Anyone who asked that this substitution be made would doubtless hear contradictory replies: 'A symbol is not important, it is of no consequence; why nag at us for something so minor' and 'It is a difficult thing to change mottos, they are a profound part of national tradition and are embedded in a people's idea of itself.' The logical reply to this contradiction would be: if it is nothing, you can change this word, and if it is profoundly embedded in the national consciousness, then again, you should change it.

13 The folklore of domination

To the extent that 'bad faith' always refers to the bad faith of the other, this concept seemed to us a macho concept: the macho always also tells us how to think. This category also indissociably reflects the hegemony of a writing subject who, in the playlets on which his theory is based, uses the position of superiority that he has outside his writing to constitute that writing as a practice of spiritual direction. The fact that Simone de Beauvoir does not endorse this category, even when she says she is adopting the existentialist perspective, seems to me to be of vital importance in reopening a certain number of debates, which I think it wise to mention before continuing to contrast her philosophy with that of Sartre. For I have already expounded this idea and been greatly misunderstood – an experience which should not be ignored. When you realize that what has been heard is not what you thought you said, you have to ask yourself where the obstacle lies and what the assumptions of your own speech are.

The first obstacle springs from a conviction widespread in the social doxa according to which there is a 'feminine intelligence' and a 'masculine intelligence' which are radically heterogeneous. So that if there is an observable difference between, for example, the work of Simone de Beauvoir and that of Sartre, this is not very surprising, or is it? The debate on types of intelligence went round and round in circles in the feminist movement of the 1970s: a sizeable section of this movement directed its attention to researching feminine specificity. This tendency thought that difference had been repressed by modern society and that work was therefore necessary to bring specifically feminine values to light once more. From this perspective the supreme insult was to say of any woman that she was 'phallic' or 'man-identified' and Simone de Beauvoir was often cited as the archetypal case of the sin of identification with the masculine. This label was fairly constantly applied to women who earned their living by some sort of theoretical work or who tried to be the theoreticians of feminism. 'Theory' was thus assimilated without mediation or clarification to the 'masculine'. Consequently, for us poor theorists the Movement was not the place of psychological reassurance that we might have hoped it would be for all women: in it we found something more like a repetition of the latent or explicit aggression that we were subjected to elsewhere in our professional fields, or in our private lives.

The first time that I mentioned the difference between Simone de Beauvoir's thought and that of Sartre, my words were received with a little too much gratitude by some of my friends: so she wasn't so identified with her man as we thought, so feminine intelligence ultimately triumphed over theoretical training. For anyone trying to problematize everything, it is a rather brutal experience to see one's ideas immediately taken up within the unquestioned categories of the dominant doxa. It is here that the conceptual distinction between the 'masculine' and the 'masculinist' is necessary. For no one knows what the masculine in thought might be, particularly given that all men do not think identically. In a symmetrical way, one would expect the fact that all women do not think alike to be acknowledged. But it is possible to recognize a masculinist position; things said from such a position can be identified and described. And while 'the masculine in thought', if it existed, should inevitably be found in the work of all men thinkers, the notion of masculinism contains no such necessity: it is a folklore which does not have to appear in a man's writings. Certainly it should not appear in the work of a woman writer.

What we notice at once in Beauvoir's reworking of existentialism is the disappearance of the masculinist elements present in Sartre's work; first not only do the imaginary productions (the little stories assuming a superiority, presumed guaranteed, over others) disappear, but so do those fundamental concepts which are entirely based upon them. Using a simple procedure of textual analysis, I

suggested that these concepts, and in particular 'bad faith', all derived from Sartre's phantasmagoria. The fact that they disappear,
along with the phantasmagoria in question, when Beauvoir takes up
the 'same' philosophy reinforces the hypothesis that the imaginary
order and the concepts are inextricably bound together.

Simone de Beauvoir's abandonment of all these things seems to me
to be both unsurprising and exemplary: that which is masculinist in a
doctrine cannot be communicated from a man to a woman, however
much in love with him that woman may be, or however much she has
pledged herself to the philosophy of her mentor; the contrary would
be pathetic. But more importantly, we can conclude from this that
'specificity' lies with masculinism and not with some hypothetical
'feminine in thought'. The latter would, in principle, be equally
incommunicable to the other sex. The difference that we observe to
begin with is one of simple subtraction which makes what is said
more universal, since it produces no excluded 'others'. And when
Simone de Beauvoir describes human realities in which she is not
involved – the black community in the United States, workers' movements or so-called primitive societies – she does so with the aim of
finding little shafts of light that will help her understand her own
position, if only by contrast. An approach where one seeks to understand others in order the better to understand oneself is a long way
from the idea that the 'European of 1945' can hegemonically understand everyone. But there is no reason why we should regard
Beauvoir's attitude as 'specifically feminine'; on the contrary we can
raise it to the level of universal, while Sartre's non-reciprocity
(I understand everyone but I never imagine that others could reconstitute my project) can in no way be universalized.

Some feminist theorists have rightly noted that when ideas of
'difference' and 'specificity' are used in everyday language it is
always woman's difference that is mentioned, since it goes without
saying, of course, that man is never different, for what would he be
different from?[66] Against the grain of that common attitude I am
trying to say that it is theoretically possible to have a community in
thought that includes everyone and I believe this to be desirable on a
human level. When we find subjects who deny this community and
seek to restrict it to include only themselves by affirming a privilege
and excluding others, it is this that we should regard as a 'specificity',
a particularism, or quite simply folklore. If rationality is (at least) the
desire to make oneself comprehensible to all, to reason in a way
which can be expounded and discussed, masculinist specificity must
be seen as reflecting irrationality. Of course in social terms the

opposite occurs: Sartre's delusions were not perceived as such while Simone de Beauvoir's non-exclusive words were greeted by meanness and an effort to deny their universality. 'I have learned all about your boss's vagina' said Mauriac graciously to an author from *Les Temps Modernes*.[67] An accusation of navel-gazing which was not transposed at random.

Simone de Beauvoir's reworking of existentialist theory is not however limited to a subtraction. In *The Second Sex* she also adds questions and expectations which considerably alter the way the problems are posed: 'woman does not claim the status of subject because she lacks the concrete means to do so'.[68] 'Women lack the concrete means to organize themselves into an entity which could posit its existence through confrontation'.[69] From the book's introduction onwards, this idea of 'concrete means' is constantly stressed and leads to a very different perspective from that of *Being and Nothingness*. Sartre was concerned fundamentally to deny that external factors could be an obstacle, a true constraint, real adversity or a cause of alienation: I am stronger than everything that is, because I am ontologically different from what is external to me and my vocation is to transcend it. Simone de Beauvoir, on the other hand, poses a problem which is clearly at a stage removed from Sartre's: it is not enough to know that one is not determined by external factors (not to believe oneself to be persecuted by them). The external world must also provide one with the 'concrete means' to assert oneself as a subject, as the subject of an action, of something. Unfortunately however, woman is shut away in the void; her social status deprives her of a world and of hands. The idea of deprivation of concrete means as a radical obstacle to the assertion of the self as a subject is one quite foreign to the viewpoint of *Being and Nothingness*. Without rights, for example, how can woman project to carry out any type of activity in the social world? Even her clothes 'were primitively designed to condemn her to impotence'. Any action assumes an object on which to act and a means of action; a subject deprived of this access to the external world cannot be a conqueror, as Sartre's understanding of the For-itself would have it.

When it is contrasted with Beauvoir's work, the enormous gaps in Sartre's framework appear. *Being and Nothingness* may seem to be a text that is 'filled to bursting', complete and closed in on itself, but it also contains omissions. One is that Sartre does not even pose the problem of the need of an external reality in which to act, and a highly particularized reality, come to that. Not a world in general, but one in which one has some hope of accomplishing one's aim.

Simone de Beauvoir talks of nothing else: for example, let us consider her discussion of 'free motherhood', which is free like love, in other words outside the institution of marriage.[70] According to her, this type of motherhood 'interests many women', but it runs up against several problems: 'illigitimate birth is a stain on the child' and free motherhood is not 'accepted by society'; 'It must be said in addition that the lack of crèches means that having a child is enough to paralyse a woman's activity entirely.' This regrettably brief paragraph shows how the lack of two social factors, one symbolic and the other practical, prevents women from 'performing in complete freedom' a certain 'feminine function', in other words that possible choice that is motherhood.[71]

14 Can crèches be of concern to the absolute ego?

The content of what Beauvoir says seems like simple common sense. Nevertheless this notion of 'concrete means', whose absence blocks freedom, places her thought on a different track from Sartre's: the 'subject' of freedom that she would like women to become has little to do with the phenomenological subject that Sartre inherited from his Husserlian days as a theoretical position. My kind reader is begged to forgive this torrent of authors and the relaunching of the analysis by a historical regression. This is because no author is a radical point of departure: of course Simone de Beauvoir uses Sartre's philosophy, but the latter derives from a transposed version of Husserl;[72] and Husserl himself laid out the basic framework of his doctrine in discussing Descartes. A little patience and here it is: Descartes, says Husserl, did not accede

to the consideration that the ego (as it was disclosed in the *epochè* as being for itself) is not yet an I that can have other or many co-Is outside itself. It remained hidden to Descartes that all such distinctions as 'I/thou', 'internal/external', first 'constitute' themselves in the absolute ego. Thus we understand why Descartes [...] did not set himself the task of systematically investigating the pure ego – hence consistently remaining within the *epochè* – to see what it might itself possess as its own actions [...] He did not come to see the important problematization which, on the basis that the world is phenomenon of the ego, consists in systematically asking in return what are the really demonstrable immanent activities of the ego to which the world owes its sense of being.[73]

Let us not go into the details of what the *epochè* is. We need only note that the 'absolute ego', the 'pure ego' and the phenomenological subject are (to say the least!) radically detached from ordinary empirical relations. The world is not strictly speaking external, the question of the co-existence of other subjects does not arise. For the world is a phenomenon of the ego, and the distinction between 'I' and 'thou' constitutes itself within the absolute ego. Husserl regards the Cartesian theory of the subject as having made all these observations possible, but says that Descartes turned away from his own discovery by rushing off to found the natural sciences.[74] For a corollary of this doctrine is that any interest taken in 'objectivism', and particularly in the idea that there is a nature which could be an object of sciences that are required to be exact, is described as a tragic 'haste' which leads to the forgetting of meaning and the appalling positivism in which modern Europe has lost its soul.

Sartre's idea of the 'subject' came out of the idea that 'I' does not exist in relation to a world: the world is posed by the 'I', hence his view that 'it is I who choose even the coefficient of adversity of things'. On the contrary in Simone de Beauvoir's writing, far from being constituted within the ego, the distinctions between 'I' and 'thou' and 'external' and 'internal' are constitutive of the particular mode of any given type of 'subject'.

15   The extinguished subject, and how, nonetheless, the improbable later occurred

A close reading of the first pages of *The Second Sex* shows us that Beauvoir is not proposing a single theory of the 'subject'; this term is used in at least three ways. There is the 'subject' who constitutes the other as inessential and as an object; this mode corresponds to 'male sovereignty'. There is the 'subject' of oppressed minorities, American or Haitian blacks, workers from the poor areas of Paris or the Jews of the ghettos, whom the white-christian-bourgeois-man regards as 'the other', but who can answer back and retain independence in relation to the dominator's viewpoint because a community exists which makes it possible to say 'we'. These minorities can organize 'themselves into an entity which can understand and place itself in confrontation'. Lastly, there is the subject who is completely extinguished as such, lost in submission to other people and in other people's point of view: women who, when they speak of women, say 'women' as men do and not 'we'; women who are scattered and whom no form of solidarity unites. These three modes are thus situated in a schema of objectifiable power relations and the text relates each of them to concrete parameters, which are seen as existing outside the account which seeks to reveal and understand them. A given mode is not chosen by a particular 'I'. It is the particular mode which decides whether the 'I' can be the despotic subject, the minority subject in struggle and resistance, or the extinguished subject, in other words woman.

Woman is extinguished because the traditional position deprives her of an external world to act in and subjects her to the other's point of view; these things may go together. 'The restrictions that education and custom impose on woman now limit her grasp on the universe':[75] if our author lays so much stress throughout the book on feminine narcissism, it is in line with this idea. The only field of action left to 'woman' is herself, and herself through the look of the other. Of course Beauvoir does not forget that there are women workers, nor that any wife-mother has to bear a heavy burden of domestic work. However the last chapter is concerned to show that this 'daily labour' is 'thankless' in the strict sense of the word, insofar as women do not receive 'the moral and social benefits they might rightfully count on'.[76] So is a person 'someone' only when the work she or he does is validated and remunerated? We could look more deeply into Beauvoir's thinking on this point. But let us see how the question of the community that she raises has been pursued dialectically by her women heirs.

The American Women's Liberation Movement, the French MLF of the 1970s and their equivalents in the other developed countries have not necessarily regarded *The Second Sex* as their *What Is To Be Done?* Besides, Simone de Beauvoir would not have liked it if they had. And even though most of the women involved in these movements have been very grateful to 'Simone', the movements themselves started around issues which she considered more or less settled (contraception, abortion[77]) and something she did not regard as possible: the creation of, if not a community then at least a movement, whose founding principle would be that solutions can only be collective. Through this, the awareness of belonging to a social group emerged, with at least the effect of enabling each woman to discover that she was a woman among other women, indeed that each woman is a woman to the extent that she is one woman among others. For once, consciousness of womanhood was drawn from the sense of belonging to a group.

Women were particularly seeking this consciousness because of upheavals in the culture, which had long been unobtrusive or piecemeal and which became more widespread after the war. The writing of *The Second Sex* and the hunger with which women readers devoured the book can be seen as signs of the times. Our great-grandmothers seldom had the opportunity to think about themselves as women – this is the paradox – because their lives could not accommodate a notion which would have gathered together categories which had to be kept separate: those of virgin, wife, prostituted, mother, widow, nun and, in some cases, 'lady'. They had first to be virgins, which was the opposite of being women, and when they later became wives, and thus women, this was as 'someone's-woman', which implies that they were never simply and absolutely women. To be only when one belongs to someone is not to be, but to have the status of a perceptible quality, like sweetness according to Plato: 'To be sweet, but sweet to no one, is impossible.'[78]

The beginnings of emancipation in relation to family structures created a new being in the social reality: it became possible to be just a woman, without belonging to someone, or being an old maid or a 'fallen woman'. This category still meets with fierce resistance in daily life: there are people who, knowing that I am unmarried, still insist on calling me 'Mademoiselle', despite my age of more than forty and my protestations. In French as in English, this is the symmetrical counterpart of the custom of calling a married woman by the surname and first name of her husband: one is either a Mrs John Smith – 'Mrs' followed by a man's name – or a 'Miss'.

Just a woman, yes, but what is that? Where were we to find the new consciousness of self which social upheavals had made necessary? Women have sought to gain a consciousness of womanhood from very different sources. Some have felt themselves to be women through partial identification with a tradition – of jam-making and seduction by frills (grandmother's life without the heavy constraints of fidelity, multiple pregnancies and obedience with which grand-mother was burdened); my generation has been greatly tempted by this tendency, which is by definition nostalgic and retrograde, since it offers a return to identification with tradition. Other women (of whom I am one) have thought it possible to feel ourselves to be women through a better understanding and awareness of our bodies – 'our bodies, ourselves' – which is the opposite of retrogression, since women's traditional position forbade them to know even the most necessary things about themselves. Still other women, manifestly drawing their inspiration from some male authors, made it their aim to feel themselves to be women through a systematic project of differentiation: since men are this, I shall be that. In my opinion, this can at best lead only to wallowing in the mire of ideology. It is very difficult to establish that 'men are this', because they differ greatly from each other; wanting to differentiate oneself from a highly diverse reality is a sad and hollow plan of action which soon leads nowhere, for is there any place that no man has ever occupied? In looking for specificity, one condemns oneself to not-much and it moreover means accepting a derivative position, since seeking to define oneself by contrast means that one has accepted that the other has the power to determine things.

The collective Movement has not supplied a unanimous answer to the question, 'How does a woman of the second half of the twentieth century feel herself to be a woman?' This question is apparently in many people's heads, otherwise the glossy women's magazines would not have so many women readers. My suggestion that the Movement and women's magazines might have something in common should and must make my readers scream, since these magazines deal with our unease in such a perverse way: they begin by making their readers feel guilty about their failure-to-be-entirely-a-woman, then suggest ways in which the consumer society can help them improve themselves by pointing to an art, not of being a woman (there is no art which can make one be what one already unfailingly is), nor of becoming aware of oneself and clearly perceiving one's experience of oneself in the world (which would be a positive thing, but which would work towards the disappearance of the need which makes women read these magazines), but the art of being very-woman, remarkably-woman, more-woman than one's neighbour, more-woman than before one read and applied the recipes. This type of game assumes the existence of a womanly essence, which, depending on her efforts, is more or less developed in every woman, a world of competition between women and a panel who make the final judgement. It suggests that every woman should throw herself into the conquest of her own femininity, into the construction, which may well become a masquerade, of a self entirely marked by sexualization, which presupposes that one started off as a zombie or as ectoplasm in need of substance.[79]

Nevertheless the unease on which this flourishing trade feeds is real. It at least relates to the fact that women were long deprived of any way of acting in the world and of any chance of initiating anything, with the result that until recently it has scarcely been possible for them to say 'I', affirming themselves as the subjects of projects. But 'I' is not as independent as one might think from the consideration of what one is at the actual moment when one decides. A concrete self-awareness is involved in the consciousness of an intention to do something. An image of 'I am' is mixed into the definition of what one is going to do. Women's oppression is characterized by, among other things, the fact that they breathe an atmosphere saturated with 'you are', 'you are not' or 'you should be', which more or less prevents them from determining what they want and what they want to be.

'Men simply are, and that's it. Whereas women are something: whores, virgins, martyrs, beautiful, ugly, modest, experienced, tall, fat, small, thin...but they are something' writes Cathy Bernheim.[80] This is true, and yet we must at the same time say the opposite. Some men have a well determined 'self-awareness', and Sartre could not have written what he wrote without his. Whereas, when women separate themselves from the various somethings Cathy lists, they are left with a big nothing. Or they were left with a big nothing, not so long ago. Hence, moreover, this famous counter-questionnaire made up by women from the Movement in answer to one published by *Elle* in 1970:

Do you think that women are women:
- down to the tips of their fingernails;
- down to the point of collapse;
- down to their hate for their sisters;
- down to the limits of men's imagination?

The Movement has always been concerned with the question of concrete self-awareness, but fortunately has not replied with any dogma adopted by all. Beyond the various answers we have mentioned, one simply finds a kind of minimal consensus: one can know oneself as a woman by being among women and through concern about what happens to other or to all women. Thus we saw lesbians joining in the struggle for contraception and abortion on demand, women who had the means to 'get by' anyway calling for their legalization and reimbursement by social security, women without children setting up organizations for building crèches, single women showing their concern for the daily problems of housewives and Western women being appalled by clitoridectomy or the forced wearing of the chador. This is what replaced nail varnish and the acknowledgement of the lord and master in women's consciousness of self: a sense of being women because they wanted more freedom, a better life and greater dignity for all women. All those who got involved in the Movement, even temporarily, thus gained a degree of autonomy and an awareness of collective belonging. Autonomy in the first instance in relation to the divisions established and imposed by the culture; for ideology always has clear ideas about gender: a man is a man and a woman must be feminine, in other words she must correspond to standards which are endlessly listed and honed, to the point where they contradict each other. Autonomy too in relation to the men we love, if there are men we love. I seem to remember that they tended (yesterday of course) to be used to telling us who to be and how to behave. Whether or not they have preserved this annoying habit, we have at least learned to avoid its effects, inasmuch as we no longer require their recognition of our being to be able to assume it.

This means we have also needed to find out about our own desires, a concern our mothers were spared. The usual course of women's lives used to be reduced to a sequence of events in which they did not have to ask themselves exactly what it was they wanted: accepting an offer of marriage, fulfilling the conditions of a role and then, for most, somehow or other confronting many contradictitory demands. Those of more recent generations who have won material and personal autonomy now need to know that, if there is a man in their lives, he is not there to meet a practical or social need, nor because they have simply agreed to an offer, but because they wanted and still want him there. The less a woman needs a man for something, including in order to feel herself to be a woman, the more it must be recognized that she (I, you, they) is a desiring subject, who is not sidestepping the life of a lover.

All this may shed some light on collective resistances to feminism. In the first place these surely relate dully to the fact that feminism wants autonomy for all women, while the dominant ideology seeks to maintain their dependency. But they also relate to the fact that a free women clearly acknowledges her feelings as personal feelings, instead of displaying a simple 'probity', in other words an attitude which arises from a given situation and is entirely shaped according to what that situation demands. Indeed feminism is a kind of immodesty, which explains why it so often arouses derision. The traditional order requires women's desire to be put out by the best possible extinguisher[81] and on no account to be the necessary condition of the relationship that a women has with a particular man.

Honey is still sweet only if there is someone for whom it is sweet, but being a woman and belonging to no one has now become possible: we have moved from the status of 'qualities perceptible to the senses' to that of beings. Who are 'we'? Some women, who want all women to share this position? Or just a potential 'we', who will come into existence when all women share this position? Whatever the case, it is no easy thing to plan to live this way without evasions, particularly when there is no tradition to support our way of thinking. Many feminists have explored the past in an attempt to find positive role models for women, and they are there to be found. This is lacking in *The Second Sex*, as is the idea of a collective women's movement and no doubt for the same reason. Simone de Beauvoir did not try retrospectively to construct a portrait gallery of individual women who were clearly living their own lives, even in the limited field of literature. She is even qualified in her praise of Emily Brontë, Virginia Woolf and Katherine Mansfield.[82] No woman wrote *Moby Dick* or *The Trial*, she says, which in itself is not to display the best possible literary taste. Her failure to feel the strength of freedom which enabled the writing of *The Waves* or *Orlando* is linked to a prejudice which is not strictly literary: no one was an emancipated woman before me. According to the existentialist view, to create is 'to found the world anew', to do which one must 'unequivocally assume the status of a being who has freedom'. It is thus essential to tell oneself, 'I am the first and only one to do this.' The great difference between Simone de Beauvoir and the feminists of my generation, including those who payed tribute to her, is that each of us took the view that 'fortunately, I am not the only one, nor the first here; but I am certainly here, all the same'.

16   How did she manage to write The Second Sex?

While we may have modified what we inherited from Simone de Beauvoir, she herself had to bring to bear a formidably astute intelligence simply to pose the problem, given the intellectual frameworks at her disposal. Hélène Védrine, who has restored to its rightful place that form of intelligence that the Greeks attributed to Ulysses and to politicians, would call Beauvoir's work a wonderful *métis*. The term refers to an art of indirect means, quite close to that of 'cobbling things together with whatever comes to hand' and also to that of seizing the opportunity. The Greeks thought that this was the kind of intelligence that enabled one to move in an unknown world.[83] But how did Simone de Beauvoir manage?

 She describes how one half of humanity is subordinate to the other. This subordination itself must then be explained. But how? There is a narrow escape in the Introduction, where she just avoids an idea much chewed over by the twentieth century – an idea that would have closed the question before it was even opened. Simone de Beauvoir reminds us of a thesis – which she believes – according to which 'the category of the Other is as primordial as consciousness itself': 'otherness is a fundamental category of human thought'. And she cites Dumézil and Lévi-Strauss in support of this. 'In the most primitive societies, in the most ancient mythologies, one finds the expression of a duality – that of the Same and the Other'.[84] Eeek! Kojève's catechism certainly has set the tone for the century on the Left Bank of the Seine. Someone does a seminar at the Collège de France and we are stuck in it for fifty years at least. Lacan, Lévinas, Lévi-Strauss, Simone de Beauvoir and a few others all took their bearings from it, directly or indirectly, and thus 'French-style' German phenomenology became a dogma, in other words an obvious truth to be taught. According to this dogma, human thought has a universal structure which can be observed equally well among the Bororo peoples as among the tribe of St Germain-des-Prés, at the time of the Pharoahs as in the age of Planck, an ultra-simple structure and so minimal that in practice it is most difficult to establish its absolute absence anywhere. As I know nothing about the Bororos, nor about the Pharoahs, except what people say, and as quantum mechanics is largely beyond the capacities of my understanding, I shall not try to prove that there are some thoughts which escape this duality of the Same and the Other. Suffice it to say that it is trivial, or rather so crude that we cannot legitimately regard it as a 'fundamental category'; for what can be founded on such a summary logic? What is really thought in the various forms of thinking requires many other things. It is not this poor duality which makes Newton's theory into one which thinks something through or makes Marx or Tocqueville into political thinkers: we can thus regard it as quite irrelevant and regret that so many people have focused on a dogma of such derisory scope.[85]

Simone de Beauvoir believes in it and her belief nearly deprived us of *The Second Sex*: if the fundamental and primary dimension of consciousness is the duality of the Same and the Other, it is only a short step from this to deduce the metaphysical duality of the sexes: man is the Same, women the Other, and henceforth where is the problem? That is how it is; let us see that it is good. Emmanuel Lévinas made a whole metaphysics out of this, which Simone de Beauvoir notes and quotes in the Introduction, but which she does not agree with: once again, she unhooks herself or turns away from what she nevertheless regards as an indisputable theoretical position; in this case she reintroduces an element which reopens the space of a problem: the notion of reciprocity.[86] Granted that each consciousness regards the other as another, 'the other consciousness [...] sets up a reciprocal claim', 'willy-nilly, individuals and groups are forced to realize the reciprocity of their relations':[87] there is no Other in absolute terms. However there is one exception to this rule: between the sexes this reciprocity has not been established because women have not (yet) done the same back to those who set them up as Others. And lastly there is a question: 'Whence comes this submission in the case of woman?'[88]

From a methodological point of view, here we can clearly see Simone de Beauvoir's technique, her *métis*, her craftiness with and towards the doctrinal philosophy she has accepted. It is a technique of reintroduction which undermines the structure. Desanti says somewhere that a philosophical utterance is an empty statement which produces closure. I do not know if this proposition is generally true but, as Desanti was very familiar with phenomenology, we can grant that his proposition may be valid for thinking about the Husserlian or post-Husserlian current. It could be said that Beauvoir, constantly faced with the closure produced by phenomenology, challenges it just as constantly, rediscovering questions that the pure phenomenologists left out: that of the concrete means necessary to establish oneself as a subject or, here, that of reciprocity.

17   On reintroduction and the diversity of otherness

By reintroducing the question of reciprocity, Simone de Beauvoir also turns otherness from something unique into something diverse. For a particular group a particular other is the Other, but for another group it will of course be different. She patiently pluralizes this monolithic category of 'the Other' and, ultimately, indirectly mocks it by using examples which do not invite her readers to credit this category with a great coefficient of seriousness. She does this while still citing Lévi-Strauss's *The Elementary Structures of Kinship*, which defines the 'state of culture' by the 'aptitude of man to understand' biological relations in terms of duality, alienation, opposition and symmetry.[89] She cites and undermines it.

At about the same time Bachelard was complaining about the narcissistic closure of supposedly clear minds. He too was seeking to reintroduce into philosophical considerations a little information that might transform the questions. The little that I want to say here about the sciences is not a digression: it seems to me that there is a parallel in method, and above all in polemical aims, between Simone de Beauvoir and Bachelard. Both challenge a certain style of philosophy which swallows up othernesses. The Other which the phenomenologists tell us so much about is only ever one dimension of 'I's consciousness, and, once again, the difference between 'I' and 'thou' is constituted in the ego, with the world as a phenomenon of that ego. This world is the vanishing point of my reverie and can be forever considered as caprice and as miniature – forever insofar as this conception cannot be combined with a project of secondary correction.[90] Neither 'the other' nor the world are to be patiently discovered by a laborious movement beyond the 'I'. As long as the sciences were 'but dependent branches of the One philosophy', which was at the time the 'universal science', then everything was all right according to Husserl.[91] But then these sciences became specialized and 'positive'. They grew away, severed from the common trunk. The phenomenologist declares this a catastrophe and a fundamental crisis, whatever the 'theoretical and practical successes of the special sciences'[92] might also have been.

There is something highly questionable in the way a philosophy thus denigrates disciplines on the grounds that they have freed themselves from its own omni-incorporation. It well illustrates its relation to difference, whatever the latter may be. The attitude of this type of philosophy towards women and its relation to the extraphilosophical can be seen as isomorphic. For the twentieth century which has talked such a lot about the duality of the Same and the Other, sometimes complaining that philosophy is a permanent integration into the Same, this philosophical twentieth century has taken care not to acknowledge fully that close by it had others, theoretical constructions which, in both their aruments and methods, are independent of the mode of philosophical work, different from philosophy and different from each other, but still close and all presenting a double face: they are rational, which implies also that they question the 'native intellect' of those who become involved in them, requiring these people to reshape their categories and concepts, and they also seek to produce an account of the world or, more precisely, to produce an account of the range of phenomena it is concerned with. A philosophy which recognized the difference, independence and equal dignity of these diverse disciplines which are called sciences would not speak of a 'crisis in science' nor of a 'crisis in philosophy', but of a fit of pique on the part of the philosopher who has to learn that he can no longer get acquainted with this fine diversity (*ars longa, vita brevis*) except perhaps in those aspects revealed by journals popularizing scientific discoveries: the philosopher has become the 'common man' or the 'layman' of the sciences.

Phenomenologists are those who, faced with this situation, prefer splendid isolation. They start by refusing to recognize the difference and the equality in difference of these other accounts which are talking about something; they go on to posit that the world is a phenomenon of the ego, just like the difference between 'I' and 'thou'. Phenomenology's attitude towards the sciences is very similar to what Beauvoir said about 'male sovereignty'; it excludes reciprocity, understands difference only in terms of subordination and thus closes itself to the existence of various constituted differences.[93] This may also explain why Sartre, in 1943, denigrated Marxism and the serious-mindedness of revolutionaries in general. A philosopher rarely accepts the existence of a politics which is not entirely that of the philosophers: 'Either it is I who command, encompass and elucidate in the final instance, or it does not exist, other than as an object of contempt.'

By contrast we should salute at least three colleagues who were all very active during the War and who all later integrated an authentic principle of difference into their work: Vladimir Jankélévitch, Hannah Arendt and Georges Canguilhem. The first always postulated the principle of the independence of the political and of good intentions from philosophy; indeed he portrays the latter as prone to hair-splitting or to 'megaro-eleatic subterfuge' at times when it is necessary to do good forthwith, and where that good is manifestly simple.[94] The third, a philosopher of biology, welcomes the foreignness of science to philosophy, saying 'For philosophy, all kinds of foreign matter are good and it can even be said that good matter is always foreign'.[95] As for Hannah Arendt, who was so concerned to explore 'the plurality of the human condition',[96] she has given us at least one theory of action as action with and among others, and thus as something affected by others and as an event whose consequences are limitless. The important thing in action is that it takes place in a milieu where all other beings can carry out their own actions; their reaction is not just a response but a new action, which in turn has effects, so that no action is performed in a closed circuit. Besides, it is an understatement to say that she recognizes the independent existence of politics: politics exists and philosophy constitutes itself both separately and in relation to it.[97] When the independent and equally dignified existence of others (other people, other levels of human life, other disciplines) is fully recognized, philosophers of either sex can reciprocally perceive their own character as other and the importance of exchanges. And they can realize that they are also capable, when circumstances demand it, of being something other than philosophers.

18   Ascetical attitudes

According to Beauvoir, women's position is characterized chiefly by its lack of externality and concrete means to act on the world. This continually resubjects every woman to another person, a man, who is himself able to enter into an active relation with the world. This situation must be explained, because there are no obvious reasons for its existence. Here we encounter the paradox of Beauvoir's theoretical position: the requirement for an explanation could be posed with true urgency only in the framework of the ethics of authenticity, which allowed her to distance the destiny allotted to women enough to describe it as a shocking contingency, something strange which must be changed as soon as possible. It is indeed existentialist philosophy she is using, but in a paradoxical fashion she turns it into operative philosophy and makes it think above and beyond its means. For existentialist subjects, defined by their transcendence, are neither beings nor essences. The effect of existentialist metaphysics is to expel from the sphere of the person all possible determining factors, these being rejected on to the external plane of a situation, which must by definition be transcended. There can be no valid existentialist anthropology or psychology, at least not in principle. Existentialist morality even requires a non-psychology and the annulment of all forms of anthropological determinedness. There is a break between the subject (who has no thickness and must be understood as a mere mathematical point, the locus of a freedom and origin of the vector 'project', in relation to which everything is alien) and everything else, which is thing, 'In-itself', immanence, etc. This perspective enables Beauvoir to avoid essentialism: there is no eternal feminine any more than there is a 'black soul', and no human nature, whether diversified or not. Consequently everything observable is simply a result: the famous words which open book II, *On ne naît pas femme, on le devient* ('One is not born, but becomes, a woman'), reflect the particular application of this idea, which Beauvoir does not fail also to use in a critical way elsewhere, against all theories of the Jewish character or the black soul.[98]

Everything becomes contingent in relation to a freedom: the issue is no longer to justify a particular state of things by reference to some nature or necessity: on the contrary, the point is to set-before-oneself all forms of determinedness, attributing them to an external situation governed by the arbitrariness of culture, and demonstrating its foreignness and potential variability. There is no destiny and everything lends itself to an objectifying description through which the subject (at least the writing or reading subject) withdraws from involvement in what is only a sign or an institution, thus depriving it of her or his subjective guarantee. The liberating force of the book no doubt arises from this movement, whose iconoclastic character seems to me very important on the imaginary plane as well.

Since existentialist ethics requires a non-psychology, it thus prohibits the posing of the question of happiness. The only value it acknowledges is that of 'the freedom which must invent its own ends unaided', the correct end for this freedom moreover being itself: the right 'free choice' is to choose freedom. The notion of happiness on the other hand can be seen as one of the ideological locks (or 'social lies') which block all investigations of dominance or of any form of subjugation: it is so easy to declare that a people whom one has enslaved are happy; it is always possible to maintain that a given group needs my guardianship in order to blossom, that they do not feel the need to be self-governing and are entirely happy in this carefree state which so suits them. The problem of happiness almost inevitably leads us back to (usually preconceived) ideas about specific psychological tendencies, which are said to be satisfied by this or that situation; it brings back the idea of a particular nature, of a set 'character', of needs that can be ascribed and known by others, and thus, in practice, determined by them.

Simone de Beauvoir rightly mistrusts the facile recourse to stating that a situation one has imposed on others is a happy one. But her wariness here is not simply tactical; her rejection springs chiefly from the rigour of her ethics, reinforced by the neo-Kantianism aspect of existentialism. Posing the problem of choice in the field of pleasures and hardships would represent a fall and a compromise with the pathologically determined will. *The Second Sex* describes not so much the unpleasant aspects or unhappiness of oppression as a more radical shattering: the absolute boredom of being confined and the non-life of slavery. Simone de Beauvoir quotes confidences from Sophie Tolstoy ('my existence is death') or Mme Proudhon ('I have nothing'), illustrating a distress which goes beyond the simple level of displeasure or even of hardship. Symmetrically, she does not say that liberation means an increase in women's happiness; she knows that 'a woman who sets out to live' leaves a deadly void for a harsh world: *The Second Sex* is free of advertisers' language and does not sing of the charms of independence. It presents liberation as a strict requirement (perhaps as an imperative of the categorical type, for a freedom must want freedom), or as something which must be sought as a matter of course: the 'woman as vassal' 'buries her will and her desires' and her life is a death, the silent solution to every problem.[99] In this context liberation is a simple 'choice to live', without any foreseeable 'guarantee of happiness', as she puts it.

However there is one point, and far from the least important, on which the question of pleasures and hardship is superimposed over that of freedom and subjection. For Simone de Beauvoir it goes without saying that a girl who is married in the traditional way ('given in marriage') has a dreadful sex life with her husband; later, with a bit of luck, she will find 'perfect happiness in the arms of a lover'.[100] Marriage is synonymous with sexual and emotional frustration, whereas a free union opens up the possibility of erotic satisfaction. The critical aspect of this idea is supported by texts by Montaigne and a certain Dr Grémillon, who each say in their own way that a husband who does not want his wife to be unfaithful to him should not give her a taste for pleasure.[101] It is also supported by very depressing accounts of women being raped on their wedding night and afterwards. On the other hand, the positive aspect of the thesis appears more as a regulatory ideal, stated with conviction but perhaps unprovable. Part IV and the chapter called 'The Married Woman' stress the idea that love and sexuality can flourish only in freedom. In 1949 it took courage to say that pleasure is a good in itself and that it is to be found outside institutions, still more to go so far as to write that 'a woman who knows the harshness of the struggle against the world's resistances' has a real need 'to satisfy her physical needs'. The author's nerve is manifest, her meaning unambiguous (it is as though, with all her heart, she wishes all women many joys, having explained where they are not found), but the idea itself is not quite clear:

A humanist morality requires that all life experience should have a human meaning, that it should be infused with freedom; in a genuinely moral erotic relation desire and pleasure are freely uplifted, or there is at least a tragic struggle to regain freedom within sexuality; but this is possible only when the other is precisely recognized as a *unique individual*, in love or in desire.[102]

The texts pitches and tosses on the page, as though battered by ideas which are noticeably different from each other: when Simone de Beauvoir tries to establish the principle that makes the experience of pleasure possible, guided by a generous intention she answers freedom, but then immediately acknowledges an element of pathos and adds something quite different, the uniqueness of the other. Not, I think, because the principles she has chosen is not the right one, but because the very project of making a transcendental deduction of pleasure is, given the current state of thinking about women, always derived from apologetic intentions extraneous to the question.

Let me make it clear: if I were participating here in an opinion-forming debate, I should quickly establish my personal sympathy for Simone de Beauvoir's 'thesis' and should say no more. Here is an idea which is very plausible, perfectly progressive and which above all offers an attractive synthesis of two values – freedom and physical pleasure – the first being described as a condition which makes the second possible. One can vigorously state one's sympathy while retaining an attitude of critical reflexion. This image of the pleasure to be gained from free love should be considered as the emblem of Beauvoir's thought, an emblem in relation to which we, of course, need to place ourselves as for or against (which means reading the book as it was written or not), but which must also be analysed as such.

The twentieth century has not been lacking in discussions of the sexual satisfaction of women. As a general rule these discussions are extremely irritating inasmuch as they are biased, like advertising slogans: they are edifying texts in which women's pleasure appears as a monogram providing a pretext for something else, an allegory whose role is to plead in favour of the fundamental values of the author, whatever they may be. It might be a 'new look' apology for conformism – a women only feels pleasure if she feels secure and marriage alone can give her a sense of security, so... Or a neo-traditional plea for 'adult responsibility', along the lines of right-thinking family planning: sexual satisfaction is only possible in the context of a clear-minded use of contraception and a stable relationship based on real commitment. We find even worse in the work of Hélène Deutsch. Thus Ti-Grace Atkinson analysed the political and ideological aspects of the sermons on vaginal orgasm which are delivered to us all. She shows that what is going on here is a displacement of the apology for marriage, a kind of substitute institution.[103] We should remember that anything said about women's sexual pleasure – or about frigidity – is liable to be a kind of hieroglyph or ideogram. The usual praise of vaginal orgasm assures us that this marvel is reserved for women-mothers who have given up all personal activity, because such activity is symptomatic of an incomplete renunciation of phallic identification. If we really must take sides, we are no doubt better off with Wilhelm Reich and Simone de Beauvoir than with Françoise Dolto or Hélène Deutsch.[104] All the same, the image of 'perfect happiness in the arms of a lover' (and no longer those of a husband) is an ideogram like any other.

This ideogram transposes on to the emotional plane the existentialist prescription: one must know and want oneself free. That is all that matters and from it one can hope to get at least sexual pleasure. Though this is (again) an ideogram, we should at any rate appreciate the fact that this is the *only* point where Beauvoir tackles the question of women's possible happiness. As I said, she manages to write two solid volumes on the position of women without resorting to the economy of pleasures and hardships, except at this point. This abstention, which we have put down to the rigour imposed by the existentialist perspective, deserves more praise than her engraving of an emblem deserves criticism. It was a challenge to produce a book which in no way colludes with 'encyclopedias for a happy life', a genre whose idea is present in many practical guides or facile novels but not in those places alone, to the point where one might think our century was avidly seeking a 'key to happiness'. This austere aspect of *The Second Sex* may explain the categorical rejection many women have given and still give it: it is a frightening book, not because it calls on us to give up a happiness we have, but because it does not promise the happiness we lack. By contrast we can see where the seduction of, for example, the work of Luce Irigaray or Helene Cixous lies: when one chooses women's bliss (in a much broader sense than that of sexual pleasure alone) as a theme, whatever one says about it, one can be sure of gratitude.

Although it seems strictly 'existentialist' ('what can I hope for from freedom?'), we cannot say that it is to existentialism that Beauvoir truly owes this emblem of the woman who finds her sexual satisfaction in free unions. It reflects an important reworking of the imaginary plane of that philosophy itself, since it contrasts as clearly as possible with Sartre's figure of the frigid woman. No philosophical thought is without its imaginary plane and it is perhaps on this level that the most fundamental changes take place. Ideas circulate and are shared; their vocation is to be assumed by others. But when they are assumed, they may be given an entirely new slant – otherwise they would simply be repeated. Much as Beauvoir may owe to existentialism her general abstention on the question of happiness, it is to herself alone that she owes the image of a sexual pleasure made possible by freedom.

19   The explanatory impasse

More paradoxically, we can say that it is to existentialism that she owes the essential element of her book, which is the theoretical failure around which it is constructed.[105] She posits a demand – the subjugation of women must be accounted for – and she seeks an explanatory model. She states that this world, as a space for both projects and intersubjective relations, has always belonged to men, but she wants to go further than simply recording the fact. In the seventeenth century Gabrielle Suchon observed that men have reserved for themselves 'business deliberations and the executive power in businesses', functions which 'women could easily have carried out if they had not been deprived of and excluded from them'.[106] But she does not wonder what they did to gain control of these interesting things, nor how they managed to make women accept exclusion. Simone de Beauvoir is in a different position because she is faced with the following question: women are, at least potentially, subjects and therefore capable of opposition, and yet they do not contest the practical and moral subjugation that men have imposed on them. How have men managed to make women accept servitude and what are the origins of power relations between the sexes? From the way that she treats this problem, it does indeed seem that in her eyes the oppression of women is so unthinkable a scandal that she can assign to it neither an origin nor sufficient cause. In the first part of her book she examines three types of explanations in turn and in turn rejects them. First biology, which according to her is not enough to form the basis of a sexual hierarchy. Then psychoanalysis, which she regards as begging the question: 'the phallus acquires such value because it symbolizes a sovereignty which is realised in other domains'. Then historical materialism, which she taxes with manifest inadequacy. And as, one by one, these explanations are mentioned and then eliminated as inadequate, oppression becomes an ever more groundless oddity.

Some readers will perhaps recall Rousseau's procedure in *The Social Contract*. What is the origin of the social order which puts man in chains? Is it God? No. Is it Nature? No. Is it the principle that might is right? The very phrase is a nonsense. Rights conferred by war? That is a *petitio principii*. This way in which a text leaves us in the lurch, refusing us the explanatory model which was nevertheless originally stated to be required, is perhaps the surest sign of its philosophical nature. Doxa never lacks explanations. Acceptance of the void or a lack-of-knowing and stress on the strangeness of what is, as of what is said, remain one of the surest traditions of our craft. And Simone de Beauvoir has been trained in this craft, which means that she learned for herself (and taught others) to accept a lack of satisfaction. Thus *The Second Sex* leaves us without an explanation. Of course a 'key to the whole mystery' is provided in the second part; but it has neither more nor less validity than the interpretations she rejected at the beginning of the book. The key she offers is the idea that at the time of the horde, women were excluded from the expeditions of war-parties; 'it is not in giving life but in risking life that man is raised above the animal; that is why superiority has been accorded in humanity not to the sex that gives birth but to that which kills'.[107] But Beauvoir founds nothing on this basis; she does not use it as the starting point to deduce a genesis or to construct a theory. To retrace the history of women's position she takes much more from Engels than from this Hegelian 'key', a souvenir of that wretched master and slave dialectic which so captivated Kojève.

We are finally left with the image of an oppression without a fundamental cause. This void has a very strong and very dialectical effect. For then it seems that, given that oppression is based on nothing, countless mechanisms or institutional butresses had to be established to create and maintain it. None of the involuntary factors (nature, economics, unconscious) maintain phallic power: it must therefore have acquired a forest of crutches for each situation, a pile of symbolic guarantees and barriers from the education of little girls to repressive legislation on birth control, from dress codes to exclusion from politics. I would be prepared to wager that Simone de Beauvoir did not herself believe in the 'key' she offers us and that this made her pay minute attention to the polymorphous network of limitations imposed on women: daily life is all the more tightly policed because women's subjection has to be constantly reinvented.

This depiction of an ultimately groundless oppression is, on the one hand, a corollary of the existentialist maxim already quoted, 'constraint can have [. . .] no hold on a freedom': it was surely not a primordial power relation which allowed men to subjugate women to the point of making them renounce asserting themselves as subjects. Certainly this is a truism: the existentialist perspective cannot think in terms of causality, being founded on a negation of determinism.

But, to be strictly orthodox, one would have had to conclude that this oppression does not exist, except in the bad faith of some women, sisters in serious-mindedness of the revolutionaries. Simone de Beauvoir does not draw this conclusion and in this I see the proof of the primacy of her involvement in the real over a philosophical frame of reference. Any philosophy undergoes remarkable modification when applied to a field of conflict by someone involved in that field who has practical aims in relation to it. In *The Second Sex* we do not find Sartre's inability to grasp oppression other than in the form of a failure of speculations on the origin of that oppression. And what, ultimately, do these speculations (which are always likely to be mythical) matter to us when the very impossibility of accounting for women's infeodation here helps the better to expose the aberrant nature of their subjection all the more strongly?

For on the background of a Hegeliano-Sartrian formulation of the problems (each consciousness seeks the death of the other, which meets it with equal hostility), relations between masculine and feminine appear as an incomprehensible exception.[108] The philosophical frame of reference which Beauvoir regards as absolutely true is the one least well equipped to explain the phenomenon and, for that very reason, the best equipped to criticize it. Or rather it always requires something more, and the search is on for that something in a kind of never-ending list. The last part, 'Towards Liberation', is highly significant in this respect, since it shows the difficulties facing a woman who has decided to reject the traditional shackles. This part, the most 'spirited' in the book and certainly the most personal, is by no means an additive-free happy end to oppression: as Beauvoir has not really uncovered oppression's 'root', she cannot show it as definitively eradicated. We cannot help wondering who gave her the idea of a 'key' or an ultimate explanation and why, in utter contradiction to her own method, she took it up. More generally, we can say that any one explanation, and in particular any explanation which locates the cause of oppression in an inaccessible place (the time of the horde) is likely to show women's position as a fate decided outside this world and to hide the structures of daily life which recreate the traditional relation of subjection in new historical situations.

Must this inquiry into Sartre and Beauvoir lead us to a kind of indifferentism? In other words, should we think that it does not really matter whether you claim to draw your inspiration from one philosophical position or another, once your practical expectations are clearly defined, for the set of values and aims linked to those expectations will reshape your perspective as you go along? Such a hypothesis has interesting corollaries regarding the nature of philosophical thinking, whose dogmatic impact, weight and structuring force must be then regarded as limited. From this viewpoint, it is not only the choice of metaphysical frame of reference that counts and a philosophical undertaking can still be defined as work, particularly in its effort to bring values into contact with a set of theoretical problems. To make a comparison: some people quote the Bible in support of left-wing politics, whereas many others use it as inspiration for solid right-wing government (and there are others who think these texts are talking about something else altogether): therefore we must conclude that the dogma it contains is apparently not absolutely forceful, unequivocal or categorical; it may encounter values and expectations which are very different since they are antagonistic. When the text is immediately assimilated to a particular political point of view, there is of course no room for philosophical work. But when people start developing a 'liberation theology' which states its case, a work of synthesis takes place, which is an effort to combine a tradition with current concerns. And perhaps those current concerns are so important that the tradition does not really matter. Our reading of Beauvoir would plead in favour of such a hypothesis.

But it could also lead us to uphold a kind of argument in favour of the worst, for the inappropriateness of the philosophical point of view to the project of a theory explaining women's position seems to be the critical force which, page by page, takes this observable but unnoticed position out of the realm of the banal, making it at last observable. 'One is not born, but becomes, a woman', yes, but how? If a constraint can have no hold over a freedom, the first one I mention is not enough, I uncover a second, and then a third...and after a thousand pages, I have still not said everything. This argument in favour of the worst plays on the gulf that exists between what should be and what is empirically observable; it is the tragic perception of a gap or an insurmountable difficulty. Our study can thus become an apology for an undertaking doomed to end in an impasse that was predictable from the outset. In this case we must note a corollary: when thought leads to an impasse or is stretched between incompatible assumptions and requirements, the writer's courage alone can overcome this tension and take us beyond the impasse. Her power to remain-in-a-lack-of-understanding and to accept the gap is present throughout the text, even if she does not mention it, and her will to theorize alone holds the two ends of the chain or, to put it another way, the two incompatible poles of her work firmly together. This corollary has the following corollary: the thought thus produced

cannot become *doxa* for others and still less for a political movement:
how could a group take up a gap whose edges are only joined by the
determination of a thinker who has taken responsibility for the tension between them upon herself? A group needs a doxa, in other
words a body of opinions which are more or less connected and
properly constituted as a dogma, never mind how woolly. Or practical objectives, which create cohesion beyond divergencies in thinking.

20   A portrait of Simone as herself

I have seen this corolla constantly open up in the feminist movement,
even among Beauvoir's admirers. 'Beauvoir, but...', Beauvoir with
reservations. Two weeks after her funeral there was a meeting of
some of her most faithful followers and friends at the audiovisual
centre in Paris which bears her name. We behaved rather badly, as
happens in the second stage of mourning, when relatives assail each
other, overstep marks, tell truths and say terrible things; funeral
feasts in the countryside provide examples of such situations where
everyone frees themselves from the solemnity of protocol and, after
the hollow speech of ritual homage, finally rediscover their true
affection for the dead person, with all the caustic and mocking
nuances of everyday fondness. This is necessary to reclaim the memory of the one we have lost from the pompous celebration which
deprives us of that person almost as much as death itself.

So it was a meeting of admirers: Christine Delphy, Liliane Kandel,
Delphine Seyrig, Anne Zélinsky and me. We were all unconditional
in our feelings about the person of Simone de Beauvoir, who had
most generously helped the Movement without ever seeking to control it. But *The Second Sex* was a different matter: Anne Zélinsky said
she had learned nothing from the book while Christine Delphy
stressed that it lacked the idea that a collective solution could be
found for the common problem. It is true that nowhere in the book
did Simone de Beauvoir envisage a collective liberation movement;
for her the liberated woman is always entirely an individual. Delphine Seyrig and I defended Beauvoir's work and the irreplaceable
things it had given us. But in so doing we were speaking as readers
and not as activists, so that what we said was not in conflict with
Christine's or even Anne's reservations. Neither of us claimed to have
found in *The Second Sex* a vade mecum for the struggles we had been
involved in: the book is not a 'Little Red Book' for militant feminists.
It is simply a book, intended to be read (to say this may not be to

state the obvious) and not to provide an ideology which might cement a group at times when there is a lack of agreement on practical aims. Simone de Beauvoir once said that she did not want to be regarded as the mother or the grandmother of feminism: this is the exact correlate of the reservations of those closest to her, not to mention the others.[109] The discontinuity between *The Second Sex* and the Movement of the 1970s was recognized on both sides.

And yet we say that *The Second Sex* was the Movement before the Movement. And yet, today, I no longer feel such a clear difference between my memories of that Movement and the intentions of *The Second Sex*. If we consider simple things, there is a basic similarity of orientation between Simone de Beauvoir's choices and those which are ours still. 'When [a woman] takes a lover, a lover is what she really wants. This lucidity is one aspect of the freedom of the choice she makes [. . .] to marry is an obligation, to take a lover is a luxury.'[110] Does the 'portrait of a lady' contained in these lines not contrast sharply with that implicitly contained in the following, by Juliette Drouet: 'I want you to stain your clothes and tear them as much as possible and I want to be the only one to mend and clean them'?[111] Doubtless we have used different words to speak of luxury, lucidity and freedom; doubtless we have not even bothered to abhor the other way of being in love. But these nuances should not hide a more obvious split: there were in 1949 and in the 1970s, and no doubt still are today thousands of women who, if they allow a little eroticism to show through, experience it as a frenzy for housework and would see no meaning in luxury or a desire that frankly acknowledges itself. We fought so that all women should have access to the existing means for dissociating sexuality and reproduction if they wish to do so. We were of course guided in this battle by the desire to prevent tragedies, by the idea that 'it's nicer to be born when you're wanted', but fundamentally too by the hope that sexuality might become strictly a question of pleasure. How many of those who benefit from the results of this political struggle (and that does not yet mean all women), would accept the latter idea and how many would say simply that 'contraception is a good thing'. A good thing, yes, but for what?

Those who fought to bring down one of the conditions that made pleasure impossible were not all intellectuals; if we had been we would never have won our case. Besides, what is an intellectual and what qualification do you need to be one? We should be wrong to assume that the aspiration to a sexuality which is not buried in something other than itself is confined to a supposedly defined social

milieu. With others, this diffuse idea found a collective space where
it could be articulated and its arguments stated. For some years
women's groups talked about the 'quality of life' they were looking
for and the many obstacles they met with. 'Double day, half pay' was
echoed by 'Love? I'm so tired!' I hope that the then new awareness
reflected in these two slogans is still perceptible in them. There is a
link between the place of women in the economy (at the bottom of
the pay ladder), their place in the domestic economy (housework is
their lot and it wears them out) and their exclusion from that luxury
which should be accessible to all. Now that this Movement has
ceased to exist and people no longer talk about the 'quality of life',
should we go back – we women who read – to a tête-à-tête with
Simone de Beauvoir? Once again, reading *The Second Sex*, Mary
Wollstonecraft's *Vindication of the Rights of Women* or the work of
George Sand or Virginia Woolf can relieve us of many burdens and
particularly of that loneliness which affects all women when they try
to understand a little of what is happening to them. But, apart from
the sadness of seeing the debate become confined in thus moving
from the street to the page and from widely differing sections of
society to the group of those who read those kind of books, a question
remains: is not a book, however brave and intelligent, or a theory,
even one which accepts the greatest number of paradoxes, always
liable to proceed towards a closure, and thus to close something off?

I am obviously ill-placed to ask this question here and now.
However it is a necessary one. Earlier I left open a choice between
two hypotheses, indifferentism (the philosophical bases of an inquiry
are not important) and an apology for an argument in favour of the
worst (the more inappropriate the bases, the more wonderful the
results that can be drawn from them). We must in all rigour ask
ourselves whether, when one is thinking alone, philosophical premises might not set up limits, no matter how remarkable the results
produced by their inappropriateness to the object of study. 'Knowledge is a light which always projects shadows somewhere' says
Bachelard and no doubt this is particularly true of thought which is
developed and written down in solitude. Although an idea which
illuminates also sets up a screen – that wall of shadows which is
merely the limit of the light – the fact remains that when several
people discuss something there may be one who will shout 'be careful!' and point out the obstacle which is being constructed, at the risk
of course of rendering null and void both the beginnings of the theory
and its shadows. We have had too much experience of brutal returns
to square one to sing the unqualified praises of collective thought;

however, when there is no one, not even a mischievous demon, to hold back the hand that is about to write *quod erat demonstrandum*, we need to recognize that the text is offering at once both a new knowledge and its epistemological obstacles. Taking one more step in this direction, we can say that ideas cannot be separated from the 'sociology' of ideas, their diffusion and reception, because the collective or personal character of a given thought constitutes the very nature of the 'thesis' which is being advanced.

The 'epistemological obstacles' which restrict *The Second Sex* can be identified by trying better to remember the hiatus between its 'theses' and the Movement's ideas or abstentions. The first thing to notice is the liberal nature of the book's perspective and of the hope with which Simone de Beauvoir closes her critique of women's position. 'In no domain has woman ever had a chance', 'it is rare for woman to have a real chance': this problem, first articulated in the Introduction, reappears throughout the book and particularly in the last part. It is a recognizable theme belonging to liberalism in its classical form. For, according to liberalism, the division of roles should never be pre-set by a law, written or unwritten; any artificial regulation of individuals' destinies prevents the free play of competition, whereas if competition is left to do its work, everyone will probably end up in the social position appropriate to their abilities. And, the argument goes on, this is an excellent thing for society as well as being fair to individuals.

Taking this kind of thinking to its extreme, we come to Stendhal's phrase: 'all geniuses who are born women are lost to humanity'. In the first place the liberal position assumes that abilities are randomly distributed (to girls and boys, children born into both the working class and the bourgeoisie, those of all origins and mixtures of origins); then it is regretted that in some these abilities should be stifled due to a lack of means for their development. And then, for the reasoning to be truly convincing, it should be demonstrated that this constitutes a loss for the collectivity. In principle this reasoning is valid for all social positions and can be illustrated by examples taken from anywhere in the social hierarchy, but this seldom happens. Liberalism shows a clear preference for 'top of the range' examples when considering these matters. Until recently jobs in the French postal service were clearly divided along sex lines: the postman was a man, while women worked behind the counter. The liberal approach could have stressed (but did not) that this pre-set distribution of roles was absurd. Now that things are different, liberalism does not hail the change as a victory, just as it did not take up the former arrangement as a 'problem'.[112] How is it that this liberal perspective sees only the top of the social pyramid or even that obscure zone in which the nebulous problem of 'genius' is posed?[113]

If there was one forbidden issue in the women's movements of the 1970s, it was that of 'woman's' social promotion. We had a vague idea that the women of the preceding generation had been concerned with this, guided by a desire to see each woman rise as high as she could and 'take her chances'. We were interested in other things, many other things, according to the situation in each country. French women had to fight long and hard over abortion and contraception: their struggle was shaped by the awareness that while some privileged women certainly had the means to find unofficial solutions, the majority did not; the establishment of equality among women regarding those things common to all was our ideal. I should like one day to see this ideal reappear in relation to the problem of crèches, which are a crucial factor in workplace equality between women who do not have children and those who do.[114] British women were orientated more towards the issue of equal opportunities at work. This concern differs from the classic liberal outlook in two ways: it does not relate only to those professions that have a high degree of social status and it argues in terms not of individuals but of proportions: when a given business is asked if it has a policy of equal opportunities in employment, the question relates strictly to personnel statistics. It is still too soon to cry victory, but a number of institutions now regard inclusion of the principle of equal opportunities in their management strategy as a matter of honour; although of course they may forget to implement it.[115]

These points show us the gap between the intellectual frameworks of *The Second Sex* and some of the guiding principles (which may have remained unformulated) of the women's movements. These movements saw 'women' as a collectivity and took as their reference point not those who seemed armed to face social life with a few 'chances' of doing all right out of it, but the least advantaged; not 'Woman' as an individual, but proportions of women to men. Women's groups also took account of many other things which it would be hard to fit into an already familiar intellectual category.

It was relatively unavoidable that *The Second Sex*, orientated as it is towards the notion of the 'subject', should not always succeed in going beyond the bounds of liberal individualism. Let us stress that this is not a criticism which should be addressed to Simone de Beauvoir: when one simply thinks, and thinks alone, one sorely lacks the arguments that people with different social experiences can bring and, above all, those supplied by practice in a group. This observation applies to everyone, *de me quoque fabula narratur*, to me also.

My agreement with Simone de Beauvoir encounters another stumbling block. At the end of the book, she writes: 'All in all, we have won the case.' Who is this 'we'? And even if it were true, how did this historical transformation take place? Here too my concern is not to criticize her optimism, for example by calling it a demobilizing illusion, but more to identify it as symptomatic of a lacuna in the analysis. The book cannot say what has been won, nor how. The 'we' soon becomes 'many of us', an expression which was to be used frequently in feminist language, but in a contrary way: to speak of the difficulties faced by most women, but not all, or sometimes in order to avoid appearing as though one were claiming to speak for everyone absolutely. And of course 'many of us' do have the impression that we have 'personally escaped' (another typical expression) some aspects of alienation. This is no doubt what Simone de Beauvoir means: when she was finishing her book she must have thought that, when all was said and done, she was less oppressed than her mother had been. A mother whose face sometimes wore the bruises left by M. de Beauvoir's blows.

This feeling of having been less unhappy than one's mother is important: in this case it is a deserved reward for the young Simone who had faced many conflicts and anxieties in order to escape a social context where a man's first right over a woman was to humiliate her. I am getting ready to speak ill of Sartre and to criticize his attitude to 'the beaver', but the wrongs here are not of the same order. Mme. de Beauvoir was at her husband's mercy every day, with no possibility of leaving him, despite his mockery and her bruises. If Sartre had been no better than this (however much we may lament his behaviour), Simone de Beauvoir would have left him. Furthermore, her life was not restricted to her relationship with Sartre, even though it was structured by it. She had a lot 'outside' that relationship: a job, travels alone, an intellectual life which was not confined simply to taking up Sartre's doctrine and, at the time she was writing *The Second Sex*, an affair with Nelson Algren. Above all, she had won one battle, that of discovering that 'home' has an outside: the life of society, the upheavals reported by the newspapers, the penal colony for children in Belle-Île and the duty of everyone, even those who are women, to feel responsible for the world. For a woman like her mother, morality consisted of taking care of the home, obeying her husband and allowing herself no other interests. Indisputably, Simone had won something.

And subjectively speaking, belief in the positive effects of time is a great support. To imagine that history is moving towards better things is, at the least, a defence against despair; it can often be a tonic that combines with action. And yet we must question this belief and ask ourselves how useful are partial or exclusive liberations, those that only affect some aspects of a situation or some individuals in a group. The fundamental right to dispose of one's pay as one chooses, which was not acquired by French women until this century, did not ipso facto put an end to the submissive attitude of women workers towards their parents or husbands, even though it gave them the means. It is true that parents still bring up little girls in a way that does not acknowledge the fact that once they are grown up they will have the means to emancipate themselves. Since education does not anticipate this situation, which is new and does not affect all women, it sadly often succeeds in taking from them the psychological means of getting as much as possible from their material independence. Moreover, when we consider the way that many people still bring up their sons, we can only conclude that it has never occurred to them that twenty years hence these sons will have to form loving relationships with women who can tell the difference between their own existence and that of a doormat, women with the material and psychic means to show the door to these despots, who have remained children because the absolute availability of their mother has deprived them of the reality-testing which makes us adult.

Even today there are no guarantees that every women will have the material means of independence, nor that many will have the psychological means, and the two are linked. We have to start by realizing that the fact that a large percentage of women are 'housewives' is not without its effects on those who are not. The collectivity of women is not as scattered as it might seem; there is a whole which must be considered if we want to understand how (and why) the common lot falls to each and every one via a causal structure linked to the social whole. I do not claim to be able to understand this 'social globalization' and in using this term I seek only to point in a direction which is not illuminated by posing the problems in terms of the 'subject'. When women's position is seen in these terms, the final result seems to be at once both optimism and pessimism, neither of which are justified.

For it is excessive to say that woman has never had a chance in any field and moreover the use of the singular 'woman' should be rejected, here as always. It hides the fact that women have been able to act and create, either because of a miraculously preserved talent (but where does this miracle spring from?), or because of a social status guaranteed in other ways, or again through a strength of character produced we know not how. When they wanted to marry her off to an old man, the adolescent Louise Michel simply quoted a famous sentence from one of Molière's characters: 'The little cat is dead', and we know that revolutionary action later offered her a field in which to fulfil herself as she wanted. Virginia Woolf, Queen Victoria or Florence Nightingale do not fit the image of 'woman' who had nothing and no chances, any more, indeed, than they fit the stereotype of a full and simple blossoming of the possibility of acting on the world, or thinking for oneself. Since images of people which lack any ambiguities or limitations are simple products of kitsch (or of the megalomaniacal voluntarism of *Being and Nothingness*), we can well do without them. By looking around a little, Simone de Beauvoir would have found examples of women who had at least some chances.

And yet, in contrast to her optimism (some have won their fight) we should say that the common lot falls to all women, in a more or less obvious way. Queen Victoria was publicly criticized by the archbishop and by public opinion when she wanted to use a little chloroform to ease her pain in childbirth. A woman *must* suffer in giving birth to her children, the Bible says so. In her childhood Virginia Woolf was more or less sexually assaulted: there is nothing to protect little girls from the incestuous desires of men in their families. Later she was not allowed to go to university to pursue her studies as she wished. These are a few visible signs of a wider phenomenon: even though women may try as hard as they can to individualize themselves and even though the men that they meet may not be 'all the same', it is still true that in the life of society any woman encounters the standard feminine position and is liable at any moment to be treated not as the individual she wants to be but as 'woman', in other words according to the average idea of what a woman is and should be. I am always meeting people who assume I am docile as if it goes without saying. They do not see me, they perceive me in terms of a model (a woman is someone to whom one can behave in an imperious manner without difficulty) and this preconceived idea is all the stronger because the number of women who contradict it is small. The model will hold good so long as the majority of women do not rebel against it. In things like that, we are dependent on each other.

We are also reminded of the common lot through social representations. The Florence Nightingale 'case' is remarkable in this regard: her portrait has been greatly retouched by hagiography and history has brought her back into line, turning her into a blandly moving 'dear angel' or a 'lady with the lamp', busily watching over the injured. This image does not tell us, nor help us to understand, that during the Crimean War she quite simply organized all the military hospitals of the campaign. First she had to besiege Ministers to make them come to terms with the idea of a corps of women nurses (in the Army for goodness sake!). Without Lytton Strachey (but who reads Lytton Strachey?), we should know nothing of the powerful and apparently rather difficult woman she was. This woman is not the one who has gone down in history, as they say: official imagery has substituted a pale figure like a cheap religious icon, who fits better with the image we are still supposed to have of 'woman', whatever real women do and however they contradict that idea. Thus we basically never inherit anything from unusual women who were not bland. Simply recognizing that we need to inherit from them (as they really were) is moreover another way of saying that all women are affected by all others and by the different approaches shown us by some others.

All in all, by saying in a contradictory way that 'we have won the fight' and that 'no woman has ever had a chance', Simone de Beauvoir seems to have missed the point that every woman's life is lived in contradiction.[116] The fact that a woman is oppressed on the one hand and on the other has a chance, her chance, explains the hesitant or split character we find in many women. We can only argue with reference to women who have gained a little fame and whose biography is therefore well-known. Virginia Woolf's fits of madness may perhaps reflect the enormous tension she had to accept in order to carry out her work – come hell or high water. *A Room of One's Own* and *Three Guineas* make this pretty clear: she was aware that there was no support for a woman's intention to be a writer and yet she thought that the most traditional thing in a woman's life, which was to be constantly and actively preoccupied with marriages, destined women to be 'naturally' at home with at least one literary genre, the novel.

These remarks on a limited subject – women and the novel – can give us ideas for dealing with the general problem of women:[117] the situation of each woman could be characterized by the fact that she has to live with a highly developed contradiction, which is writ large in the overall situation and appears concretely in small print in every woman's daily life. Every adult Frenchwoman may vote, be elected and have her own cheque book (I remember a time when this was not true for married women). She can take someone to court or buy anything she can afford without asking anyone's permission and rent a flat herself (my friend Marguerite Cordier remembers a time when, as a single woman taking up a teaching post in another part of the country, she had to ask her father to travel with her and rent her a room, single women tenants being regarded as unseemly). In principle, but only in principle, any adult Frenchwoman can avoid an unwanted pregnancy. But many Frenchwomen are still entirely or partially dependent on their husbands for their subsistence, so that many have not reached even the lowest level of independence. In families where there are both boys and girls, parents are often less willing to make sacrifices to pay for the girls' education than for that of the boys or else the girls are made to feel what a sacrifice is being made for them, which is not much better. Teachers and families alike more or less automatically steer girls towards shorter and uninteresting careers. The inadequate number of crèches means that women must choose between motherhood and a job. And in any case, a woman continuing Marie Curie's work may be raped when she goes home late at night from her laboratory.

Since we are on the subject of the cruder aspects of collective life, let us ask ourselves how public monies are distributed. If we accept that military parades involving low-flying jet fighters constitute a show giving pleasure to an audience consisting mainly of men, if we also agree that a televised football or rugby match is of interest to an audience made up of 90 or 95 per cent men and if we then ask ourselves what is the cost of these shows, whose only real point is to reassure a narcissism which we can call either macho or violent, we can say that the media and national budgets will stretch to any sacrifice for something that is entirely psychological, since its purpose is to flatter a self-image that some men want to have by proxy. Nothing is refused them. If we now compare this with the funds accorded by the collectivity to the building of crèches, an issue fundamentally concerning women (although some 'new fathers' support them too, and praise be to them), we have to conclude that the reality of women's lives counts less than the imaginary needs of a certain type of man.

So at the global level we can see enormous contradictions. This said, why should I be surprised that for me (and, I assume, for all women) social life blows hot and cold with a mixture of socio-intellectual recognition and reminders of the old order or standard? Here is an extreme example: one day the Royal Institute of Philosophy in London invited me to give a paper. You see, women are no longer necessarily excluded from even the most 'chic' places where ideas circulate, so what have you still got to complain about? However, after my paper the first contribution from the floor somewhat reduced my optimism: a gentleman stated that it was appalling that women should engage in philosophy when it is their vocation and responsibility for the future of the species to give birth to children. Of course I did my best to make mincemeat out of him (in such circumstances you have to let rip), though asking myself where and when I had cultivated this art of impertinence.[118] In a public debate – and is not any debate public, even between two people over breakfast? – the only diplomacy is to make your opponents feel how isolated and ridiculous they are, which you do by winning to your side those who are there for a laugh, the people with sense and those who appreciate courage. That makes more people than you might think, and one should never despair of humanity. All the same, this anecdote well illustrates my contradiction: if I were purely and simply oppressed, I should never have had the opportunity to develop such an aptitude for defensive insolence; if I were not oppressed at all, I should never have needed it.

It may well not be possible to understand this contradiction at a purely individual level. It is easier to grasp it at first at the level of institutions and society.[119] To return to *The Second Sex*, we should perhaps link its failure truly to pose the problem of contradiction to the fact that it noticeably sidesteps the issue of institutions in favour of an analysis of relations between individuals. Thus concerning abortion Simone de Beauvoir gives a remarkable description of women's painful discovery of the 'social lie': they have always been deluded with the idea that motherhood is to be their greatest accomplishment only to find that their lover or husband does not want the responsibility of a child and asks them to have an abortion. She finely details the psychic and relational aspects of this problem and the hatred or contempt for 'males' that women acquire in such a situation, but lays no stress on the state policy to increase the birth rate. She presents what we call the 1920 Act as basically an element of custom law, undated and undatable, springing from 'the hypocrisy of the moral code of males', which contradicts itself with 'careless cynicism'. The rebellion whose flag she waves, while not calling for a collective response, is aimed against 'men' or 'the man' and not the state. She sees individuals rather than socio-legislative structures. If we regard *The Second Sex* in this light, we cannot really uphold either of the two readings proposed above – neither indifferentism regarding the choice of theoretical frame of reference, nor the argument in favour of the worst. The particular philosophical framework of the inquiry leads to omissions: here the discussion lacks at the least an analysis of institutions and also a concept of exploitation.[120]

Thus the theoretical perspective which enabled Beauvoir to work, and which she reciprocally reworked, held her thinking within the limits of a relatively classic model: because it focused on the individual, existentialism could not quite manage to pose the problems, even at the level of the individual. And, significantly, Beauvoir moralizes that which she has not managed to analyse. *The Second Sex* seems to be saying that once a crack has opened in the wall, it is the duty of the woman who benefits from it to use it to the maximum to establish herself at last as a subject condemned to be free. Every time Beauvoir mentions a woman who had some means to assert, create or emancipate herself and did not exploit that chance to the full, moral reproof is not long in coming. Themes such as complacency, self-satisfaction, narcissism and above all the solution of taking the easy way out appear. The analogy between oppression and moral fault finally proves to be a boomerang. It reinforces a misunderstanding reminiscent of the very widespread moral condemnation of failure at school. If Beauvoir had come out and said that she was angry with women who did not push their opportunities for freedom as far as possible, if she had argued that the more women there are who seek to be free, the easier it is for each woman and thus for her, Beauvoir, to find her own road to freedom, her critique would have been more acceptable. But in order to think through this type of problem – the social whole and the interdependence of people engaged in a process of liberation – one needs a different problematic from that of the subject, and a different perspective from that of morality.

So how else should the problems be posed? I have no idea. Let us simply note that in the 1970s Beauvoir's language and concerns were different from those of 1949. She paid a great deal of attention to the ideas which sprang from the social movement in France which was soon called the 'MLF' (Women's Liberation Movement) and she synthesized them in such a way that, in a preface she wrote to a collective work on abortion, she could make the connection between the ideology of motherhood and the 'invisible' and unpaid work of 'the private production of domestic work': 'It is hard to present doing the washing up and washing dirty clothes as sacred functions to the little girl. But if a woman is confined to the home by her children, she becomes at the same time the housewife whose labour power is extorted from her for practically nothing.'[121] And in this text the power of the law forbidding the control of conception is at last challenged and described as 'criminal'. 'Bring the law to book': this phrase from the same preface no longer has anything to do with the existentialist perspective.

This is a different 'genre' from that of *The Second Sex*, one whose format is characterized by brevity: articles, interviews, prefaces or accounts given during a sensational trial. It should be stressed that between 1949 and 1971 Simone de Beauvoir constantly wrote on the position of women. She did not put down her pen and then wait until our dear Movement began. However in content the new genre was the same in the 1960s and 1970s: she listened, first to writers like Lagroua Weill-Hallé or Andrée Michel, then to the collective thoughts of groups from the Movement, sometimes to women factory workers.[122] She caught hold of emerging ideas, hearing both their social critiques and messages of hope. With Andrée Michel, she stressed that the structures of French society had not changed since the First World War.[123] With the women workers of Hispano-Suiza, she spoke of the feeling of dignity that women get from working. And of the women activists during the war of Algerian independence, who combined leafleting with work and motherhood, she said – and it was also to be true of others – 'the nervous breakdowns caused by this kind of overwork, however spectacular, are curable',[124] while the gradual fading caused by domestic slavery and the disgust and resentment linked to it are not.

So Simone de Beauvoir talked with other women throughout the 1960s and 1970s and the content of what she said changed. Above all I think what changed was her use of the word 'world'. At the beginning of this study, we cited a passage from *The Second Sex*: woman 'finds herself living in a world where men compel her to assume the status of the Other [. . .] her transcendence is to be perpetually transcended by another consciousness which is essential and sovereign.' In 1978 she says to Pierre Viansson-Ponté that she has begun working with 'young feminists' with whom she is 'entirely in sympathy' because they want 'to change the world that has been made by men'.[125] There is a tenuous but fundamental shift between these two formulations. In the first case, 'the world' is simply the name of the place where consciousnesses meet, or where some transcend others, and where subjects ('men') are subjects of a will that they impose on others. In the second case 'the world' is a reality: it has been 'made' and can be 'changed'. No longer simply the place of agonistic intersubjectivity, it is a thing, or more precisely a production, and 'men' are no longer regarded as the subjects of simple wills, but as artisans – of laws and institutions for example – whose artifact is this world which now needs changing. An agent or an artisan cannot entirely be assimilated to a 'subject'. Looking beyond Simone de Beauvoir's last texts, we can of course ask ourselves whether the artisan is really 'men' taken as a whole or whether the genesis of institutions might not be more complex; nevertheless, during those years Beauvoir's thought crossed the frontiers of existentialism and took a new direction. It was no longer an analysis of intersubjectivity, but institutional analysis.

However we must return once more to the metaphysics of *The Second Sex*. 'Woman [...] finds herself living in a world where men compel her to assume the status of the Other...' The effect of these words is to synthesize the results of the minute examination undertaken in the book and to make the facts in some way eloquent. Philosophy 'gathers up' the conclusions of specific remarks on, for example, education, fashion or sexuality and tries to express what it is that is fundamentally wrong with the situation in which women live, to address this problem to someone's consciousness, that of the man or woman reader. This type of language increasingly disappears from Beauvoir's later writings; her thinking becomes more closely tied to the factual. We see her bringing to the fight the weight of her reputation and the intellectual strength of which she is capable, but we no longer hear a particular voice of hers, which expressed her desire to escape the sphere assigned to her and to participate in 'human *Mitsein*, or co-being'.[126] At the beginning of this study, we contrasted her philosophical framework with the actual remarks she makes. We must now say that if *The Second Sex* were rewritten in the form of a catalogue it would lose its efficacy as a book, an efficacy which was and still is great. However, if we consider that in this book philosophy makes the facts speak in order to address them to someone, then philosophy may have a function not so different from that of poetry.

'But what exactly were you looking for in *The Second Sex*? A theory, or the voice and support of a big sister?'

'What are we looking for in any philosophical text if not the theoretical support of a forerunner? Although, of course, we may not find it.'

Third Notebook

which is reflective and biographical

which is concerned with the characters in the philosophical drama; where we see the philosopher being substituted for philosophy and where it is insinuated that this is not necessarily a good thing for the mind; which attempts to define the conditions necessary for an unbegun and unfinished work, but in which it is admitted that there is always something of the philosopher in philosophy and that thus the latter remains an indiscipline.

1   The Medici fountain

'I have never forgotten the distress signals which I, as an adolescent, sent out to the woman who was to absorb me, body and soul. Nothing would be left of me, not so much as a pinch of ashes...' writes Simone de Beauvoir about her *Memoirs of a Dutiful Daughter*.[1] She goes on: 'I lent my consciousness to that child, to that girl, who had been left forlorn in the depths of the unrecalled past.'

Memoirs of a Dutiful Daughter, which is the most highly wrought of Simone's books, reveals to us a childhood of pain now soothed; it is a distanced account of much suffering, perhaps governed by the hope that such things will never happen to anyone again. But the book also records a memory of an 'extraordinary richness', which the author describes without once becoming pretentious: a fantastic appetite for books, debates and encounters with other people, an impatient impetuosity. Beauvoir was a brilliant student, but this is not what she tells us about: 'I want life, the whole of life. I feel curious; I am keen to burn myself up in no matter what flame'.[2] Therefore, Kant, Hume and Leibniz, despite odd moments of disgust, Léon Brunschvicg's lectures (even if the excellent man 'kept repeating himself'), the Bibliothèque Nationale, the cafés, evenings where everyone sang at the tops of their voices, and all this sprang from the same *joie de vivre*. And Simone de Beauvoir slides over the result (she was awarded the *agrégation** in philosophy at the age of twenty-one, but she hardly mentions it), to describe only this euphoria mixed with anxiety which drove her on.

Then came a certainty: Sartre 'would one day write a philosophical work of the first importance'.[3] Oh. And then this:

> Day after day, and all day long I measured myself against Sartre, and in our discussions I was simply not in his class. One morning in the Luxembourg Gardens, near the Medici fountain, I outlined for him the pluralist morality which I had fashioned to justify the people I liked but did not wish to resemble: he ripped it to shreds. I was attached to it, because it allowed me to take my heart as the arbiter of good and evil; I struggled with him for three hours. In the end I had to admit I was beaten; besides, I had realized, in the course of our discussion, that many of my opinions were based only on prejudice, bad faith [oh] or thoughtlessness, that my reasoning was shaky and my ideas confused. 'I'm no longer sure what I think, or even if I think at all,' I noted, completely thrown. My pride was not involved. I was by nature curious rather than imperious and preferred learning to shining.[5]

There follows a very sad page which shows her 'suddenly uncertain of [her] true abilities' and fascinated by the gang formed by Sartre, Nizan, Aron and Politzer who 'impressed' her for all sorts of reasons, some better than others. It is an astounding tale, which shows that even if one knows an enormous amount of philosophy, one never knows enough to remember, at the right moment, that 'shining' or 'impressing other people' is not the point of it. 'Not being sure' and 'learning' come closer to what is called 'thinking' in the ethics of the discipline. And ever since Democritus, in principle, people have taken pride in not seeking glory.[5] So this text tells us about a defeat in terms which (for us) put Sartre in the wrong – so he wanted to show off? – and would put Simone in the right, if only she could see what she was saying. All her life she kept repeating that she 'left the philosophy to Sartre', as though there were room for only one person. Here is a first group of misunderstandings which concern the discipline they had in common.

* The highest-level competitive exam for teacher recruitment in France (trans.).

The second group is biographical. For Simone de Beauvoir the 'finished woman', as she puts it, plunges the girl into nothingness: there is nothing left of her, not even a pinch of ashes. This means that for her, the meeting with a lover brings with it a tragedy worthy of Sophocles: one must supress oneself. Thus, describing meeting Sartre again after the summer holidays of 1929, in other words shortly after the beginning of their affair, she writes: 'I had liquidated my past; I threw myself unreservedly into our story'. And in the original French edition there is a footnote, which stresses the point again: 'I described this liquidation in *Memoirs of a Dutiful Daughter*'.[6] Suppressing oneself in order to commit oneself to 'our' story 'unreservedly' (she could not have put it more precisely). So was *that* how, at the beginning of the century, a young woman formed a relationship with a young man? It seems that the couple did not consist of a relationship between two formed and changing beings, but between a formed, self-assured man and a sort of tabula rasa.

The third misunderstanding intersects with the first two and involves me, long afterwards. Again in *Memoirs of a Dutiful Daughter* Simone notes: ' "From now on, I'm going to take you in hand," Sartre told me when he had given me the news that I had passed the first part of the *agrégation*'.[7] In 'Women in/and philosophy' I discussed these words that are at once both banal and terrifying. For being 'taken in hand' by someone else takes one out of philosophy, to the extent that the latter is the confrontation of a will to think with a lack of both knowing and a master. Simone de Beauvoir, whom I did not know personally at the time, gave me to understand, through various intermediaries, that she did not agree with this interpretation, which she regarded as excessive: Sartre's words meant, 'I'm going to help you prepare for the oral of the *agrégation*', or, 'I'm going to teach you to play Japanese billiards' etc. I still thought what I thought, and I referred to Sartre's words again at a conference which she knew about. She wrote to me saying that what I said was interesting, but that she did not agree with all of it, without, however, telling me exactly where she disagreed with me. No doubt she had disliked my criticisms of Sartre, but I did not know for sure. Then one day she rang me up and suggested we meet. After all, there were not many Beauvoirologists. So we met, and talked of other things. Not about our particular dispute, nor about Beauvoir's work. This is understandable for many reasons. She never explicitly challenged her theoretico-loving admiration for Sartre; it would have been an act of violence on my part to ask an elderly woman about the thing that had structured her life, for better or worse. She did not open the subject and it was not for me to do so. As for her thought in general, how could we have discussed that? My place was that of a commentator, or a historian of philosophy. I was not about to ask her to produce a commentary on her own work with me. The more since, like Sartre, Simone de Beauvoir never revised any of her books: they have always been reprinted without alteration. And she, as an author, had no wish to enter into a debate on a work which she saw as far back in time. 'Since then,' she said, 'other women, particularly Americans...' the sentence remained unfinished, suggesting a distance in relation to her post-war work. That was all she said to me about *The Second Sex*. She had lost interest in her own work, although she was probably pleased to see that someone had taken on the task of its exegesis. But this exegesis in itself reinforced the distance in time. People produce commentaries on past philosophers.

So this non-meeting left me with all my questions. In *The Prime of Life* she records some of Sartre's words: 'I shall follow no one'.[8] The context is a political one, but the words are also valid as a condensed version of a philosophical position opposed to the attitude of those who let themselves be 'taken in hand'. 'I shall follow no one, I shall examine as closely as possible all available traditions and ideas' could be the words of someone who has decided to think philosophically. Sartre's meaning is noticeably different: 'I shall follow no one, and if anyone wants to follow me, that's up to them.' Sartre trapped Simone de Beauvoir by insisting that she follow him. And if, later on, she managed to produce a philosophical work, she did so indirectly, without explicitly occupying the position of a philosopher. Discreetly. No matter that the Introduction to *The Second Sex* is a real conceptual analysis and a far more considered analysis than three-quarters of that which calls itself philosophy in the twentieth century, the fact remains that Beauvoir did not seek to have it recognized as such. Of course this does not really matter, since the fundamental thing is to be a philosopher whereas to appear to be one is a derisory aim. However, 'little sisters', of which I am one in relation to Beauvoir, would be pleased to see women publicly appearing to be philosophers. Blessed be Geneviève Rodis-Lewis, as much as Hipparchia and for the same reasons.

This third notebook will be devoted to these questions I am left with and which I was unable to discuss with Simone de Beauvoir. They have more to do with the everyday aspect of intellectual work than those discussed in the previous notebook. They are concerned with the subjectivity shaped by philosophy, which is partly social, and there are basically three of them: first, how does the issue of *appearing* to be a philosopher discriminate between women and men and in what unexpected and remote places does it lurk? Second, what is the relationship between a commentator and a writer; what definition of philosophy should one propose to locate Beauvoir's work as philosophical, even though she claimed nothing of the sort? And third, to return once more to the Sartre/Simone 'case', how did the emotional aspects and the modes of their relationship as lovers become fixed around an event, a branching off which can only astonish us? They were two students, a man and a woman, who were more or less equals in the university system, and yet, in being together, the first became the century's most visible philosopher and the second a tremendously well-hidden philosopher.

In the previous notebook we suggested separating two aspects of philosophical work: the first is the reworking of thought and can be shared by all, thus in particular by both sexes, and the second is the assumption of hegemonic privilege, which is present and indeed weighs heavily in some of Sartre's writing, expressing itself as a masculinist assertion in the little scenes, in other words at the imaginary level of the system. And we used the term 'masculinism' so that men who refuse to see themselves in this type of configuration do not have to do so.

The observation of everyday life in philosophical institutions also invites us to make this separation. It is the second aspect that makes women leave the field in great numbers just before their studies take them to the highest possible point. Women, and no doubt a certain number of men for whom an assertion of privilege in thought seems either laughable or in bad taste. The fault of theoretical masculinism is not to be found in all men, even those who are philosophers. Nevertheless it is part of the idea that the philosophical community has of itself. As a result it is always somewhere around in the daily relations we have with each other. While some men can happily hold it at a distance, with no other form of trial, women have to determine themselves in relation to this phenomenon, on pain of being determined by it. In this regard, the scene at the Medici fountain has much to teach us: Simone de Beauvoir must have been well aware – if she had thought about it – that philosophy was not all about being 'proud', 'shining' and 'impressing people', that these were just aspects of it and contingent or indeed foreign ones at that. She seems to have fallen victim to metonymy and, in her fascination, to have taken these parts for the whole.

2   *There is more than just the Luxembourg Gardens*

In ten years of teaching at an Ecole Normale Supérieure,* which at
that time admitted only women, at least in principle (but where
anyone who wanted could come to the classes), I saw many indisputably good students and I saw most of them give up their research.
While those young women had all the necessary qualities to undertake their own philosophical work, they would decide that teaching in
schools was 'good enough' for them, or would move into a discipline
whose position was less dominant in the hierarchy of knowledges or
one that was more recent, which usually meant that they wrote a
thesis in psychoanalysis. Sometimes it was simply a question of
fluctuations of mind: a decision was taken to begin research, then it
was abandoned, then taken up again with some changes, etc. in a
long dance of hesitation which I experienced myself until the point
when orders and constraints gained the upper hand over uncertainties of spirit.

These uncertainties are partly related to the state of the discipline
itself today, which does not encourage people to shout, 'Nothing is
vanity, let us get to work and move forward!' But for a woman there
is also something else. It is as if it were forbidden to say to oneself,
out loud, that philosophy should continue and that one feels called to
take up one's responsibilities in this continuous creation.

'Of course it is a matter of interdict!' I am assured by a young
woman who is highly qualified in our discipline, 'and don't say "as if
it were", say "it is".' In the first analysis, she is only superficially
right. While there really is a problem of things being forbidden, this
is no doubt the subjective version of something else, which is harder
to overcome. In the discipline as it displays itself there is an element
that must be internalised if one is to posit oneself as an author-to-be
of philosophical work and is to place oneself in advance in the camp
of those who are not going to repeat other people's philosophy, but
produce their own. This camp is, moreover, quite the opposite of a
camp since, in adopting this attitude, one also shows oneself to be
ready to fight and more than happy to cross swords with anyone else.
This element is a sort of self-assertion as a super-consciousness, a
light set above some or all others, and it is an assertion which women
and many men cannot and will not make. I am thus tempted to reply
to my woman colleague that bans are there to be transgressed or
subverted, whereas a structure such as the one I am trying to

---

* A university-level college for training teachers (trans.).

uncover firstly cannot be overcome unless one escapes its logic and secondly has nothing nice or desirable about it. The task is then to find out whether it is possible to get rid of it, not so much to be able collectively to invent a new form of philosophy as to test the creative power of abstention from the point of view of both theory (what is reintroduced when one drops the project of enclosing systematization?) and relations between philosophers: in the traditional practice of philosophy, everyone is at war with everyone else; is it possible that abstention could offer the necessary conditions for a community in which men and women could communicate? Oh Utopia, you won't let go...

In any case, there are some advantages in the idea that the ready-made philosophy we encounter contains an element which means that it only suits a certain type of man, and that this problem is intrinsic to it. Thinking that the intellectual modes at our disposal are inappropriate or insufficient leads us to conclude that we must be inventive. And what could be more pleasing, since this is the most classic way of stepping into philosophical creation? If Descartes had found all that he needed in the methods of thinking he had been taught by the 'good fathers', we can easily imagine what we should not have had. However, it is wise to beware of ideas that are too advantageous, and pleasing truths should be proved several times. The hypothesis (which I still support) that what turns women away from philosophical production is intrinsic and indeed structural comes into this category. On the other hand, if we simply assume that they are forbidden, we regard the obstacle as coming from outside: there is philosophy and then, literally outside it, there is someone (but who?) who has the task of saying to every woman: 'Thou shalt not come near'. Thus, chatting with my young colleague and raising objections to what she says, to her idea that women are forbidden, pleading the case that the situation is even worse, I realize that my way of seeing things is recognizable: it is the one that has always provided a prelude to individual decisions to take on the reorientation of philosophy, a fairly constant phenomenon since at least Pythagoras' day.

Intrinsic and extrinsic. Deep in my examination of the relations between Simone de Beauvoir and Sartre, suddenly I no longer know what the difference between an inside and an elsewhere might be. Sartre 'would one day write a philosophical work of the first importance'. 'A philosophical work', fine; 'of the first importance', what is this? But we move from one to the other using ordinary syntax: a-philosophical-work-of-the-first-importance. Sartre thinks and his thought is brilliant. He sets himself to tearing my ethics apart (a desire to forbid), he impresses me and I am sent reeling with the idea that I do not think. In Simone de Beauvoir's case, there certainly was someone who took on the task of making her understand that she was forbidden. And it worked, to the point of making her forget all that she had learned. A sad end to an initiatory journey. The young Simone seems first to have discovered a little about philosophy as it is taught at school and university. She liked it and it did her good. Reading the best authors gave her a better idea of this form of thought, she understood it and the institutions validated her understanding. At the end of the path, when the apprentice was on the point of leaving her alma mater to become responsible for transmitting that thought in her turn, a scene takes place where she is administered what she thinks is the ultimate elucidation of the question of 'what is philosophy?': it is a garden where people test themselves against each other and where anyone who is not tough enough is 'ripped to shreds' and has to withdraw.

3   Each to her own primal scene

Mine took place far from the Luxembourg Gardens, in Quimper on the south coast of Brittany. As the philosophy classes at the girls' school were too full, I and some others were sent to classes at the boys' school. This was my first experience of being 'the only woman', hence a singular person in a masculine world, which did not simply become mixed by virtue of my presence. The teacher was an elderly man who took the content of his classes chiefly from wide circulation magazines on science (for the 'philosophy of knowledge') or sport (for the 'philosophy of human action'). But he got us into class on time, always kept our homework books up to date, maintained order and discipline and gave us written tests every Monday if his football team had lost, which was a fairly frequent event. We must assume that the institutions asked no more of a teacher. The basic task of a secondary school seemed to be to discipline us, sometimes offering us knowledge as an additional extra. In this situation, my schoolmates and I adopted masks of great placidity. This teacher disgusted us, but he was not the first to do so. And in Quimper in 1964 it was out of the question for there to be open conflict as a result. Or almost out of the question.

To compensate for his classes, I read everything I could lay my hands on, understanding what I could, gleaning little bits whose meaning I could grasp from the *Gorgias* or Pascal and skipping the rest, which was beyond me, then going back to it, reckoning that my faculty of comprehension would have opened up a little in the meantime as a result of other things I had read. I wanted to get my teeth into something more substantial than the bland gruel we were served at school and I was sure and certain that something more substantial existed. The teacher and I did not get on well, particularly after the day when, completely forgetting myself, I was naive enough to want at all costs to explain to him a passage from the *Discourse on Method*. You have to be most ingenuous to believe that, just because you have a piece from Descartes in front of you, a statutory equality of intelligences has been established, so that it matters little that one is a teacher and the other a student; the text is there, the point is to understand it and as long as he has not explained to me why it does not mean what I thought it did, I shall stick to my point of view. *Veritas non filia authoritatis.* Without even knowing Bacon's words, as soon as one enters philosophy, one gathers that truth is not the daughter of authority; hence moreover the fact that all institutions of philosophy, be they schools, universities or 'research' bodies, are unsound.

About once a week the teacher had literally to put me in my place, which was defined by a task such as: learn Messrs Huisman and Vergez' manual off by heart. It really was a question of place: once I went too far and the teacher got really angry, 'if you want my place, say so at once and take it!' said he, banging his desk. But that was not exactly what I wanted and when, a few years later, I had to teach in my turn, occupying that place made me suffer many torments. After this outburst from my teacher, I kept a better hold on myself and my penchant for impertinence became discreet, in other words it developed. I still thought that philosophy was something other than what we were told it was, but I tried to keep this belief to myself. And I decided to study philosophy to test out my belief: I wanted to know if I was right about Descartes and about the discipline in general.

One day I came upon a schools' edition of *The Bases of the Metaphysics of Custom* and I was overwhelmed. I had found the substantial thing I was looking for. It was rigorous and it was about something – how wonderful! The preface told me that this excellent author had written other works, in particular three *Critiques*, which the preface writer greatly praised and which he thought should be read in a particular order. At the back of the classroom there was a huge cupboard: the library. Once a week we were allowed to borrow books if we asked the teacher. I therefore asked for the *Critique of Pure Reason* and my esteemed future colleague refused to give it to me:

'That is much too hard for you. Kant...Kant...you know... Here is something for you instead, which will also be useful to you for the lessons we shall be doing on the training of the will... Kant is very difficult, and he exaggerates, his is the morality of the hero, the sage and the saint, perhaps, but not a decent man's morality'.[9]

The book he gave me was a biography of Marie Curie, written by her daughter Eve, if I remember rightly. A week later I gave it back.

'So you saw,' he said, 'how cold she was in her attic room and how she put her suitcase on top of the bed covers...'

'What a woman she was! She could dance non-stop for three days! So that afterwards her shoes were only fit for the dustbin!' replied she who is always suspicious when people start talking to her about edifying sacrifices.

I have never read the *Critique of Pure Reason*. Twenty-five years have elapsed since that last year at school and I have still not read it. I have never been able to, except by cheating: reading the end first, and then what came just before the end, a little of the beginning, a passage from the middle...that is not what reading is, particularly for a book like that. I have to admit that my teacher's assessment of it as 'too hard for you' has had an effect, and that is very strange. For years before, when the school library refused to let me have Shakespeare (regarded as dangerous for a little girl's morals), I went immediately to the town library, where the librarian always gave me anything I wanted, even precious first editions which were not to be taken out on loan. Why did I not immediately do the same with Kant? The following year, in Brest, I was lucky enough to have a real philosophy teacher, Mme Eon. She gave us a good lecture on Kant's philosophy. I could then have disregarded what the other one had said. Soon afterwards I was earning my living and had enough money to buy books for myself without having to ask anyone's permission; at that point I should, simply out of a sense of duty to my work, have devoted two months of my time to reading the *Critique* from cover to cover. So we have to admit that prohibition was paradoxically effective here: a few, totally unjustified words uttered by someone I did not respect still prove insurmountable years after-wards, even when they are counter-balanced by duty.

So is my young colleague right when she says that prohibition, the 'inter-dict', the word that comes between you and the object you want to approach is enough to explain the phenomenon? Even if the initiative for the ban does not originate in some great system of symbolic distribution and is only the result of an individual, anecdotal event, in this case simply a word of retaliation, it has its effect. For refusing me the *Critique* was basically an act of vengeance: I had too often plagued the poor man who explained the cogito's self-evidence by the chimpanzee's insight and refuted the methodological separation of body and mind with tales of planarians being conditioned to positive phototropism.

Because I find it hard to understand this story of mine, although it is very real, I shall use it to support my reopening of questions often considered outdated. One hypothesis would enable us to make sense of my autobiographical episode: it is possible that girls and women have a powerful sensitivity to prohibition – a sensitivity which nothing affects – because their education is more closely watched and entirely centred on negativity. In my childhood and adolescence, parents and teachers feared a number of things from us which were regarded as disastrous, but did not expect anything positive at all. Taking things a little further, it could be said that, fundamentally, we were treated as potential nuisances. Our educators seemed to think chiefly of the disturbances we might cause, the foolish things we might do and the serious headaches we were liable to give them. These various worries were expressed by the all-embracing term 'behaving badly', which is all the more effective because it refers at once to not sitting straight in one's chair, using slang, making noise and, last but not least, having sexual relations at an early age and thus possibly making the adults face the terrible problem represented by a pregnant adolescent. Our intentions were implicitly on trial at all times, as though we were little things to be feared, which had to be stopped from doing damage: preventative precautions were thus the primary concern of educative procedure.

This attitude of prohibition had two features: the first was that it was presented to us in a purely negative form, in other words with no compensation by positive prescriptions. We were not charged with fulfilling a hope, dream or ambition; we were not destined for anything much apart from one day leaving 'the family' to enter another. The aim of all the bans was to make this departure possible, which explains, moreover, why nothing positive was invested in us. One way or another, the point of view of parents and educators basically came down to that of a prefect, who asks nothing more from the child than that he or she should sit still and take up as little space as possible. Even the need to prepare ourselves for employment was suggested to us, if at all, in the negative and indeed in a way that made us feel guilty: we were not to be a burden on our parents until we got married, if we got married (they could no longer arrange it themselves), or worse, forever. Hence we needed to grasp the idea of 'being a burden for as short a time as possible', something made explicit to many women of my generation.

When I read Rousseau, I again find the pure interdict which characterized our education, formulated in an abstract and general way which also corresponds to the reality: 'Girls must be restricted early'.[10] A general restriction which can take any given form, depending on the time and circumstances, and even apparently senseless forms. Because any early restriction – on language, manners or bodily positions – is instructive and provides the right foundations if a female individual is to learn restriction in all its forms and is to accept without argument those that are imposed upon her. According to this hypothesis, a little girl's relation to prohibition simply has nothing in common with that of a boy. For if we are to believe psychoanalysis and everyday observation, the latter encounters bans which are clearly defined and thus, by contrast, define a space of possibilities which is then structured by expectations and permissions, what is prescribed being an element in what is permitted. For a little girl nothing is either prescribed or permitted.

The second characteristic of bans as they are inculcated into girls may well be their indirect nature. For assuming that the fear of seeing girls behave badly is basically the fear of a sexual life which could only be untimely, we must still recognize the fact that this ban, which we may regard as fundamental, is never or seldom expressed as such. It is metaphorically signified by all the other restrictions. 'In my day', adherence to sexual morality, which was absolutely required of girls and women, was a matter for conversations between adults only. No one talked to girls about it, because no one talked to girls about sexuality at all, as though giving them an idea of it meant immediately running the risk of giving them wicked ideas. But if we accept that this morality was inculcated indirectly, we can better understand the ill-defined or unbounded nature of the prohibitions. When the articulation of a ban is in its very principle metaphorical, nothing can halt the proliferation of its variations and metaphorical derivatives, for any restriction will do to signify the one that is not to be mentioned. This situation can moreover have ironic consequences: many women freed themselves from sexual morality more easily than from the metaphorical restrictions meant to signify it. One sees this a lot among my contemporaries, at least in the circles I move in. It may even be that some women, who are now the mothers of daughters, are still transmitting metaphorical bans to those daughters, while talking to them about the free and fulfilled sexuality that they hope will be theirs when they are grown up, but not necessarily now.

I wanted simply to explain why I never transgressed the particular refusal of the *Critique of Pure Reason*, which was certainly a form of interdict, despite the fact that I pride myself on my spirit of contradiction. I have answered with far more general hypotheses, which might explain the insurmountable nature of any such refusal. Thus a localized question sometimes allows us to shed some light, of a hypothetical kind at least, on the universal it contains. And the hypothesis is enough to trigger debate on something which normally goes undiscussed. But I must now return to the precise problem: is the fact that women very seldom adopt the position of creator in philosophy linked to a ban (it would be enough that they should be given to understand that they were not capable of it), or to the structure of the act through which one establishes oneself as someone who is going to produce one's own work, an act which seems to involve assertion of oneself as a super-consciousness with an overview of everything that has been thought until now or is being thought at the moment, in the streets, in other fields of knowledge and in the works of one's predecessors? Theoretically I tend to favour the second interpretation and yet my personal experience tells me that prohibition is a force which unsettles our understanding. We must conclude that the problem has been badly posed, since there is a contradiction between theory and personal experience.

We must go further and state that a question like mine has no meaning, since philosophical thought is an unstable thing that is hard to grasp. Even if we say that it is a critical re-examination whose aim is to apply reasoning consciousness to all sorts of ordinarily accepted principles, such as those of morality, intellectual thought, politics or religion, this definition is still too vague to define a particular activity. It is also too impoverished to include some works which bear the name of philosophy, and at the same time too generous, for there are realities which philosophers have not approached in a critical way at certain times, or concerning which they have not opposed custom with their reason, nor the law with their consciousness. The definition of philosophy as, for example, a desire to rethink everything freely, is only clear, precise and sufficient for rather blinkered opponents of any philosophical undertaking, for Anytos, who accused Socrates of thus leading young people away from the respect they owed to the laws and customs of their country, or for Cato the Censor, who asked the Roman Senate to expel Carneades for similar reasons.

4   Still further from the Luxembourg Gardens

But it is precisely at this point of vagueness (which disappears only when philosophy has to struggle) that we need to place ourselves in order to reformulate the problem. I should like if I may to mention one of the earliest figures in Greek thought. Long before Socrates there lived in Lindos, on the island of Rhodes, a certain Cleobulus, who may have travelled to Egypt to learn philosophy. We do not know for sure. At any rate, the doxographers regard him as one of the seven sages of Greece. The essential part of his work (three thousand obscure lines of poetry, it seems) is lost, but some phrases which were famous in Antiquity have come down to us. One of these, 'Moderation is best', has had a fine career. Another is 'We ought to give our daughters to their husband maidens in years but women in wisdom', on which Diogenes Laertius comments, 'Thus signifying that girls need to be educated as well as boys.' Even daughters. He had one, Eumetis, whose name means something like 'happy intelligence'.[11] Some called her Cleobulina. She acquired a degree of fame by pursuing the same type of studies as her father, writing enigmas in hexametres.[12] This story seems to me exemplary in more ways than one. As we know, the social status given to Greek women, even those of the free classes, was far from liberal. It was not customary to educate girls and, long afterwards, Diogenes Laertius stressed the originality of Cleobulus' thinking. The same Cleobulus is also said to have stated: 'It is want of sense that reigns most widely among mortals and multitude of words; but due season will serve.' He noted a situation which was simply shared and voiced a hope for all.

Thus, at the dawn of philosophy, we find an important gleam of light: a philosopher could dispute his society's custom concerning an important aspect of women's position. And we can also see that, against custom, philosophy was the only means of appeal. When philosophy is the only way of challenging custom, it acquires immense power. Just think: the only means of appeal! If that appeal is now blocked, there is no way of challenging what is. This is why the philosophical utterance of a ban is so effective against someone who has already identified philosophy as their only means of appeal. Any rebellion which is looking for a language and an opening and finds a lock instead is lost. We must seek our freedom outside philosophy, or else expose ourselves – in our complete vulnerability – to the refusal that this mode inflicts on us simply with words. The extrinsic and the intrinsic meet here: when the world outside philosophy offers no support to someone seeking their own freedom, that same someone is at the mercy of what happens in their relation to the philosophical world. If Simone de Beauvoir proved so receptive to the block that Sartre erected against her, this is a judgement not only upon Sartre and the philosophical manners of the time, but on the standard situation for a girl, even an educated girl, at the end of the 1920s. She had nothing else: look at the rest she describes in the *Memoirs*, the genteel teas, the crushing weight of the family. And so, when something began to go wrong in her relation to the world of philosophy, she was defenceless. In the same way I, who had only a premonition of philosophy to use in my opposition to everything, was shattered when the philosophy teacher uttered the words 'too difficult for you'. I was lucky that this affected only one book (but what a book!).

There is something else to be learned from the story of Cleobulus and Eumetis: they wrote verse enigmas. Their activity seems at once both similar to and distant from what the later Socratics practised under the name of philosophy. But no closer nor more distant than the work of Saint Thomas Aquinas in relation to Socratic enquiry. If it is hard to tell what philosophy is, whom can one certainly call a philosopher?

What is philosophy? Who is a philosopher? I do not know which of these two questions is of greater concern, but I find that *The Dinner of the Seven Wise Men* illustrates them particularly well. On seeing Eumetis-Cleobulina, one character says: 'Is that the very intelligent girl whose enigmas are famous as far abroad as Egypt?' To which Thales replies that, for her, riddles are above all an occasional distraction; she is also gifted with astounding wisdom, a power of reason adequate to govern a state and a philanthropic nature; she has encouraged her father to govern Lindos taking account of the needs of the people. As this dinner is a work of imagination written centuries after the death of the characters it portrays, it would be a risky thing to attribute to this passage the status of a historical document on Cleobulus and Cleobulina. It may be that it primarily expresses the opinion of Plutarch and shows how much the idea of wisdom changed between the seventh century BC and the first century AD: in Plutarch's time riddles were no longer enough to 'be philosophical'; one also needed a goodly dose of *noûs politikòs* and *èthos philanthrôpon*.

The question reappears later in the text, after the dinner has settled into its rhythm and the banqueters have said funny and wise things (such as how a king can drink the sea and how this is easier than making his government potable to the people). A doctor called Cleodorus, who has also been invited to the dinner, protests: 'But what difference is there between all this and Eumetis' riddles? It is no

doubt suitable for her to weave them and then offer them to the
women, as girls do with belts, but it is ridiculous that men [*andras*]
should take this type of thing seriously.' This sally is aimed chiefly at
the aphoristic replies (referring to time, death, space, hope and so
on) offered by Thales to questions which Cleodorus calls impasses.
He cannot see that Thales' replies are superb and calls on the sages
to stop bothering with this type of enigmatic questions. To do this, he
personalizes things, if I may be allowed to say so. His first argument
is 'leave that to the Barbarians' and his second, as we have just seen,
is 'leave it to the little girls'. When the aim is to eliminate a form of
wisdom, Greek men are invited to mark themselves out from Barbarians and women. We can note here that the question 'who is a
philosopher?' removes the need seriously to pose the other one, 'what
should philosophy be?'. But Cleodorus is shown to be in the wrong:
Plutarch energetically defends his old world, and thus Thales and
Cleobulina. Aesop, who is supposed to be present, ridicules Cleodorus and a little later Cleobulus introduces his thoughts on moderation
with the words: 'as my daughter says'.

The sages seek neither to establish nor to assert a difference between Lydians and Greeks or between men and girls, and this fact
can be related to an aesthetic of thought as xenophilic and self-
expatriating, which is outlined in the same text. The master of the
house declares that he praises people, states and governments who
protect foreigners' property first and that of their own citizens afterwards; he suggests that, in the same way, the guests' *logos* (speech or
reasoning) should no longer keep to its own domain and should
concern itself with giving the king of Egypt the help he has asked for.
Later, Solon says that the best state, the one which best achieves
democracy, is the one where criminals are pursued by those who are
not their victims as much as by the victims themselves.

My readers must surely feel here the extent of my delight at
questioning what remains to us of ancient memory on the question of
women in philosophy. Seeking vestiges of accounts of women philosophers, even of an indirect or belated kind, one finds, in conjunction
with a sympathetic portrait of Eumetis-Cleobulina, a doctrine of open
society, a very fine morality, a great vocation conferred on thought
(concerning itself with that which is not its 'own backyard') and,
better still, a kind of subjective assurance: philosophy is all this so
there is no need for anxiety about its form. I say 'better still' because
I believe this serenity permits non-exclusiveness. With this kind of
wisdom one can mix the *éthos philanthrôpon* with riddles and can

consider that in her fable about the moon Eumetis has given a fine exposition of how one cannot dream of governing if people lack all measure. Even Solon's idea that 'laws are liable to be revised', gains its full force in this context. Things such as a society open to strangers, Greeks who assert the similarity of Hesiod and Homer with the Barbarians and men who accept the idea of a community which includes both themselves and girls also imply a state open to its own changes.

I believe we must choose: either we opt for this ethics and this aesthetic, or we must accept a labyrinth of questions which may turn sour or ridiculous. For the problem we have posed – if it is hard to know what philosophy is, how can one be sure of being a philosopher? – relates to the concern (which I do not wish to judge) with being able to say 'me too'. Me too, I'm one! The easiest response to this type of concern is to build up one's image as a philosopher. This means not letting oneself be judged simply on one's work (as a contribution to the collective effort), but setting oneself up as a sovereign consciousness, bringing to bear the force of one's own person, in work as elsewhere, in a tone suitable to the holder of a super-knowledge and thus not forgetting to indicate in what way that knowledge has an overview of others.

The funny thing is that this attitude can be adopted before one has even started to form the supposed 'super-knowledge'. In crushing Simone de Beauvoir, Sartre was getting into practice, playing at stingrays, imitating Socrates and not without presumption. And yet, in 1929 Sartre was simply a young man taking the *agrégation* who had not yet started his own work. Had he even found the theme to which that work was to be devoted? Quite possibly not. That year the subject for the general philosophy essay was 'Freedom and Contingency' and Sartre proceeded to discuss it for thirty years. At the time that he 'ripped' Beauvoir's ethics 'to shreds', he had just fortuitously encountered his life's subject, or was on the point of encountering it, to know we should have to be able to date the scene to within a week. We cannot take him seriously at this time. But he was already acting out the philosopher's relationship to 'popular opinion', latching on to Simone's little personal ideas (which were no doubt in an inchoate state) and judging them in an entirely recognizable way to be 'confused', 'at fault', 'prejudices' and 'hastily formed concepts'. This is exactly how Socrates regards young Meno's ideas, even though he says so more politely. Greenhorns can always act the Socrates, once they have found someone to butt.

5 *The wheel*

Let us leave aside for a moment the presumptiousness of this and simply consider the question of the distance and overview of philosophy in relation to the doxa. For this question 'breaks us on the wheel', as Montaigne would say, in other words we are caught in contradiction and suffering. On the one hand, if philosophy does not grant itself the possibility of offering a distanced form of truth which can win the fight against opinions backed up by the force of custom and numbers, it is hard to see what reason it still has to exist, for its *raison d'être* is to create something divergent and remote. In this respect Cleobulus' existence is precious. If all philosophers had always known how to cut themselves off from common opinion concerning women's position, a woman like myself would be overflowing with acknowledgements. I should be grateful to philosophy and I should literally recognize philosophy insofar as it would be acting in accordance with its vocation of providing a distance and the theoretical strength to maintain that distance against the strength of prejudice. So then what is the difference between this formulation and that of the sovereign super-knowledge, theoretically hegemonic and in any case superior in terms of reason to popular belief? Let us be honest: not a lot. And yet, the first formulation leads us to something we regard as 'good' and the second to something reprehensible, which we have attributed to those who experience themselves as superior in the human community, such as white Europeans in relation to Chinese or black people, or men in relation to women.

We can only draw a dividing line by acknowledging the importance of appearance. For one can put on a show of ascendancy, of superiority, in which nothing at all is at stake, whereas the power of a theory to maintain distance can only be acquired after uncommonly arduous endeavours. A young man who has not yet thought anything for himself can play the former trick on a young woman. But if one distances oneself from what everyone else believes in a meaningful way, one has to pay a price. The heliocentrism of Copernicus and Kepler is a perfect example: this idea, which went against 'universal agreement', as they said at the time, required a patient effort of thought whose aim was the idea itself and not the pleasure of singling oneself out from the common herd. Hence the fact that it could be articulated, even at the imaginary level, without need of support from the authority of a socially valued personage: Kepler chose not a bearded old white European sage to endorse the hypothesis of the earth's movement, but a young lad, who had been well battered by life, and his mother, a herbalist and witch. And the story is presented like a dream, a mode which is not credited with an incontrovertible dogmatic power, but has the merit, in the author's eyes, of being that of free fantasy.[13] On the other hand, those who ballast what they say with the full weight of what they are in society would seem thus to betray the fragility of their words. History shows us thinkers who moved in the highest circles and whose theoretical efforts are still important to us because they represent what no one else was saying. These people were often able to cast a humorous doubt over the worth of their great efforts; in any case they have left their theories to plead their own cases, without the support of pomposity or personage at the imaginary level.

And this is indeed the paradox I am trying to uncover. Pomposity does not indicate involvement in the continued creation of philosophy; on the contrary it is rather a sign that one is imitating the master by whom one was fascinated at an early age and whose fascination was so great that one has been unable to escape it. Let us consider, for example, the followers of Althusser or Gueroult, the followers of Alain's followers or Heideggerians competing to be the most faithful disciple. When we scratch someone's veneer of self-assertion in thought as the holder of a super-knowledge, we often find that this assertion masks an emptiness, in this case that created by the absence of personal thought. The partisans of a 'great' (whom they consider very great) Other are the most intractable dogmatists of the Republic of Letters and they are so because they feel destined to perpetuate this person's work. Since our times are not very propitious to fertility in the field of theory and since philosophy is not in very good health, emptiness is very widespread and so also are dogmatism and magisterial posturing. Little is created, but this lack is compensated by giving more status to the person of the philosopher, who decrees the fundamental and moral principles of any theoretical undertaking, without their having any exact relation to any current problem or any specific undertaking now in progress which could be debated.

It is understandable that women should find it almost impossible to identify with this empty superiority, or to imagine inheriting the master's authority in a game where the point is to reincarnate a personage and not to carry on a debate. I say 'almost' advisedly, for the pronouncement of an absolute impossibility would be open to challenge on more than one ground. It would amount to projecting on to 'women' in general something which I basically think about myself, and thus to reintroducing the idea of a nature common to all women and defined by its incompatibilities ('women absolutely cannot identify with . . .'). Worse still, to assume a nature is to think that things happen directly between a particular person and a particular intellectual situation, without the complex mediation of one's experience of oneself in the social whole and in one's professional group. The experience needs to be grasped, while at the same time leaving open the question of whether or how the mediation is restricting. There is also such a thing as an 'imaginary view of oneself', which is powerful and does not always take account of the data of experience, even experience one has of oneself in other people's eyes. Many of our contemporaries admit to the belief that they are subjects of a long epic of 'metempsychosis' or 'metemsomatosis': they imagine themselves to be a poverty-stricken porter of ancient times, then a Roman patrician, a rat in Ireland at the time of Ptolemy, then an Inca princess or a parrot on the banks of the Amazon; they picture themselves in another body and an entirely different situation, assuming that their essential self is continuous. Of course this type of belief remains clandestine, but its existence tells us that anyone can fantasize themselves as different, while continuing to be 'themselves'. To assume that any woman is always aware of the fact that she is a woman, down to the last detail, is to attribute an attitude of psychological rigidity to half of humanity, when we know that human beings can imagine themselves as swans, geese or white elephants. All I am saying is that the young Sartre could integrate his fantasy into a reality (a network of interrelations) whereas any such claims on the part of a young woman would instantly be dismissed.

When women become involved in philosophical work, the first thing they encounter is incredulity. This partly relates to the fact that they are assumed to have neither a capacity for authority nor indeed a critical mind, but are seen as embodying docility, as though their relation to prevention described above were vaguely understood by all. Such massive sensitivity to prevention constitutes us as under-consciousnesses from the outset, as is fitting. As is fitting, first of all, to a social order that extends beyond philosophy: it is important to remember Anytos and Cato precisely because they reveal something which is not internal to the discipline. Here are two greybeards saying that young men (men, but young ones) should not even encounter philosophy because they should have absolute respect for received customs and practices and it would corrupt them. We find the attitude of the politicians of Antiquity towards young men reflected in what most men, philosophers or not, think about women:

both young men and women must piously absorb the principles they
are given as imperatives.

In contrast to philosophy this submissive position makes the former seem to be something which overcomes imperatives and principles. And of course, in return this tells us why young men were the
ones who crowded round Socrates or Carneades and why today there
is a particularly strong demand for philosophy from women: philosophy is bound to arouse passions in those to whom piety is prescribed.
However, the project of overcoming principles remains an ambiguous
one, if it does not go hand in hand with an ethical ideal of egalitarian,
democratic or better still libertarian values. For by establishing a
point from which they can look down on society's imperatives, philosophers can at any time constitute themselves as super-authorities.
The desire to free themselves which led the young man or woman to
become students of philosophical thought then suffers the dreadful
fate of falling prey to another type of dominance, or of identifying
with overviews and attitudes of mastery, which amounts to the same
thing. We certainly are about to be broken on the wheel.

Before abandoning this ambiguity to its sad fate, let us simply note
that the consequences it has had for young men differ from those it
has had for women. Politicians seek to drive philosophers from society, and even to kill them, so that they stop corrupting young men,
because they are aware of the subversive aspects of philosophy.
Philosophers will just about accept women as immediately docile
followers, which is already a way of depriving them of philosophy or,
more often, drive them as far as possible from the philosophical
domain. It is in relation to these supposed 'under-consciousnesses'
that philosophers can best see themselves as 'super-consciousnesses'.
Overall, we can see that the relation between women and philosophy
is just a dramatized version of their original relation to prohibition, a
relation which philosophy did not invent but on which it sets the seal.
Challenging is something both desirable and more difficult for someone in a very subordinate position; the simple and direct relation of
a former little girl to what she knows of philosophy is marked by
contradiction from the outset. To the extent that this relation is
mediated by a social structure – there are teachers, students and
institutions, that is to say dramatis personae and stage – the whole
story may indeed become a drama about a kind of *sociale bellum*, a war
between allies:[14] the *socius*, the companion or associate, sends one
back to precisely the point one wanted to leave. But can we content
ourselves with reading books in secret in a barn somewhere, or with
having a strictly institutional relation to the state's universities and

no friends at all? My experience is close to that of Simone de Beauvoir: it is infinitely easier for a woman to take the *agrégation* than to get herself taken seriously by the people she associates with. But which is more important?

In secret. We have noted that it is possible to act the philosopher, a simple posture which does not correspond to actual personal work; as a hypothesis we should posit that the opposite is also true: the possibility of underground or secret philosophical work, which does not label itself philosophy. If it is hard absolutely to identify the philosophical nature of something generally regarded as such, we must admit that philosophy may also exist where it is not particularly obvious. In some works by ladies, for example (but not only there). Should we perhaps say that prevention ultimately functions only in relation to appearance?

6 The body at work: problems of identification

I have sometimes wondered about the relation of philosophers' bodies to their work. Not the relation of their hormones to their conceptual activity, which is the unspoken background to what is said by all those of our contemporaries, women and men, who postulate a self-evident and radical duality between 'masculine' and 'feminine' thought, but the theatrical question of how the thinking body is staged. As others see it, the body may be young or old, that of a woman or a man, thin or rounded, and of course people's sub-jective attitudes to their own bodies can be read even more directly than objective data. Léon Brunschvicg very carefully trimmed his beard to a point and placed his fine symmetrical head above a white shirt collar which rose from his waistcoat, whereas Gaston Bachelard's face was all undergrowth. Is this purely fortuitous? Two portraits frame the latter's work: the first, taken in 1924 in a physics class, shows a fine forehead between a shock of black hair and a black beard. The head is in harmony with the place: it is serious, but straightforward, exactly the right kind of head for a serious scientist, too serious not to be uninterested in any form of affectation and not to prefer the freedom of austere comradeship to the 'personal groom-ing' which must be displayed by anyone who intends later to enter the Academy. This style of appearance corresponds to the *Essai sur la connaissance approchée* and *La Valeur inductive de la relativité*. At the end of his life, we see Bachelard sitting in patriarchal style, a brimming library behind him, with a book on his knees and a scarf over his shoulders like a stole; his hair has turned white and is much longer than the Sorbonne usually permitted in its professors, his mouth is completely hidden by a moustache which overhangs his beard. This is the portrait of the Father of Solomon's House as described in Bacon, without the luxury. The archetype of the old sage. There can be no question that *The Poetics of Space*, *The Poetics of Reverie*, and *The Flame of a Candle*, were written by this body engrossed in meditation.

Doubtless it is always easy to find correspondences between face and work after the event. But I have set out these ideas simply to establish their counter-proof. Imagine a stylish young woman, put her into a Laura Ashley dress or give her the means to dress more expensively; give her also the project of writing a modern equivalent of *La Connaissance approchée*; for example, a work devoted to the epistemology of superconductivity. In a flowery dress. Is there a discrepancy or not? That is the question. Of course, when we get right into our work, we forget ourselves; concentrating on the object of our study, we think, at most, of the readers whom we hope to address and sometimes forget even those, remembering them only when we reread and thus rewrite. But in the course of any kind of work there are other times besides those when one is 'buried in it'. There is the moment when one chooses the subject and, every morning, the bizarre quarter of an hour when the person and her or his work meet up again; every evening there is the point when they part. There are the times when one sees one's friends, the formidable *socii* to whom one tells a little of what one has done during the week. In this daily life of the philosopher, there is more than enough space for something which is not work, but a web of questions about the appropriateness, credibility and legitimacy of that work. 'Is this what needs thinking about today?' 'Will this be of interest to even one reader?' Everyone is familiar with these questions and their fellows. But there is also the one that goes, 'Is it credible that I should be the one to think about this?' 'Is it plausible?' 'Am I in the right role?' We shall not go so far as to say that we are all the novelists or playwrights of our own lives. The crucial question of the plausibility of the meeting between a person and a piece of work is crucial only because it is a crossroads of social involvements.

Social divisions are greatly implicated in this space of multiple doubts which preceeds, accompanies, surrounds and follows a piece of work. Often without the person being aware of it, a sense of plausibility or implausibility is enough to fix choices according to an

unformulated perception. This is where the question, 'who am I?'
settles the question, 'What shall I undertake?', for there is a hierarchy in the subjects one can work on and differences which are not all
of the same order as the hierarchy. So do we choose our theme and
method according to the role we should like to play or feel able to
assume? Do we let ourselves be guided by what is credible, depending on whether we are old or young, a man or a woman, good-looking
or ugly? I do think, at any rate, that individuals tend to rule out the
unbelievable and abandon projects which they could undertake on
the basis of their training and intellectual abilities alone, but for
which they do not look the part.

How can we say they are wrong? For one thing seems certain: if
one chooses a subject on the basis of one's intellectual capacity to
deal with it properly, disregarding sociological plausibility, the quarter of an hour every morning is more difficult, more weighted with
conflict. A loss of energy usually follows. In students one can already
often make out confused states which hinder their work. I remember
a time when the *agrégation* was organized on a single-sex basis; so
when the state announced that it wanted a recruit forty-five women
for the philosophy *agrégation*, it was a very public matter: forty-five
women had to be found. In such circumstances for me, a woman, it is
obviously legitimate and necessary to prepare for this competition; if
I am moody in the morning, at least it will not be linked to my sexual
identity. Then the *agrégation* became mixed, at a time when there was
also a spectacular drop in the number of jobs. Women students'
commitment to preparing for it then became more difficult: a new
cause of conflict came between them and the syllabus, which nevertheless continued its usual round of the 'great authors', from Plato to
Nietzsche. Anyone who remembered the previous situation would
have linked the women's unease to the new extra-intellectual factor:
the fact that they were now competing with men, when moreover
penury was a feature of the situation. But this social or institutional
element was doubly internalized, as an intrinsic difficulty in the
relationship between women and the work expected of them and as a
personal difficulty: 'that is not for me'.[15]

A crossroads of social involvements. Let us now consider how
completed pieces of work are received. Here too the work is not seen
in isolation, it is the work and the relation of the author to work
which is considered. And the relation will be approved or criticized
more than the work. 'When I read her book, I was sure it had been
written by some sour old spinster and when I met her later I

wondered what could have got into such a pretty girl to make her think of writing that.' How fortunate that the author of the thick and scholarly work on which this comment was passed was an indisputably good-looking woman! She was criticized for the dissonance, but at least her person was not fantasized on the basis of her work. But here is another story: take a field of research (again in philosophy) so valued that in order to venture into it one must be a man, have the highest possible academic credentials, be white and from a Christian family which has been wealthy for several generations. In contempt of our theories, a woman had the cheek to enter it, for the simple reason that she was intellectually capable of so doing, and as she was very bright, she was brilliantly successful. 'When you're an ugly old hag, there's nothing else for you.' My word of honour, I'm not making it up, but I beg my woman reader not to see herself in this vicious portrait: it cannot be you, for the great lady who had the courage to listen to nothing but her intellectual passion and whom I always found more pleasant to look at than the speaker of these appalling words, this figure whom I put forward as a role model for her intelligence and courage, will never open this book, or I should be most surprised if she did.

If such things were said about me, I should prefer them never to reach my ears. For I am not sure that I should be strong enough not to be mortified by them. 'Once you start saying something interesting, you are no longer seen as a woman', sighs a woman colleague and friend. Often we feel we are in the opposite position to that of Scheherazade: she had to keep telling fascinating tales to prevent herself from being murdered by her mad husband, while we are 'annihilated' as women when we manage to make people listen to us – I used the notion of mortification deliberately. However, we should not separate this problem from a more general fact: does a *young* man allow himself to write a book intended to be authoritative? So if we accept that, in general, it is not purely a mind that is involved in a piece of strictly intellectual work, but that the choice of subject, the determination and energy one devotes to it and the reception given to the result are also governed by a kind of sense of what is fitting – one is more or less obliged to establish a harmony between the person one obviously is and what one writes – we can begin to understand the weight of even arbitrary social divisions and their effects on individuals and their behaviour.

The reader will long ago have understood that I am not upholding the idea of the existence of feminine writing and masculine writing, woman's thought and man's thought. Indeed I utterly refuse to give any credence to this dualism, which is however dominant in contemporary thought and is an avatar of the doctrine of the Ideologues or of a sort of 'materialism of temperament', according to which thought comes from the brain that produces it in the same way that the liver secretes bile. What bothers me in all this is not so much the zoological aspect that such opinions sometimes have, but the point that if thought is related only to the person who utters it, all sorts of important considerations fade into irrelevance. Thought is thought about something: is this something properly understood? Does one's thinking reflect the current state of the problem? Does it show a sufficient level of information? Has it questioned itself enough? Is it accompanied by critical thinking? Does it open up new perspectives? When questions of this type can be asked of thought, it can be regarded as thought and not just as a verbal opinion or a quiet delusion. Because I want to be able to ask these questions, the author's sex is the last thing I am concerned with, at least in the first analysis.

7   Questioning roots

Something else in this conception should bother our contemporaries: the fixity of the differences thus assumed. Rooting them in chromosomes or the hormonal system would imply that men are all the same and women are all the same, in all places, at all times, and that there can be no freedom for subjects. Say you are born in Brittany in the mid-twentieth century. You are lucky: you are not shut up in your folklore. Because no culture is entirely self-governing, indigenous and turned in on itself; all are shot through with elements which have come from elsewhere and, since the project of preserving a cultural or individual identity seems to you devoid of meaning, you can try to discover that which was not given to you at the outset. You can enjoy changing and bless the fact that the notion of being rooted in one's region or locality is badly formulated: one is not attached to one cultural place as by a root. But those who say that everything is determined by which sex we belong to are also saying that there are no possibilities for change, one is what one is: 'I am me, believe me', says one. 'Oh really? well believe me, I am me', replies the other, and may add, after a moment's thought, 'Let us part good friends'. For one corollary of difference at all costs is indifference. However there is also another, which is the complete forgetting of the principle of cultural arbitrariness. Far from being applied to the question of the sexual division of labour and attitudes, the idea that customs and practices are largely conventional, differing from one side of a border to the other, and that there is a great diversity in the way that people respond to elementary or social necessities seems, on the contrary, to be suppressed by this dualism of the fixists.

'On the beach, trousers have become feminine' notes Simone de Beauvoir, as though pointing to a great victory. Not that deprivation of the right to wear trousers was painful, but the fact that something has become gives us the aesthetic pleasure of mobility, which is so rare. In a symmetrical way, think of all the complaining or sarcastic comments there were during the 1960s when boys started wearing their hair long. Gender fixism is built on incompatibilities: one cannot be a boy and have shoulder-length hair. The idea that one cannot be a woman and create philosophy is perhaps of the same order: an idea so derisory that to refute it also seems totally derisory. And yet it has social and individual effects which go beyond understanding. For once, let us greet a fragment of rootedness with fondness. For a while my grandmother worked as a docker; she was also astoundingly beautiful. It was she who taught me that there is no such thing as incompatibility, except in the 'dreams of dreamers', and that a woman can even, for example, permit herself to do embroidery, an activity which was in principle the preserve of men in Brittany.

In the First Notebook we wondered what the consequences of a sexist or racist remark might be. This question should not make us forget that sexism, racism or antisemitism can be silent; it takes longer to become aware of people's antisemitism when prudence keeps them silent; it takes longer to realize that someone is the victim of constant ostracism because that person is Vietnamese, Jewish or a woman when the ostracism is not combined with malicious comments. We live in a rushed world and it is quicker to catch someone in the act by picking up on what they say rather than listening to their silences and reticences. There is however a great difference between sexism that is spoken and that which is kept silent. The second retains its status as a private opinion, which may, of course, have effects in social life, but does not directly call on others to practise discrimination themselves. Sexism that speaks seeks to be shared – by women as well as men. In the preceding pages we have tried to explain that an action, in this case a piece of intellectual work, can contain a representation of oneself, as is clearly suggested by everyday language. Expressions such as, 'I can't see myself doing that,' or 'Yes! I can just see you doing that!' tell us that there is a visible element, a screen on to which is projected a harmony or a discord between 'me' or 'you' and an action; these expressions tell us that harmony is a good thing and discord a bad one, worse, that if there is discord, the action will not be done. 'I can't see you doing that' comes into the category of prophecy and 'I can just see him...' is an almost visionary vision: I can see it so well that it is certain he will do it.

This kind of regulation of what is projected by what one thinks one is or would like to be seems to me highly applicable to writers like Sartre and Simone de Beauvoir, insofar as they did not separate the production of a work from the construction of their own personages: they incarnated the figures of 'great modern intellectuals' as much as they wrote books. If there is such everyday regulation, both before and after work is produced, then the sexist words of men colleagues who say that women cannot be philosophers has an anchor point, a mode in which it has effects. One must decide to be an oddity, must find it interesting to act the part of the paradox and deliberately go against the grain of plausibility. This implies not only a change of aesthetics – preferring discord to harmony – but also a great outlay of psychic energy and a lot of disappointments. Not accomplishing what is expected of you and pursuing an idea because you are gripped by it, even if the relationship between that idea and yourself can only come into the category of the bizarre, creates tension; however the 'you' involved here is not your deep self, the one you may know nothing of, but an obvious, social self, the one that people see at first glance, like that of Bachelard in the photographs. And what others say affects that self, because the image we have of ourselves is largely exogenous.

8 Status

So what happened to Simone de Beauvoir, the brilliant student who later left philosophy to Sartre? This question is a crossroads for me. More than ten years ago I classified the event in the category of 'Heloise complex', where a woman establishes herself as a philosopher's loving admirer; the situation is profitable to him and fatal to her. She sees the master's philosophy as complete in itself and does not therefore feel condemned to invent or to think something that has never been thought of before. He, on the other hand, benefits from her look, in which he sees his own thought as a perfection (as no thought is). I should like today to re-examine this idea, which must, I think, be complicated and requires at least two corrections.

The first concerns the couple of Abelard and Heloise. At the time when I wrote 'Women in/and philosophy', I had thought only about the beginning of their story, when they were still merely clandestine lovers. I had considered their intimate relationship, isolated from the world by secrecy. The rest of the drama contains different elements. Here it is, read over Etienne Gilson's shoulder.[16] Heloise's uncle, learning of her pregnancy, demanded a wedding, something the two lovers resisted with a stubbornness which needs explaining: at the time not to be married was regarded as a perfection which was part of the status necessary for any philosopher who wanted to be admirable. This is what Abelard wanted and so did Heloise, perhaps even more so than he. Anyone who gets married *'de superiori ordine ad inferiorem descendit'* ('descends from a superior to an inferior order').[17] He acknowledged his sexual needs to the whole world, and thus a shameful alienation in the body. Worse still, a wife would prevent him from getting on with his philosophy: a philosopher burdened with a wife might not devote himself entirely to his books. It is better to employ a good servant, said Theophrastus, and these words are quoted in the correspondence of the unhappy pair. Speaking of an 'Heloise complex', I stressed Abelard's need of his disciple's look, without grasping the even greater need he also had of the eyes of the world (scholarly Europe in this case), in order to feel that he was a 'great philosopher' and thus necessarily unmarried, following the code of the time. As we know, the two lovers did in the end give in to the uncle's demands and get married, but they did it in secret, in the small hours, in the presence of almost no one but the uncle, which then allowed them to swear to everyone else that no wedding had taken place. In so doing they preserved Abelard's image and his audience; if the news had got out people would no longer have crowded to hear the master. Who would have retained their confidence in the quality of his teaching?

This is the reason for the secrecy they maintained around their marriage. However, as the offence was public, Uncle Fulbert wanted public reparation. To dissimulate the wedding still more, Abelard sent Heloise to spend some time in a convent, letting it be understood that she was to become a nun. This gave rise to the anger and revenge of Fulbert, who sent his henchmen to surprise Abelard in his sleep and castrate him. This tragic episode was however denied as such by Abelard at the level of the 'real'; he even went so far as to write that it was not such a painful thing. He still recognized pain and tragedy only at the level of status: it was no longer possible for him to be a public figure, the great philosopher of Europe, when everyone knew what had happened to him. He thus bade farewell to the teacher's role and regained a self-image by becoming a monk. Through his conversion, he regained an image of himself, this time as a Christian philosopher who, 'in the place of salvation' where he found himself, no longer feared the 'hatred of men' who acknowledged him as a 'great logician' and accepted the 'keenness of [his] mind', but where Bernard de Clairvaux suspected him of heresy. It would seem that by becoming a monk, he found a way of effacing the disastrous effect his mutilation had on his image. But when one is married, one can only enter holy orders if one's spouse also does so at the same time: Abelard obtained this (too!) from Heloise, who had absolutely no vocation for it. She herself agreed to take the veil on Abelard's orders, as Gilson says.

Thus the concrete existence of three people – let us not forget their son Astrolabe – was subjected to and shattered by a desire for glory and the construction of the persona of a genius: 'a passion for spiritual grandeur which never seems to have been entirely pure', writes Gilson. The origin of this pitiful tragedy lies in the idea – itself pitiful – that, since the 'science of philosophers' was not enough to generate admiration, those seeking admiration had to court it in ways other than through their works, on a stage where a scholar's greatness and state of perfection were made absolutely visible in that scholar's person by imaginary parameters (single life). Some philosophers are mad about something other than philosophy and thus simply mad.[18] One hesitates to write such things, which border on invective, but I cannot be content just to acknowledge, by contrast, the exemplary wisdom of Democritus who, when staying in Athens, remained incognito.[19] It is true that he thought that nothing existed but emptiness and atoms and that all the rest was nonsense, starting with glory.

The first correction to make to the concept of the 'Heloise complex' is thus the following: the self-sacrifice a woman agrees to in her veneration of a mentor is part of a wider configuration: the mentor is seeking general admiration (which is not commensurable with philosophical work) and wants not only to produce philosophy but also to be a philosopher. The second correction concerns Beauvoir. I think that, despite everything, she did produce philosophy. But she 'did not see herself' doing it and, when one reads what Sartre wrote about women, it is easier to understand why.

Being and Nothingness puts forward an image of philosophy coloured by masculinism: a power of the ego-philosopher whose megalomania is based on a contrast with, and then endangered by, something Sartre thinks of as 'feminine'. Where could the poor woman have placed herself in such an account? Neither on the side of the super-power, which transcends feminine bad faith, nor on that of the slimy In-itself. There is no place for a woman in such a system, and even less for a woman who produces philosophy; she cannot see herself in it and is permanently expelled from it as a figure of bad faith or as an undoer of the For-itself's conquests. She would have had to flee and find a place of reference somewhere else. There now! Is it this that gives rise to the question posed by many of my contemporaries: 'Are there some philosophies which are more appropriate than others to thinking about women's liberation?' Basically these women are looking for an ecological niche: a sector, any sector, of intellectual life in which a type of thought exists which allows them to place them-selves within it.

Simone de Beauvoir did not flee; all the same she saved her skin, at least partly. The Heloise complex seems not to be so crippling as I formerly meant it to appear. Can one escape it on the quiet and produce philosophy independently, on condition of course that one does not attempt to pose as a philosopher? Producing philosophy unawares? Clearly my thesis can lead imperceptibly to a strange position. Simone de Beauvoir and I could not talk about it. This was because the question I wanted to ask her was crazy. 'Simone de Beauvoir, do you think that you wrote philosophy unawares?' I did well to keep quiet. One scruples to force someone at all costs to say that they have accomplished something without realizing it. Of course, it is no lack of respect to suggest that philosophy never quite lets go of a woman who has studied it at an advanced level, at a time when this was not a common thing, and then taught it for several years, even after this woman, Simone de Beauvoir, had decided to leave the philosophy to Sartre as though there were room enough for only one, which indeed seems to have been the case. But the argu-ment turns back on itself: she had devoted enough time to philosophy to be able to decide for herself whether her work was philosophy or not. She knew my theory about *The Second Sex*: if she had wanted, she could have spoken out clearly against my reading or in its favour; she never did either and her silence, in which there was perhaps a slight touch of malice, could have meant either, 'Let me have produced philosophy unawares' (it was such a good compromise between her-self and Sartre) or simply: 'Sort it out for yourself.'

9   On philosophy and its history

If I must sort things out for myself, I shall begin with the ethics of
the trade: as I said, one scruples to try and reveal something that
was accomplished without its author being aware of it. But can we
require readers to see in a work only what the author thinks he or she
put into it? And to see this work exactly as the author thought they
should see it? Behind this simple question lies the double problem of
the status of philosophy and the history of philosophy and also that of
the relation between them.

Traditionally speaking, as we have already recalled, the specific
property of philosophical thought is regarded as being that it entirely
understands itself: it has no hidden content which might have
escaped the author. Philosophers are thus people who know absolutely what they are saying, and in this they take a firm stance as
'textual father'. The absolute transparency to themselves of what
they say guarantees the strict definition of the origins of their
thought: the latter does not rest on or arise from an unthought
(non-thought) which could be explored in order to elucidate what
they have said. In short, because what they say is founded on nothing
but itself, it is self-founding and thus a founding discourse.

This conception of philosophy has been disputed during the
twentieth century. The debate can be traced back at least as far
as the linguist Emile Benveniste. Benveniste tried to show that the
categories of Aristotelian logic corresponded to those of ordinary
Greek grammar.[20] His work gave a precise content to the idea of
an unthought element in philosophy. In his view what precedes
philosophical thought is natural language, from which philosophy
then arises; in other words it is because of this given that philosophical thought can exist. There followed a Quarrel between the Ancients
and the Moderns: some philosophers gave Benveniste's work a very
poor reception, while others poured their own predilections into it. If
one says that something ('X') precedes philosophy one can regard
this 'X' as the situation of class struggle at the time the philosopher
was writing: thus historical materialism took on the task of revealing
the concrete conditions that enabled the production of a given work.
The Freudians took 'X' as the unconscious and analysed fantasies
and repressed desires, so that philosophical texts acquired a status
analogous to that of dreams, slips or puns. As for the Nietzscheans,
they had every reason to feel triumphant because the idea of something 'anterior' to all philosophy can already be found in Nietzsche.
But this is where the Moderns rejoined the Ancients: since it is

philosophy which has understood that all philosophies arise from forces which pre-exist thought, should we not recognize once more that the challenge to philosophy comes from itself? If it is internal, it is a trick of philosophy; thus philosophy still entirely contains itself, including any challenges to it. The Derridians have made much of this detour which returns to the point of departure, with all the imaginable consequences for the defence of the pre-eminence of philosophy over all the other disciplines. The newest social sciences, they claimed, cannot possibly reveal hitherto unknown aspects of philosophical discourse, since they are only by-products of that discourse itself. Thus, discussing the question of a possible 'metaphorology' of philosophical texts, Derrida writes: 'It is impossible to dominate philosophical metaphorics as such, from the exterior, by using a concept of metaphor which remains a philosophical product. Only philosophy would seem to wield any authority over its own metaphorical productions.'[21]

Dominance, authority, once again this is exactly what is at stake. On the other hand, if there is an immense unthought element in philosophy, then clearly the history of philosophy, as a discipline, can adopt the task of reconnecting texts to the outside. This project suggests that the exegete understands a work better than its author, since the former knows both the work, its outside and what links it to its outside. If, on the other hand, a philosophical work understands itself, then the aim of the history of philosophy is to understand Plato's thought as well or almost as well as Plato did and, naturally, to explain it to the dear students, who need a bit of a hand. This idea of the history of philosophy goes hand in hand with a certainty that there are errors to be corrected: those of earlier interpreters or the ones that beginners cannot fail to make. Everyone knows the familiar portrait of Descartes which appears in almost all editions. According to Alain, the philosopher is looking humourously at anyone who is about to give an interpretation of his work and saying: 'Another one who's going to get it wrong!'. This anecdote contains the whole melancholic odyssey of the history of philosophy as an academic tradition: Decartes is looking at his commentator, not the other way round, and, if the commentator is clear-sighted, he or she will bow and say, 'I am not worthy to have a conversation with you, sir' (it is I who am continuing Alain's tale here). From this point of view, the history of philosophy is a relation to the sacred and an odyssey in the strict sense of the word, for it aims to return to the native land of truth. Sadly, in practice, and no matter how cunning we are, we must suffer the tribulations and wanderings of Ulysses.

10 Tertium addo

The alternative thus presented could be turned into a dilemma, since the two contradictory cases lead to the same conclusion that someone has a total knowledge, either the author or the commentator. But this alternative does not exhaust the whole range of possibilities and there is at least a third way of conceiving of philosophy and the history of philosophy: we can regard both as work, and thus as a dynamic, which can lead to and from each other. From this point of view, a philosophy is neither a monument nor an effect which is blind to its origins and thus in relation to itself, but an effort to shift thinking from one state to another. There is thus something upstream of it, for thought began before any philosophy, and downstream, for its work can be continued. The continuation may take the form of that discipline called 'history of philosophy'. The advantage of this perspective is, among other things, that it regards the history of philosophy as a philosophical activity.

Philosophy would then exist in the mode of that which has neither completion nor beginning, but is rather impulse and movement. It would also be interdisciplinary: if we accept the idea that philosophy does not launch itself, we can see it springing from anywhere, from science for example, through a perception of the fact that the way a science thinks encourages rethinking. And this has its symmetrical counterpoints: philosophical questions may also relaunch investigations in fields with different methodologies and modes of administering proof. We hope to do justice to Bergson in illustrating our case with the example of biology: between *L'Evolution créatrice* and Jean-Pierre Changeux's lectures at the Collège de France, via the work of Canguilhem and his students, almost a century of philosophy and biology in France was marked by this important interaction. We can also do justice to Bergson in remembering that Gilles Deleuze is one of his great readers and that, in Deleuze's work, the interaction between philosophy and the history of philosophy owes a great deal to the way that Bergson replaced the notion of philosophy as a monumental system with that of thinking-on-the-move and saw thought as something alive and ever-changing that emerges from a real which is there and then detaches itself from the place whence it arises, turns away or goes on a long detour, but may ultimately turn back towards the place it thinks it started from.[22] When Bergson says that contemplative thinkers 'are born detached', this is neither an apology for a flight from the world nor, conversely, a critique of conversion in the style of Plato or Plotinus, but the idea of a primal bursting which contains attachment and detachment: for life itself demands that we dissociate ourselves from that which carries us. We are perfectly within our rights to regard these words on 'life' as mythical, but we must then give them to status of a regulatory myth: thought is neither completely 'detached' nor completely 'attached', the two aspects mingle in spurting forth, which is also an activity.

By seeking a model of this type in Bergson, 'I am sorting things out for myself'. Indeed, if we adopt the conception of philosophical thought as something ever-changing, which started elsewhere in several places at once and is moving towards an elsewhere or else-wheres which cannot be foreseen, the boundary between what is 'philosophy' and what is not loses its clarity. This seems to me important for more than one reason. We have already indicated that in history many different forms of thought have laid claim to the name of 'philosophy', each in their own time; if we consider the past as a whole, it is almost impossible to ascribe a meaning to the word 'to philosophize'. With the model I am proposing, this ceases to be a problem and becomes on the contrary a sign that the dynamics of thought are getting themselves reorientated. We have also suggested that the fact of not accepting the inascribable nature of the philo-sophical could lead to a desire to make the invisible visible at all costs. This desire could have all sorts of unfortunate consequences, since one becomes more concerned with being 'seen as a philosopher' than with thinking something. 'In wanting to enclose a vast domain, one ends up by demolishing one's finances' said Democritus; the full meaning of these words merits contemplation. The enclosure of the field of philosophy could, in practice, lead to its greater exhaustion, from all points of view.

Let us imagine 'philosophy' cutting itself off from all the other disciplines; let us imagine that a particular philosophy decides that all the others, past and present, are counterfeits which should be thrown into the muddy ditch surrounding the true domain and lastly let us imagine that something stated by many exegetes in philosophy is taken seriously and applied, namely the idea that the only legiti-mate philosophical mode is that which is strictly theoretical, that which has been entirely thought through, so that the presence of images and little stories is something totally illegitimate. By strictly applying these hypotheses we should obtain not a pure form of philosophy, but a hollow one, with nothing to say, except, 'look, I am'. I have tried to show elsewhere that no thought can do without images, whatever some philosophers may think about the boundary between the rational and the imaginary. My de facto argument is that those who say that there are no myths in Kant must have skipped a good many pages. But the principle must be generalized: when work is in itself unbegun and incomplete, one must be connected to various spaces outside it, and thus to that which one has not entirely thought through; reciprocally, one cannot understand oneself through and through.

11 *Heterogeneous genesis*

To my way of thinking, the idea that a thought always begins elsewhere is of no interest unless that 'elsewhere' allows us to introduce a plurality: the specific effort of one thought would then be to constitute one coherence (approximate at least) from an initial diversity. Starting with this line of questioning, I can situate both Simone de Beauvoir's undertaking and my own work on *The Second Sex*. There are many things upstream of her thought: existentialism, values that existentialism could not predict and a great deal of other reading. In one sense my thinking is downstream of Simone de Beauvoir's work: it would not have been possible without the things that can be learned from reading *The Second Sex*, nor without many things I have learned elsewhere. This idea of polygenesis allows us definitively to rid ourselves of the blinding mode of the master–disciple relationship; there can be a master only when there is a single master. When, for the entry S. de Beauvoir, the Petit Larousse dictionary of times past put, 'Disciple of Jean-Paul Sartre', the wording seems fine but it is false. A master is necessarily a single master, we might say in a pastiche of Leibniz; once there is a plurality within the origin, the other's mastery fades away.

This also allows me to situate Beauvoir's work both as philosophy and as defying the boundaries of 'philosophy', following the example, moreover, of the most precious authors of times past. It is philosophy to the extent that she uses categories inherited from that tradition (which she reworks in doing so); but at the same time she works beyond its boundaries, trying to reach a reality beyond the dreams of philosophy, that of the concrete existence of women. When we return to what I call the most precious authors, we can see that they are precious because they too are not clearly circumscribed; some of them had one foot in philosophy and the other in the scientific world of their time, others worked on the border between philosophy and theology, others still tried to combine a philosophical inheritance with discussions of political conflicts which philosophy had not invented. All in all, the concern to define the 'strictly philosophical', this mania of always wanting to be able to state the 'great difference' between philosophy and everything else, is a modern one.

Reciprocally, such a conception allows me not to bow to what Simone de Beauvoir thought of her own work, without thus having to set myself up in the delusional position of the commentator who understands better than the author what the meaning of the latter's work is. What I have proposed is not an ultimate and retrospective elucidation of Simone's thought, but a reworking which begins partly with what she gives me to think about, but also draws on many other things, turning back towards that partial origin of my own set of problems. The perfect elucidation as dreamed of by the commentator-who-knows-best, would have to be exhaustive, total and totalising, so that there would no longer be any need to read Beauvoir, as the critique would be an improvement on the work. This is not the case; I have not exhausted the content of Simone's thought, and I only have to open one of her books at random to discover a little stretch of blue or yellow wall that I had never seen before. The same thing happens every time I go back to my study of Bacon; the same thing when I open Cicero or Descartes. I have never given myself entirely to any author and I possess no author entirely. In all of them I seek a little bit of support, without expecting that any will offer me the key to an ecological niche in which I could curl up and settle down.

The idea that all thought has a kind of polygenesis also allows us to return to a question raised in the first notebook. I mentioned a simple belief that in any theoretical enterprise some values are merely assumed and are not generated or checked by the reflexive or theoretical aspects of the work. *The Second Sex* starts from the collision of feminist values with intellectual models inappropriate to uphold those values and shows us all the more clearly exactly what a theoretical effort entails, when we appreciate the work that goes into holding these divergent 'data' together. The defininition of thought as an effort, or as work, acquires meaning in this hypothesis of polygenesis.

And since everyone else indulges in metaphor and the imaginary, I should like to offer an image: in the social system of kinship, children appear to be produced in a unilinear way. Even though we know that children are not just their fathers' progeny, the principle of patrilineal parenthood means that this knowledge is repressed at the symbolic level. And if the child must be absolutely 'the father's', then the mother must be closely watched, appropriated by her husband and reduced to no more than his continuation: a receptacle, a living incubator. Unilinarity in the social sphere is a problem for feminists. However, in seeking to shatter this reduction, there is no reason for us to stop at a recognition of bilinearity. Children are of course the children of their fathers, mothers and a whole family tree when one traces back through the generations; but, genetically speaking, they are also the fruit of infinite chance and continual micro-mutations and thus are not immediately tied to what is called the 'genetic inheritance'. In this sense, all children are unpredictable beings who are not strictly their parents' childen; then each enters into relations with other adults and other children, with institutions and a language which extend far beyond the progenitors. 'Are we just our parents' children?' wondered Descartes, who answered the question by referring to God. We can leave God alone and say that, as soon as unilinearity is challenged, multilinearity appears and all human beings have to face it and must indeed confront it to constitute themselves.

This should of course be understood as a metaphor: to constitute oneself as a quidam or quaedam who thinks for 'oneself', one has to let go of the idea of unilinearity in thought (the master whose disciple I am) and try to deal with polymorphous data, confident in the thought that in any case one is a unique and improbable creature, irreducible to one's multiple geneses and fundamentally the fruit of their chance entanglement. This gap in causality (everyone is a mutant) is the crack which establishes the divergence of all from each of their geneses. It matters little that the gap is only a hair's breadth, as tenuous as a clinamen; this minuscule difference is enough to constitute freedom, a densely inhabited freedom, with body, substance and the considerable power of a relation to all that produces us. I was born just about everywhere, under the now shattered sky of the Greeks, in a Brittany farmer's clogs, in an Elizabethan theatre, in my grandmothers' famines and destitution, and in the secular, compulsory and free schooling that the state was so good as to make available to me, but also in the rebellions that were mine alone, in the slaps that followed or preceded them, in Simone de Beauvoir's lucid distress and in Descartes' stove. And there is more to come.

12   Aristotle, the Ottoman prince

In Bacon's writings one repeatedly finds a fierce judgement of Aristotle, the 'scholars' dictator', who, 'as though he had been of the race of the Ottomans, thought he could not reign except the first thing he did he killed all his brethren'.[23] Bacon also often decribes him as a ruffian, a Vandal for knowledge, like Alexander, who ravaged the earth with his conquests. Aristotle wanted to dominate, to establish his authority, and not to seek the fragments of truth. Since he sought magisterial success and professorial pomp, he cites other philosophers and scholars only in order to refute them, never to think with them, says Bacon.

This idea deserves recognition insofar as it proposes an interpretation of hypertrophy of the power of denial in philosophy, which is here called murder of one's brothers: the aim is to reign alone, to establish oneself in the position of master, notably that of school master. In the eyes of the Elizabethan philosopher this attitude implies a kind of repressed recognition of brotherhood: the philosopher certainly has brothers, but it is precisely because they are his brothers that he thinks he has to murder them. If Bacon were alive today, he might say something similar about the attitude of the phenomenological current regarding the sciences and 'others' in general, including 'woman'.

In fact this current works to blur the kinship that still exists (along with differences) between various forms of thought and philosophy. We have already given a simple example which we shall now rapidly recall. According to the general introduction to a resolutely phenomenological series of books, philosophy 'can only continue in the face of an impasse, welcomed by it and pushing up against the unknown. It is only this that radically distinguishes philosophy from the sciences, which are located in being and sure of their method'.[24] It takes courage to talk about 'method' in the singular at the end of the twentieth century, and a method which means that the sciences are 'sure'. This imagined radical opposition between philosophy and sciences echoes Husserl's complaint that the different sciences have gradually become detached from the 'all-embracing', metaphysical project of 'universal philosophy'; they have separated from each other and have each built up their own autonomy on a model which Husserl at first calls 'positive'. But the vocabulary soon shifts: these 'simple factual sciences' are then taxed with being 'positivist'. They appear as devoid of meaning, a view Husserl upholds in two ways. First he says, 'This science has nothing to say to us. It excludes in principle precisely the questions which man, given over in our unhappy times to the most portentous upheavals, finds the most burning: questions of the meaning or meaninglessness of the whole of this human existence.'[25] Then, a few pages later, one reads this: 'It is surely enough in the inseparable unity of philosophy that the factual sciences possessed the relative meaning they had, in other words their meaning as truths for simple territories of being'.[26]

The second argument renders the first frankly suspect. Has Husserl first won the reader's agreement with a rhetoric of pathos – Newton has nothing to tell us about war, death or the smothering of passion – only surreptitiously to slip an 'imperialist' content into the agreement thus obtained: the problem stems entirely from the fact that the provinces have emancipated themselves from the 'universal philosophy'? It is not difficult to find equivalents of this type of reasoning in relation to women who are emancipating themselves.[27]

This point of view seems to me not only imperialist, but quite simply false. Against it one can argue that the autonomy of the different sciences obeys a principle of diversification or pluralization of thought which we have no reason to regard as catastrophic. Why should a unified thought have something to say about the burning questions of an unhappy time? A unified knowledge has nothing precise to say about anything. Moreover one wonders when this fine totality, nostalgically evoked here, ever existed, since complaints about the dispersal of disciplines go back at least as far as Cicero. But since we are dealing here with value, we could, contrary to the phenomenologists, regard the differentiation and growing complexity of the intellectual adventure as a wonderful thing. And we could dialectically recognize also that it is true that the sciences are dispersed only if we look at them from the point of view of their results or accomplishments; it is far less true if we look at them in the light of their incompleteness, the way that they pinpoint (through a complex process) what is still unknown, or the way they incorporate what has just been successfully understood, against all expectations.

As I am not Pico della Mirandola, I shall not boast of having direct experience of all scientific practices. A contingent and highly absurd political event led me to rub shoulders for more than two years with young researchers from all disciplines, all of us victims of a ministerial comedy beyond anything that would be condemned as an unlikely fiction if it were acted out on stage.[28] For once, biologists, mathematicians, anthropologists, physicists and a philosopher saw a great deal of each other. Because they were researchers, my friends in misfortune were placed at the exact point where their branch's 'knowledge' enters a process of self-destabilization. We had a common relation to the crucial difficulty, that which is problematic in the latest state of a question. Our disciplines were certainly different, but our intellectual subjectivity was noticeably identical.

The contrast between the 'impasse' which is supposedly the preserve of philosophers, and the 'sciences sure in their method' is completely false, except in classical mechanics and 'critical criticism' as both are taught in schools. Of course, if some thought it easy to discuss a given question because there was a good theory available enabling them to explain absolutely what they wished to explain, if they put simple confidence in these extant methods and in the fact that explanatory schemas and 'theoretical positions' abound, this would indeed provide philosophy with a very different 'other', if we see philosophy as a lover's search which is never satisfied. And this would come down to assuming that there are no lacks, nothing is missing, and that we can comfortably install ourselves in a system of references and a certain knowledge. Such a cosy certainty does not exist (except, perhaps, in science teaching in schools), a sense of the unknown remains common to philosophy and the other forms of investigative thought. Reciprocally, the 'impasse' has never in itself constituted a mode of thought, even a philosophical one. The taste for that which has not yet been thought should not be confused with an impasse, and in any case, in order to pose a problem (in whatever field), there are always many things it is better to know.

When critical enquiry is informed and knowledge is problematized, they come together. Unfortunately I cannot go deeper into this idea: it is only as an informed amateur that I can follow what is said at a conference on astrophysics where impasses are explored, such as those in the theory on the formation of the galaxies; it is only by hearsay that I know that a central problem in biology or physics is liable to be reworked, not because there is some new data, but because intellectual perceptions of it can be modified by new thought, so that a problem of this type can be a subject for debates on orientation. However we need to recognize that in such cases philosophical reasoning is in action, away from the books, teaching or seminars which are duly labelled philosophical, as soon as people get to grips with the fringe of unknowing which borders every field of knowledge and overflows from it. The inappropriateness we uncovered in Simone de Beauvoir's work is not specific to the position of a feminist woman philosopher. This characteristic applies to all investigators who ask questions in the context of theories that already exist (who do not play the part of the *tabula rasa*) and thus commit themselves to an adventure which is, of course, their own but which integrates and acknowledges other people's earlier efforts. If formidable questions arise against a wide background of acquired understandings, anyone who takes on the task of enquiring and rethinking cannot adopt an attitude of intellectual solipsism: the predecessors are there and cannot purely and simply be strangled. They are components of what constitutes the very thing that enables me to detach myself from them. However, someone undertaking to reorientate thought is not in a comfortable position either, since this project is not one of managing an acquired capital of sure and nicely arranged references or a good store of legitimate and recognizable capabilities.

Discomfort. We indicated at the very beginning of this book how difficult it is to speak when one is a woman, a philosopher and a feminist. But is this difficulty any different from a far more widespread precariousness, a difficulty occurring in many other situations of theoretical work and which constitutes philosophy pure and simple? The problem of difficulty creates a gap between Simone de Beauvoir and Sartre. She experienced contradiction; she had to play the part of derived subjectivity, make herself the echo of her master's voice to preserve Sartre's interest in her as a lover. She was torn between her project as a speculative thinker and her love-life, between the nature of her enterprise and what she was in other people's eyes, which stopped her from establishing herself as someone taking on that kind of project. Not to mention the gap between the theory she received and the values that she wished to promote.

Sartre, on the other hand, appears to have found no difficulty being a philosopher, finding from the outset a harmony between his work and his social being, that is, his image and status combined. We cannot say that this led him to produce very good philosophy, nothing we have referred to here invites us to place his work in that category. However we have not referred to all of it and the question of the value of Sartre's work can be left hanging. For, whatever the case, we have still to see that for this phenomenologist man being a philosopher without difficulty went hand in hand with a solipsism established by destroying others. I should like to return once more to Sartre's everyday relations with Beauvoir and a few others, bearing in mind Bacon's picturesque judgement of Aristotle. Is killing all the others in order to reign alone a unique event in the history of philosophy? In the most banal incidents of Saint-Germain-des-Prés, we can hear the rumblings of a fearsome repetition of this philosophical attitude. (From there it is a small step, and one which I shall accept responsibility for taking, to the view that, just as the slaughter carried out by Aristotle founded the 'Philosophy of the School', so phenomenology makes possible the foundation of a new scholasticism.)

13   Letters to the Beaver: continuity and discontinuity

The twentieth century will certainly have been kept informed of the story of relations between those two. In 1983, two volumes of *Lettres au Castor et à quelques autres* were added to the thousands of pages of Simone's memoirs (in which she frequently makes herself the great man's bard), to several films, to *La Cérémonie des adieux* and associated interviews, not to mention some passages of the *Carnets de la drôle de guerre or*, the autobiographical basis of *She Came to Stay* and even some allusions in *Words*. In view of their idea of testimony, Sartre and Simone de Beauvoir chose to acknowledge their smallest deeds and gestures in public, thus inviting people to give the most banal ups and downs of their lives a meaning applicable to humanity as a whole. And, as a number of people saw this couple as a model of liberation, the phenomenon should be analysed as required by the two protagonists themselves and their doctrine. When one fully assumes a choice, one presents it as exemplary: one presents it and publishes it as an example to all others.

All the same, the letters do not strictly constitute an addition to all the rest, if we are to judge by the collective reaction that followed their publication. They caused a shock, as though the love story of Sartre and Simone de Beauvoir, particularly in the latter's memoirs, had until then been portrayed in an over-sympathetic light. Retroactively, because they appear as unprocessed documents, these letters give the memoirs the status of an official version. One might form the impression that we were long fooled by this version and that, now that we have been undeceived, we can see what lay underneath this model of a successful synthesis of freedom and love which we had until now been offered, and precisely as a model.

Some elements in the letters encourage such bitterness, if only the earliest note preserved from Sartre to Simone de Beauvoir: 'Charming little Beaver, would you be so good as to give my washing (bottom drawer of the wardrobe) to the laundress this morning? I've left the key in the door. I love you dearly, my love', etc. Right, 'My love and dirty socks to you': such a love-letter cannot fail to arouse a certain degree of feeling in circles closely or distantly influenced by feminism and where people thought until they read it that the mode of relations between Simone de Beauvoir and Sartre was different from that of a marriage. Let us acknowledge Simone de Beauvoir's courage (in publishing this letter in 1983 she must certainly have known that it would be said that she had been taken in), but take note of the lesson: it is always important to subject any discourse, whether it rhymes love with liberty or adopts the religious tones of eternal feasting, to a trivial question: and who, in this tale, is responsible for the laundry? All the rest is ideology, be it elegies on the emotional warmth of home or the metaphysics of the meeting of two transcendences among the existentialists.

These *Lettres au castor et à quelques autres* are in any case invaluable for a rereading of Simone de Beauvoir's memoirs, in other words to identify what is not said, the silences, the blanks in these narratives, or further to ask oneself in what sense Beauvoir can ultimately be regarded as the author of these memoirs whose scribe she was. Are they *her* memoirs when she discusses her relationship with Sartre? Is it her point of view and her subjectivity which are expressed there? It will be said perhaps that here I am using an outdated conception of writing, as if texts, and particularly memoirs, should or could 'express the personal point of view' of their authors. But although the relationship of subjects to their (own) words does indeed pose complex problems, a relationship of control exerted by someone else over words is far easier to describe. Nothing is more false than John of Salisbury's remark: 'Who can claim to have power over another person's tongue when it is so hard to find anyone who can master their own?' And we should regard as scholasticism any procedure which takes the fact that the relation between subjects and their own language is problematic as a reason to forbid analysis of the dominance exerted over what somebody says by another person or by an institution.

We could moreover maintain that the philosophical problem of our time is the lack of correspondence between what calls itself avant-garde or modern in theoretical work and the progressive aims of practical action. Modern suspicion has deprived us of a language which would make it possible to give at least an approximate articulation of these aims; but, as they have to be articulated anyway, we have seen inverted commas springing up everywhere and our educated contemporaries talk about 'rights', 'subjects', 'free choice', 'humanity' and so on. One can withdraw from this contradiction, as Barthes did in 1956, by taking the political mickey out of the avant-garde.[29] One can also, as I am doing here, try to make at least some distinctions or, better still, to turn suspicion on to itself. But the philosopher of this end of the century would be the one who managed radically to resolve the contradiction between the loss of language among the learned and our need to articulate urgent problems with people other than academics.

Sartre's letters draw attention to certain aspects of Simone de Beauvoir's memoirs, to elements which were certainly always there, but were seldom noticed. To fragile signs which allow us to regard these memoirs as censored, or self-censored, it matters little. Here is an example: the first volume of Sartre's correspondance opens with a collection of love letters addressed to Simone Jolivet; then we come to the heading '1929', where we find the note quoted above and a remark by Simone de Beauvoir: 'The letters Sartre wrote me during the summer of 1929 have been lost.' What a coincidence! Let us remember that the summer of 1929 was not only the crucial moment when their relationship began, but also the exact period that elapsed between the last page of the *Memoirs of a Dutiful Daughter* and the first page of *The Prime of Life*.

At the end of *Memoirs of a Dutiful Daughter*, they are taking the *agrégation* and drinking cocktails. It is summer time and 'when I left him at the beginning of August, I knew that he would never go out of my life'.[30] *The Prime of Life* begins at the start of the following term and there has been a change, which is glossed over by the apparent continuity of the narrative. They are still drinking cocktails, but Simone de Beauvoir describes them as a 'novice couple'; the rules of the game are more or less set between them. Of course, some brief flashbacks evoke the summer and the way in which these rules were established: through Sartre's 'little phrases' describing the type of relationship they were to have. 'What we have,' he said, 'is an essential love; but it is a good idea for us also to experience contingent love affairs', 'let's sign a two-year lease' and so on. Sartre no longer uses 'you' and 'I', but 'we', and he unfolds the canvas on which their story will be played out in advance.[31] The crucial moment when the mode of their relationship was (perhaps) discussed has been left out of the narrative; we shall never know if there was any argument, if the 'morganatic marriage' they contracted was a compromise between two contradictory projects, or exactly what they both wanted, or Sartre's will imposed on Simone de Beauvoir. The always difficult transition by which 'you' and 'I' become 'we' is left out by the way that Simone de Beauvoir's memoirs are divided into volumes. It has often been said of the moment when the pact is made in *The Social Contract* that it is almost impossible to make out the transition between the time when individuals are separate beings and that when they have come together as a collective whole. Here the difficulty seems to have been avoided, but perhaps it is not of the same order. Perhaps an 'I' becomes a 'we' through the annexation of a 'you' who is thus reduced to silence. Simone de Beauvoir will never tell us how she projected their relationship in the future, before it became fixed. The letters Sartre sent her during the summer of 1929 might in no way have altered the image given to us by the memoirs, where she simply records what Sartre said at the time. However by losing them, at the least she reinforces her silence: these letters might well have contained comments on what she herself was saying at the time.

In the *Lettres au castor et à quelques autres*, we find long pages where the author, a certain Jean-Paul Sartre, teacher of philosophy, gives a blow-by-blow account of his unappetizing café meals in Laon or his rounds of the cafés of Montparnasse, 'and with Poupette I took a taxi because it was raining': day-to-day froth, the flattest accounts of immediate experience. But there are also some remarkable passages (where Sartre, who always knew he was a good cheat, plays at being an author of epistles, as others play at being café waiters?) for example on the pure time of boredom, which must be sipped from a teaspoon like codliver oil, or the letter to Olga, written from Naples, a very carefully composed letter in which something of essential importance for all the letters is articulated. Something of essential importance also for the subject that concerns us.

In the streets of Naples in 1936, Sartre discovers work confused with private life and this horrifies him. Neapolitans, he writes, live in all-purpose rooms on the ground floor: they sleep, eat and work there. But these rooms overflow on to the street, people put their chairs on the doorstep, half inside, half outside, so that there is no longer any inside or outside.

> The outside connects to the inside in an organic way, it reminds me of a somewhat bloody mucous membrane which has protruded and is doing all its little gestations outside. When I was working for the PCN,[32] I read that starfish 'devaginate their stomachs', in other words they push them out and digest outside their bodies. That horrified me.[33]

The inside outside and the obscene proximity of an anvil and a nightshirt.

Disgust for women's genitals, breasts and so-called women's attitudes is expresses in Sartre's writing and thus in his professional life. 'Organic obscenity', 'devagination', 'immodest rooms', 'Naples' belly is everywhere', 'gestations': as this letter reveals, the everyday and indeed holiday images through which Monsieur Sartre expresses himself are in harmony with the imaginary productions employed in his philosophical work. But the 'Neapolitan' situation also reproduces this continuity of work and private life in miniature: if Sartre was as much fascinated as horrified, it is probably because there he encountered, as in a mirror, that which precisely was to make him Sartre. For, without deliberately seeing inside and outside as continuous, how could one think that the great categories of the necessary and the contingent, freedom and bad faith make their mark in the choices of so-called private life? In Naples in 1936, Sartre was revolted by that which he was to affirm in *Existentialism and Humanism* (when I get married, I commit all humanity to the monogamous path), and in various passages of *Situations*. And with the publication of the letters, it is Sartre's life, Simone de Beauvoir's and those of dozens of other people that become Neapolitan and thus 'open on to the street'.

As a result, the problem of the value of continuity between ordinary life and one's work is squarely posed. If, in practice, we say: 'it is possible for a man philosopher to be the same in his daily life as in his philosophical work', what exactly do we mean? That this is a good thing? And that, symmetrically, it is a pity that this is less easy for a woman in the present state of things? A woman is never recognized as both woman and philosopher at the same moment. Some other time we shall give samples of theories maintaining that a woman who thinks or speaks always feels split and which strongly invite women to cease thinking, describing this split as an appalling tragedy. But, supposing that this is how things are, how is it that when Sartre encounters an image of non-division, of continuity between private existence and public activity, first of all he hates it (so is this not a pleasing image of his position as a man-philosopher?) and then metaphors of the female body persistently occur in his writing. Continuity, immanence, the relationship between inside and outside, are these things perhaps the feminine par excellence? Can my reader still make anything out of this? I'm completely lost. But wait, the overall meaning is becoming clearer: whatever the case, women or the 'feminine', they are both wrong. Women (or the feminine) are wrong, the proof being that they are split, and continuity, which is feminine, is obscene. Anyone who found any logic in all this would have grounds for talking about 'masculine logic' and for slipping from there to the idea that all logic is masculine! It would be better to agree that it is more fundamental to see things in terms of value than of theory. The latter sometimes goes off the rails and may uphold A and non-A at the same time. But the apportionment of values does not suffer these accidents or random effects. Women are like this and it is a bad thing; women are like non-this and it is a bad thing.

So, after all that, are we now in our turn going to debate the value of continuity between life and thought? Or reject this issue in its entirety? Before deciding, it would be a good idea to give greater consideration to the example which is liberally spread before us. 'The finest thing I have seen as regards the mixing of work with private life, was an empty room, last night.'[34] This sentence seems enigmatic – from mixing to emptiness – but, when everything is mixed together, how indeed could one not dream of an empty room? Besides, one feels a longing for solitude, for emptiness if necessary, running through this account of a life overburdened with acquaintance, 'people are eating me up, good Beaver'. The boat that takes him to the Cap Nord is, says Sartre, transporting 'a desert island, which is me'.[35] But this need is not truly insistent in the letters, no doubt because it is metamorphosed into a positive cathexis of distance. How Sartre loves the Beaver or Simone Jolivet for being so far away! And how he despises 'these pigs of couples who dare to sleep in the same bed!'[36] The distance at which he holds the person he is writing to is all he needs to constitute himself as a nucleus of solitude in the café La Coupole or in a station foyer. To be a 'room of his own', all by himself, anywhere.

On the other hand it is not so easy to see where the mixing of work and private life comes into this correspondence. It is not where one would expect it, at least if one has in mind the coded genre of the philosophical letter: Descartes writing to Elisabeth or, in Rousseau's fiction, Julie writing to Saint-Preux. It is not until around 1939 that the correspondence starts to contain philosophical discussions: in the preceding years Sartre seems to comment on his passions and projects just like anyone else, to the point where one catches oneself thinking that if one did not already know that it is Sartre who is giving us all the minute details of his travels, one would soon have had enough of them.

14   The only speaking subject

And yet, even in the gossip of the first thirteen years of this correspondence, something of the writer's position shows through, and not only in the compulsion to write, to try and write everything down to the point of impossibility: 'It is decidedly impossible both to live a little and to recount what one experiences. Imagine, I have already written four pages, I have all of today to tell you about, and it is already ten past seven'.[37] Something else, and something rather unpleasant to boot, is taking shape in these letters, showing us the writer becoming the true author of his private life, namely the way in which Sartre is establishing himself here as the only speaking subject and as master of the circulation of what is said.

He writes to Tania, to Simone Jolivet, to Simone de Beauvoir or to Paulhan. He writes to Simone de Beauvoir that he is writing to Tania, to Simone Jolivet or to Paulhan; he copies out passages from these letters. He reads letters he has received from Simone de Beauvoir to Guille and Poupette (Hélène de Beauvoir); he passes Tania's, Gégé's or Lionel de Roulet's letters on to Simone de Beauvoir and he even sends her a card written by Merleau-Ponty to Martine Bourdin, which the latter has given to him. He tells personal stories: one day he has a pathetic scene with Martine Bourdin, he gives 'Mme Morel a good laugh telling her the whole story', then he writes to Simone de Beauvoir that he gave Mme Morel a good laugh, and so on.

Does all this point to a radical subversion of the intimate, justifying the later publication of these letters? 'I thought to myself that those letters might be published... I had an idea that they might be published after my death', said Sartre in 1974 and Simone de Beauvoir, in the preface to the letters, recalls this and remarks: 'By giving this correspondence over to the public I am simply fulfilling one of his wishes.' But is it established in the letters themselves that the private can always be circulated? Not quite: in order for it to come to the attention of a third party, the intimate must be judged so by Sartre. Of the correspondence he receives, he passes on what he wants, and only what he wants, to whom he wants. He recounts his life and that of those close to him, but on the express condition that he keep a novelist's control over the narrative. On no account can anyone else take the initiative of reading a letter from, say Sartre, to a third party. Everything has to go through him, otherwise he would not be the author of this strange story of human relations. It is a story consisting of words rather than deeds, but in it what one says is supposed to be a kind of act producing effects which, when something is put particularly well, have force and constitute an event in subjectivity. Sartre moreover never assumes that a letter can have any effect other than the one he intends: 'Although short, my letter will please you.' He writes to Simone de Beauvoir that he is going to write to this or that person, noting the tone ('I shall give him a friendly

answer') and what will result from it. The idea of such control over
the effect produced by a text is doubtless among the illusions necessary to any writer's work. But in the case of a letter with a supposedly
single addressee, things should be different. Sartre never seems to
have experienced the fact that every message is an adventure.

If to say something is to produce an effect, to say to someone that a
third person has said this or that is to transmit an effect while at the
same time redefining it. Thus Sartre creates a whole series of microscopic events, but these events are certainly not a cloud of particles
moving at random in many different directions or according to
unpredictable collisions. For he keeps himself firmly planted at the
centre. Each letter and each meeting creates a one-to-one relationship
in which a world supervised and orchestrated by him is established.
He then brings this world into contact with the other micro-worlds of
his other one-to-one relations. As a result, each of the friends to
whom he writes, whose lives are commented on or whose letters are
passed on to other people, becomes like a character in a novel written
by him. 'Once one is incorporated into your world, one can no longer
get out of it', complains one of them rebelliously. Sartre, recounting
this anecdote to Simone de Beauvoir, comments: 'Ultimately it's just
as I said [. . .] He doesn't want to be involved in our stories any
more.' No doubt the term 'stories' should be given its full and precise
meaning of 'narrative construction' here: Sartre constructs his relations with other people like a novel and with each other person like a
scene or episode of a serial. He also wants to construct the different
elements of his being; 'I want to talk about the case of a necessary
Jean-Paul Sartre who would be to my impressions and my feelings
what Spinoza's attribute is to the modes it underlies'.[38] Let us recall
that the attributes Spinoza speaks of are attributes of God, a unique
substance. We can link the idea of a necessary Sartre to Nietzsche's
words: 'Nothing will happen to you but what you are.' However such
an idea precisely assumes that nothing happens, since there are no
relationships with other people or even with things.

On the other hand, if one of the correspondents sent one of Sartre's
letters to someone else, the event that this letter represented would
change its meaning. Everything would slip from Sartre's control and
he does not like that one little bit. In February 1940, it happened that
Martine Bourdin, with whom he had had a brief affair two years
previously, spoke of that affair to Tania and showed Mouloudji the
letters that Sartre had written at the time. Sartre hears of this and he
really blows his top. He is so furious that he sends an 'open letter'
to Bourdin, as we know notably from a passage from a letter

to Beauvoir: 'I am sending an open letter to Bourdin which Tania is to post and in this letter I tell Bourdin the story of Bourdin as it really was.'[39]

The next fifty pages of the *Lettres au castor et à quelques autres* have shocked more than one critic and more than one reader by their bad taste, as have the letters of eighteen months earlier, in which Sartre recounts his nights with the said Martine Bourdin to Simone de Beauvoir. I see in this something more serious than bad taste: Sartre does not realize that what Bourdin has just done (told the story, passed on the letters) is exactly what he himself has always done and is doing once more at the very moment when he describes Martine Bourdin's indiscretion as 'vulgar'. Not only does he send his poisonous letter through the intermediary of Tania (in order, he says, to calm her down in passing), he gives a copy of it to Beauvoir, which means that today we have it too. Sartre thus gives himself the right to pass on what he likes to whom he likes and the right to render the private relatively public, but he does not acknowledge that others have this right: 'That woman who undresses her doings in front of anyone, it's like incontinence', 'she is dirty enough to go into the details of our sex-life'.[40] His is a right to speech which, because it is a monopoly, renders his speech itself execrable.

Given the nature of what is said, we might be seriously tempted to hold this 'right' up as an example of something we have no reason to 'demand'. But the problem is infinitely complicated. Let us make it clear first of all that the term 'right' here of course does not relate to a strictly legal situation, but to a psychological, and thus social, position which an individual adopts in daily life: one considers that one has, or does not have, the right to do something and this issue arises every day, in the least relations between human beings. All situations of power, intimidation or submission involve an intersubjective dissymmetry where one person 'considers they have the right to do something' and the other does not, the former usually reinforcing the latter in non-recognition of the right. It is this dissymmetry, produced by a relation of dominance, which creates impudence and bad taste. What Sartre says when he recounts his 'sex-life' is utterly sickening not because it concerns his erotic life (we can imagine fine confidences addressed to a third person), nor because he displays eccentric attitudes in this area (is that directly our business?) but because he awards himself a monopoly on the right to tell. He speaks for other people, as though they were not other people and thus liable to speak themselves, establishing them as not-speaking and thus as abject. In other words, the details he picks up when remembering a

night, and possibly his very way of making love, is not unconnected
to the fact that he denies the other person the right to speak. And
more generally, it could be said that when someone considers that
they themselves have a right they deny to other people, even if it is a
right to something good (like speech), the very fact transforms the
thing itself, rendering it obnoxious.

At this point it should be said I have been considerably surprised
by the rather puritanical commentaries critics have given on this
passage in the *Lettres au castor*. They no doubt reflect a common or
bourgeois view, according to which it is of course the sexual aspects
of the relationship with Martine Bourdin, and then of the conflict with
her, that are shocking. From my point of view, only question of the
legitimacy of speaking is of concern here and one could (should)
disregard the fact that it is a sexual liaison which is being discussed,
the better to grasp Sartre's immorality in this business. For it is
eminently questionable to criticize anyone's mores directly. The
sphere where morality and immorality acquire meaning is that of
relations between people and their subjectivities. When I say that
Sartre sets himself up as the 'only speaking subject', my aim is to
formulate a moral critique which directly concerns not the structure
of his erotic life, but his relations with other people in general. Of
course what is called intersubjectivity (perverse or not) also fully
affects sexuality, or at least what emerges of sexuality in a relationship. Thus it is possible to have an ethical viewpoint on sexual
relations as well, without this being strictly a viewpoint on 'objective'
mores.

I should like to stress this point: a first version of this essay was
given as a conference paper at the university of London. My audience
were astounded that I did not raise the question of the respective
values of monogamy and 'polygamy', of multiple relationships and
fidelity. This is a common experience: one tries to develop a complex
way of posing problems and one is brutally dragged back into frivo-
lous debates. The question of the respective values of monogamy and
diversity seems to me utterly trivial, since oppressive intersubjective
relations, much boredom and very little love may exist in either case.
The choice between fidelity and multiple relationships can be seen as
a simple matter of preference, individual whim or temperament. This
can be given a philosophical formulation using the good old Socratic
method: there is oppression in some monogamous relationships; there
is oppression in more diversified lifestyles; oppression is a bad thing;
thus what makes a relationship good or bad is not the fact that it is
exclusive or allows for multiplicity but something else, which we still

have to discover. It is also possible to approach the problem from the other direction, this time with the Stoics: some things are morally good, others are morally bad and yet others are indifferent. Having an odd or even number of hairs on one's head is the paradigm of absolutely indifferent things. The strength of philosophy, if it has one – what makes it able to bring joy and affirmative strength – is that it can postulate that many things generally considered good or bad are in fact morally indifferent; we can thus feel free in relation to them, ignore them and concern ourselves with other things. The Stoics went a long way down this path, since some of them maintained that a greater or lesser length of life was one of the indifferent things, even though it was everyone's duty to take care of themselves. We should take from them at least the idea that the more we put things into the 'indifferent' category, the freer or less involved we feel and thus available for the important things. If we stopped adopting polarized positions with regard to sexual morality, we could at last concern ourselves with what matters.

Sartre's immorality is thus that he denies other people a right which he has always granted himself. Formally speaking, this attitude destroys the very principle of all ethics.[41] The puritanical commentaries which appeared on the publication of the *Lettres* shocked me because they disputed everything except this point, considering, like Sartre, that someone like Sartre 'had the right' to set himself up in such a dissymmetrical position. They ignored the fact that no morality is possible without at least the principle of reciprocity, without mutual recognition, and that everything else flows from this, or is indifferent.

In reducing other people to silence so that he could be the only one to speak, Sartre was both unjust and violent. We could also say he was immoral even in his repentence, immoral squared, for he ultimately criticized himself not for this injustice, but for his sexual habits and for having had 'sordid little affairs'. It is rather comical to see him promising to reform, to stop being a 'bastard', to apply the maxim: 'One should only do what one is able to assume' – and the existentialist meaning of the word 'to assume' is already there – in relation to a situation in which he is shamed by a scandal that would also make any conformist blush. So is the redefinition of values by philosophy sometimes just a long trip that leads back to where it started?

Sartre also denies other people the capacity to speak the truth: 'I tell Bourdin the story of Bourdin as it really was', he writes to Simone de Beauvoir,[42] and to Martine Bourdin: 'So this is how you must tell the story. Also the last time you wrote to me saying, "Why do you think I am vile?" Well now you know: because you tell obscene, unworthy and invented tales'.[43] The letter opened with the words: 'Do not go shouting our story from the rooftops in a revised version. Your indiscretion, which has come to my ears, obliges me to tell you what I think of our affair, so that if you can't help telling it, you can at least tell it properly.' But Sartre the master of truth is also Sartre the master of illusion, for in the same letter he mentions what he wrote to Martine Bourdin during the time of their affair: 'My letters, which were exercises in love literature and which gave the Beaver and me a good laugh, did not entirely fool you at the time. Deep down you knew that I did not love you.' He is thus the only one who can invent what he says, with the aim of fooling someone else, because instead of being what it is supposed to be – a personal letter from a particular man to a particular woman – the text is a schoolboy exercise in lover's discourse, sent to a woman whom he did not even like. He tells Martine Bourdin to relate their story 'properly'. But to tell their story 'properly' is to say that it never happened, which is literature indeed.

A portrait of the lover as a literary tyrant: if this approach to reading makes sense of all the details provided by the correspondence, we can say that the mixing of personal life and work is perfect, in Sartre's Montparnasse as in Naples. And of course, when he chooses to copy out a particular passage from a letter he has received, it is as though he were the author of an epistolary novel who thought it right that the imaginary character X or Y should write that letter. Hence the pertinence of Tania's request: 'Yesterday evening, at a point when we were happy together, she did her best to get me to say that I would not tell you what she was going to tell me [...] I put on a crestfallen air and ended up by promising.'[44] That was indeed the only way to ask Sartre for love, in other words to ask him to recognize the other as a real person, thus limiting the despotism of his fantasy. He was somewhat distressed by this vow of silence and later on did all he could to reprocess the event (as he reprocessed the war in the autumn of 1939, finally saying it was his war); but he did not quite succeed and began to be afraid of Tania, whom he suspected of being nosey: 'I got your two notes,' he wrote to Simone de Beauvoir, 'I quickly tore them up, I tore them all up, including the ones you wanted me to keep.'

As I see it, this assertion of control over the circulation of what is said makes irrelevant the regret expressed by many that this correspondence is truncated because the replies are not given. Simone de

Beauvoir has been criticized for not publishing her own letters at the same time. Of course we should like to know how Simone de Beauvoir really reacted on particular occasions, instead of only guessing from Sartre's remarks, which, necessarily, interpret, reformulate or retranslate. But this regret is pointless.[45] If Sartre wanted to be the only speaking subject to give testimony on his life, the absence of answers was necessary so that the whole collection of letters should ultimately constitute a text.[46]

Since Sartre behaved as a literary tyrant in relation to Martine Bourdin, there is no reason not to assume that he behaved in a similar way with Simone de Beauvoir. There is even one detail which seems to prove that he did: the letter written in Naples from Sartre to Olga in 1936 may have a familiar ring to some readers. Anamnesis on their part: the end of the first volume of *The Prime of Life* is a resumé of this letter. In 1960, when Simone de Beauvoir wrote this volume of her memoirs, (*her* memoirs? her *memoirs?*) she clearly had a copy of it in front of her and one looks in vain in *The Prime of Life* for any inflexion, detail or tone which would show that she had gone through some process of personally reformulating the text. The only difference seems to be the mark of the passing of time: in 1936 Sartre emphasized disgust, while noting the fascination that the confusion of inside and outside exerted on him. In 1960 Beauvoir writes: 'Humanity stands revealed in its organic nakedness and visceral heat: it was this aspect of life here which dazed, disgusted and bewitched us. [...] We were pleased to find that poverty had broken down all barriers; the words 'inside' and 'outside' had lost all meaning.'[47] She places a greater emphasis on fascination, but this is 1960 and the existentialist critique of so-called intimacy 'behind the wall of private life' has been developed. We shall now always have a doubt: when Simone de Beauvoir wrote about her relationship with Sartre, did she also tell the story 'as it should be told'? And what should we think about the following detail from one of Sartre's letters in 1939: 'When I come back on leave, *together* we shall write your journal and my notebook, in the evenings before we go to bed.'[48]

This is an intermixture of work and private life, insofar as Sartre's work was that of a writer. But there is also a congruence of his personal position and his philosophical theory. In this regard, one letter from December 1939 is irreplaceable: it provides the best possible resumé of Sartre's philosophy, and it enables us to understand what was lacking both in the philosophy and in the man: '(Today) I have been busy with various things [...] among which I have completed my ethics.'[49] And he goes on to expound it. First he wonders which beings are concerned by morality, answering that these are beings 'who are their own possibilities', neither angel nor beast, but Man, man in general or generic Man. This is in itself unsurprising, since humanism has been a basis for ethics for a good four hundred years. But what is specifically Sartrian in the new brand of humanism provided here is that 'Man', abstract Man or Man in general, is the sole reference point or principle.

For humanism as a basis for ethics usually takes account of (at least) two principles: the idea of humanity as a general and generic horizon and the idea that this humanity is dispersed and scattered in a great number of individuals, each being, at least potentially, the full essence of humanity. Among these individuals there is one that is me and I become human in the strict sense of the word by recognizing the fact that every person around me and I myself are humanity in itself. Without these two principles or theoretical dimensions, that of generality ('humankind') and that of dispersal (humankind is scattered in persons) it seems to me impossible to understand the major works of the humanist tradition. The principle of dispersal is very important because it makes it possible to formulate the idea that there is morality when I become human by acknowledging you as a human being. If it is to have a meaning, the category of 'other people', must be seen as derived from this principle of the multiplicity of people, each of whom is all of humanity. In this multitude, there is one who happens to be me, in relation to whom the others are Others and each of these others is another, any other, referred to in French by the single term *autriui*, meaning 'someone who is not me'. It should, moreover, be seen here how the notion of *autrui*, which is derived from dispersal, can be considered as a deviation: all others become any other, anybody, who is not me, as massive in their uniqueness as the 'I-me' to whom they are a pendant. Life suddenly becomes a stage on which 'I-me' and 'not-I-me', called 'other people' or *autrui* meet in a duel. As my English-speaking readers may know, *autrui* is a key concept in French philosophy. It was coined as a philosophical concept at the cost of a linguistic blunder. For it is a genitive or dative, which has been properly used as such for centuries, *les biens d'autrui* being 'someone else's property'. Used as a noun, I suspect it is not only a linguistic blunder but a philosophical one as well. Nevertheless, we make our students turn pale with the classic and lapidary essay subject: *Autrui*. So, says this topic, tell me about a person who is defined as anyone-not-me and who occupies neither the strict relationship of 'you' to me, nor the position of 'he' or 'she', but is something between the second and third persons of the conjugation, a half-'you' whom I discuss half as 'he' or 'she', a 'you' whom I distance into a 'he' or 'she'. Ultimately, any essay on *autrui* always ends up being nothing but a long waffle about 'I-me' and this is not surprising, since the category is constucted simply as a contrast to 'I-me'.

Whatever the case, what is unusual in Sartre's version of humanism is that the principle of dispersal as a necessary and positive condition for thinking in terms of ethics is not to be found there. This version of humanism, which only retains 'man' as a principle, was of course proposed long before the autumn of 1939 by Pico della Mirandola, in his *De Hominis Dignitate*. Pico recognizes, or considers as a subject-agent of ethics, man in general and him alone; he names him Adam, obviously a solitary and unique being if ever there was one. In Sartre's philosophy, 'man' as the sub-ject of a moral pro-ject is also an Adam or a Robinson on his desert island, which is the same thing, for one is king of the world as long as one is alone. But this absence of the principle of dispersal and the pluralization of human subjects as a creative and positive principle, a lack which shows through in Sartre's major works, is clearly emphasized in the resumé sent to Beauvoir. Sartre takes care to describe his ethics by explaining what it is and what it is not. In particular he writes that it is not 'an extensive humanism in the sense that men, individual particles of humanity, are said to be an end for man'.[50] If 'men are not said to be an end for man', if one can claim to have produced a moral philosophy without concerning oneself with the fact that there are human beings, then Man in general is the only remaining principle, a true Adam indeed. And in this case, the problem of the relation to other people is not even posed as a problem for ethics to work on. Of course in Sartre's work we find instances where the existence of other people is mentioned, but these always refer to an agonistic situation and in such cases it is not a relationship which is involved, but death, which is quite different. If 'hell is other people', or if every consciousness seeks the death of the other, this is because the relationship with the other, as a relationship, cannot be grasped by the system. More generally, it can be argued that when philosophers say that something is 'death' it means that they cannot formulate a thought on it.

In Sartre's ethics there is only room for one ego, who represents humankind as a whole – the 'I' of the phenomenologists – but to whom that humankind is reduced. This hypertrophied subject, who appears in the philosophical works, reappears in the biography in the form of a single speaking subject, one Jean-Paul Sartre. And what we can call the Adam complex surfaces in his relationship with Beauvoir to the point of being almost explicit. One letter says that he imagines 'a diverticulum of myself: you'.[51] So was Simone Eve, a spare rib turned cavity? In this we can again see the link between a philosophical and a feminist critique: what is unpleasant in Sartre's attitude towards Simone de Beauvoir is nothing other than the weakness of his moral philosophy. Men are not an end for man, and a woman is certainly not an end for this man: she does not even have an independent existence, she is merely an appendix of her philosopher lover's 'I-me'.

'Human reality is ethical to the extent that it is without God.'[52] This insistence of Sartre's philosophy on detaching itself from what it calls God is one of the best known aspects of his thought; the correspondence sheds new light not on the negative reference, but on the insistence. Many philosophers before Sartre proposed theories of ethics which did not need to be based on God. What is different in his work is the necessity he feels constantly to recall the absence of God. When related to this leitmotiv, the notion of the 'Adam complex' which I am putting forward can acquire a sense which goes beyond the purely psychological: for Adam is the man who only feels himself to exist by always remembering that he is henceforward alone without God, recently abandoned, very recently condemned to be free, the man who only exists by meditating on the imperceptible gap between his hand and that of God, that focus of the fresco of the Sistine Chapel. The man who, at least for a time, was also truly the only speaking subject and, even more important the inventor of words, the namer of the beasts.[53]

What the *Lettres au castor* have to show us is the breadth of a philosophical position. A theory, 'man who is his own possibilities', is also a specular image, 'I want to talk about a necessary Jean-Paul Sartre', and a mode of relationships, or non-relationships, with other people and the opposite sex. It apparently governs all daily life, to the point where details seem to become heavily significant: 'My persistent silence on the subject of James's *The Portrait of a Lady*, which I could not finish, should show you that I can see no other use for this book than the worst (sic).'[54] Sartre is in the army and has been mobilized. In all his letters he clamours for books and devours everything that comes to hand. But he cannot finish *The Portrait of a Lady* and he says so surprisingly aggressively. Why does this portrait of a charming but exceptionally gifted woman arouse such rejection in him? We shall never know for certain, since Sartre does not explain himself, but we can always recall a passage from the novel in which Osmond, who is on the point of marrying Isabel, says:

'I like her very much. She's all you described her, and into the bargain capable, I feel, of great devotion. She has only one fault.'

'What's that?'

'Too many ideas.'

'I warned you she was very clever.'

'Fortunately they're very bad ones,' said Osmond.

'Why is that fortunate?'

'*Dame*, if they must be sacrificed!'[55]

Osmond fails to reduce Isabel's independence of will and spirit and soon comes to hate her. Sartre seems to have had more success and Simone de Beauvoir tells us herself that he tore her pluralist morality 'to shreds'. *The Portrait of a Lady* may have given him a horrible image of the failure that could have been his. And what phantasmagorical consequences would such a failure have had? 'You reason like a woman. You're a twat,'* said Sartre to one of his army comrades.[56] This is an example of the most widespread, everyday sexism; but the context is interesting. These charming words were addressed to a comrade who, because he was talking next to him, was preventing Sartre from writing. Let us stop here, before we are overtaken by nausea.

Not, however, before drawing the following conclusion: if this were the psychological position that always went with philosophical activity, there would be nothing either desirable or enviable about the latter. It is too often said that when women demand the same rights as men it is just the expression of a psychic problem identified by psychoanalysis as the sublimation of 'penis envy', which is supposedly the force underlying unhappy female sexuality: the suffragettes thought they wanted the vote; in fact, the right to vote only interested them as a metaphor of what men have. This idea, which is very popular in intellectual circles, has sometimes been attacked by feminist theorists; however it has also been upheld within feminism and plays a very precise role there, that of bad conscience. If the 'feminism of difference', which integrates this bad conscience, flourished so well in France during the 1970s, it was because in this country recent memory did not offer any historical experience that invited us to shrug our shoulders at this confusion between the analyst's couch and the public square. In the United States, the women who launched the Women's Liberation Movement had come straight from the battle for black people's civil rights; this had given them a simple

* In French *con*, a common insult implying stupidity and referring to the vagina (trans.).

and clear awareness of the importance of fighting for rights that are just and the psychoanalism of the problematics of 'envy' could only make them laugh, along with the women of the anglophone countries who had carefully followed the course of this long battle. This was not the case in France, hence the ease with which so many women allow themselves to be made to feel guilty by this ideological argument. And now that the black civil rights movement is long over for everyone, the conditions are right for addressing this savage criticism still more often to women engaged in an activity that is not traditionally feminine. Something of the sort was hurled at me recently. All that I know, all that I am saying is that the unqualified and unquestioning conferral of great value on philosophy is an illusion, that the philosophy practised by some of my men contemporaries is exactly what I do not want and, to my mind, is something nobody should want, either from a theoretical or a humanist point of view.

'I want all that you have, simply because you have it, even if I don't care about it', this is how Claude Habib defines the process of envy as it is played out between the sexes.[57] In opposition to this, we must bring in the principle of choice: I want what is good, or better than other things, independently of any considerations of the fetishistic 'value' added to the thing by the personality of the person who traditionally has it. If philosophy ceased to teach us to discern values, independently of what general opinion may add to them, it would also cease to be worth a moment's trouble.

Such a risk exists and is probably the only risk that philosophy always runs. All the same, it is from philosophy (but not from it alone) that I have learned what I needed to know in order to reject all that I have described of Sartrianism.

15   Protagoras

Let us end our long stay in the land of the existentialists with an admission of surprise: how can so closed a way of thinking, which cannot become diversified through encounters with different levels or fields of experience or with contingent facts, which has no content other than itself, which expresses only the violence of the writer's position as soon as the latter regards speech as his preserve or privilege, how could such a form of thought occupy the collective stage in a way that philosophies rarely can? To what extent is the monopolistic violence which, in Sartre's work, is structured around the position of the writer, specific, in other words unconnected to other more common and less literary forms of violence, such as ordinary domestic violence? Might not the great echo which Sartre's philosophy found in the collective consciousness arise from the fact that, far from displacing the models of social relations, it recycled their subjective quintessence using language in which they were unrecognizable?

'He explained the matter to me in his favourite terminology. "What we have," he said, "is an essential love; but it is a good idea for us also to experience contingent loves." ' For, at the age of twenty-six, Sartre did not intend to deprive himself forever of the seductive diversity of women, explains Simone de Beauvoir. So be it. But what must we then think of 'his favourite terminology', when what we hear in his words is the popular idea put into practice by so many others: 'there are good girls and fun girls, the ones you take out and the one you marry'? It is easy to shift from Sartre's words to the language of everyday ideology, as though there were a fundamental and depressing similarity which made it easy to translate between philosophical utterances and things said everyday on the streets. If this were true then philosophy would truly be a pointless passion.

But who said: 'My claim is that I am one of these, rather better than anyone else at helping a man to acquire a good and noble character'? It was not Socrates, but Protagoras, the man the crowd greeted with enthusiasm. Of course as these words were recorded for us by Plato, we may well doubt their authenticity.[58] Nevertheless, Socrates defines philosophical effort in contrast to Protagoras' fine self-assurance. There are three points in his reply which deserve mentioning here. First, he says, 'It is true that if a man talked on these matters with any of our popular orators, he might possibly hear similar discourses';[59] then he claims kin with the Seven Sages and the Lacedemonians who 'conceal their wisdom [...] and pretend to be fools'[60] one of whose maxims, 'It is hard to be a good man', he particularly praises; lastly Socrates notes, apparently in passing, that among the Lacedemonians and Cretans it is not only men but women also who rejoice in the education they have received. This all goes together: someone who thinks it is hard to become a good person (and quite impossible to be one at all times) knows that to state one's superiority is a crazy pretension. One might as well disguise oneself as an ignoramus and recognize that all men and women are in the same boat. Virtue is equally difficult for all, therefore all can make an equal effort to become good people, at least intermittently. On the other hand, once someone is convinced of their superiority, what they say resembles what is said elsewhere in any position of control. The reference to the 'political orator' shows no contempt for the political sphere on the part of philosophy; the orator is singled out as someone who always says the same thing: 'I shall lead you to good, follow me, I am the master you need.' Could not the objections Socrates makes to Protagoras also be made today to Sartre's position and to that of many others?

I do not want to return here to the idea that sophistry (or scholasticism) is the 'other' of philosophy. We must accept that the boundary is shifting and ill-defined, so that there is a kind of recurrent problem: it never takes much for philosophy to veer off towards the thing from which it wanted to separate or to distinguish itself. The sign of this wandering is when it teams up with a power which allows a desire for authority to be satisfied. Magisterial power for Aristotle and the scholastics, magisterial glory for Abelard, the power of the word and the popularity of the man who knows how to state his superiority for Protagoras, a little of all of that for Sartre and in the end the big names all meet up on the same side as the doxa and political orators. If we were only to consider Cleobulus, Socrates or Cleanthes, we should see that philosophy can, when it wants to, distance itself from what society thinks of women. If this capacity for distance is so easily forgotten, it is because there is nothing so fragile as philosophy, nor so prone to drifting off course and right back to the very place it originally wanted to leave. So that, once again, people are quite within their rights to laugh at it.

16   The game is not up

'The present outcome of our talk is pointing at us, like a human adversary, the finger of accusation and mockery. If it had a voice it would say...' The *Protagoras* ends with a prosopopeia which mocks both Socrates and Protagoras. But it is Socrates who breathes life into it, while the other still has the candour to refer to the 'faults from which he flatters himself he is exempt'. One can, of course, accept that there is great kinship between sophists, scholastics and philosophers, at least when they all come together in the position of instructors of the people, believing that their thought is better than common opinion, even though they have never disentangled themselves from the latter or from the badly reasoned ideas they believe in. However, unlike the sophist, the philosopher here seems able to imagine a nameless, faceless person by whom he is assimilated to the others, who guarantees that everyone is equally incoherent and, above all, who laughs. A little demon who brings to light their common lot by taking both the philosopher and his opponents down a peg or two. If we are to recognize this demon by its laughter, it may well be that it once borrowed the features of the little Thracian servant girl who laughs at Thales.[61]

From this point of view, philosophy is not identified with ultimate consciousness, nor with absolute control; on the horizon there is always an imaginary point that is better, liable to prove everyone wrong, including the philosopher; so that the philosophical consciousness ironically finds itself overlooked by something: a demon for Socrates, a God for Pascal, the unreason of experience linked to the unpredictable excavations of the 'dust-covered labourer' for Diderot and perhaps the future historical reality for the Marxist. We do not need to go so far as to define philosophy as that which knows that something else can laugh at it, nor do we need to regard all thought which flatters itself as being faultless as being like that of Protagoras. If such were the case, we should have to expel from the philosophical pantheon a very great number of authors who are in fact important to us. We do not need to demand an absolute and well-delineated oneness from 'philosophy'. But we can retain a precious idea from Socrates' humour: no one can pride themselves on always reasoning better than the protagonist or otherwise than the ordinary person; whatever one does, outside the field there is always a point from where someone unforeseen and unidentifiable can perceive an at least partial or occasional similarity between those who think they differ.

Such a conception allows us to set aside some false problems, such as this: I have sometimes wondered what sort of service learned men render, and to whom, by producing masculinist ideology in their own language when such ideology really has no need of scholars to come into being. Formulated thus, this is a functionalist and indeed finalist question, since it leads us to think about the social impact of intellectual production. Of course any macho gives a jubilant welcome to the fact that a great man puts his signature to some everyday sexist notion, hence the republication of Schopenhauer's vicious remarks in anthology form. But this jubilation no doubt relates to the fact that nothing guarantees in advance whether or not such support will come. Sexist idiocies are to be found in the work of Sartre, Rousseau or Hegel, which proves that one can never be certain that philosophers will distance themselves from every aspect of widely-held opinion.[62] Like other people, 'sages' are bogged down deep in what is defective and unthought; like other people, they make us laugh. Yet

their efforts are directed at getting away from what is immediately
obvious and thus to betraying consensus and common notions. Montesquieu attacks ideas which lend legitimacy to slavery; Cleobulus
and Aristippus thought that girls could be treated more generously
than was the common practice. The uncertainty is thus complete: the
learned are liable to betray social practices and the ideas which go
with them or to 'theorize' in their own way. There may be a Montesquieu or a Gobineau on any question, which is why racists do not
regard the latter as superfluous. Thought is sometimes risky for
collective certainties; not that often, of course, but an awareness of
the possibility is all that is needed for conformist notions from a
philosopher's pen to be greeted as an improbable good fortune, a
narrow escape, by a conscience that has in fact only just got away
with it.

17   *A very brief history of philosophy, or what does it mean to*
     reorientate oneself in thought?

According to the *Tusculans*, first of all there were people who bore
the name of Sages: *sophoi* in Greek and *sapientes* in Latin. Thales,
Solon, Bias of Priene, Cleobulus and a few others devoted themselves
(again according to Cicero) to contemplation and their wisdom was a
'discovery of things divine and human', as well as the principles and
causes of those things. There were at least seven of them, but since
the list of the Seven Sages of Greece is a changeable one, we can be
sure that there were more than seven.
     As for Pythagoras, he decided one day to state definitely that he
had no knowledge of any of the arts, but was a 'philosopher'. A man
called Leon who ruled Phlius expressed surprise at this new word, for
'philosophy' was a neologism. He asked him who philosophers were
and what difference there was between them and the rest of men.
Pythagoras answered with a long metaphor.[63] But the story does not
end there. Pythagoras's project, which consisted of carefully trying to
determine the size of the stars, the spaces between them, their movement and everything else concerning celestial phenomena was described by Cicero as 'old philosophy'. Was what Pythagoras called
'philosophy' similar to what nowadays we call 'scientific research'?
This is because 'scientific research' is a rather long and heavy translation, as any word for word version is, of philo-sophy. In any case,
one fine day a man called Socrates 'was the first to call philosophy
down from the heavens and set her in the cities of men and bring her

also into their houses and compel her to ask questions about life and morality and things good and evil'. But the story does not end there either: this page from the *Tusculans* notes that the variety of subjects Socrates dealt with and his various ways of discussing them produced many sects of philosophers who were at variance with each other. And the fact is that since then we have not stopped arguing with each other and with ourselves as well, for the mind talks to itself, sometimes in hard words.

We can take many things from Cicero's narrative, and notably that the discipline from which we rightly or wrongly believe we are descended is the result of more than one reworking. It is always renewing itself and creating neologisms. Consequently, any time it distances itself from its origins or traditions, this is a form of fidelity. It is fidelity to a dynamic, a vocation of freshness or a dizziness, but certainly not to a native land or to a capital's omphalos, albeit that of Delphi. Hence variation is by definition that which is most permitted and even, we might say, absolutely required.

We can note also that this variation takes the form of an abandonment which is not destruction. Pythagoras distanced himself from the Sages, but Pythagorean research did not 'liquidate' the intellectual position of the *sophoi*. Wisdom as the knowledge of things divine and human continued to be claimed by others. In later Antiquity, the *Corpus Hermeticum* reflects this idea fairly clearly and it was to become very much in vogue during the Renaissance. The idea of an evangelic philosophy (or one linked to revelation) also occupied the place of the knowledge of things divine and human for centuries. In the same way, the Socratic reorientation did not suppress the Pythagorean project and although 'scientific research' has had a broken history, there are other reasons why this is so. The movement allows that which it abandons to go on existing.

But how does a reorientation take place? The page of the *Tusculans* gives us to understand that Pythagoras and Socrates each made a kind of absolute decision: the first 'decided one day to state definitely that' and the second seems to have done the same. However, in the case of Socrates, we know from elsewhere that he was obeying his personal demon. We can see in this the allegory of an unconditioned principle (no one invents their own demons), a prescriptive principle, which imposes itself, gives orders and speaks within the philosopher's own subjectivity.

We know, overall, what the principle of orientation is: when the compass needle shows me north, I know where west and east are because I know which is my left hand and which my right. A practical subjective principle is necessary to orientate onesef in space. On the basis of this rudimentary requirement, one can, of course, develop far more sophisticated means; nevertheless the use of maps, compasses or sextants and techniques using the stars or landmarks all require this minimum. We should however distinguish simple orientation from reorientation. The first assumes that you know where you are (Piazza Navona) and how your body is located in space (your favourite café is on your right and thus the path in front of you leading out from the square is the one going to the Corso). But sometimes it happens that one does not know exactly where one is and thus experiences disorientation. In general this disorientation is overcome. On the sea, one needs to know *grosso modo* where one is and by means of this dead reckoning one can determine the vessel's exact location. Maps, almanacs, compasses or books of lighthouses are used to correct the approximate knowledge called dead reckoning, but cannot replace it. It is thus possible to imagine experiences of radical disorientation.

After a long drive, you arrive, very tired, in an Italian city. You rummage about in the glove compartment and take out a plan of the city. When you stop at a red light, you read a street name which tells you you are at the beginning of the Via Cavour and you know that you are travelling towards the city centre. You glance at the plan: to get to where you want to go, you must therefore drive to a large square and turn left. You drive on, but you do not come to a large square. You want to find out if it is still far; you catch the name of an avenue which has just crossed your Via Cavour, look at the plan and discover that, according to it, no avenue of that name crosses the Via Cavour. You made a mistake when you were rummaging through your map collection and have been trying to get your bearings in Milan with a plan of Turin, Rome or Florence!

What we call reorientating oneself in thought means realizing that one is walking around somewhere with the wrong map because one had not been aware where one was. The little Thracian servant girl laughed at Thales' disorientation: he was wrong to walk about the earth with his eyes on a map of the sky. He had misunderstood where he was and that is why he fell down a well. As a result, Socrates called philosophy back down to earth and made it into research into life and common practices. Research indeed: once one knows where one is, one discovers that the map for that place does not yet exist and there is nothing for it but to invent one.

Another element in the Phlius story intrigues me: who whispered to Leon the precise terms of his question to Pythagoras? 'He asked him who philosophers were and in what they differed from the rest of men.' Here is someone who, in principle, does not yet know what philosophy is and innocently asks to have this 'astonishing' word explained to him. And yet he asks the question in a way that crosses twenty-five centuries of philosophical effort. Defining what philosophy is means defining who philosophers are and how they differ, in general, from 'other men', sometimes collectively referred to as 'the common herd' or 'the common man'. Cicero must have twisted the story a little and put into the king's mouth a question formulated in such a way as to be exactly the one that Pythagoras was ready to answer. However, our detection of this trickery should not distract us from the essential point: there may be no answer to any question other than the one which seeks a definition of how the philosopher is different. Let us imagine that the king had asked for a definition of philosophy, or simply for an idea of the thing, backed up by a few examples. Would Pythagoras not have been in as much difficulty as we are when we are in a schoolroom facing students who, in principle, do not yet know what philosophy is either and, equally innocently, ask us to explain it to them before they start on their course of study? I used to get out of this awkward situation by saying: 'Today, all I can say to you is, "you will see", and at the end of the year I shall say, "I hope you have seen."' I did indeed hope that the nature of philosophy would appear to them through the few samples of it that I could give them. As these words seldom satisfied my students, I left them to answer the question themselves. Without necessarily knowing anything about either Pythagoras or Rembrandt, they always unfailingly spoke to me of the philosopher, a wise old man with a white beard. One might challenge the age, sex, wisdom and beard, but could I say that they were wrong in substituting the philosopher for philosophy? The day before I began teaching, the person in charge of our teacher training, Mme D. Dreyfus, said, 'You must understand, colleagues, that you will teach not with what you know but with what you are.' These words caused great anxiety (does that mean any pedagogical failure is a personal failure?), but as far as I can tell they were true, and the students always know it.[64]

Leon of Phlius' question personalizes the discipline, asks about difference and contrasts the 'philosopher' with the 'rest of men'. These things have now become to some extent 'self-evidences'. However, if we allow these terms to be dictated to us, our answer, like that of Pythagoras, will reflect the structure of the question: the philosopher is the only one who wants only to see.[65] As this personalization establishes difference by postulating a 'rest' of humanity, it opens up the possibility of saying all sorts of unpleasant things about the nature of the 'rest'. But it also implies that the discipline does not exist beyond the individuals involved in it or, to put it the other way round, that in place of a common theoretical configuration, there are philosophers. Their stature or calibre hides the incapacity of philosophy to constitute itself as a shared rationality. There are schools or sects which quarrel with or deliberately ignore each other, and in any case they do not have a sufficient common stock of principles, ways of defining their objects or modes of determining proof.

Jeanne Delhomme discussed this question before me, but in a quite different way. She notes that the philosopher cannot be seen as the individuation of philosophy or the singular incarnation of collective work; philosophy constantly comes down to the philosopher (and back to him as well), which is what distinguishes it from the simple and continuous history of 'ideas', or rather lifts it from that history by the power of negativity.[66] I shall take care not to pronounce on the implication of this thesis, which is that the history of ideas is a place of continuity. In proposing earlier a model for the polygenesis of all thought, I suggested seeing continuities, and thus dicontinuity, more or less everywhere. But I should like, above all, to recognize not just the diachronic, but also the synchronic aspect of the question, by saying that the figure of the philosopher is substituted for an impossible community, by which I mean the impossible community of the discipline. It would be false to say that philosophers are by nature antisocial animals with a psychologically based propensity to keep themselve to themselves. The need for friends 'whose cheerfulness dissipates your gloom, whose very appearance gives you joy', is expressed, once and for all, in ancient philosophy.[67] And Cicero is even clearer: some people think, he says, that if society magically ceased to be necessary for subsistence and material life, then anyone gifted with an exceptional mind would fly away from it, dropping his business and confining himself to knowledge and science. 'This is not true. For in his desire to avoid being alone he would seek some companion in his studies, so as to profit from teaching, learning and discussion.'[68] Nevertheless, even in this praise of friendship, we still find sectarian aspirations (each one seeking out a *socius studii*) rather than the hope of a community of all seekers after wisdom, or of a global community (even though stoicism declared itself inspired by the concept of cosmopolitanism). We could add that, because there is no overall intellectual community, everyone does indeed need friends, in other words a close emotional community.

We can explain by the fact of reorientation itself why the personalization of the enterprise goes hand in hand with the non-existence of philosophy as a common property that transcends individuals. Simply getting one's bearings, in space or in thought, supposes a subjective principle which is not itself individuated. Telling right hand from left and thus being able to establish the points of the compass is something universalizable and we can understand why the philosopher of the abstract universal should have become so attached to this model.[69] But the space in which we move is not simply the great homogeneous geometrical space for which this principle is enough. We are also always in a precise space of reference (Milan or Rome), which is the space of a projected journey. The possibility of reorientation depends on a second principle in addition to the first: that of the recognition of how the precise space connects to the intention of travelling.

In accounts of intellectual explorations, this second principle appears as arising from somebody's will: 'Pythagoras, one day, decided that', 'Socrates brought philosophy back down to earth.' The reference to proper names is not out of place: the narrative calls on decisions which can of course then be explained, justified and shared, but whose origin seems to be hidden in the impenetrable folds of the will. After the event the decision in favour of reorientation may seem to be an excellent idea in which one wishes to participate; but at the time it is a kind of manifestation of a sense, similar to the sense of direction, which compares its awareness of a vector – 'I am here and I want to go there' – with the available cartography, thus proving the latter deficient. What is surprising in all this is that once the reorientation has been stated (enough of the sky! I am on earth and I want to concern myself with towns and houses) it may become entirely obvious, but not necessarily to all. From an intellectual point of view, its obviousness is no doubt related to the fact that the decision itself causes the space of reference (where are we?), the desire or project (that's where I want to go) and at least a rudimentary road or sea map to appear all at once. But no reorientation has ever been welcomed unanimously: adherence to it thus still requires a subjective principle in the receiver.[70] All in all, if we accept that 'philosophy' is that which debates theoretical reorientation, we can understand that it is never strictly speaking a discipline, in other words a collection of rational principles which are shared by all its agents. The personalization of the project thus appears as an irreducible point. There is always a grain of it, like that in 'a grain of common sense', except that it is in the nature of this grain that one can never tell whether it is common sense or fantasy. Personally, I think it is both.

However, it must be realized that personalization can operate in many ways, depending on whether philosophers put the minimum necessary into their reorientation, without an 'I-me' occupying the whole field of their project, or whether they choose the opposite course. Any of them (of us) is liable to push personalization so far that it takes up all the space. It would be a clever person who could mark out the line that must not be crossed and even how quantity can be measured in this case: this is another question which we can leave hanging without regret.[71]

We have not lost sight of the 'subject' of our enquiry, on the contrary: if this discipline, which is not one, implicates the people who take it on, we can grasp the acuteness of the initial problem. What about women and philosophy, if the latter does not exist as a common property which transcends individuals? It is the figure of the philosopher that exists, as we have seen, in place of the common discipline which is always lacking. Around this figure crystallizes a question which should not be asked: that of the failure of philosophy to keep its fundamental promise to constitute a rationality in common. But there are two contradictory things to be said about the missing community: first that it does not exist and secondly that at the same time it excludes people, for example, women. Since personification has to hide the failure, we can see why the idea of a woman philosopher is repellent to so many colleagues: she does not have sufficient stature to conceal the lack, her shoulders are not broad enough. The non-existent community may also give itself the illusion of existing by excluding people: once there is someone outside, it becomes possible to imagine an inside in which everyone is together. Correlatively, if 'the philosopher' is the mode of philosophy's existence, then only one is needed per century or half century and it is that philosopher's person which counts and is of interest.

In opposition to all this we need to establish the idea of collective philosophical work which has moved and moves on from age to age, is orientated in different directions, taken up, pursued and redebated, which does not have the strongly structured unity of a tradition (the tradition which a real community would keep), but is not constantly being radically undermined either. Reorientation never means absolute discontinuity.[72] It seems to me that with this type of image of philosophy, one can regard the people involved in it as working on a continued or discontinued creation, in other words a permanent effort towards reactualization. These women and men need to be sufficiently numerous to pursue a task which is constantly being reset.

All this only takes on the problem in its corporatist aspects: what should be done so that women who get involved in philosophy can be better integrated into their world? But perhaps there is more to look for. If we accept that in the society as a whole women are generally oppressed, the fact that some women approach the pole of theoretical reorientation could have appreciable consequences for the exploration of that oppression, if (of course) the women in question show an interest in so doing. This is only now beginning to happen: while gratefully acknowledging the fifty or so women of Greek or Hellenistic Antiquity who produced philosophy, we must accept that their status was strictly that of exceptions: they left the social order outside the walls of the sect unchanged.

'Do you think I have done wrong to spend on the getting of knowledge all the time which, because of my sex, I was supposed to waste at the loom?' replied our Hipparchia to an imbecile who was criticizing her precisely for having neglected her first duty and left the shuttle idle.[73] These words, the only ones I have found uttered by a woman philosopher of Antiquity concerning the ordinary lives of women, seem to me to be of crucial importance. By introducing the issue of our life-span, which we know to be limited, and the idea that it can be either pleasantly used or irretrievably wasted, Hipparchia brings to bear a point of reference which lifts the question above the conventional division of labour as dependent on, particularly, sex. It is indisputably better to use one's time than to waste it. This settles the question, but it also leaves aside any consideration of the usual position of women.

Far be it from me to 'moralize' on this attitude. Custom prescribed that women should burn up their life-spans; those who were able to forget custom and prescription were right to do so. And what if this simple opportunity were offered to a woman today? No one should find anything to complain of in that. But does this opportunity exist and has it ever done so? This is far from certain, for intellectual reasons and not simply because of the misogynistic attitudes of the profession. Hipparchia's choice is linked to an admirable method which is however inappropriate. Methodologically speaking, her remark suggests that if one opens a debate taking existential differences (sexual difference, the distinction between the slave and the free man or whatever) as a starting point, it is impossible to open a theoretical debate. At the time of the Greeks as in our time, the doxa was bogged down in relativism. There is one form of virtue for the free man, one for the woman, one for the child, one for the slave, one for the old man, and so on. Menon sets a whole swarm of virtues buzzing around Socrates' head, just as our contemporaries keep finding new ways to say 'everything is relative' and 'each to their own truth'. This relativism is the death of thought. To the extent that Hipparchia first brings in an external term, time, she shows a sense of method which Gabrielle Suchon makes explicit: 'instead of immediately establishing what can be said about women (on the subject of the deprivation of freedom), I discuss essence, nature, the different species and the properties and benefits of freedom at length'.[74] This certainly is the only way to pose the problems in a theoretical mode.

But philosophy is not purely and simply a theoretical activity. The complete forgetting of oneself in favour of the subject under discussion may perhaps just about apply in mathematics; Canguilhem notes somewhere that, while we can imagine angels taking up mathematics, to do biology we have to have something of the dumb creature about us (être 'un peu bêtes'). It is the same in philosophy. Although the act of philosophical thinking absolutely requires theorization, it arises out of something else, which we have called the reorientation debate. Such a debate assumes that consideration of what one is is brought into play with objects which can be perceived theoretically. 'What one is' cannot, of course, be strictly defined in advance ('I, Baruch Spinoza, earning my living making glasses'), on the contrary. The consideration of 'what one is' is extremely problematic. An 'I' seeks itself and tries to determine where it has got to after acknowledging its exile or, better still, its non-location, which it seeks to escape. When one omits to ask the question of what one might be in relation to the objects one elects, this is no longer philosophy so much as conversion in the professional rather than the religious sense, in other words redeployment.

On one side the loom, on the other, the getting of knowledge: Hipparchia abandons the first in favour of the second. In so doing she finds a better way of life, but she wins exile and, if I may be permitted a neologism, she unfinds herself. It is understandable that a very unhappy situation should give rise to a desire to flee; since her conversion to philosophical study seems to have made Hipparchia into a person of joyful and caustic temperament, this flight from an overly determined identity is amply justified. The interest manifested by some women for philosophical study may well proceed, not from a desire to find themselves, but from one of losing themselves. Any conversion promises this forgetting of self, insofar as the chosen object and it alone takes up the whole field; one leaves behind at the threshold the identity one had in relation to one's former activity 'because of my sex, at the loom', and lastly all reference to identity. Which can be a cause of great joy.

We can indeed assume that, until at least very recently, women suffered from, among other things, an overloaded identity. Without even trying to show the vexatious nature of this identity, which was highly artificial and full of prohibitions, we must observe that it is hard to bear being in a situation where one is not allowed for a moment to forget what one is supposed to be. One might well be filled with a desire to be nothing, when every action is stifled by a coating of 'you are', and always the same thing.[75] Seeking oneself ('know thyself!') presupposes that the voice that says 'you are... and thus' has spluttered or fallen silent at least for a moment. That which a Greek or Thracian girl asked of philosophical studies was in all probability the opposite of what someone like Socrates expected of them. But today? Today the plethora of exogenous identity still exists and men philosophers still hold forth on 'woman' as much as ever, to the point where is no longer possible for anyone who finds this burden unbearable to escape it simply in philosophy. But some women are no longer seeking their salvation in flight; they are recognizing their disorientation. Some are looking for an identity which is not that proposed by social representations, others are trying to identify what it is exactly that they want when they think they are fighting for 'women's liberation'. Is it forbidden in philosophy to acknowledge a historically specific collective disarray? Is it not on the contrary obligatory to set one's disarray to work? For that, one must begin by recognizing it as one's own.

18 Post-script

April 1971: sales of the 12th issue of a journal called *Tout* ('Everything') published by the group *Vive la Révolution* ('Long Live the Revolution') are banned due to its 'pornographic nature'. A certain Jean-Paul Sartre gives this journal a cover because of his fame; he is its fictional 'editor in chief'. Jean-Paul Sartre was charged with 'offences to public decency' in April 1971.

If we are to judge by the extracts printed in *Génération*, what was said in this issue by the homosexual men and lesbians to whom *Tout* gave the floor was not very aggressive and definitely not comparable with the metaphors of *Being and Nothingness* or the confidences published in the letters.[76] A leaflet from the FHAR[77] contains the gay challenge: 'Yes, we have been buggered by Arabs, we are proud of it and we would do it again', and a group of lesbians states: 'Girls who kiss each other are powerful'.

'What conjectures are you going to lose yourself in now to explain why the police called these words an outrage to public decency whereas no one raised a stink about *Being and Nothingness*? You can't mean to suggest that Pompidou's French Republic was more repressive and pernickety than the Vichy regime! Of course, it can be argued that the expression of masculine heterosexuality of whatever kind is less repressed than that of homosexuality, whether masculine or feminine, or assumed that the Vichy censors had not read *Being and Nothingness* from cover to cover. Or that the seizure of *Tout* was just an excuse to harass the VLR activists, who were a nuisance for other reasons.'

'Actually I think we need to refine our concepts.'

'That's professional conditioning for you! You want to use your pen to draw a tenuous line between notions, while, off your page, society decides "as one man" either to send in the cops or to regard freedom of expression as sacred.'

'What other hope is there? Let us draw a distinction between the idea of 'pornocracy' and 'erotography'. A thing is pornocratic when it talks about sexuality only in accordance with established power relations in the social sphere. *Pornè* is a prostitute, and what could be more socially authorized than buying, buying in general and thus this form in particular? Nothing except perhaps for the assertion of an equally general power of men over women. That is pornocracy and it transforms any subordinate or anything that can be bought into a humiliated woman and all women into subordinates who can be humiliated or bought. Pornocracy always slips through the censor's net, because that net was not designed to catch it. And pornocracy does not really have much to say about bodily pleasure: it talks about the pleasure of domination. Erotography is a far rarer thing and far more open to censorship; it is often censored at source, so that we can only give fairly anodine and literary examples of it. What would be disturbed or put in danger if one described one's pleasures purely as pleasures, I should like to know? In any case, 'porno' always goes with 'crat' and, if 'eroto' existed, it would go with 'graphic' or would belong to the genre of 'lyrical art'.

'All the same, there were naked men's bodies on the cover of that journal, and women's knickers. People could have been shocked.'

'On the walls of French towns at the moment there are plenty of posters showing a near-naked siren praising some brand of men's underpants. That is considered innocent enough for the eyes of children and everyone else, because the image is an invitation to buy and is in no way a celebration of the feasts of Eros. It's just more pornocracy, and the most ordinary form of pimping.'

'In other words, pornography does not exist, because what is called pornography, or can be related to buying and power, is pornocracy, or else is erotography, which you regard as perfectly licit.... Where will it all end if we can't even rely on feminists to be puritanical these days?'

'The puritans were, and still are, merchants.'

Fourth Notebook

which is prospective and retrospective

*juridical, uchronic and utopian; in which some questions of practical philo-
sophy are resolutely broached, without neglecting the analysis of small and
insignificant facts; and in which there are more complaints about learned
personages.*

In a work devoted to 'women-philosophers', one M. de Lescure tells
the story of how a girl scandalized her convent companions with
her religious scepticism.[1] The abbess asked Massillon, a famous
preacher of the time, what remedy would be appropriate for this evil.
He prescribed a 'tuppenny catechism', which would teach the delin-
quent, along with the necessary truths, the humility of learning them
from a 'summary within the grasp of all'. The future Madame du
Deffand (for it was she) must learn to kneel and adore the teaching of
'the children's book'. The remedy failed and the marquise left, to
hold the most frolicsome and brilliant salon in all Paris according to
some, according to others, to join the band of those women who
'prided themselves on being neither wives nor mothers nor women'
and whose sole ideal was to be an *honnête homme* (decent man), a type
incarnated, as is well known, by the famous courtesan Ninon de
Lenclos. M. de Lescure discourses at length on this anecdote and
contrasts the women philosophers (those 'debauchers of the mind',
those 'shameless hearts' whose 'impiety calls for thunderous reproof',
etc.) with the Christian mother and her virtues. This book may still
be found on the secondhand bookstalls by the Seine.

If one has to read something – since in any case we all live in a
cultural universe – it is assuredly better to read Voltaire than some
bland and mediocre text designed with the aim of cultivating the
presumed simple-mindedness of its readers. Madame du Deffand

gave proof of her discernment and chose the best available. Since one has only one life, from an intellectual point of view as well as any other, this is a basic reflex. The resolution to choose for oneself what to esteem among things to hand is akin to the founding act of free thought as opposed to religious faith which, as Bossuet stresses, rests on the testimony of others and the authority of the person who instructs you. When Madame du Deffand rejected both the religion and the authority of Massillon, she was entirely consistent. But her choice of independence (I choose for myself), however admirable and commendable, remains half-way between the usual intellectual position of women (passive acceptance of directives) and philosophy.

She distances herself from the former because a good woman is always delighted with anything she is given; in this she duly guarantees the value of the gift and that of the giver. Among the attitudes usually expected of women, next to obedience and pliability to the desires of others comes adulation, or at least an automatic and reguired admiration which, need we state, is quite the opposite of admiration. When a woman goes into ecstasies over something of little value, it sometimes raises a condescending smile on the faces of some of those present: how absurd! But the smile itself expresses satisfaction that all is as it should be. The more she is delighted by a household gadget or transported by a childish catechism, the more bland novels she reads, the less difficult she will be and the more she will conform to the expected standards. Philosophers, whether graced with a sense of humour or not, are contrary spirits, as regards both theory and more or less everything else. 'How many things I can do without!' Socrates is said to have exclaimed at the Athens market.[2] Did he mean the vegetables, carpets, statuettes and more or less valuable vases or the chitchat at the stalls, the murmur of projects, the agreements made, news exchanged and more or less benevolent comments on one's neighbours' lives? What was it exactly that Socrates was asserting that he did not want? He might have repeated these words at the Agora in relation to the hollow pronouncements uttered and the political manoeuvres that were planned there. Let us simply retain the abstract possibility of declaring that one does not need something judged desirable by the culture of the time; it could also be Thalès' astronomy. Seneca did not have the opportunity to perform the scene he was capable of; let us imagine him all the same, planted firmly in front of the forty thousand volumes in the Alexandria library and describing the whole collection as a pile of useless courgettes in those terms which belong to him alone: 'the student is loaded down, not instructed, by the bulk', 'there was no refinement or benevolence about it but only a studious luxury – and not even studious'[3] Besides, they were all more or less copies of each other, said Francis Bacon, much later. Reorientation does away with town plans and road maps which do not fit with the planned exploration.

Some knowledges leave the mind unsatisfied, some intellectual food does not nourish, some theories block intelligence or screen out awareness of something which absolutely must be known. The idea that there can be a culture which does not educate – which I do not need – seems to be a constant factor in the opening of a philosophical project. Madame du Deffand did not go quite that far, but she nearly did. All that was missing in her case was the acknowledgement of an 'I': I don't need. Despite the scandal caused by her rejection of religion, the operation by which she exchanged convent beliefs for the ideas of the philosophers was almost silent; she did not present herself as the one performing this gesture, did not make it explicit or become self-aware in doing it.

One of the leitmotivs of the Women's Movement in the 1970s was to complain about a culture which women had nothing to do with. Many thought it urgently important to create art and literature 'by women, for women, about women', because, they said, all available forms were 'about men, by men, for men'. Let us not discuss whether this rejection is well-founded or not; it is a fact which we must acknowledge. It marks a radical disorientation, which can be re-garded as classic, but which remains a rare thing in the history of protests by individual women or feminists: among the great ladies of the past, one more often finds a desire to leave behind inferior forms of life and culture for the better ones, which already exist. Hipparchia preferred study to the loom and the studies she took up were surely the most fascinating of her time; our marquise rejected the infracul-ture that others tried with all their might to make her accept (she was not even offered Saint Augustine!) and ran off to seek more intelligent and stronger stuff elsewhere. The right to education seems to have been one of the great constants of feminist demands. As early as 1693 Gabrielle Suchon made a strong link between the 'freedom of the mind' which she wanted for 'persons of the Sex' and the conquest of a consciousness 'enlightened' by the light of reason and the finest authors.[4]

Adorno would deal with this attitude by saying: 'Those whom repressive culture has held at a distance can easily enough become its most diehard defenders.' At the opposite pole from this flat apology, he describes a 'state of mind' which 'presupposes experience, a his-torical memory, a fastidious intellect and above all an ample measure of satiety':[5] satiety in relation to a tradition which one carries within oneself and which one must have in order to reject it. We shall grant

him satiety (with which we are familiar), without thinking him right
to distinguish those he calls 'savages' or 'newcomers' from those he
calls 'us', in other words, and he does not hide the fact, students from
the Third World who attend American or German universities on the
one hand and on the other the heirs to the European intellectual
tradition. This contrast is incorrect. The distaste for culture manifested by the highly cultivated is inverted in the wink of an eye as
soon as any of them is faced with a reality of lesser intellectual acuity.
We need only listen to what our school students have to say about
freedom, society and the individual's relation to the latter and however disgusted we may be with the inheritance, we suddenly forget to
reject it: we think they need (oh?) to know about some passage from
Spinoza, one of Kant's long notes or one of Hegel's analyses. We
catch ourselves wanting to save their souls from a woolly doxa and it
is ourselves that we are saving, and the brilliance and relevance of
our inheritance. The value of a culture is perceived through contrast
and one can easily rediscover a passion for Brecht, Stendhal or
Shakespeare by reading one Mills and Boon novel.

If the privileged heirs' aversion can cease instantly when they
encounter something else, we must understand that the 'newcomers'
are, reciprocally, the defenders of a strong culture because they so
well remember what that culture has allowed them to escape from.
After a tuppenny catechism, any philosophical nourishment seems
like a feast for the mind. True disgust can come only later, when the
'newcomers' are sufficiently sure that they will not fall back into the
infraculture; and yet it is these newcomers, and not the heirs full of
'historical memory', who may find that the available culture, even in
its strongest forms, does not allow them to find out where they are or
to get to where they want to go. The more anarchistic criticisms of
'culture' from women in the 1970s reflect a historical confidence:
none of us were prevented from attending a secondary school or
university as Virginia Woolf was – or at least not in the same brutal
way. Of course, the difficulties have not all been magically removed.
But there is a world of difference between a pure and simple impossibility of studying and sly discrimination.

1   The other means of appeal

If we can hear discontent with the available culture and a radical
disorientation in relation to current politics in the rumblings of the
feminist movement, it may be that the conditions necessary for re-

orientation are coming into being and that women are now able to illustrate what is called the 'migrant's creativity' by suggesting a change of chart. It would be easy to maintain that women philosophers are now facing the completely new and historic task of changing the course of culture, reorientating it in such a way that it can at last enable a woman to know where she has got to and how to get where she wants to go. I might as well acknowledge that I find the idea of producing a counter-culture very tempting, but I no doubt already have too much historical experience and too many memories to charge head down into this kind of self-apology. For we must first note the specificity of the current situation: we no longer have to turn to philosophy as the only available means of appeal against disastrous ideologies and social oppression.

Where racism is concerned, we are no longer in Montesquieu's times. Of course it is an intellectual joy to read a study like that of Albert Jacquard who, making good use of his knowledge of genetics, pulverizes pseudo-scholarly twaddle supposedly based on that science. His *Praise of Difference* is a fine example of the way in which a scientist can produce philosophy, by making public the fact that his discipline is still problematic on certain points, setting out the share of non-knowledge which it contains and analysing the intellectual confidence tricks that lurk in this obscure zone and are repugnant from a human point of view.[6] However, it never occurred to Albert Jacquard to portray the geneticist as the providential one who would alone carry out the task of combatting racist ideologies. He considered it his responsibility as a scientist to advance a critical clarification of the problem and to demonstrate the madness of experts when they export their expertise to precisely those domains where they are incompetent. The perspectives he opens up concerning the importance of diversity are remarkable and yet the book ends with a note of extreme humility: to build a world where human beings are less at the mercy of other human beings requires an effort of imagination, which is already being made, according to Jacquard, by the 'much criticized generation which is getting ready to succeed us'. From this praise of 'our children', we can at least understand that here is an intellectual who knows that his thought is not enough and that historical change depends on the collective will and not – just – on readjusting concepts.

A purely intellectual effort can no longer stand up to social practices that alienate all the 'others'. What is required are social movements, which are effective not only because of their ability to articulate ideas that challenge the established order, but primarily because of their weight and number. When one takes as one's aim to make the collective consciousness accept something which it precisely does not wish to know, one is heard more or less clearly depending on whether one is one of five or fifty thousand people and also depending on whether or not one represents a diverse range of social groupings. Once one starts to think in terms of political movements, it is clear that it is not just a question of thinking and writing; it is fundamentally important to be able to invest time, energy, determination and intelligence in the pursuit of a collective project.

These are no longer the days of Eumetis alias Cleobulina, nor even those of Simone de Beauvoir: critical theorization no longer bears alone the responsibility for providing an appeal against custom. We should welcome the new situation gladly – a social movement for the liberation of women has emerged, with no unified doctrinal base and functioning on different bases from that of theorization. A quite different form of appeal, which grew out of simple expressions of exasperation: 'we've had enough'. When several hundred thousand people are all out in the street saying that they have had enough of this or that, some deaf ears are obliged to hear. The Movement never sought leadership from its intellectuals; on the contrary, it carefully guarded against any type of leadership or star system. In the First Notebook we saw how foolish it is to seek to make philosophy govern what takes place in a non-doctrinaire movement. Any attempt similar to that of Janet Radcliffe Richards, more intelligently conducted though it might be, would be condemned to a similar absurdity, which stems from a failure to recognize that a social movement does not conduct itself in the way that theory theorizes. It is a fairly futile mental exercise to seek to 'reclaim' a historical fact, unless one explicitly gives the attempt a uchronic form: let us imagine that we can start again and that I can draw the outlines of a reworked history on my blank paper...

2   A trip to Uchronia

When I start dreaming in this way, it is not just the recent history of the feminist movement that I reshape in my mind, but all policy affecting women since the French Revolution. 'What if our dear Sans-culottes had not excluded women from citizens' rights in December 1789?' 'What if they had not dissolved the women's clubs in September 1793, nor guillotined Olympe de Gouges and Mme Roland?' 'What if they had not banned women from political meetings on 24 May 1794?'[7]

On the other hand, what would have happened if, at that time, the state had listened to some women's demands for free education for all children in mixed schools? If marriage had been abolished in favour of the social contract between man and woman proposed by Olympe de Gouges in 1791? This is a wonderful contract, for it preserves the rights of women and children and enables us to see, by contrast, how the real legislation at once sacrificed both women's freedom and children's interests to what is commonly called patriarchy. I shall sum up de Gouges's contract briefly: We, A and B, come together of our own free will for as long as our mutual liking lasts, on the following conditions: we place our wealth in common, while still retaining the right to divide it in favour of our children and those each of us may have as the result of any other inclination, in the mutual recognition that our property belongs directly to our children, in whatever context they were conceived, and that they all have the same right to bear the name of the father and mother who have acknowledged them. In the case of our separation, we shall be obliged to deduct our children's share as indicated by the law.[8] In the name of the cherished principle of freedom of expression, which was called at the time a freedom of 'communication of thoughts' her contract states, 'any citizen may freely say: "I am the mother of a child who belongs to you", without being forced by barbarous prejudice to conceal the truth'. The contract was intended only to protect the rights of children, in particular by removing the legal difference between those who were 'legitimate' and those who were called 'bastards' under the Ancien Regime. But for women this changes everything, because it allows them to be open and encourages them to ensure that they have independent means of support: the father, and indeed the mother, are expected to support the children, but the husband is not told to 'take responsibility for his wife' as marriage no longer exists. The man has no particular rights over the woman whose bed and life he shares as long as their 'mutual liking' lasts; and if one of them had a child as a result of another 'inclination', no one would be forced to lie about it.

In the abstract, I am convinced that women's liberation requires anti-patriarchal legislation, in other words a reform of the law concerning filiation which would substitute puerocentrism for the patricentric system. For many forms of women's oppression stem from the anxious appropriation of children by the father-husband, who jealously appropriates the wife-mother in all possible ways and in particular so that he can be sure that a child is definitely 'his'. To suggest, as Olympe de Gouges's contract does, that adults have only duties in relation to children, with no possibility of appropriation, makes it possible to eliminate at least some aspects of the appropriation of a woman by her man. Yes, I should like to award our Olympe the prize for genius, while also pointing out that she had had little education. By her own admission, she could hardly spell. But this did not prevent her from understanding the philosophico-political ideas of her century better than many others, nor from writing (or rather, dictating) that, since the law is the expression of the general will, all citizens should be involved in its formulation.

My praise should not be taken as a declaration of anti-intellectualism; on the contrary, when I note that she understood the notion of 'general will' better than generations of 'great intellectuals', this is equivalent to noting, once again, that intellectuals may have extremely good ideas which they do not themselves understand. The idea that the law should be the expression of the general will had an author, and Olympe de Gouges clearly knew her Rousseau. Let us remember that, at that time, learning to write and learning to read were sometimes still separated. To say that a philosopher was read by people who knew only how to read is to pay that philosopher the greatest compliment possible. The ideas of the *Social Contract* proved comprehensible to readers who had not been to school; but Olympe de Gouges did not endorse the limits that Rousseau then placed, implicitly in the *Contract* and explicitly in *Emile*, on the generality of the general will. She took the concept of general will literally, without the assumptions that 'went without saying' (the general will of all except...) which restricted the generality of the concept in the minds of, for example, those who drew up the Declaration of the Rights of Man. She understood every aspect of this concept except those that were unspoken. And as her interpretation of it could not be refuted, those for whom the implicit assumptions were more important guillotined her.

On the 22 December 1789, the term 'Man' contained in the expression 'declaration of the rights of Man and of the citizen' was clarified: it meant *vir* and not *homo*, the male and not the human being. Olympe and a few others tried in vain to make the French Revolution their revolution. To imagine, uchronically, that they succeeded, around six generations before we came into the world, is to allow oneself the pleasant dream of being born into a very different world from the one we actually found. The phenomenon of battered women would long ago have disappeared, since it is basically a problem of married women who are economically dependent. If, in

1920, the French electorate had included women, the appalling law banning contraception, abortion and information would never have been passed; distribution of contraceptive devices throughout society would have directly followed their technical development and might even have hastened it. We should be more certain that we had been deliberately conceived by men and women who were free in relation to each other. And how different our childhood would have been with parents whose only obligation to each other would have been to watch over their common offspring (you, me), without either's regarding themselves as the 'owner' of those offspring! And if every child had the right to 'bear the names of the father and mother who acknowledge them', the girl-child would later have been as able as her brothers to pass on something of a family name; among the offspring, there would have been no individuals seen as having greater worth because they were heirs to the patronymic while others were seen as having lesser worth because they were not destined to pass on a few fetishized syllables.[9]

At a more global level, if political, school and 'familial' equality had become a normal aspect of society two centuries ago, we should all be different from what we are. I am very sorry not to have been brought up by people who were themselves born to people (etc.) whose mutual relations were defined by Olympe's Contract, rather than by the Napoleonic Code. I am even sorrier not to have lived among people brought up in this way; I should have preferred to have met men who had never experienced the authoritarian appropriation of their mothers by their fathers and who did not ask me to prove myself worthy of 'coming into their families' (a ridiculous idea, which has always put me to flight), and therefore to bow before the most absurd idiocies of their fathers and mothers, etc. In the relationship between a man and a woman, the reference to earlier generations weighs heavily and it sometimes feels as though you are in conflict not with a man himself, but with what was imposed upon him by his grandfather, which he deferentially accepted and is now imposing on you. The weight of the family past is not simply a matter of psychology: it is supported by the legal framework, which was set up by the political structures. The various bourgeois revolutions, of which the French Revolution is one, democratized or popularized the notion of 'lineage', in other words of a family that continues from one generation to the next, with a name and property to bequeath. Thus the aristocratic model, which was already widespread in the upper middle class, came within everyone's reach. A couple relationship is not formed in the one-to-one relationship of a man and woman. It passes through things, institutions, people and so on, and these mediators are themselves ordained by history; hence the pleasure to be had in dreaming of a different one. The real history which weighs down on us turns every woman into simply the means by which a masculine lineage can perpetuate itself at the level of the imaginary. 'Thou art thyself' says Juliet to Romeo, 'that which we call a rose by any other name would smell as sweet.' 'Romeo doff thy name.'[10] And she says she will do the same. When shall we also be able to say, 'Thou art thyself'?

3   The great disorientation

In talking about the position of women in terms of 'mediations', we are already setting off on the path of theorization. Let us hold back from this a little longer. For women theorists involved in the women's movement the feminist experience has been a true experience, in other words an encounter with an unexpected reality, in which a truly different and manifestly non-theoretical 'appeal' was created. With hindsight we can see that in the women's movement of the 1970s women had extreme difficulty in identifying who they were in what they were doing, and indeed in precisely describing the theoretical or practical basis of the action they were taking. Of course in the abstract it is not incorrect to say that feminism tried to bring to light a discontent,[11] or unacknowledged sufferings and hardships:[12] a difficulty of being which the collective consciousness refused and still refuses to see. It was research, 'in groups which formed, became deformed and then undone', into ills that were hidden even from the consciousness of the woman who suffered them, ills that she had always learned to hide and ignore. This research could only be carried out in small, informal groups and it often began with a kind of 'exchange of impressions'. Things that the available conceptual frameworks do not enable one to understand, nor current language to articulate, can still manifest themselves in the form of vague impressions, often first regarded as strictly personal, until others confirm them and add their own thoughts, remarks, tales and so on. By means of this mirroring relationship (which sometimes gave rise to panic and was at any rate hard to accept) gradually a collective awareness could emerge of what had been repressed by each woman.[13] This is my most vivid and most precious memory from those years: having gradually learned, with other women, to put a name to what was hurting me, through the discovery that I was not the only one being hurt. This enabled the rather lost woman I still was to face up to things; but for me as a woman philosopher it was also a positive experience of disorientation. When one thinks one has been trained in 'rigour', which, in principle, forbids one from advancing something which has not yet been entirely thought through and well-founded, the discovery that whispered, impressionistic stories and openly subjective viewpoints can lead the way to an understanding of the most vital things is a real lesson, which I have not yet fully integrated, but which teaches the following: it is better to allow yourself to start speaking before being completely sure that you can justify what you say; otherwise, you will never speak at all.

I digested this lesson philosophically by avoiding the easy rationalization which was on offer of thinking that women are destined to be impressionistic, while men have access to rigorous thought. The value of impressionism lies in a particular situation: when everything conspires to stop people from becoming aware of what they are experiencing, it is essential that they give voice together to little perceptions and intuitions, no matter how faltering. As for 'rigour', I have come to realize that the idea I had of it came from an impoverished tradition of philosophy, which can be contrasted with another. In the works of some Greeks, some seventeenth-century authors or in *Capital*, one finds a demand for exploratory rigour: when one investigates and tries to proceed with as tight an argument as possible, it seems necessary to go beyond what is commonly said in the hope of finding a coherent understanding. In the training we received, 'rigour' only ever meant a way of pruning everything that is not acceptable to all at the outset. It only suppresses that which risks appearing whimsical or freakish. This companion of the wisest conformism (as though wisdom was conformist!) produces both boredom and illusion at the same time: no one succeeds in pruning as much as is necessary.

So, from my experience of the methodological subjectivism of the Women's Movement, I learned to draw on a more adventurous idea of rigour which tears the fabric of acquired ideas and moves towards lands whose very existence is not guaranteed in advance. *Capital* is made of bits and pieces, Descartes recounts his life story and his dreams, Bacon weaves his project with biblical memories, Greco-Roman myths and quotations from Virgil and Socrates often calls on strange bursts of imagination to help him in posing problems. Everything must be brought in to undo a world of commonplaces and at the forefront of the project is the demand for rigour: a tonic rigour, full of juice and very different from the safe rigorism, the self-censored (and always ready to censor) puritanism that we have learned. The imprecise and hesitant words proffered in women's groups took me back beyond my training to a rediscovery of the groping and stuttering contained in the project to produce philosophy: many clumsy attempts and much improvization are needed before a clear and distinct idea is formed.

Disorientation then. Even if the Women's Movement can be characterized by its effort to bring to light aspects of the difficulty of being, it must be acknowledged that this is not a definition. Many women before me have said that the Movement was characterized by various rejections but that it did not articulate what the women involved collectively wanted. Two tendencies could broadly be identified: a feminism of equality and a feminism of difference, which often, moreover, declined the name 'feminism' and sought to separate itself from earlier struggles such as that of the suffragettes. However, these two currents (and anyway, were there only two of them?) coexisted and formed what was all things considered a single reality, whose type had never been seen before simply by reason of its lack of definition: the Movement never delineated its edges in any way. It did not form a party, with cards, membership and a manifesto, so that the issue of whether one was part of it or not remained deliberately vague. A woman from the 'Women's Movement' could be more or less anybody: a regular participant at meetings, a trade unionist who realized one day that her role in union delegations was purely decorative, or the wife of a revolutionary activist who discovered that her husband thought it absolutely right that she should be busy with the pots and pans while he debated the liberation of the masses with his comrades.[14] If the Movement had any particular effects it was due to its diffuse nature: it spread the idea that whatever the 'woman question' might be, it is not something strictly for specialists. Any woman who begins to rebel, to think it unreasonable that she should do all the housework and for this to be regarded as her responsibility, was and is 'in the Movement' and the Movement would have no meaning if it had not led women and men who never went near a meeting to rethink some aspects of their relationships.

Of course there were some women who carried the Movement and others who were more carried by it, but this is a distinction we can make now. When we speak of the Movement in the past, we refer to the former, who, without exception, have stopped meeting to explore issues together; but I do not think that the diffuse diffusion of the

Movement is over. People still talk about it and, most importantly, they do so in their everyday private conversations: the fact that a neighbour is beaten by her husband is regarded, not as a subject of derision, but as a problem which needs tackling somehow or other. The very small number of women elected to the French National Assembly in 1988 was noted as an embarrassing fact by many journalists. And those of my friends who have daughters, whether children or adolescents, are very concerned about the lives these girls will be offered. It seems that my generation alerted at least a section of public opinion and sowed ideas which are still causing questions to be asked, even though we almost never meet these days.

This is truly something to marvel at, since, without any very clear definition of who was or was not a member, the Movement also lacked any precise boundaries in relation to its objects and projects. It was not based on a clear definition of what was wrong with the position of women; it was always polymorphous and scattered in groups that differed greatly from each other. Moreover, at the best moments, it began to speak a language which did not respect the usual rhetoric of political demands: many banners and slogans were judged incomprehensible by people who were otherwise well disposed. When confronted with these slogans, many men and women laughed heartily, finding them full of meaning and spice, while others really could not see what they meant and wondered if such phrases were worth the cloth and paint used to make the banner. 'Amnesiacs of the world, forget us' was one for the First of May; another, mocking leftist comrades, was 'One solution, something else'. Many were unhappy about 'A woman without a man is like a fish without a bicycle',[15] 'Democracy for men means demography for women'[16] and the wonderful, 'I'm a woman, why aren't you?', which is worth twenty years of surrealism, to my way of thinking. A British Christmas card which said 'The birth of a man who thinks he's God isn't such a rare event'[17] was fairly successful among my friends, while the one I particularly liked, *Nous mourrons de n'être pas assez ridicules*; which means something like: 'we are not ridiculous enough and it may kill us', was judged opaque by almost everyone.[18]

This was, from all points of view, an experience of strangeness: to our way of thinking, all these phrases were equally meaningful, but some people thought they were all weird while others adopted one but left the rest. You could never tell in advance which would be understood and by whom. Hence what I have just suggested: to our way of thinking, they were meaningful, all of them equally so, but without our ever being able to tell whether or not their meanings would be grasped. One of the great things about the Movement of the time was that it did not concern itself with the public plausibility of what it said. The possibility of incomprehension was accepted as a pendant to speaking freely despite the acknowledged impossibility of entirely justifying what one says. This is far from being the preserve of feminism: underlying every utterance are decisions which cannot be totally justified to everybody, but which make it possible to speak. No discourse can build its own foundations and thus anything that is said may seem 'strange' or 'weird' or devoid of meaning, at least to somebody. Even if it is said by Nabert, Sartre or Hamelin, when they are stripped of the connivence which makes what they say digestible. We can start with Socrates: 'strange' (*atopos* in Greek) says Glaucon of the description of the cave in *The Republic*. Like the disorientation we have described, strangeness has a status in philosophy: that of an indispensable opening. That which is *atopos* is bizarre, but it is also 'without a place' (a-topos): the term marks the unlocatable nature of what is said in the accepted frame of reference. This does not mean that its meaning need not then be made as clear as possible. We have managed to sow a little disorientation. If we did not make clear what project was bearing us along in the Movement, this was due to some underlying reasons, which should now be presented.

4　Two inappropriate ways of thinking in one movement

The feminism of difference is based on the idea that women's true femininity is suppressed, has been so for centuries as a result of our sex's submission to the other or to patriarchal structures and is now even more so because of a modern social life which erases differences and makes everyone the same. From the 'Psychanalyse et politique' group to the journal *Sorcières*, via the work of Luce Irigaray, women have tried to uncover a womanhood which is neither the distorted femininity of the slave-woman of yesterday, nor the afemininity of the modern woman (if she really exists). Moreover this tendency thought that in this it was doing a service to the whole of society: by bringing authentic difference into existence, women would accomplish an important historical task, for they would remind the uniform society that difference exists.

To borrow an expression from Hélène Védrine, many feminists, including herself and myself, stated their 'hesitation' at embarking on such a project.[19] But to hesitate is not to produce a polemic and this fact should be noted. It seems that we felt we should let these things be said, basically 'just in case' – just in case something important arose from this current of thought which did not appear likely to have any worrying negative consequences whatever the case. Anyway, when a group collectively analysed the ills women suffer, it recognized a sad difference. If, in a symmetrical way, some women were trying to uncover a difference which it would be pleasurable to think about, perhaps this was a necessary counterpoint. Of course there were sometimes debates between feminists of equality and partisans of neo-femininity, in particular because the latter were rather free with their (Lacanian) insults. One could easily find oneself being called a 'phallic woman': I remember a day when Catherine Deudon, one of the Movement's photographers, was very violently reproved because of a camera. The debates between the two tendencies never proved productive, a common problem in internal debates and one which scarcely encourages people to pursue them. Moreover, there was also certainly a common base of agreement, in relation to which these debates were trivial.

The feminism of difference and the feminism of equality have remained precariously adapted to the situation and the confused feeling that they are inappropriate may have done much to ensure that they coexist more or less peacefully (less rather than more, all the same). The former has not managed to prove itself, it has remained at the stage of programmatic utterances because it has run up against intrinsic problems. The most important relates to the problem of the sign, which is no small thing. For this neo-femininity wanted to be a language, a language in which 'women can speak their sex'.[20] Certainly sexual difference has always been largely a business of signs, regarded by some as not arbitrary (which means that their nature as signs is forgotten) and by others as revocable, though with difficulty. It is important to realize that they truly are difficult to revoke. It is an illusion to think that one can be an absolutely free spirit, soaring high above convention and paying no attention to the 'rest of humanity', a rest who feel uneasy when little girls are not dressed in pink slippers and little boys in blue. Like everyone else, I need to recognize that the absurd strength of convention is within me. After all, for thirty years I could not bear to part with my very long hair and it took the life or death question of chemotherapy to make me sacrifice this distinctive sign which I had chosen as such in childhood. Of course we can find philosophers, both men and women, who have not felt tied to the marks of sexual identity: Hipparchia left her loom behind and Descartes nicely writes: 'I am not one of those who think that tears and sadness belong only to women and that, in order to appear as a man of courage, one must force oneself always to wear a calm expression'.[21] And ultimately the idea that we should be able to ask that freedom of philosophy must be defended. But in that case I need to know ('I' being anyone here) that I cannot identify with 'philosophy', in other words I cannot claim that it naturally speaks through my lips. For there are no known examples of people who have tried in a completely unbiased way to explore the entire system of signs governing the manifestation of 'femininity' and 'virility' in a different society or, a fortiori, in their own. It would take an angel or a perfectly balanced mixed group set on a libertarian project to do it. We might as well acknowledge the gap between radical freedom of thought, which philosophy promises, and the narrower freedom of which 'I' am (anyone is) capable. In relation to the question of sexual difference, no one is the Great Subject of philosophy or theory and this is why work can and does take place, started by one, continued by another, disputed by many.

The basic criticism to address to the neo-femininity current consists in noting that it represents an extreme form of voluntarism: it supposes that one can purely and simply repudiate an old system of signs – when it is hard even to be aware of fragments of it – and invent a new language which, far from being conventional, would be invented by nature and secreted by 'womanhood' (for why should one substitute one convention for another?), a language which would at once bring what it said into existence since, still according to the same current, one is located in relation to the gender split only when that difference is expressed. For if one were ipso facto differentiated in that way, all discussions of the question would be a waste of time.[22] Such a doctrine seems contradictory in its principle, like a sort of cratylean dream applied to oneself.

Moreover, how can one hope to bring to light an authentic femininity, whose difference from what has gone before and from all former identities is certain? Identification with our foremothers was an integral part of the discovery we made in childhood of our place within sexual difference. With a bit of luck, we then found models for identification which were less restricted to the family circle, a few breaths of fresh air: we travelled, through space, through the social classes and, by reading, through history, thus realizing that, even within 'alienated femininity', different forms exist and wondering therefore if some might not be more pleasing than others. Above all, aside from these problems of specularity, we were drawn to things and activities, according to our tastes. When we reached adulthood, the state that Simone de Beauvoir calls that of a 'finished woman', the chance elements of our different journeys meant that there were perceptible differences between women; so much the better and there could be more still. In such a situation, to look for a language in which 'women can speak their sex' is, in fact, to reduce this diversity to a sameness, to speak in terms of a single femininity and thus to bring in a problem of models. For, once one accepts such a perspective, the old models come rushing forward, following the logic of the archetype according to which the older the model, the more of a model it is. Unsurprisingly, the neo-femininity current led to a return to pre-1940s fashions, crocheting, jam-making and motherhood considered as a fine art. One may like jam and knitting and think that motherhood is indeed only justifiable if it can become one of the fine arts, but it is a big step from there to accepting even for a moment that every woman should conform to this model. And then many men have started to enjoy devoting part of their lives to jam or children: to want this type of 'difference' would mean forbidding them these choices.

Moreover, there is no way that this idea can support a collective democratic movement. If every woman cobbles together some idea of what a woman is, depending on her personal fantasies and chance experiences, not all of which are very pleasant, there is no reason why any group of women should agree, unless it is structured around a guru who can impose her speech as the speech of women. When there is freedom of speech and everyone tells her own story, we discover a kind of liberating differentiation. Even those physical events assumed to be most similar in all women, biologically speaking, can be experienced in extremely different ways. When Beauvoir talks rather sadly about puberty, she is speaking for herself alone and the chapter on this issue in *The Second Sex* should be read in the light of the *Memoirs of a Dutiful Daughter*. She recounts her experience twice: once in the mode of the universal and once in that of an autobiographical narrative. Obviously for her it was a sad fate. In women's groups, we discovered together that we cannot be certain that there is something that can be called puberty. It is the same thing with periods: some women from the preceding generation, including Annie Leclerc, thought that a woman should feel discomfort; women who felt no pain were suspected of having lost touch with the dark zone of femininity. However, others brought up their daughters in the strict belief that any woman who complained of headaches or other ills merely proved by this that she had fallen for obscurantist mythology. In the end, my generation understood that everyone is different. But as long as we stick to one model or another, there will be no serious medical research to try and find the painkilling drug which is needed by some women, but not all.

Trying to produce and impose a model of woman, however 'new', prevents one from getting to know and understand the plurality of the womanhood of real women. It quite simply prevents people from wanting to know about this plurality. For this reason we can link it to religious or political doctrines which have for centuries aimed to define the new man, inviting everyone to strip themselves of the old man to take on this new character. The idea goes back at least as far as St Paul;[23] stalinism and fascism brought it up again this century. Such a project is no doubt appropriate to the foundation of a religion or a tightly controlled political ideology, or to a form of association in which any variation appears as heresy or dissidence.

It matters little that the 'feminism of difference' has never had the practical means to be that much of a threat: it concerns us here only as an illustration of a permanent impasse, that of the ideology of difference, which arises from a contradiction. It starts by assuming that the existence of difference is valued, but then, by concentrating on one particular difference, it turns against its original programme, suppressing all differences which might exist on either side of the great dividing line which it has drawn. The only consistent way to give value to the fact of difference is to uncover differences by their thousands, or better, as Albert Jacquard suggests, countless differences which defy all lists. I believe, with him, that the quality of our existence depends on these differences, from all points of view. This being so, a binary system is of no use: it is the closest thing there is to pure identity.

However, this ideology could just about be justified on the grounds that any historical movement produces its own myths and ideology, which must be coped with somehow. Yet this myth was never appropriate to the Movement as it was. It might have suited an inactive movement: it had nothing to do with the various battles which women were starting and some of which are still going on. Groups which took up the issue of rape had primarily to deal with the police and medical and legal institutions which, instead of taking the charge seriously, tended and still tend to blame the victim. These groups also had to give psychological support to most of the rape victims when those around them failed to do so, to put it mildly. How could the praise of difference in any form have been an appropriate ideology for such a battle? A battle which taught many that there is no such thing as homogeneity when it comes to crime (an act of arson is imputed to its perpetrator, a rape to its victim) and that some individuals are less protected by the law than others (or than was thought), certainly less protected than property. The women fighting around this issue seem to me to be driven by not an ideology but a morality which acknowledges a de facto solidarity with and a duty to help those women whom society does not protect as it should. This morality deserves to be conceptualized and taught. If I have the strength, I shall try to do this.

All the same, the feminism of difference has coexisted with another, more classic current in the history of feminism, which is the one we can call the 'feminism of equality' and which, in my opinion, was also precariously adapted to the precise situation. It was no more appropriate than the other for understanding the discoveries of the social movement of the 1970s. Equality is only a simple notion to the extent that it refers to the field of isonomy, in other words the sphere of rights defined by the law and the state. The principle of isonomy is respected when everyone is equal before the law and when the law includes this principle in its very formulation. At the beginning of this century feminism could easily understand itself and find its bearings in relation to the discrimination enshrined in the law. At this time French law did not respect the principle of isonomy. All women were excluded from citizens' rights; married women were excluded from taking a large number of legal actions, a situation the Napoleonic Code graciously called 'the incapacity of the married woman'. But reform followed reform and more or less erased that particular aspect of inequality: women now do as they choose with their earnings, vote and can be elected to public office; married women no longer need their husband's permission to do paid work, open a bank account or take someone to court. One might think that the issue of isonomy is now settled. And yet there are still all kinds of disparities, which lead to power relations being established in relationships between men and women. So where do these disparities stem from?

Here we are reaching the nub of the matter, both philosophically and historically speaking. The usual approach to this question, using received concepts and the maps available, prevents us from understanding the issues and produces a set of false problems or a loss of intellectual direction – not in the Women's Movement, but in everyday discussion. As disparities are seen to persist, despite the fact that isonomy is apparently an established principle, the phenomenon is

explained by constructing a different arena from that of the law and
the state. These disparities are then imputed to 'attitudes' and 'mentalities', to the well-known complexity and particular inertia of the
world of customs, to civil society (which, in the liberal Western
world, would object to too much state regulation), or else to the
education given in families, in which the state would be embarrassed
to intervene too directly. In arguing in this way, one begins to believe
in the existence of entities which are then seen as responsible for the
persistence of inequalities, as though the education given by families
existed in itself and for itself, distinct from what happens in the
political arena; as though the relationship between parents and
children was in no way mediated by historical realities. All these
considerations lead people to throw in the sponge.

But do we really have to give up or should we try to realize that
these explanations are based on categories which we urgently need to
challenge? The Movement was a school for disorientation. In it one
could gain the feeling that neither frameworks for understanding nor
ordinary language were suited to what needed saying. We need to
push this disorientation to its limits, to try to realize that the very
categories in terms of which we ordinarily see politics must be transformed. If, for example, Tocqueville's thought, that great source of
today's commonplace ideas, blocks the necessary anlysis of politics,
or simply does not help us to undertake that analysis, then, although
it is more interesting to read than twopenny catechisms, it must go
the way of the Athens courgettes. It will henceforth be my concern
(and I should be pleased if others would become involved too) to give
at least some samples of the intellectual reorientation required by the
historical existence of a movement which was able to convince a
great many people of the fact that there is a problem.

5   My funny old life again: the public employer

I should like to be allowed a flash-back here. During the summer of
1981, I wrote an essay aiming to show two connected things: firstly,
that we have not acquired isonomy, and, secondly, that the 'woman
question' leads us to wonder what the distinction between the 'state'
and 'civil society' is worth. I gave this piece to my friend Liliane
Kandel so that she could put it forward for publication in *Les Temps
Modernes*. Thanks to her and to Simone de Beauvoir, it was scheduled
in record time and appeared in November of the same year. But
Liliane Kandel did more: she gave a copy of it to the Ministry of

Woman's Rights who passed it on to the Civil Service Ministry. Then I heard nothing more about it. Later, when I was shopping for a pamphlet on the new women's rights, I discovered in it a circular signed by two Ministers, Yvette Roudy and Anicet Le Pors, which proved that I had been (very partially) heard. This circular itself has its weaknesses, and the major failing of being almost unknown. It is a sad thing that none of us followed the matter up more closely Our grand-daughters and great-nieces will have uchronic criticisms to make of us: 'What if the feminists of the 1980s had shown more conviction. . .?' I reproduce this sample here, with only stylistic changes, because there is no doubt that this matter will have to be taken up once more.

Few people in France today are likely to remember Mademoiselle Bobard.* In 1936 she gave her name to a ruling by the Conseil d'Etat, the highest national court hearing disputes between citizens and the state.[24] A few years earlier she had been ingenuous enough to seek employment in an executive civil service post at the Ministry of War. Then, when she was refused the post (on a pretext the reader may easily guess), she appealed to the Conseil d'Etat.

That Council's answer was sublime, if we agree that the sublime is the extraordinary in ordinary life, the ordinarily extraordinary and vice versa. The ruling stated (thereby laying the first legal foundations of sexual equality in France) that, like men, women are fit for the civil service, but that the particular nature of some jobs requires. . .need I go on? I am told this is called a decree of principle. Basically this type of ruling states or defines a new principle, while at the same time declaring that the principle does not apply in the case of the particular litigation which gave rise to the appeal, and hence to the judgement and hence to the statement of principle. It is a perverse situation and very frustrating. You are not included in something which is nevertheless in part your work. The exception prompts the declaration of the rule, which then exempts it.

Thus the principle of sexual equality entered French History not on the triumphant path of the progress of Enlightenment, but rather with the crooked gait of the cows that Homer describes advancing reluctantly to the sacrificial altar. To return to Mlle Bobard, you may have thought that the motivation of the judgement had something to do with the Ministry of War, the imminence of the Second World War, women and weapons, women and secrets, secrets and soldiers, women and soldiers, Mata Hari. . .did your thoughts take

* By coincidence, *bobard* also means a tall story in French (trans.).

you right back to the Amazons? No need to look so far afield: actually it was just a question of grammar. Someone could write a fine thesis on 'howeverism in juridical texts concerning sexual equality from 1936 to the present day'. It would offer an opportunity to draw up a list of the various ways of retracting what is said as it is said. All the texts of the laws proclaiming equality – the Bobard ruling, the Law of 19 October 1946,[25] the Law of 10 July 1975 – are in fact constructed on the same linguistic model. First comes the principle, which is proclaimed or reproclaimed whenever necessary, pleasant or useful to a government's image. Then comes a new paragraph, or simply a comma, and at once the vessel is scuppered: 'However, when the nature of the functions or the conditions of their exercise justify it...', 'nevertheless, the particular régime in force in the...', 'subject to provision for the discretionary right of government to waive...', and so on. Each time that the principle is proclaimed, what is in fact being reproclaimed is the imprescriptible and inalienable right of the government to ignore it. And since these laws concern only the employment of civil servants and thus place obligations upon the state alone, this means in effect that they are written, debated, amended, published, taught in Law schools and learned by budding jurists all for nothing; except that they repeatedly accredit the crooked idea that henceforth in France everything is resolved and that moreover any outstanding difficulties are being actively worked on.

Women and public employment: a study of a case that is at once both extreme and exemplary. For, outside officialdom, anyone seeking good reasons for some manifestation of the sluggishness of history will always find them. It is so easy to argue that a law is never enough to create parity (non-discrimination) because, you understand, a legal text is ineffective against implicit customary precedent or ingrained social attitudes of mind – the mechanisms of civil society. The legislating state pleads that it can do no more. Not long ago Monique Pelletier, the Minister for Women's affairs, told a women's magazine, 'We have made enough laws, now people's attitudes must be changed.' Of course, attitudes and mentalities must also be changed, but by what miracle can this be brought about while the institutions themselves contrive to remain unchanged? Analysis of the state as employer enables us to challenge the excuses of the state as legislator: that at any rate is what I hope to show here.

For the state is not just a body which regulates a social domain external to it, it is also the largest employer in France. There is no need of statistics: it is common knowledge that in every branch of the public service (hospitals, teaching, post office and telecommunications, tax office, etc) large numbers of women are employed at the bottom grades of hierarchies and salaries, and exceedingly few in decision-making posts. Even so, posing the problem in terms of hierarchy obscures the essential point and leads to an easy, all too-easy 'explanation', which completely exonerates the public employer: families, the argument goes, encourage social ambitions in boys, while girls are encouraged to set reasonable limits to their aspirations and to content themselves with some place that is seen as 'natural' for them. True, one has often heard the consoling words 'That's not so bad for a woman'. But before incriminating some obscure and confused 'civil society', whose inert mass hinders the emancipation of women, notably through education, it might be as well to ask whether the good laws which customary sexism is supposed to be so strongly resisting are as perfect as we are told. Or whether the attitudes that need to be changed are not quite simply those of employers, starting with state recruitment officers. In broader terms, the dossier that feminists need to reopen today is that of the theory of relations between the state and what is termed – perhaps merely through intellectual laziness – civil society, that Other of the state whose existence is supposed to ensure that the state is not sole and absolute master and has not (yet) taken over all aspects of collective life.

To return to the precise problem of women in public service, the investigation is unnecessarily hampered if all attention is focused on the hierarchical aspect of discriminations. Of course, to repeat, in every branch of the public service women occupy the majority of badly-paid posts while men can contrive to rise to higher grades. Moreover, this does not differentiate the 'public' from the 'private', since more than half of unskilled workers are women. But I think it better to emphasize first of all that the scarcity of men in low-status jobs and the scarcity of women in better-paid positions each have very different causes. And moreover that these two scarcities are not on a numerical par.[26]

Everyone is agreed that if men are few in some types of public employment (but how many is 'few'?) this is due to a lack of applicants. I have before me the conclusions of one Jean Massot, high commissioner of government, which were addressed to the Conseil d'Etat with regard to another appeal which I shall discuss below. I note that in one sense they coincide with my own opinion: 'The simplest and most legal way once more to recruit a high proportion of men into primary school teaching would doubtless be to make this

career more attractive and to put an end to a situation in which a
primary school teacher's salary can only provide a supplementary
income (*salaire d'appoint*) for a household'.[27] The moral is that 'few'
(how many?) men are recruited as primary school teachers because
few men present themselves for the entry examination. Women
accept jobs that scarcely interest men (unless there is nothing better)
because they are doubly unrewarding, being both unattractive and
badly paid. This implies that the need for women to marry is analyti-
cally contained in their job description, which is what 'supplementary income' means. If, on the other hand, there are few
women at the top of the ladder (but again, how many? as few as the
other few?), it is because few women are accepted. Rather than
starting from the number of women employed at these grades, it
would be better first to consider how many women apply for the
posts. We should then see that the number of women with long, even
brilliant academic records behind them, and hence eligible to sit
the highly selective recruitment examinations, is, I maintain, much
higher than one might think, to judge merely from the proportion of
women who actually occupy high-ranking administrative positions.
We can now invert the currently fantasized picture of the relationship
between families and the state. Do fathers, mothers and the educational establishment clip the wings of their daughters' ambition? No,
the academically-minded middle and lower-middle classes of the
1980s have advanced a fair way in their views on such matters. As for
the popular strata, the consensus there is perhaps even stronger:
among the urban and rural working classes it is regarded as self-
evident that both girls and boys need to make themselves employable
and here ambitions are even more markedly orientated towards the
public sector. For, as is obvious from everyday social experience,
disadvantaged and oppressed groups tend to place a special value on
civil service jobs, whatever they may be, because they represent an
escape from insecurity. All the more reason to encourage their daughters to apply for such jobs. And in that case, they might as well
aim for positions at a level where life is comfortable – what could be
more logical as a strategy of escape from the trap of precarious
marginality?

I therefore consider it pure mystification to say that the hierarchy
of the sexes in public employment simply reproduces a pre-existing
hierarchy in traditional civil society. Whatever level of employment
one looks at in the public sector, a woman applicant faces stiffer
recruitment conditions than a man. At the bottom of the ladder
women are driven into fierce competition with each other.[28] At the

top they face the sexism of the selection panels. We therefore need to consider the problem not so much from the point of view of hierarchical pyramids as from, if one may put it thus, a lateral perspective, looking at the numbers of applications, chances of success and actual levels of recruitment or exclusion of women public service staff.

The state, which is generally regarded as progressive (although powerless to put its generous principles into effect), also benefits from a grossly flattering public image, in that its recruitment is supposedly conducted in the most democratic way possible, free of sly discrimination, by means of public competitive examinations, than which, as well all know, nothing on earth could be more equitable.

On the face of it, this would seem to be yet another reason why women would choose this particular employer; especially since the (so-called) legislation for the protection of women's rights (not to mention the provisions of the labour Code) is said to be having catastrophic effects on women's employment in the private sector: employers know in advance if they hire a woman that, should she have a mind to repopulate the nation, they will be subject to obligations which are fairly strictly defined by law; and many employers automatically regard a woman as a potential mother. I do not believe that this legislation is the real cause of existing discrimination in private-sector recruitment.[29] But it does at least make it easier for private-sector management to shrug off its responsibility: it can blame the state which, with its over-protective laws, makes the avoidance of discrimination practically impossible for employers whose good will is, naturally, not in question.

Whatever difficulties may exist in the private sector, public sector recruitment by competitive examination is itself far from being above all suspicion. To support this contention I shall consider here just two examples which are characteristic precisely because of their diametric contrast. There is in France a National School of Posts, Telecommunications and Broadcasting (ENSPTT), which is microscopic in terms of student numbers, but has the status of a *grande école** by virtue of the careers it opens up. Its graduates leave with the rank of top administrators. Those who apply for admission have already completed long years of higher education, such as a master's degree, a diploma in political science, or even a full course of study at another *grande école*. The entrance examination consists of a written part (two papers each valued as two points) and an oral, also

---

* Prestigious university-level college with entrance by competitive examination (trans.).

comprising two tests: a language exercise (two points) and a 'conversation with the selection panel'. Is the latter a minor component? Far from it: it is the decisive part of the examination, since it is valued as five points, in other words almost the equivalent of all the others put together, although the latter can claim an academic rigour which any imaginable 'conversation with the selection panel' will lack.

It is easy to carry out an institutional analysis of this type of selection procedure. Everything hinges on a 'conversation' whose aim is to establish the applicants' 'profile', with the help of information taken from their files and curriculum vitae. This type of selection can be termed both impressionistic and substantializing: at the ENSPTT oral, a candidate is chosen on the grounds not of what she or he knows, but of what she or he is. And it makes a big difference whether it is a she or a he. Let us look at the evidence: in 1981, after the written papers of the examination exclusively for graduates of the grandes écoles, fifteen were selected to go forward to the oral, eight men and seven women. After the oral six men and just one woman were finally accepted.[30] Thus on the basis of two written papers testing knowledge, which were of course anonymous, we find real parity between men and women. In itself, this is very reassuring. In any case, it backs up my thesis that explanations for the scarcity of successful women applicants will be found not by looking at the attributes of the women candidates themselves (inhibitions, lack of self-confidence, half-hearted support from their families or whatever), since the outcome here can be traced entirely to the misogyny of the selection panels officially mandated to select not abilities but persons.

Incidentally it is worth adding that such a mode of recruitment, where the socio-substantializing principle (who are you?) replaces the rigour of an academic standard (what do you know?) is utterly discreditable for a republican state. I use the term socio-substantializing principle because assessment by file, curriculum vitae and conversation does work haphazardly, even though the impression the candidate may give is taken into account. For the 'impression' one gives is an integral part of one's social identity. As a result, the social hierarchy as the panel members understand it becomes the decisive criterion for selection. Never was the adage that 'the school chooses the chosen' more apt than here, where privilege is bestowed on those who are already privileged through membership of a dominant or prestigious social group. What is being evaluated in a test by file, CV and conversation is a person's imaginary worth in terms of a set of opposites: man rather than woman, 'well-groomed' rather than 'vulgar', white rather than black? Parisian rather than provincial? Reproducing social stereotypes current in the wealthy districts rather than the poorer ones?

To this it may be objected that, apart from a few top-level admissions procedures, the recruitment of state employees is not conducted in this way. My reply is, first, that I should like someone to explain to me why it is precisely the 'top-level' selection procedures that are so impressionistic. This is not how nursing auxiliaries are recruited for the hospitals. It would seem that the democratic or republican principle has to except its own oligarchy from its own system. In other words, substantializing recruitment, however contrary to republican procedure, seems to be 'necessary' at the top end of the hierarchy, the person's imaginary status being drafted in to confirm and reinforce the prestige of the posts and indeed to guarantee the excellence of the functions their occupants perform. Of course such guarantees operate purely at the level of fantasy. If competent women are passed over in favour of less competent men, we can only hope that the institutions will run themselves, which moreover they usually do. Condorcet once amused himself listing the fatuities of some of the Ancien Régime's politicians.[31] Gross as these may have been, they did not bing about the collapse of the state. We might also recall Charles VI, who was mad for years without this having any serious consequences or compromising the monarchy. He was King by divine right, and that was enough since his symbolic presence was all that mattered. It may be that the French Republic (which, if we are to take Pompidou's word for it, also needs its princes of the blood) can likewise afford to have among its top administrators people whose presence is purely symbolic. Indeed this would be excellent proof of the solidity of its institutions, but the thought makes your blood run cold all the same.

The dualism of methods of public-sector recruitment (according to precise abilities or substantializing personalization) exactly reflects the distinction between what are called posts 'with personal responsibility' and jobs which merely involve the execution of decisions and policies arrived at elsewhere. If you have a civil service job which amounts to performing duties and tasks set by others, your ability to put the code of operations into practice will alone be taken into account. But if your job is to define other people's tasks and to determine the broad guidelines of an organization, or to have a symbolic role as one who takes these decisions, we lapse into notions which are predemocratic and prerational, belonging to the category of the magical. The term candidate's 'profile' barely conceals the evaluation of a charisma which is in itself nothing other than the interiorized membership of a socially and symbolically dominant group.[32] I once heard a government Inspector-General declare that it is not legitimate to expect genius of a functionary. That remark indeed constitutes a rigorous definition of the modern status of the functionary, something which is of decisive importance in the history of our institutions. But overshadows the fact that the image of the functionary as someone who is simply competent to carry out clearly defined tasks presupposes the existence elsewhere, at the upper end of the chain of command, of a completely distinct system which creates definitions of tasks. Doubtless this act of creation is itself a myth, but no matter. What all this means is that the democratic, republican notion of the civil servant absolutely requires its converse, its contradiction: a place within the system where different and indeed radically opposite values prevail, in this case the person's personality (in other words the set of social parameters which define it) and not the individual's knowledge and trained capacity.

The apparently vague method of recruitment (not rigorous from the point of view of abilities and kowledge) of a 'conversation with the selection panel' is in fact perfectly suited to that place, since it enables the examination to be personalised to the highest possible degree. Sexist prejudices (like those of race and class) will inevitably be given free rein here because they are not counterbalanced by any precise assessment of knowledge. The ENSPTT selectors demonstrated this in masterly fashion: the oral reintroduced the parameters which the marking of the written papers had not taken into account. I shall say someting below about the steps which could immediately be taken to limit such shameful discriminatory practices. But even then, the real solution can only be attained by dialectically transcending the notion of the functionary post itself. It is because there are executants who are regarded purely as executants that an imaginary virtue, a symbolic snob-value is required in 'top-level' officials. If, as the idea of self-management suggests, the so-called lower grades of officials were allowed to define collectively both their own tasks and the conditions necessary for the proper functioning of their service, it might perhaps be possible to dispense with recruiting the others according to some spurious and archaic quality of charisma.

That is not all. For if, conversely, we look at those practices of competitive recruitment which can actually lay claim to a real degree of democratic rigour, it transpires that here too the situation is not as acceptable as we might have hoped. Few people are likely to remember the case of Mesdemoiselles Bachelier and Niol. Sadly, they too have bequeathed their names to the annals of the Conseil d'Etat. In 1975, the Teacher Training College of Morbihan in Brittany held a competitive entrance examination to recruit ten men and fifteen women. The joint panel of examiners for the two examinations only succeeded in filling five of the men's places for lack of adequately qualified candidates. The fifteen women's places, on the other hand, were filled without difficulty and the selectors even suggested enrolling the next five women candidates on a supplementary list of acceptances. The names of Mesdemoiselles Niol and Bachelier were on this list. But instead of allocating the women on the supplementary list the unfilled places from the men's exam, the education authority's inspector decided to fill those places with male candidates from the supplementary lists of other regions. Niol and Bachelier took the case to the administrative courts: a tribunal in Rennes found in their favour. The Ministry of Education appealed against this ruling to the Conseil d'Etat. Jean Massot, who has already been mentioned, wrote a report which is incredibly hard to follow for a lay reader such as myself. One becomes lost in the maze of jurisprudence and indeed this extreme degree of juridical complexity is ultimately part of the problem. It is relevant to and revelatory of the current state of the position of women in France. In 1978, when the Conseil d'Etat ruled in this case, despite the 1936 Bobard ruling on sexual equality, despite the 1946 law, the 1975 law and so forth, the problem of whether or not a woman is equal to a man was still giving rise to complicated mental and judicial wranglings. And things turned out badly for Bachelier and Niol. Despite the Rennes tribunal's decision and Jean Massot's conclusions, the Conseil d'Etat decided in favour of the Minister, and thus of the regional Inspector, who had wanted to take men from another department. The wording of the ruling was a masterpiece: 'Since recruitment of men and women primary school teachers by separate examinations is inevitably prejudicial to sexual equality, its legality should be appraised in the light of a well-established series of precedents which has been worked out over the last twenty years by the most solemn rulings of the Conseil d'Etat.' The uninitiated reader starts; but you and I have naturally perused our Legal Reports. Given that in any case the principle has been violated from the outset (and no one seems bothered by this), behold how this violation is solemnly legitimized! Certainly it was well and good that in 1975 Giscard d'Estaing's government proclaimed the principle we all know. But since all laws on sexual equality in the public sector include exceptions, it is plain here that legality can only be contrived within the framework of a wider state of exception! And if this legality proves unfavourable to women, then too bad. Frankly I cannot make head or tale of this, nor can I square it with the little I thought I understood of the notion of principle; but the result is clear: Niol and Bachelier are not school teachers. There are around nine million housewives in France and 60 per cent of the unemployed are women. Let us hear no more talk about the intertia of customs and mentalities while laws are so made that men, and only men, are protected by the arsenal of jurisprudence.[33]

A legal protectorate: one might indeed imagine that a country both democratic and realistic would take measures to protect certain social categories who are disadvantaged or handicapped from the outset. Thus in the case in the United States, where university places are hard to come by, a fixed quota of places is reserved for young people from oppressed ethnic groups. This type of provision is actually calculated not so much to protect from as to correct certain effects of social inequality. Without getting diverted into a discussion of the practical effects of the American legislation, let us simply note that in France the opposite occurs: the quotas protect the privileged.[34] Recruitment by separate examinations for men and women primary school teachers has this effect when the quality of women candidates is avowedly higher than that of men, so that if open competition were allowed then women would be the winners. Let us restate the main points: in an admissions procedure like that of the ENSPTT, an impressionistic selection method gives a free rein to the spontaneous sexism of the examiners. But where women are allowed to deliver proof of their abilities, strict and overt segregation is maintained.

This is not the end of the story. An official decree dated 19 April 1977 formally ended all distinction between the jobs offered to men and women primary school teachers. Was this a victory? Not at all; for on 22 August 1978 a contradictory decree was promulgated bearing the prestigious signatures of Raymond Barre and two other senior ministers and stating, 'Separate recruitment procedures are to be provided for male and female candidates in those regions where the proportion of teachers of either sex in post in nursery and primary schools was greater than 65 per cent of the total number of teachers on 31 December of the year preceding the recruitment.' The ministers must have deemed it necessary to combat the excessive feminization (how familiar and plausible that formula sounds!) of primary education. Yet strangely enough it seems never to have occured to anyone to set quotas of this type for admissions to the Ecole Nationale d'Administration, the Ecole Polytechnique or the *agrégation* in philosophy, nor to coin some phrase like 'the excessive masculinization of certain occupations'. The parallel is never drawn, though it could and should be argued for. If one is going to say that it would be unfortunate for young children to form a mainly feminine image of primary school teaching, one might equally well say that it is deeply pernicious for adults to have an exclusively masculine image of administration, technology or intellectual work. The more so since there is no shortage of high-quality women applicants, in contrast to the case of male primary school teachers. All that is lacking is proper safeguards to protect against the sexism of selectors.

Whatever legal counterweights we might devise, the principle which must be absolutely respected is that of the homogeneity or universality of the legislation. As we have seen, once it becomes possible to breach the principle, it is the breaches and not the principle which become the norm. Furthermore, rumour has it that once an avenue of professional qualification becomes 'feminized' its prestige declines. It would be a waste of effort to try to prove that this opinion, far from being a perception of an independently existing form of sexism in society, it itself a generator of sexism. It is much simpler to require that all professions be equally 'feminized' – which is what I meant by a principle of homogeneity. Supposing that for the moment it were true that the status of a profession is inversely related to the number of women working within it, this would remove one of the modes by which a hierarchy of professions is established, which would give cause for rejoicing. As has often been said, women's struggles converge with global struggles against social hierarchy. I am not convinced that a homogeneous 'feminization' of occupations, or in concrete terms a feminization of decently paid work, would have a substantial impact on the overall inequality between jobs. But I am certain that a homogeneous masculinization of very low-paid jobs would bring about the disappearance of so-called 'supplementary incomes'.[35]

The necessary safeguard can be imagined in various forms. Strict quotas could be set, in which case they would have to be the same for all forms of competitive recruitment. Or it might be decided (if this better reflected the spirit of the times) that a supervisory commission would meet each time that the proportion of women passing at a public examination fell below a certain threshold: since examiners hate nothing more than measures which might put them into the position of examinees, the deterrent effect can easily be imagined. Lastly the legislation currently applying to primary school teachers could be extended to cover the state sector as a whole. When it was published, no one regarded that decree as outrageously coercive. It is objectionable merely because, as I have said, it privileges the privileged. If it were extended to the whole of public employment, it would become perfectly progressive. It could even be regarded as a temporary expedient, destined to fall into obsolescence as soon as the much-touted attitudes-and-mentalities had changed to the point where all professions were 50 per cent composed of women, in other words, in practical terms, with the disappearance of the unacceptable phenomenon of 'supplementary income' and of that equally unacceptable social phenomenon of the confinement of millions of women to the home. The latter is, moreover, the only area where we can still see attitudes-and-mentalities at work. If we leave aside the upper-middle classes, housewives are unemployed people in disguise, effectively on a par with conscripts on national service. Acceptance of the travesty, which military constraint alone manages to force on young men, is still imposed by ideology on many women. Rather than exhausting themselves making pointless job applications, they resign themselves to a totally unsecured and unpaid condition as domestic workers. And this resignation is sustained by the mythical figure of the mother-and-wife. What would happen if, having noted the 'spontaneous' phenomenon described above, the Women's Movement launched a campaign for all housewives to register as unemployed? What if the campaign was vigorous enough to be heeded? It would be a bad day for national statistics, but sooner or later we ought to think about it, and the ideological work of women's struggles will necessarily have to be directed towards encouraging the largest possible number of 'housewives' to see themselves as unemployed. Very hard-working unemployed, needless to say. Even if one does not agree with the call for wages for housework, we should concede to those who are fighting for them the merit of constantly recalling attention to the existence of this invisible and unpaid work.

Feminist thinking today has the good fortune to be able to draw conclusions from more than a century of struggles and debates. That century has been marked by a variety of partial, discontinuous or fragmented offensives, from individual battles to enter a particular profession to struggles for the right to vote, for citizen's rights or for free access to contraception and abortion. But it happens now and then that some of us, downhearted at the end of the day, end up feeling that 'nothing does any good'. The waves of hope rise and fall: 'The grey cloth becomes barred with thick strokes moving, one after another, beneath the surface, following each other, pursuing each other, perpetually. As they neared the shore each bar rose, heaped itself, broke and swept a thin veil of white water across the sand. The wave paused, and then drew out again, sighing.' These opening sentences from Virginia Woolf's *The Waves* might well contain the poetics of our collective historical experience. Successive waves of women have joyfully fought, convinced that once we had at last gained the right to, for example, a job, education, citizen's rights, or a sexuality freed from the chains of reproduction, something fundamental would have changed in the general female condition. A thin veil of white water across the sand: those gains have hardly even yet been gained and the radical transformation that we expected along with civil equality or birth control has not come. Besides, like harbour pools governed by a complex system of locks and sluices, particular social spaces open to us and then close off again. Of course, we rejoice when careers in the judiciary or administration, places at the *grandes écoles* or work as a sculptor open up to women. That always amounts to something won back from the twilight zone of unemployment or housework. It means a little less competition between women at the bottom of the ladder. But we can no longer put out the flags when it happens because we no longer see these advances as irreversible steps foreshadowing other, vaster mutations. When Julie Daubié won the right to take the *baccalauréat*, she was a true pioneer, inaugurating a collective movement;[36] she was a messenger of hope. Unfortunately, the various minor breakthroughs we see today cannot be interpreted in the same way. Since the Second World War, the number of women doctors in the United States has fallen slightly every year. It is as though defence mechanisms quieter and more complex than brutal exclusion had taken some time to get under way, but then gradually gained in effect; or perhaps an implicit *numerus clausus* defined a tolerance threshold, a hidden point where the alarm bells sounded and beyond which the holders of power in society go into action to keep women out. Simone de Beauvoir says it is harder for a young woman to be a writer today than it was when she was thirty. One can easily believe her. The overall number of women in work is lower now in France than it was in 1900, if we include all the women farm labourers of the *belle époque*. The proportion of unmarried women has also decreased, which is a bad sign, or rather is in tune with everything else.[37] A century of victories and collapses. The second sex, that shock absorber of social swings, never makes any certain gains. Inward migrations, exoduses, expansions, recessions, fresh waves: whether economic, cultural or political, the waves break more of us than they keep afloat. And even if they did

keep us afloat, they would be deceiving us. There are enough ideological or political eddies in the Movement, enough inquiries going
adrift, to make sure of that.

For, inevitably, we keep returning to the same question: where
is the root of the evil? What obstacle must be shattered in order to
trigger irreversible progress? What is really worth doing? Naive
though it may be, the question is unavoidable, even when one knows
from experience that the answers one might find to it soon turn into
nebulous mythmaking.

Where is the radical solution? What is the underlying bedrock of
the problem? I have no idea, unless it is once more a question of
thresholds: perhaps we have not yet accumulated enough partial
successes to ensure that each is solid and definite. It may be so; but
how can one tell in advance? We have to take a gamble, in the
knowledge that if there really is a threshold to be crossed, we cannot
allow ourselves to neglect anything at all. 'I scorn almost nothing',
said Leibniz, who rightly held that the sound of the sea was composed of the sum of an infinite number of minute imperceptible
noises. A dual strategy could at any rate be tried: both to neglect
no demand as too small to be significant, and to demand that all
measures be always global in scope.

To neglect nothing: sometimes a group in the Movement takes an
initiative and receives nothing but criticism from the rest. 'Running a
campaign against the gutter press wasn't the most urgent or necessary of priorities': one has often heard that verdict and others of a
similar kind in the Movement. Everything is urgent and everything is
necessary, including the campaign against the gutter press, even
though one still needs to think carefully about the exact tactics to be
used. Is it best to seek to have a sexist newspaper banned, or instead
to see whether it is kept afloat by public subsidy and in that case to
demand that state handouts be cut off? We may argue about how to
attack, but the act of fighting against humiliation and discrimination
of whatever kind is always justified. I shall scorn nothing: to return
to women in public employment, I shall not even scorn the reform
of requiring that all competitive recruitment panels (and indeed
examiners' panels in general) should be strictly mixed, men and
women, half and half: in other words isomorphous with the composi-
tion of the society in whose name they act. This is definitely the case
for the panel of examiners of the ENA (National School of Administration), where there is usually one woman to ten men. You shrug;
that's the ENA, there are so few people whom that affects. Except
that this school is a training ground for politicians. Members of

Parliament, Ministers, senior executives and others all tend to be ENA graduates. Therefore the whole state machinery is provided with servants who, from the outset, know this is a world of men among themselves. Anyway, there is no reason to tolerate any discrimination whatsoever, especially in places where decision-makers are educated. On the philosophy *agrégation* panel one may just find, in a good year, the odd transient woman members, sometimes there is only one; and the women candidates whisper, rightly or wrongly, that these women members are hand-picked so that their presence will make no difference to what happens. The simple fact is that all selection panels could now be half composed of women.[38] Since this is possible and does not happen, these backstairs rumours have a basis in fact. And more power to the mischievous rumours as an opening weapon of attack! After all, reform of the selection panels should not require a campaign by the Women's Movement, no matter how small-scale. It is the job of women academics who are aware of the anomaly to make known their discontent to those responsible; and it should be enough to argue that what is both possible and legitimate ought to be instituted straight away: since we now have a republican government, one in other words which is more capable of grasping the meaning of a principle.

To neglect nothing, because that means tolerating nothing. But also because it means that parity between the sexes must be made a universal law, without exceptions. For a century we have been fighting partial, discontinuous offensives. Homogenizing them today would involve a kind of blanket strategy, a maximal deployment of feminist critique, so that it becomes coextensive with the social space. We could all then work together in peace, since there is enough for everyone to do, once we all agree to let nothing pass. No Mount Athos must be left standing on the social terrain, and the words 'however', 'nevertheless' or 'with the reservation that' must not appear in the next proclamation of sexual equality. Because there is going to be one, isn't there? What do you mean, it's not certain? If the next proclamation is not already on the timetable for the National Assembly then we were taken for a ride at the last elections.[39] But no: Yvette Roudy and Simone Iff[40] are now working on a reform of the law on prostitution, which is a most important issue, and they seem to be adopting a good approach which pays attention to what the women prostitutes' collectives are saying, and which takes account as well of the state's own implication in the affair. Rather than treating the state as a force of order regulating a society which exists outside itself, they have directly posed the question of whether the state is not the country's number one pimp. From the viewpoint of political philosophy this is crucial, a first pointer towards an innovatory perspective. The state carries a heavy responsibility in what concerns the phenomenon of prostitution, not least because it is the state which has always been the protector of the client. The repressive measures it adopts are always aimed solely at prostitutes and the men they live with, never at the clients whose demand creates the market and hence the phenomenon. And some of the repressive measures which affect women are even primarily designed for the purpose of making the contract of purchase less risky for those same clients: the obligatory health inspections, for instance. By directing its measures only against the women and their procurers, the state is effectively acting as a pimp for the client. This innovatory approach adopted by Yvette Roudy and Simone Iff ought to lead them to draw the logical consequences from this state responsibility and draw up a radical plan for legislation capable of starting to set in train the elimination of prostitution.[41] Subject to the proviso, of course, that such an undertaking will depend for its success on the greater or lesser extent of measures undertaken elsewhere to better women's concrete social conditions and their overall social image. For once we have time on our side: six and a half years in which to accomplish an irreversible change; but we need to make haste, since only the accumulated weight of reforms will serve to make each one of them effective. So when shall we see the extension of the anti-racist law of 1972, to apply the same sanctions to sexist attitudes and utterances? And when will there be decrees which give real effect to the Weil law on freedom of abortion and contraception? In the highly unlikely event of the new government being hard up for ideas, we should be ready to provide it with a well-stocked list of legal measures that are urgently needed now[42] – regardless of how rapidly attitudes-and-mentalities, for their part, prove disposed to change.

6   *Partial dispensations and a little circular*

These words date from 1981. At that time a simple, clear idea had not yet become widespread in groups working for the liberation of women. This idea is in the same spirit as my essay, but is only just today beginning to be a subject of debate. I shall formulate it like this: French legislation on contraception and abortion is structured in a completely absurd, twisted and Jesuitical manner. On the one hand, under the law passed in 1920, which has not been repealed, abortion, information on abortion and propaganda – meaning advertising – for contraceptive products are still offences under the law. Two family planning activists were charged with them in January 1988, for giving out addresses of foreign clinics. The Neuwirth law, which permits the prescription of contraceptives and their sale in chemists, and the Veil law which permits abortion in certain circumstances, are simply dispensations, and quite restricted at that, in relation to the law of 1920. This means that the right of women freely to control their own fertility is still not legally recognized. Together, the underlying principle of a penalizing prohibition and two dispensations posit a non-right combined with minimal concessions. If women's right was recognized, we should have laws that were more rational, in other words more simple and logical. The issue of abortion and contraception would disappear from the Penal Code and would only figure in the context of legislation on health, which is perfectly able to define the necessary conditions for any form of medical intervention.

We should also recall here the correct formulation of an old legal adage: 'The exception proves the rule for non-excepted cases.' From this point of view, the dispensations provided for by the Neuwirth and Veil laws correspond to a reproclamation of the 1920 law. The ban on anything not included in the dispensation, such as the advertising of contraceptive products, is reaffirmed and 'confirmed'. The legalization of an exception amounts to letting go of one element in order to uphold the fundamental point. Unfortunately, the fundamental point here is that the right of women to control their own fertility is still not enshrined in the constitution. I do not know when we shall have a government brave enough simply to repeal the 1920 law and I write this sadly after some years of a Socialist legislature. 'We shall keep our hands off the legal framework of women's position' seems to be the motto of any government, as soon as it is in power. In any case no government ever does anything for women unless it is pushed very hard. When it is pushed, there is always a great loss of energy and a blunting of ideas. When it is not pushed, the clock starts going back. When one considers the number of street demonstrations, meetings, posters, manifestos and petitions, all the fundraising, pamphlets and the millions of hours of effort we put in between 1971 and 1975 to win a mere dispensation from a repressive law which is still in place, one has to admit that the notion of a waste of energy is, in this case, a gracious understatement.

It is important that the administration does not discourage potential
women candidates by the image of itself that it gives them [...] The
presence of both sexes in the selection bodies is a factor in enriching
the criteria for selection of candidates by the diversification of points of
view corresponding to the needs and realities of a mixed society. At the
present, panels are largely composed of men; it is your task to solicit
and encourage the participation of women who display the necessary
abilities. At the very least it is necessary to avoid panels composed
entirely of members of one sex [...] Statistics show that in all bodies,
even those that have a high proportion of women, the number of
women who reach posts of responsibility – at any level – does not
correspond to their percentage in the workforce. Deliberate and re-
lentless action must be taken until these anomalies have been reduced.

This last sentence, almost Churchillian in style, is enough to make
one laugh till one cries: it is completely contradictory to demand
'deliberate action' in a circular which has no power over anyone.[43]
Not only does it 'recommend' without prescription, it was also quite
simply never any more than a circular, while the panels are
appointed by decree. Now there is a hierarchy of legal texts: as a
decree is more important than a circular, it cannot be attacked in this
way. Moreover, this circular, which simply recommends, does not
even set out the threshold above which a group is considered mixed.
Such a text comes into the category of bizarre legislation which is
careful not to legislate, although it appears to be doing so. The
resistance put up by the state to the integration of women into its
structures never fails and we can see the extent to which we are given
fake reforms.

    As a result, we must take up the cudgels again and seize the
opportunity to make our demands, or mine at least, clear. French has
the term *mixité*, which mainly describes any situation where women
and men, or boys and girls, are together. We use it to describe the
principle of co-education, for instance. But in my experience the sexes
are never really 'together' when one of them is in the overwhelming
majority and the other merely a token presence. Therefore, I believe
that real *mixité* cannot exist without the additional principle of a
balance of the sexes. From conceptual explanations, let us now return
to politics. There is no reason why a well-disposed government
should refuse to bring a law establishing a balanced community of
the sexes before parliament. (It is not within my powers as a utopian
to know when we shall have a well-disposed government, but I shall
risk the following prediction: any government would be obliged to act
as though it were well disposed if the collective movement were

strong enough to make any other attitude burdensome to it.) This law should state that sexual balance is one of the fundamental principles of the Republic, whose aim is to make concrete the fundamental rights of women and men. At the same time the necessary spring cleaning would be carried out by repealing article 317 of the Penal Code, otherwise known as the 1920 Act, and the word 'fraternity' would be replaced by that of 'solidarity' in the Republic's motto. The law would state that a perfect balance is reached once there is an equal number of men and women in a given body and that the balance is no longer even approximate as soon as representation of one of the sexes falls below 35 per cent. Of course, such considerations might make the government and parliament feel guilty, their proportion of women being way below 35 per cent. To ease their consciences, they would be shown, during the debates that would follow in the newspapers, that there are also very few unmarried male politicians. This job seems to require a wife–auxiliary who takes care of all the domestic problems and is able to second her husband discreetly and effectively in local public relations. Not to mention the unconditional moral support which even the likes of Pericles possibly needed. There are few independent men in political or cultural decision-making bodies.[44] We could explain this publicly to those who govern us, always supposing, of course, that the media are prepared to let us speak, which is becoming an increasingly rare thing.

This law would apply to all bodies linked in any way with the state, which would make us realize all of a sudden that there are a thousand and one such organizations. It is wrong to think of collective life in terms of either a contrast between the state and a liberal, spontaneous 'civil society', or a set of individuals directly gathered into one single corpus, which is the state. The state is linked to a fine collection of bodies, which it regulates or refrains from regulating, which may at any moment turn into lobbies or pressure groups and which are the agents of discrimination in everyday life.[45] To prove its good will, the state would, of course, at once have to enforce its law on sexual balance in the civil service, which would change the face of France's largest employer. It goes without saying that any local authority, and particularly regional authorities, would have to complay with this basic law, but so would any organization which receives public funding in whatever form.

In France some private educational establishments benefit from a 'contract' with the state; in other words large grants: those which were not yet mixed (mainly Catholic schools) would have to choose between their 'homosexity' and the assistance they took from the public purse.[46]

This law would also affect the various councils of the corporatist professional organizations, such as that of the doctors or lawyers. These associations have a legal constitution conferred upon them by the state, which grants them considerable local legislative and executive power: they establish their professional codes of ethics and can strike members from their professional registers. The power accorded to them by the state is quite surprising, since it makes membership of these associations compulsory for anyone who wants to exercise the profession concerned. These guilds are careful to preserve their own masculinity, as though their dignity and status were involved. Truth to tell, these corporations from a bygone age (that of Pétain) could easily be abolished; democracy would gain from their replacement by parliamentary and Ministerial commissions, who would enter into dialogue with consumer organizations and trades unions, whose prime advantage is that they do not have compulsory membership. All those who fought for free abortion know that the Mount Athos of the Council of the doctors' association is a formidable ideological power.[47] But it is also a 'legislative' power as regards 'professional ethics', which is even more unacceptable.

To look at all decision-making bodies connected to the state in terms of their sexual balance and their ability to create a community for men and women is to pose that of their appropriateness or character. In the case of the corporatist Councils of professional associations, their power is certainly obvious, but their appropriateness is far less so: the corporations do not have to be organized in this way. The state should therefore either impose upon them as perfect a sexual balance as possible or (at least) restrict the powers accorded to them, if these associations cannot bring themselves to apply the laws of the Republic. More generally, the question of sexual balance would be a good test for all organizations set up or funded by central government.

Assuming, of course, that it is correct to say that when an institution has an aim and a role which is not repressive or honorific and needs to run as well as possible or to maintain itself at the highest intellectual level, it is in its interests to eliminate as far as possible any extra-intellectual criteria which might limit its choice of people to whom it can grant responsibilities. On the other hand, when its function is more symbolico-repressive than creative or forward-looking, its members tend to be selected according to imaginary or in other words socio-political criteria. A rapid comparison of two

Academies will illustrate this. I certainly feel awkward at putting forward arguments based on such special cases; but if, by arguing my case from apparently 'elitist' examples, I can shed light on more widespread phenomena, or on an aspect of social life, there is no reason not to do so.

7 Huygens or Conrart?

The Paris Academy of Sciences still has justifiable intellectual importance and the role it has played since its foundation is undeniable.[48] It is notable that since it was founded by Colbert in 1666, it has included members who were not French nationals; the great Huygens was even brought especially from Holland, in advance, so that the Academy could benefit from his precious advice on the organization of the 'Assembly of Physics'. In 1962, this Academy opened its doors to women, without making a song and dance about it. The Academy of Sciences co-opts its members according to scientific criteria (not according to their identity), because there is intellectual work to do.

Thirty years earlier, in 1634–5, Richelieu founded the Académie Française on a quite different basis. This Academy has never had a clearly defined intellectual role, even less a role that could be defined as intellectual and creative. As early as the 19th century it was noted that from the outset it has always been composed of thirty-five nobodies, two or three token writers and two or three chairs to fill. On the other hand the non-intellectual (substantialist) criteria are still very strict to this day. 'Tokens' aside, to be a member of the Academy you must be French and of high-society, Gallic origins; the constitution demands that you be in sympathy with those in power: in principle, you have to be a Catholic and, until recently, you had to be a man.

It is a bad sign when an institution includes a lot of obscure people of this type and fewer real writers than can be counted on the fingers of one hand, who may themselves be non-men, non-Gallic and non-Catholic.[49] About once every three years, the Academy apparently recounts its tokens and decide one is missing: so in 1973 it elected Claude Lévi-Strauss, in 1978 Georges Dumézil, in 1981 Marguerite Yourcenar, in 1983 Léopold Senghor and since then, probably, one or two other writers of similar importance. This does not change the proportion, nor the profile, of the rest.

This situation did not come about all by itself, by some unfortun-

ate chance or because of a natural tendency of institutions to de-
generate. The constitution signed by Cardinal Richelieu states that
'political and moral subjects shall be discussed in the Académie only
in accordance with the authority of the Prince, the state of the
government (sic) and the laws of the Realm'. As far as 'holy matters'
are concerned, 'the Academy shall submit the approvals it grants to
the laws of the Church'. A literary equivalent of Huygens would have
been excluded by these words, for Huygens was a protestant. George
Sand, swearing that she is not 'making it up', sees in this principle of
conformism the origins of some of the publishing contracts of her
time: 'Monsieur *** agrees to write us a novel of manners which will
deal neither with religion, nor property, nor politics, nor the family,
nor any current social question.'[50] She concludes that men who yearn
in vain for one of these venerable chairs 'cry that those grapes are
sour'; women on the other hand might have a few good reasons for
calling them over-ripe.

There is more: the first sentence of the Constitution says that 'no
one shall be received into the Academy who is not acceptable to
Monsieur the Protector', in other words to Richelieu himself. This
man who liked to frequent the house of Mme de Rambouillet, of
whom it is said that 'the century's greatest writers were her nurs-
lings', chose the first academicians from a very bland set, that of
Valentin Conrart, who was the Academy's first secretary.

An example like that of the Académie Française is of interest only
because it allows us to articulate a choice: should we be outraged at
seeing such an institution reject women (although never just women),
or should we rather take it as a sign that we need to carry out an
institutional analysis, which may well give us some entertaining
results? Of course it was hard watching those men, most of whose
work will be ignored by history, deliberating endlessly over whether
they should admit one (just one) woman who, whatever one may
think of her, was a first-rate writer.[51] But is it not wiser to see this as
a chance to grasp the true nature of the Académie Française, an
institution completely devoid of intellectual location which, as a
result, makes do with the mediocrity of its members?

From a theoretical point of view we can take the Académie Française as a paradigm; otherwise I should not be concerned with it
here. Any institution founded by the state which is sociologically
similar to this Academy will probably resemble it institutionally, in
other words it will be a place without any very necessary function
and its attributes will be more or less illusory, or worse. The only
function assigned to this official mediocracy was to centralize and

freeze the language. We can reasonably assume that the function of immobilism (anti-inventiveness, anti-pluralization, anti-openness to the conflicts of the concrete) is always confided to a group of people who are the natural, in other words the sociological, guardians of restriction and order.[52]

However, from a practical point of view, we need not choose immediately between a reformist line (perfect sexual balance in, for example, the Académie Française) and a more radical attitude which would call for such institutions to be abolished. Of course, their abolition would be no great loss. But to force bodies that owe their entire existence to the state to find a new balance reflecting social diversity would be to say to them: either you think you are important, in which case will you please indicate why and accept a fifty-fifty membership of women and men (and non-Gallic men and women), or you are an unimportant group, in which case there is no point in continuing to support you.

This is a rather more drastic version of the dilemma I suggested above in relation to the Republic's motto: either a motto is important, in which case it should be changed at once, or it is not important, in which case it costs nothing to change it. For one is wrong to make one's own judgements of the importance of some things, as Louise Michel did. She rejected the various attempts to give women the vote and the right to stand for election, saying that these were 'illusory privileges' and 'ridiculous honours'.[53] That there is an element of illusion in universal suffrage is more than likely. However, if today the right to vote was taken away from any section of the nation, it would provoke an outcry. It is a classic response to quibble endlessly about the 'reality' of something when the issue is raised of according it to minorities or to the excluded. Such an intellectual attitude should and must be overturned, either by the suggested dilemma, or by the following test: either the thing is important, in which case everyone should participate in it, or it is not important, in which case the thing in question should be abolished for all. Unless we go so far as to say that a thing only has reality at the time when those excluded from it win it for themselves. Nevertheless, an intellectual change in relation to the degree of 'reality' of institutions is not enough: I want absolutely to see my legal framework on sexual balance and the transformation of the Republic's motto come about; but we cannot hope for them to be debated in parliament simply because of what I alone write. My responsibility as a utopian stops where collective responsibility begins.

I can predict only this: without a movement that is sufficiently strong and determined, this question will again end up in the limbo of non-legislative law. A recent individual experience will illustrate what we can expect to win by fighting at the level of 'attitudes and mentalities' alone.

8 Theory and practice: interlude

With his philosophy *agrégation* in his pocket, young Sébastien wanted to get work setting exercises or *colles* to students preparing the competitive exams for the *grandes écoles*. This work is usually done by colleagues who have just passed those exams. The school's head of department in each discipline is responsible for recruiting these people, known as *colleurs*, for the year. The salaries for those just starting out in state education being what they are, setting *colles* is a worthwhile activity: it is, moreover, a good way of staying in contact intellectually with a high-level educational establishment.

Sébastien first discussed his idea with a lady who taught philosophy in a school in the Paris suburbs and they made an agreement. Then he thought of the greater charms of another establishment in the centre of Paris and went to see the teacher in this second school, a gentlemen who received him very warmly and who was precisely looking for a *colleur*. Of course this decent man said he would have preferred to give the job to a woman, because it is better for the students to have a teacher and a *colleur* of different sexes, so that they associate philosophy as much with the figure of a woman as with that of a man. However, since Sébastien was there and the new term was due to start, such considerations could be left to one side. An agreement was thus reached.

Our young man could hardly set *colles* in two schools at once. He rang up the first teacher, apologized for breaking his word and told her that one of his colleagues, a woman as well qualified and competent as himself, was prepared to take his place. The lady categorically refused: the students had to have a teacher and a *colleur* of different sexes. As she herself was a woman, it was out of the question that the *colles* should be set by a woman, and too bad if the new term was about to start.

Similar guidelines figure in both cases, but with opposite results, giving an overall result in accordance with tradition: a young man finds work and a young woman does not. In the first case the sexual balance of teachers was suspended, as being a kind of ideal which it is not always possible to apply; in the second it acted as an absolute principle of exclusion. This anecdote at least teaches humility to anyone trying to fight discrimination and the perverse order of things by the pen alone. We strive to create currents of opinion, to sow the seed of ideas, and no one knows in advance whether or not they will be favourable ground in which to germinate. But even if these ideas do, by chance, become widespread, they do not directly change social practices. Once we start looking at the detail of phenomena, we see that women are excluded because of a theory which is in itself legitimate and that men are accepted despite the same theory, which still remains legitimate.[54] Are these just anecdotes? The same thing is enshrined in the law, since it is still the case that the only French law with the power to enforce sexual balance is the ruling on the recruitment of primary school teachers, which aims to keep the profession at least 35 per cent men.

9 From the 'personal' to the political: in search of mediations

Someone who is a woman, a philosopher and a feminist has an urgent need to speak on such particular situations and what they might have to teach us about, for example, individual, or so-called individual, decision-making. How are we to understand that an anecdote contains the same data as the law? We shall surely find the right article to explain this isomorphism in the department store of philosophical theories – the Treasury of History. We even have a choice of Plato or Leibniz. The former, in *The Republic*, formulates the hypothesis that 'that which is written in small letters in the individual soul is writ large in the constitution of the city'.[55] He is talking about justice, which is an attribute both of the individual and of the whole society. The latter thinks that every created thing, or 'monad', contains the whole universe, of which it is 'a perpetual living mirror'.[56] In lapidary style, the American feminist movement formulated what is clearly an analogous idea: 'the personal is political'.

If there is one idea which has formed the common base of all the different 'tendencies' in the European and American movements, it is most probably this, which can moreover be seen as the guiding idea behind any possible form of feminism: what takes place in the details of daily life, the tiny elements of relations between men and women or between institutions and people, can be seen as linked to politics. From this point of view, feminist theory is a long way from exhausting its programme. However, such an enquiry does not necessarily lead us to postulate that the individual and the political mirror or reflect each other; there is no reason why we should follow Socrates or Leibniz absolutely on this point, particularly since their theories necessarily suppose the existence of a soul on which a text is engraved and which is the mirror image of that of the society or the universe. Such a hypothesis is not quite economical. One only has to suppose that the relationship between two individuals is mediated by certain factors, or that in the individual decision-making of a person (P), (P) is not the only agent: there are other present–absent agents, imaginary allies with their full social and historical weight. This is what I call trans-subjectivity; to clarify this concept, we need to construct yet another paradigm here and beg the reader to forgive its length.

The fierceness with which the Vatican has long kept up its propaganda campaign against all forms of contraception except continence is well known. The feminist movement has always regarded this as a shocking interference in people's, and particularly women's, lives, and one which has tragic consequences: unwanted babies, abortions and various kinds of anxiety neuroses. So when John-Paul II announced his first visit to Paris, women from the Women's Liberation Movement decided to hold a demonstration. As was required, they went to the police, who refused the permission they were seeking. At this level of reality a certain arrangement of historical forces is writ large. Need we then be surprised at the behaviour – 'individual' this time – of many Catholic doctors who manage not to hear their patients when they ask for contraception and who seek to make them believe their request was based simply on whim? Or at the attitude of some chemists? One became famous at the time for refusing to supply any prescription for contraceptives which was not written exactly according to the rules; the exact rules for a prescription are very weird indeed and no doctor has ever prescribed antibiotics in an impeccable way. The chemist in the village of Fouesnant decided the moment had come to practise intimidation: he boomed the directions for use of the contraceptive pills I had gone to collect right across his dispensary, so that the entire village might know what to think of me. His behaviour that day greatly interested me. It could not be regarded as strictly personal, because it was supported by reference to many other subjectivities. As a result of repeated declarations from the Catholic hierarchy, he could feel the strength-giving presence at his side of his priest, his bishop and his pope. And when the Head of State deferentially received the latter, he did nothing to challenge the idea that the Church could speak out on any subject with authority and in particular could, in matters relating to fertility, prescribe a 'duty to be imprudent' (sic). The chemist was equally sure that his other customers would share his unhappiness at being mixed up in something as embarrassing as sexuality and, worse still, having to serve that of an unmarried woman. Habit is defined as 'that which one does because one has often done it'; in a similar way there is room for a concept of instant collective habit: that which one person does in the knowledge that the majority of other people would do the same or would not object. Women (but not women alone) are constantly confronted with this phenomenon, which is one of the most important aspects of trans-subjectivity. Here we can start to understand the impact of ideology.

In the First Notebook we wondered what the consequences were of sexist, repressive or racist language. We can now answer at least that such language is a mediation involved in the construction of trans-subjective habit. It tells individuals who their allies are and establishes a difference between that which remains a vague desire and that which becomes a decision or an action. Our period has discovered that the publication of statistics announcing that a given percentage of Americans sleep without pyjamas (or that a particular political party is going to win so many points in the elections) usually has the effect of increasing the phenomenon described – the American textile industry still has a painful memory of the Kinsey report. I do not think that we should dismiss such phenomena as sheep-like behaviour or the decaying effects of bad faith. They are a problem only for post-Cartesian psychology, which assumes that people are all individually-wrapped egos: atoms, free subjects of their actions in the spiritualist perspective, or subjects subjugated by their drives, according to some Freudians.[57] Before Descartes, philosophers recognized that fear, like all sorts of other emotions, is catching; for the imagination was regarded as being largely responsible for the fact that subjective states and convictions could be passed from one person to another.

In the Middle Ages and the Renaissance, the body was the chosen field of application of this theory of the imagination. It was thought that one person's suggestion could, if strong enough, have an effect on another person's body. This model was supposed to explain both seduction, fascination and cures by allosuggestion,[58] which was the effect most hoped for from the phenomena whose existence this theory assumed. Today, when psychology is built on the Cartesian model of insularization of the person (at least where the body is concerned) and such insularization that I have to make an effort of thought to believe that I have before my eyes not just coats and hats

but other living beings, other people, this type of thinking is relegated
to the clandestine fringes of what is called 'parapsychology'. I must
confess that I am no less sceptical about 'psychology' than 'parapsychology'. The former is linked to Descartes, the latter to
Avicenna, and I am unable to decide which of the two theories
promises more enlightenment and more aberration. Avicenna's
doctrine supposes that the connection between people is more
fundamental than their individuality and inner life: it insists on
communality. Cartesian doctrine attributes to each person an independent existence as substance and (more or less surreptitiously)
structures our modern cultural ideals. This is why the residues of the
former system are regarded as insanity while questions are seldom
asked about the validity of the latter, which presents people as
though they were, or should strive to become, walled gardens.

Contemporary culture is extremely contradictory on this point: it
insists on the atomistic model of the person, although, in practice, it
knows that things are not like that and that individuals are 'atoms'
only in very particular conditions and partially. They are assumed to
be such when they stand in a polling booth on election day, or in a
test-tube, when the psychologists take them as objects of study. It
takes as much technical precision to isolate a person as it does to
isolate a chemical substance and the result remains problematic.
Furthermore, our societies make massive use of propaganda and
advertising, as though Avicenna were still the dominant philosopher.
Where does the efficacy of advertising come from? And why do
almost all advertisements show one or several people? They proceed
by displaying a subjectivity strongly manifesting an emotional state
supposedly connected to a given object or to the lack of it: an ecstatic
jubilation or a horrible unease which must be eliminated. When an
individual walks towards a shop, the emotional state of the imaginary
'person' on the posters has become an element of that individual's
subjectivity. Just as Avicenna's followers never claimed that suggestion worked every time, so advertisers know that the effects of their
campaigns vary. However, both start from the principle that a
person's subjectivity is open to influence by that of another person.
It is in terms of power and power relations that the effects of this
transmission can be, if not understood, at least identified.

Let us assume that a given behaviour is the result of a debate
between several passions, impulses, willingnesses or intentions, depending on how we wish to name the forces present. Some of these
appear as positive elements of will, while others have the negative
power of inhibitions, but all enclose an at least obscure perception of

other subjectivities as anchor points or obstacles. Everyone has had the experience of feeling one of their vague desires suddenly transformed into a conscious choice, as though the support of other people had acted as a multiplier. At the opposite pole from this phenomenon lie thoughtlessness or ingenuousness, in other words the degree zero of perception of how others are disposed. This is a rare thing, as is the degree zero of anything. The point of arguing in terms of forces and perception is that it enables us to introduce a consideration of degree and quantity. The 'big world' influences the 'small stage of the individual', at least as a quantifier. If, in the big world, two contradictory ideas are in conflict and one is clearly winning out over the other, its 'victory' is also present in people's private discussions. Without wishing to put forward an agonistic model of human relations, characterized by some 'unsociable sociability', we can say that any relationship is a debate, at least as long as no one has given in. In parentheses, we can understand why, at its height, the 'Women's Movement' was greater than the number of its 'activists': because it was a public movement, it gave distant support and the beginnings of a language to vague desires which had seldom until then had the chance to make themselves felt in private discussions. I am thinking in particular of the equitable sharing of housework.

In reference to distant support, whose effects are felt in the period of hesitation which precedes an action, we must plead absolutely in favour of the importance of the symbolic. This is what I mean: it may appear simply an elitist version of feminism to want the philosophical republic, the Academies and the Council of Ministers to include as many women as men and if I took so long to decide to write the present book it was because my 'subject' did not seem to me one of the issues feminism regards as urgent. But if we think that the social whole influences individual situations, in other words everybody's everyday life, then it really does matter that the main social reference points, including the particularly visible top of the social pyramid, should show a balance of the sexes simply because they are visible. A Marie Curie or a Simone Veil, one individual (one woman) here and there and from time to time, is not enough: they are seen as exceptions to the rule. It is the ordinary proportion of women in prestige or decision-making bodies that matters if we want to build real equality in the society as a whole. The symbolic is only part of the problem and is important only if the pedagogical value of the visible symbolic, or its ability to rectify the blockages of education, can be argued.

Clearly the first area in which support is relevant to the constitution of a conscious intention or desire is that of the relationship between parents and children and thus particularly between mothers and daughters. In this light the idea of support is depressing, since we should have to assume the existence of a whole generation for whom the problem was solved. For if in the current state of things the daughter often does not receive support for her freedom from her mother, she will not give it to her own daughter either, and so on. Looked at from a wider point of view however, the issue of support allows us greater hope for change in the situation. This wider angle can be seen in the following tale of a teacher's influence. Of course, it is a story, and reference to 'experiments' known by hearsay, whose precise method is never given, is one of the worst habits of pseudo-scholarly sexist 'theories'. I should be ashamed to mirror this procedure. I therefore beg my reader to be so kind as to regard the following story as a depiction of a possible experiment which deserves to be carried out and not as something that has already been done and decisively proves what I say. After all, any experiment should be repeatable and repeated.

Some years ago, a mathematics professor at a British university and a feminist sociologist found a class where the girls' maths results were clearly lower than those of the boys. They then met the girls' mothers and suggested teaching them the modern maths they had not learned while they themselves were at school and with which they saw their own children struggling. A term later, the results of those girls whose mothers had agreed to the experiment had improved spectacularly. A mediation between the girls and mathematics had been transformed: family language and the subjective attitude of their mothers had become one of, 'I can do it, so you should be able to too.' We should add that most of these mothers were housewives in a rather depressed industrial town. Perhaps they also liked these classes because they got them out of the house and away from their isolation. In any case, if teaching the mother bijections transforms the overall ability of her daughter in mathematics, the idea that it is the child, as a discreet entity, who is sent to school needs revising.

Although failure in maths at school is an issue of the greatest importance, it is not the only reason why this experiment, which as I said before I know of by hearsay, remained in my mind. Nor was it only because it illustrates the idea that if one wants to give support to girls, a good way to start is by supporting their mothers. What interests me in this story is that the main thrust of the action was to demystify something, in this case maths, which had until then seemed mysterious and prestigious, a sacred zone which was overvalued by those excluded from it and from which people were more or less right to feel excluded because such a high value is placed upon it. If no woman is completely separate from the common lot of women, and since we live in a 'society of spectacle', making women's presence an ordinary thing in particularly highlighted areas of the social spectacle could provide remarkable support in what is called continuous and 'incidental education': the education which is not provided by schools but by the world as we can all see it. There is much to be said in favour of exceptional women but, since they are seen as exceptions, their images do not help to change the rule.

10   Perverted intersubjectivity, trans-subjectivity and institutional mediations

'Were there a species intermingled with men, which, though rational, were possessed of such inferior strength...', Judith Seton-Woolf put the book by Hume back on the table. This page, she thought, does not start well. Another 'species', linked to 'inferior strength', what a pity! 'If an explorer should come back and bring word of other sexes looking through the branches of other trees at other skies, nothing would be of greater service to humanity; and we should have the immense pleasure into the bargain of watching Professor X rush for his measuring-rods to prove himself superior'.[59] And yet, Hume was never one of those angry professors who discourse on the physical, mental and moral inferiority of women before going into ecstasies over some sallow stable lad, as noted by Virginia Woolf, godmother to us all.[60] Let us turn the page, 'another species, inferior strength' is surely an oversight.

'The great superiority of civilized Europeans above barbarous Indians', what's this? What has got into dearest David? I shall protest to the Dean of Sorbford. First *Being and Nothingness* and now this Enquiry; this degree course is a fine mess. What are we being prepared for here?

However Judith picked up the book once more and had to admit that, although the page was hard to swallow from all points of view, it was worth reading and should not be put in the same category as the flattering opinions on women expressed by Oscar Browning, Sir Egerton Brydges, Auguste Comte or St Thomas Aquinas.

Were there a species of creatures intermingled with men, which, though rational, were possessed of such inferior strength, both of body and mind, that they were incapable of all resistance, and could never, upon the highest provocation, make us feel the effects of their resentment; the necessary consequence, I think, is that we should be bound by the laws of humanity to give gentle usage to these creatures, but should not, properly speaking, lie under any restraint of justice with regard to them and, nor could they possess any right or property exclusive of such arbitrary lords. Our intercourse with them could not be called society, which supposes a degree of equality; but absolute command on the one side, and servile obedience on the other. Whatever we covet they must instantly resign [...] This is plainly the situation of men with regard to animals [...] The great superiority of civilized Europeans over barbarous Indians tempted us to imagine ourselves on the same footing with regard to them [...] In many nations, the female sex are reduced to a like slavery and are rendered incapable of all property, in opposition to their lordly masters.[61]

This analysis probably concerns women more directly than animals, whom it is hard to imagine exercising a legally defined 'right', which makes denial of this right meaningless. We cannot be sure that the analysis properly applies to the American Indians, since Hume distances himself from this idea ('has led us to imagine'), and if it did, the expression 'creatures intermingled with men' would be obscure. Strictly speaking, it is better to assume that this text is about women, or rather about the difference between the laws of humanity and the laws of justice, women being the apposite example of beings that should be treated with humanity, though not with justice. Animals and Indians are in there partly to pad out the meaning (Hume owed too such of his philosophical success to the ladies to permit himself to legitimate their 'slavery' too brutally), but also to clarify the theoretical aim of the text. Hume, and it is entirely to his credit, sees the 'slavery' of women as the result not of some qualitatively definable 'nature', but of comparative strengths, and thus of a simply quantifiable issue. If he had given only one example, things would have been read into his analysis that were not there. Furthermore, the intention of his words is not so much to 'legitimate' the oppression of women as to illustrate the fact that, in some cases, 'we' ('we' indeed!) are not bound by the constraints of justice, justice being less general and fundamental than the 'law of humanity'. That there is a smattering of suspect pleasure in all this is certain, but it should be seen above all as a secondary gain.

It is prudent to take this as a statement of fact. In all likelihood Hume is right (empirically speaking) to link the capacity to resist with the issue of justice, or rights, 'a certain degree of equality' and the fact of forming-a-society-with. All we would criticize in this text is the order of the arguments. This supposes that a creature's capacity for resistance is the primary factor, from which all the others stem, but which is itself not engendered by anything. We could just about grant this if Hume were discussing only utterly brutal power relations, of which the genocide of the American Indians by the Europeans would be an appropriate paradigm. We can interpret the text to mean that the superiority of the Europeans' brute force over that of the poor Indians certainly enabled the principle of justice to be forgotten, but that to forget the law of humanity is, in this and every case, absolutely unforgivable. For, according to Hume, the obligations of humanity always apply.

However, the notion of the capacity to resist as a primary entity is false as soon as one considers any state of right, even one that is iniquitous. For here, a dialectic is established between all factors, so that greater or lesser capacity for resistance stems from the law to the same degree that the law arises out of power relations, while the perfection of equality depends on integration (forming-a-society-with), just as the first steps to integration presuppose the beginnings of equality. We can also sense an issue of this type surfacing in the fact that the 'right to resist oppression' which was written into the French Revolution's 1793 Declaration of the Rights of Man was soon removed and did not figure in those that followed. Were the rulers afraid that a few words in a text might reinforce the capacity of the oppressed to resist? or their determination to fight? or their ability to gain support?

I have not finished with my Fouesnant anecdote. The chemist's attitude still contained a belief, ill-founded as it happened, that I should certainly lose my nerve, blush, or in any case not dare respond to his 'highest provocation'. My subjectivity (assumed to be weak) was assessed as one of the conditions making the aggression possible – for the less retaliation or response they expect, the more violent they are. Generally, by 'intersubjectivity' we mean something good: a recognition of the fact that the other person is also a subject. But intersubjectivity is only moral when at least a potential relation of equality and reciprocity is assumed. What happens from day to day is quite different: the greater or lesser capacity of the other person to react enters into any choice of action in a context of conflict. The capacity to react is not a strictly personal affair either. That day, summoning all my courage, I pointed out to this blessed chemist that he had forgotten to tell me an important element of the directions for use. I was not alone in this affair either: all those who, between 1971 and 1975, had devoted their time to publicizing the disasters of back-street abortion and helping distressed and confused women were there by my side in an almost palpable way, with our shared convictions and words: 'contraception is better than abortion, even legal abortion; it is time it was developed'. Had I been alone I should not have been able to show that man that he could no longer count on total impunity.

In analysing Simone de Beauvoir's mode of thought, we noted her concept of 'profound insignificance'. I think that the concept of trans-subjectivity can give this idea its full meaning. The trouble I had that day might have long deterred me from behaving like the aware and responsible woman I try to be. From everyday experience, we know that unfortunately this kind of disuasion is fairly often successful. It appears to be nothing, or not very much, almost nothing, and yet many unwanted pregnancies are caused by the 'personal' beliefs of a third party, conveyed indirectly though without a great deal of delicacy. The insignificant is effective because it conveys a profound disproportion which is politically regulated. On the one hand, the state compromises with the ideological apparatus of a dominant religion and prohibits public criticism of the damage done by this power, so that any old chemist feels justified in indirectly denying a right even though it is granted by the state. On the other hand, there is still a ban on direct advertising and information on contraception, something few people are aware of. The small posters which flourished under the Socialist government ultimately reinforced this unawareness: 'Contraception is important, make sure you are informed', they said, giving a box number. You have to go and ask for the information in question; it does not come to you like everything else. In 1986 when the legalisation of advertising for condoms was passed in Parliament as a result of the AIDS epidemic, Mme Catherine Trautmann, who was then the Socialist deputy for Bas-Rhin, judiciously asked that the contraceptive effects of sheaths be advertised as well. This was categorically refused by the Ministry of Public Health: only the capacity for preventing the transmission of AIDS could be mentioned. Every autumn in chemists' windows we see signs recommending vaccination against flue and encouraging people to visit their doctors. A compaign saying something like, 'When Cupid lets his arrows fly without warning, you have seventy-two hours to see your doctor' would be liable to prosecution. This is compulsory natalism with minimal concessions. We are still waiting for progressive legislation that translates into clear legal terms the idea that the control of fertility is a need and a right for women. Just as doing all we can ourselves to preserve our bodies from accidents is a need and a right for all.

The AIDS epidemic is gradually highlighting the issue of doing things for ourselves. In casual relationships an aware and responsible man can take the initiative to save himself from this risk. A woman has to ask her partner to be so kind as to preserve her from it, which comes down to giving the choice to the other person. The social, real or phantasmagorical effects of this dissymmetry are beginning to be felt. It seems likely that the spread of AIDS will be controlled more quickly when men alone are involved, in male homosexual circles therefore, than among heterosexual adolescents, where the disease is currently spreading in an alarming way. Those of my friends with children are keenly aware of this dissymmetry: it is fairly easy to admonish a fifteen-year-old boy without using the kind of warning that would be understood as an oblique prohibition on the multiple experimentations of youth. It is harder to prepare a girl for the same situation. Mothers would like to be able to pass on the right words with which to ask him to use a condom, but when they try to find them, when we try to find them together, we stammer, no doubt because to us this request seems aggressive. In what tone, with what words (at what point?) should an adolescent girl force a decision (because that is what it is) on her youthful admirer? How can we find a nice way of putting what is basically an order? If women of forty cannot find words to suggest to their daughters, we must hope that the latter will themselves display a greater inventiveness. But how many of them will be more imaginative than we are, and is it fair that only the imaginative ones should be safe? The fear is that the majority are running a lethal risk, or that many are adopting a similar attitude of rejection of and disgust with sexuality to that of their grandmothers, who were equally dependent on the goodwill of their husband for contraception. By contrast it is now easier to see the importance of feminine contraception, which gives one the independence of not always having to ask for something so vital. But this independence 'both of body and mind' had to be obtained through the law as a right.

Furthermore, I can see anxieties developing in some women of my generation which must be similar to those of the wives of yesteryear. However faithful they may have been, the women of the nineteenth century were exposed to venereal diseases, which were then incurable and could be passed on to them by their less faithful husbands. Freud sees this as one of the roots of depression or of the housewife's neurosis. When my contemporaries are told of the joys of conjugal fidelity some reply that they are sure of their own behaviour, but depend on their partner's word concerning his. The answer might end with some words from Shakespeare: 'men were deceivers ever since summer first was leavy.' The fact that their partner is in an analogous situation and depends on the woman's word does not help the situation: mistrust is not lessened by being mutual. While my generation thought it could abolish surveillance of the other person, that sad practice of so many conventional couples (it was understood, at least in principle, that the other person's freedom was respected and that, as a result, no one had to hide anything), the generation after us may well find itself returning to those tensions linked to the other person's word and the words that must be found. Psychologically and culturally the problem is likely to be dreadful for everyone, but particularly for the little women who are today playing hopscotch. It is an old feminist proposition that the fact of being a woman is an aggravation of problems common to both sexes.[62]

This can already be seen in the small government-sponsored posters that have been put up on chemists' doors and whose restrictive nature saddens me. A young man is saying: 'AIDS won't get passed on through me.' This me would not have been me at the same age. As it is an unhealthy thing to keep one's sadness to oneself, I confided mine to Monique, my local chemist, who said that there may be someting for girls too: some doctors are beginning to prescribe, in conjunction with 'the pill', a local contraceptive which is less effective as a contraceptive but has long been known to be a contact antiseptic and is now thought to be possibly effective against the AIDS virus. However no one yet knows to what extent this may be true. Is research well under way to check its efficacy and to perfect it as soon as possible? Shall we have to wait for the foundation of the sexually balanced university of Sorbford before the effects of this excellent molecule, called 'berzalconium', a quaternary ammonium I am told, are subjected to scientific testing? And if it is proved to work, when will a permanent law be passed that will allow the manufacturers of CdB (the brand name of the local contraceptive in question) to boast that they have found a fragment of the philosopher's stone? For the time being, women are stuck with 'people assume', 'it is possible that' and 'we don't know to what extent', always assuming that they have a nice chemist. We have only vagueness, hearsay, or rather what is not heard said, and legally imposed silence, since any advertising for a contraceptive product is still forbidden.

11   Let them resolutely approach the problem of practical philosophy[63]

Since I have confessed my penchant for utopia and uchronia, I want here to set out a few ideas which we could have supported over the last fifteen years and more when, fighting against backstreet abortions, we said 'contraception is better'. As long as access to information on contraception is not absolutely free, people will have no chance of finding out the things their doctors will not tell them. This maintains an ideological atmosphere in which contraception tends to be seen as something clandestine which has been smuggled into social existence. Snippets of information circulate, superstitions still spread and, if this leads to an unwanted pregnancy, responsibility ultimately lies with the authorities.

Some contraceptive techniques have the merit of being open to demedicalization: they are already freely sold, since they do not require checking by a doctor and present no risks of undesirable 'side-effects'. The only side-effect they do have is that they are also a more or less effective barrier against some sexually transmitted diseases. Condoms and some spermicidal creams come into this category. If the ban on advertising contraception were abolished, nothing would prevent us regarding these as parapharmaceutical items, halfway between hygiene and cosmetics. They could therefore be as widely advertised as vitamins, sun creams, medicinal infusions or Ginseng powders and other wonder remedies. Of course, they do have the disadvantage of being rather expensive, but it should be possible to negotiate a price reduction with the manufacturers in return for access to a much wider market. Since such measures would lower the annual numbers of terminations, public finance would benefit from them.[64] It might be argued that these methods are not entirely safe and that is true; but the coil and even the pill also have their failures. All that would be needed to prevent the consumer from being misled would be the requirement that an indication of the method's efficacy should figure on the advertisements and packages themselves. As for the pill and the coil, which cannot be used without the involvement of a doctor, direct information campaigns should be run on the prevention of unplanned pregnancies. Medical contraception could be assimilated to the category of the various vaccines.

There is more. Since current methods of contraception are not completely safe and the range of possibilities is restricted, so that it is

sometimes hard to find a method which perfectly suits individuals
and their lifestyles, we should be asking ourselves what level of
funding the state has allotted to research which could develop these
techniques in the necessary way. The answer is absolutely nothing,
and certainly not enough to buy themselves a bomber, nor a test-tube
baby.[65] Large sums are still being poured into the research which led
to the scandal of 'wombs for hire' and the transformation of poor
women into 'good time mothers', but there is never any money for
research which would open the way to greater freedom.

We should also have questions to ask of past, present and future
Health Ministers: there is a clear discrepancy between the current
state of medical theory concerning the detection of risks that babies
will be born prematurely, how births should be conducted, neonatal
medicine and so on on the one hand and, on the other, the reality of
antenatal care and perinatal medicine in many places. A pregnancy
monitored by X hospital has more chances of leading to the full-term
birth of a healthy baby than another monitored at Y clinic, and
reasons can be given for this. The measures enabling such disparities
to be reduced would certainly be expensive for the Social Security
budget; but the spending would bear no relation to the defence
budget – this example being of course chosen at random from the
various areas where the budget is not made particularly public.

12   *On a slight disadvantage of practical philosophy*

At the end of October 1988, the definitive draft of this manuscript
was almost ready to be passed to the publisher. And at this point of
the argument, the following words were to appear.

> People will counter this by pointing out that at INSERM, the state-
> funded institute whose job is to carry out research in the field of
> applied medicine, a research team led by Etienne Baulieu has de-
> veloped an abortion-inducing molecule, RU 486, which will no doubt
> be used as a replacement for other techniques in many cases. It has
> the advantage of requiring neither anaesthetic nor surgery. When a
> woman becomes aware of an unwanted pregnancy at an early stage,
> she can ask to use this method in a family planning clinic. RU 486 is
> taken in tablet form, followed by an injection of prostaglandins. Since
> it is rapidly eliminated by the body and the use of prostaglandins has
> long been mastered, this new technique is not at all risky from a
> medical point of view. For many women it will thus reduce the
> physical shock of abortion. It is therefore a very good thing, and yet I
> am afraid that it is merely reinforcing a mistaken orientation. This

mistake is partly due to the fact that, when we fought against back-street abortions in the 1970s, we were taking first things first, which was hard enough in itself. Given the intellectual terrorism of the opposing side, we did not have the time to clarify our ideas as much as necessary. Now that things are no longer so urgent, let us take the time to look at them in a new light.

On the afternoon of 26 October, I discovered that all this was simply an illusion: the pharmaceutical group Roussel-Uclaf, who had long been working with the INSERM team and had started to distribute the pill in question to family planning clinics, announced that it was ceasing to do so because of 'the outcry from a section of public opinion'. This was an obvious lie, since the newspapers had registered no public outcry on this matter over the preceding weeks. They had merely recounted attacks by catholic fundamentalists on cinemas showing Scorsese's film *The Last Temptation of Christ*. All the same, it was time to take up practical feminism once more, to stop work on finishing the book and to observe that the time for calm debate had not yet come.

From one day to the next the reflections of 'practical philosophy' are liable to be elbowed out of the way by historical reality, for at least one fundamental reason: such reflections certainly concern present-day events, but at the same time they presuppose a basic condition which those events almost never grant, and that is a moment when things are not urgent, a quiet space in which one can try to understand a world which gives us no respite and thus constantly imposes its own way of setting the terms of a problem upon us. In the calm space that a page represents, in the pauses between battles, we can find conditions which allow us to construct a set of problems whose categories are different from those of our opponents. When our most urgent priority is defence, we cannot really choose our categories. Let us therefore give the present what it needs and otherwise try as best we can to defend that space of thought which is 'practical philosophy'.

The farce of the withdrawal of RU 486 lasted a few days. It was very instructive concerning the relation of women to the state in France today. In the first stage, the authorities refused to intervene in Roussel-Uclaf's unlikely decision. The Ministry of Health said they 'could see no reason to make a statement on this decision taken by a private laboratory for their own reasons'.[66] Worse, throughout this affair the Ministry of Research remained silent: and yet this was a case of the concrete commercialization of a discovery made by a publicly owned research establishment. While the Family Planning organization was preparing to mobilize on a large scale, and 'historical feminists' were feverishly contacting each other (while moaning about those who 'weren't lifting a finger'), while Professor Baulieu, supported by his colleagues, was protesting furiously from a conference on obstetrics and gynaecology in Rio de Janeiro, two former Ministers had the time to declare themselves against Roussel-Uclaf's decision before the Minister of Social Affairs finally decided to intervene and to oblige the pharmaceutical company to begin distribution of the pill in question once more. The government left famous voices to respond – and a section of the media to howl – before adopting the only possible attitude on pain of discrediting itself completely. Women cannot therefore count on the authorities to act as such in defence of their freedoms. In the heat of the action (petitions, meetings, organization of demonstrations, as usual), we also learned that Family Planning had received not a penny of state funding in 1988, neither from the right-wing government before the month of May, nor from the Socialist government afterwards.

As for me, having been transformed into an activist and politico-scientific journalist for a few days, I became interested in another aspect of the problem. Why were Roussel-Uclaf explaining their backtracking in ways which varied from hour to hour? The Roussel-Uclaf researchers with whom I managed to talk discounted all the explanations given. Anonymous letters received by managers and containing death threats? No more than usual, and it had been going on for years. The threat of a boycott of other Roussel products in the United States? Two American anti-abortion groups had certainly told the French embassy that they were planning such action; but since Roussel-Uclaf markets many of its products under other names and those products are not all pharmaceutical, the threat of a boycott meant very little. The people I talked to maintained that there had been pressure from within Roussel-Uclaf itself.

Years ago the group's laboratories began to work with Etienne Baulieu and INSERM because the molecule promised (and still promises) to be rich in potential applications, such as correcting some of the undesirable side-effects of cortisone. The irony is that its use to bring about abortion is an epiphenomenon, which was easier to develop, and this Baulieu thought to do, to the great displeasure of the pharmaceutical group.[67] It turns out that the group's shareholders are conservative believers in nation and family and that some of them might belong to Opus Dei. Internal pressure to halt the research thus began about eight years ago. But, since the work was being carried out in collaboration with INSERM, a publicly-financed organization, and since Baulieu's team showed its ideological independence, the pressure exerted during the molecule's development failed. It did not fail in the case of another molecule: a few years ago, again according to Roussel-Uclaf personnel, some of the group's researchers found one which promised to be a good male contraceptive. Everything was going well on the experimental side when the researchers received the order to stop their work immediately. Despite its great importance, the early work on this discovery was abandoned overnight. Since the research involved had not been carried out in collaboration with any other team from a public-sector establishment, there was nothing to protect it from the shareholders' whim.

The relations between people's lives, the state and the ideology of those who always vote against other people's freedom are complex. On the one hand we saw a government ready to bow to a 'private laboratory's own reasons', with no concern for what the discovery might mean to women who want abortions; on the other we realize that only publicly-funded research can resist the obscure forces which think it a good thing that we should be slaves to our fertility and who were pleased that the new technique was withdrawn because it was a 'clean' and 'antiseptic' form of abortion.[68] Given these things, how should we analyse the fact that the publicly-funded research bodies devote so little of their scientific potential to seeking new forms of contraception?[69] We cannot say that this failure is due to the simple fact that they are impermeable to the idea of 'science for the people', nor to the fact that their decision-making committees consist mainly of men and are thus insufficiently motivated where contraception is concerned;[70] we have to realize that the French state humours the dominant church as far as possible and that it is, moreover, equally natalist. Nevertheless, the public sector provides individuals with the possibility of going against the tide and one day the state should certainly become representative of all women and men. While waiting for that day, we all have the task of obliging it to provide the means to freedom.

I shall now return to my space of calm debate, in the hope that nothing will disturb it in the next week. And with a belief which has grown stronger through all this disruption: by constantly keeping us in a position where urgent action is required, our opponents are preventing us from posing the problems in our own way. For natalists, contraception and abortion are practically the same thing, both obstacles to their own project. For more than fifteen years we have been fighting for women's right not to be living incubators and to decide freely whether or not to have a child. We have always said that contraception is much better than abortion and this idea has been heard by women and couples. Now we need to make the authorities hear it and make them understand why contraception represents true freedom for women. Perhaps I shall be granted this without having to prove it; perhaps my readers will think that I am stating the obvious. But as long as laws continue to forbid information on contraception, this subject cannot be regarded as unimportant.

When one fights for free access 'to contraception and abortion' and when one states that 'contraception is better', the language itself reflects a structure generated by technology: in practice, contraceptive techniques and those of abortion have the same empirical effect (enabling sexual relations without procreation) and were thus linked together in and following the 1920 Act, which suppresses both. They are still linked, whether in phrases such as 'abortion and contraception' or 'contraception is better', given that only comparable things can be compared. However, many vital points get lost when the notions are set out in this way, beginning with what comes between the failure or absence of one and the possible request for the other, in other words the unplanned pregnancy and the way it is experienced. Many good souls have stated again and again that abortion is a trauma from which women never recover. This is a sly way of saying that they should never get over it and suggests guilt and self-punishment. At the time when I was dealing with women seeking abortions, I should I think, had my ears had been sufficiently finely tuned, have heard something quite different from many of them: the trauma lies in finding oneself pregnant when one has neither chosen nor obscurely wished to be so.

I may be wrong – no one can advance what they have heard in someone else's distress as an absolute truth – but I am sufficiently convinced to offer an analysis of the trauma and to suggest that we stop speaking of contraception-and-abortion always in the same breath as a technical pair and look instead at what happens in an 'unplanned pregnancy'. If we accept the assumption that this is what causes the real shock (whether the pregnancy is then taken to term or terminated), we must still ask ourselves what exactly makes it traumatizing. We should be wrong immediately to imagine that the trauma lies in the fact that the foetus and hormonal changes are seen as an intrusion. It is more complicated than that, as can be shown by looking at the cause of an unwanted pregnancy, which makes a great difference to the degree of 'physical shock'.

Women sometimes conceive while using the pill or coil. I have seen others who, when I asked them 'why was no contraception used?' told me terrible things stemming from the interference of another person, such as a doctor, husband or superstition-spreading mother.[71] Others explained that they had had sexual relations after a long period alone which had made them forget such considerations. Others still thought they were going through or had finished the menopause and had stopped worrying about contraception. Unplanned pregnancy seems to be experienced in very different ways, depending on the case. Clearly the social and emotional contexts in which they occur are also very different, but even given this, the most painful psychic crises were linked to situations where a third party had interfered (I am referring here to the crisis linked to finding oneself pregnant and definitely not to the decision to have an abortion). Women using contraceptives on the other hand seemed able to manage the situation fairly well.[72] Those who thought they were undergoing the menopause seemed simply to feel an easily overcome resentment towards 'the ridiculousness of nature'. This leads me to think that the intrusion which is experienced negatively is that not of the foetus but of the will of another person, who is perceived as having inflicted conception, through inattention, natalist ideology, loutishness or an attempt to force a marriage. For if the classic idea used to be that a woman would try to get herself married by getting herself pregnant, nowadays the reverse has become more frequent, since women's average enthusiasm for marriage has perceptibly fallen.

It is understandable that this intrusion of another person's will, treating the woman as a living incubator, is very ill-received. The discovery that one can be treated as a simple receptacle is, in itself, a violent experience; the realization that one's own will has been manipulated without one's being aware of it, combined with self-criticism for not having looked after oneself better, is another and can give rise to a sometimes lasting doubt. Long afterwards the questions remain: who really wants me to conceive? My doctor, because he also does births? My man, because he'll do anything to keep me? My mother, because she wants to see me married and producing grandchildren? My mother-in-law, through her son, for more or less the same reasons? Such ideas can mark the future long after an unwanted pregnancy, erasing the only right answer ('I do, my man and I do, and if I don't really know why, who cares?'), sometimes leading women to reject all thoughts of pregnancy out of fear of being manipulated once more by the wishes or thoughtlessness of whoever it may be.[73] On the contrary it may also lead them to repeat the trauma, by adopting an attitude of helplessness and having many more unwanted pregnancies.

Contraception has never given rise to such conflicts, although a woman may use it because someone else tells her to ('pass your exams first, my girl!'). It only ever involves a fixed period and situation. It may cause 'fluctuations of the mind' as Spinoza would say, when unconscious and conscious desires conflict. This sometimes produces highly welcome mistakes. But these should not be confused with 'unplanned pregnancies', since, whether they are soon terminated or end in births, they do not pose the problem regularly produced by the latter of 'who wanted this?', or at least not in the same way.

In the case of unplanned pregnancy, the question of 'who wants this?' is then posed a second time: who decides on termination or who wants it to be continued? If we could answer that in all cases it is the woman concerned and she alone who takes the decision, then feminists would have won a battle. Unfortunately, this is far from the case. We see it most clearly when the decision is to abort, but the complementary phenomenon must also exist. Doubtless, often it is the woman who decides not to continue with a pregnancy to the end and if there were many of us who demanded the legalisation of free abortion, it was because this corresponds not only to many women's experience, but also to their wishes. However, I have heard and seen too many things to cry victory. 'To have a child or not is a decision for the couple' said a pro-abortion doctor one day. Yes, but what is a couple? Some men have a knack of saying 'we' which is petrifying because that 'we' means: 'I, and therefore, as an appendage, of course, she'. 'To make a baby, two people must vote in favour, since there cannot be either an absolute or a relative majority; and I am voting against, so it has to end with an abortion.' Anyone, man or woman, who thinks that there is no longer any need for feminism, should be required to be mentally present at the conversations in which a decision to continue or abort an unplanned pregnancy is taken. They would discover what kind of a society it is that we live in without realizing, and the power that men maintain over women, including that form they maintain by the extraordinary means of thoughtlessness. Who takes the other person's viewpoint into account? This question has almost made me misandrist in all kinds of situations. If, in a debate between a man and a woman, she regularly takes his point of view into account, but he only ever thinks about his own, of course they will always be a united couple, but it is a pretty depressing picture all the same. Morally, she is right (it is always better to place oneself at the intersubjective level) and he does what he likes with her. Thus one may wonder whether women are not basically victims of their own qualities, indeed of their virtues, and one is tempted to take an epic tone and cry out: 'Long live bad women and their impious acts; what is the point of being accommodating and gentle?'[74]

But let us leave epic anger aside for a moment; we still need to analyse the issue of abortion, for it reveals many things which need to have light shed upon them. We know that backstreet abortions used to cause about three thousand deaths a year in France. Legalisation has ended this mass slaughter and, in the medium term, has had the effect that many predicted: since then the number of abortions has decreased every year, thanks to the fact that a termination in hospital offers, at least in principle, an opportunity to be given information on contraception. So must women have abortions to have proper access to this information? For many working-class women this is unfortunately the case and the inadequate legislation on contraception is to blame. This still-restricted legislation shows that the state still wants to see the greatest possible number of unplanned pregnancies and is succeeding; we must assume that the legislators are counting on the fact that some of these pregnancies will be carried to term, which seems to be the case. Current legislation can thus certainly be called 'natalism with minimal concessions'. But we cannot be sure that the latter are always made to women. Formerly, when men were told of their impending and unwanted fatherhood, some did not hesitate to make their mistresses or wives run lethal risks: so keen were they to get rid of the threat, they were ready to throw out the living incubator with the threat itself. Technical and legislative advances now enable them to dissociate the two issues. From this women have, of course, also gained, as though tangentially, firstly their survival, and, secondly, the freedom to refuse the role of incubator-by-constraint which the state used to force upon them. But true freedom lies not in this, but in the authentic control of one's own fertility (in the fact that every conception is wanted, at least obscurely, by the woman involved) and in a recognition of the fact that it is the woman and not the couple (in other words the man, who is generally dominant in the couple), who is the person concerned.

13   The bones that take the pains...[75]

When one regards a decision to terminate or to continue a pregnancy as a matter for a couple, this is linked either to economic and social considerations, or to an image based on the (false) idea of the private ownership of gametes in which the man and woman provide one each and the foetus is imagined as though they were its shareholders, each owning a half share. We find this idea in its crudest form in the recent phenomenon of 'surrogate mothers', since the embryo and later the child is considered the property of the couple who provided the two little seeds and not of the woman who carried the future treasure, using her muscles, her bones, her blood and her endocrine system.[76] The formulation may vary according to the speaker's socio-cultural level, but the underlying meaning when an abortion is the result of a man's unilateral demand is: 'I do not want one of my gametes to go wandering about like that!'

The challenge to this and to the actions of couples who rent a womb comes from the argument that a gamete that 'I' produce is neither 'me' nor 'mine'. Indeed genetically speaking it is false to regard anyone as anyone else's 'offspring'. An individual's genetic stock is made up of an enormous number of genes; one gamete contains half of them, taken at random from that stock, some of which carry characteristics which do not appear in the progenitor, in other words in that person's 'phenotype'.[77] In the fusion of two gametes, a new hand of cards is dealt with the mixture of genes, which makes each individual an original creation. When a child is born, those around it try to see how it resembles its parents or, if necessary, uncle Fred and great-grandmother Amelia. The integration of a new being into 'its lineage' is a social activity of prime importance and should be recognized as being as social as naming, which is the prelude to the work of psychological identification and the constitution of the child's sense of self. But all this is constructed after the event, at the imaginary level, and sometimes against the temperamental grain of the child involved.[78]

The view that a child is not strictly ontologically dependent on its progenitors – its parents as providers of half the necessary genetic stock each – allows us to shift our viewpoint and leave behind all issues of private ownership of a microscopic bundle produced by each of the two bodies. Instead we can turn to the consideration of the work involved. Carrying a child is very tiring for a body. It is an activity, a fact hidden by the representation of the pregnant woman as a passive 'incubator'. In everyday language we say that a woman is 'expecting' a baby, as if this meant no greater effort than langorously and patiently staying in a place where something is going to happen. The fact that pregnancy involves effort on the part of the spinal column and the heart (in no way an exhaustive list), as well as the mind, is completely erased by everyday language. And yet other bodily events are rightly perceived as activities. Some years ago I had a long fight against a vicious cancer. No one imagined that it was enough for me to let myself be treated, even by the best medical team possible: everyone around me saw me as engaged in an active struggle, comparable to climbing Everest, in which even my mental strength was involved because nothing could be left to chance. Everyone saw my determination and capacity for vigilance as factors in my cure, and I should have not have liked things to be otherwise. So why are pregnant women not recognized as playing a personal and active part in bringing a pregnancy successfully to term? It is because, if we take account of 'the bones that take the pains', it is obviously women and only women who should make the decision of whether to continue or to terminate a pregnancy.

Once again, the problem should not be posed, and is not posed when contraception works; the project of conception is then discussed by both parties and passed or rejected unanimously. Unwanted pregnancies (with the exception of contraceptive failures) reflect a situation which is, from the outset, one of conflict interwoven with surreptitious interference. The fact that the decision to terminate or to continue is taken in an equally conflictual and alienated context is not surprising. Nevertheless, the legislation should give women the means to realize that on this matter they need consult only themselves.

Since abortion was legalized, we have known more or less how many there are each year. We should aim to apply different measures to ensure that the number drops constantly and we now have the means to make a quantitative assessment of the impact of the measures in question. We thus have a real touchstone of social action. The measures to be taken differ greatly: publicity for contraceptives and the organization of a real discussion between the pregnant woman and someone who clearly understands that she alone is the one to decide[79] would probably have a measureable effect.

We also need to improve the code relating to filiation and make it better known. In the old code bequeathed to us by Roman law, *pater est quem nuptiae demonstrant*, the father is the one designated by the ties of marriage. When a married woman was 'expecting' a baby conceived in relations with a man other than her husband, either the latter 'disclaimed' paternity, or he was designated as the father, unless the woman gave birth anonymously (called 'X') and the lover declared the child as being 'of unknown mother'. In France this law was reformed in the 1970s: a married woman may now declare a child as her own and that of a lover, on condition that the husband

agrees, or that she can prove that he could not have been the father.
Cases of abortion have been known which were entirely caused by
the former or present legislation. The ties of marriage still have their
effect because of their disymmetry: the same legislation states that a
husband can, without asking his wife's opinion, recognize a child
conceived out of wedlock. If the same right were granted to wives,
and this was widely known, women could make the decision for
themselves in a calmer way. And this was widely known: some laws
are posted up so far above people's heads that we have every reason
to suspect that the legislators deliberately intended them to have no
effect. Such a procedure has, since ancient times, been regarded as a
feature of tyranny.

14   The choice of ethics

People will say that all this ignores the tenderness of emotional
relationships, the ineffable charms of altruism and everything that
gives real value to human existence. But the law's job is not to govern
irenic relations which, if they occurred generally, would make it
unnecessary. Perfect intersubjectivity is a fine ideal, but unfortunately it is easily perverted, as happens when there is no reciprocity. And
then it is perverted for everyone, for it is precisely in the breakdown
of egalitarian reciprocity that unchecked trans-subjective phenomena
are found. When there is no honest debate and one person does not
properly recognize the other's subjectivity, certainly the former uni-
laterally adopts a position of power over the latter; but, at the same
time, that person deprives herself or himself of the possibility of
freedom in relation to the action of the trans-subjective forces. On the
contrary, when two people who are both driven by a common desire
to have an honest discussion meet, they each see this as an opportunity to strip themselves of at least some of the obscure and irrational
elements buried within us all; reaching an agreement with somebody
always means overcoming idiosyncrasies and fixedness which, far
from being personal, have usually been shaped by the diktat of some
force. Only another person can mediate these fantasies, in other
words establish, through discussion, a minimal distance between
oneself and these automatisms. Whenever a man has power over a
woman (unilateral power, by definition), it is possible that he will be
manipulated by many different things: the wishes of his forebears, his
neighbours' opinions and anything else one might care to imagine.

Here is a theory that might be based on a passage from Genesis, no less! (I am of course entirely responsible for my unauthorized interpretation thereof): 'Therefore shall a man leave his father and his mother and shall cleave unto his wife'.[80] The converse of this excellent project, which is rarely fulfilled, might be the following: he who does not regard his woman as his absolute equal has not left his father and mother; he will always remain their little boy and will carry out their wishes. All this can be rephrased by transposing what Marx had to say on the Irish question: 'A people which oppresses another is not a free people', and a sex which oppresses another is not free either. When there is absolute command on the one hand and servile obedience (to use Hume's words) on the other, the one who commands may of course have the illusion of exercising a 'lawless will'. But since there is then a lack of the discussion with other people which introduces thoughtfulness, that will is very likely to be subject to orders from who knows where.[81]

At this point the moral perspective of intersubjectivity clearly appears insufficient. It is easily twisted and in order for it to be defined as a good thing, something must always be added to it, notably the idea of equality and reciprocity, in other words a reference, however elementary, to the very different perspective of justice. A simplistic apology for dialogue is mystifying to the extent that dialogue often proves eristic, and the same is true of the simple ethics of relations with others. We have seen that if one of the protagonists in a discussion acknowledges the other's point of view and the latter does not reciprocate, the result is the worst possible situation in which one person is ultimately the victim of her or his own morality. Of course we need to keep in reserve the idea that there may be situations in which one gives oneself up to another person's cruelty for moral reasons, but this is valid only when the sacrifice is made in favour of a third party and not of the dreadful tyrant. Otherwise, it is a sure sign that the moral problem itself has been badly posed. And it is badly posed when considerations of justice or of universality are left out.

What these two considerations have in common is that they require the moral person to take herself into account as well as others. Universality demands that I respect humanity in others and in myself, while justice relates to the idea that people's relations between themselves and with things can be impersonally defined and that that definition includes me. We shall allow ourselves to stress this point, because the ethics of the twentieth century have quite simply buried and forgotten it, seeking a more noble doctrine. May I be forgiven my lack of finesse: preoccupation with nobility is a luxury which, in the current state of things, is not within everyone's reach.

In *Le Paradoxe de la morale*, Jankélévitch develops the idea that 'everyone has rights, except me'[82] and expounds the view that human beings must 'become a kind of nothingness in the eyes of the other'. 'That the extreme rarefaction of [their] being might make them translucid! Then my fellow, who did not know what to expect of me, will begin to hope again'.[83] This doctrine of absolute altruism may be a welcome antidote to the depression which overcomes us when we have seen selfishness and egocentrism reign for too long; it may even have validity as a superb and dialectical way to go beyond the problem of justice. But it is a theory of mad passion, or its aesthetics, and not an ethics, for at least one reason: if I posit that 'everyone has rights except me', since every other person is also a 'me', should I, if I regard you as such, tell you to see yourself as the person who says 'everyone has rights except me'? Never! I have to say to my fellow: 'Please take care of yourself and look after the interests of humanity, in others and in yourself.'

Many, if not all, women have been moulded by altruism to the point where they have indeed become 'a kind of nothingness in the eyes of the other'. Not any old other, of course, but in the first instance someone in the sphere of the family, attitudes towards other 'others' being later derived from that first person. The sinister thing about the structure of altruism (when it excludes the problem of justice) is not only that it prevents people from including themselves in the projected good, but that it also surreptitiously particularizes the other person to whom I am being sacrificed by self-denial. The morality which is usually inculcated into women leads them to leave out two elements: themselves and humanity outside the family sphere. All their duties are fulfilled once they have devoted themselves to 'their own'.[84]

It can be argued that the attitude of ignoring humanity as it exists outside the family sphere has the same origins as that of ignoring oneself. Since the assumption that 'everyone has rights except me' cannot be articulated in the second person, it establishes a heterogeneity of people and thus a suspension of the principle of their interchangeability before the law. This generous maxim denies isonomy and once that denial is accepted there is nothing to stop me imagining that (and behaving as if), although 'everyone' has rights, some have more than others or, which comes to the same thing but is worse, some have far fewer than others.[85] Making the other person into the point of reference for morality, as doctrines of intersubjectivity recommend, ultimately means doing away with the basic meaning of justice. In feminism we should see a desire, however awkward and groping it may sometimes be, to return to the ethics of justice now that women have the means to see themselves as citizens and no longer just as their fathers' daughters, their husbands' wives and their children's mothers. This ethics of justice requires one to be concerned with the interests of any part of humanity: of strangers, friends and relatives and oneself. By becoming concerned with one's own rights one can relearn strict universality – everyone, without exception, has rights. As I see it, this attitude contains a double hope, however confused the relearning may be.[86]

The first hope is that many more women will rediscover and practise this morality. The women of the French Resistance and those who fought for Algerian independence have already given us examples of this. While the domestic virtues of the wife–mother are bourgeois inasmuch as they lead to an attitude of 'that's none of my business' in relation to the urgent issues of history, recognition of the question of justice – for oneself as well as for others – goes hand in hand with an awareness of the extent of the principle of justice, which includes everyone, absolutely. It is not a pure coincidence that many feminists are also active in anti-racist movements. One rediscovers universality by rediscovering isonomy, for oneself as well as for everyone else.

The second hope that I have of women's relearning the morality of justice is this: the fact that women are subjected to men has doubtless constituted a moral anti-education for the latter. If, every day, a man has at his side an 'other' who never resists him, who, 'upon the highest provocation' does not make him feel the effects of her resentment, in such a relationship he learns that he has arbitrary power and a lawless will (to use Hume's language again), and he loses the idea that human rights are universal. The phenomenon of women who are 'battered', sometimes to death, by their husbands and that of 'paki-bashing' must be seen as linked in various ways, so that one can trace the abstract outline of a single phenomenon, a violence whose object is individuals who are less able to defend themselves than others, who do not always have the reflex to defend themselves because, obscurely or not, they know that society will not defend them. The phenomenon can be indiscriminately transposed from one category of people with less resistance to another, so that it can be said that racist violence is a school for sexist violence and vice versa. Sexism, racism, the ostracism of homosexuals and so on should not be seen as self-producing attitudes, nasty attitudes which well-meaning people would like to correct by some kind of enlightened education. They must be seen altogether as made possible by the non-homogeneity of the social, in other words by the fact that some people are less protected than others by the collectivity and find little support from witnesses in a situation of conflict. In a correlative way, others receive too much support and, from time to time, learn the terrible lessons of impudence and lawless will. If I allow someone to go unpunished for their injustice towards me, I am encouraging them to be equally unjust to everyone. Even if this were not the case, I should not allow my own humanity to be mistreated. But, in defending my rights, I can hope also to teach the other person that one can never be sure of going unpunished.

15   Introduction to the notion of passive collaboration

One Sunday afternoon, in the street, a man was beating his wife. The assault and battery had started in their home and she had come out to seek refuge in public, but in vain. Passers-by silently stood and watched this news item happening 'live' before their eyes. There were at least six spectators: they therefore could have physically overcome the aggressor without risk. This is called non-assistance to a person in danger and is, in principle, punishable under article 63 of the Penal Code. But the article is rather vague; and then one would have to have the names of the witnesses. I am not at all athletic and so my intervention was purely verbal. It proved enough. However, I arrived a bit late. If someone had taken the trouble to intervene a little earlier, they might have prevented the affair ending in the woman's suffering a fractured skull.

Summer 1987, one example among many: a murder was committed in Nice; six criminals beat a Tunisian worker to death and the local papers were extremely indulgent towards them. *Le Monde* was less so; it reported what they said: 'We're racist, we don't like Arabs', they explained to the police, without the slightest signs of remorse.[87] The fact that they explained the 'motive' for their deed to the police so directly and without remorse shows that they expected to meet with the same indulgence there that was shown to them by the local papers the next day. Or the same understanding. How many people are guilty of this murder, besides the six criminals? All those who do not regard them as absolutely guilty. Those who kidnap a company director know the risk they are running; those who beat to death a

North African, who is moreover working-class, think they are risking far less. They count on the at least passive complicity they can expect from others.

Le Monde notes that the six Nice 'skinheads' had earlier amused themselves (sic) molesting homosexuals. The article is thus wrong when it says that they 'eased their racist feelings'. Do 'racist feelings' exist? Does not talking in terms of 'feelings' require one to ask what the causes of those feelings might be? This then leads to some great provider of excuses being found and indeed to the trial of the victim, who proved unworthy of liking. The victim seems to us to be contingent and the 'feeling' transposable. It was homosexuals one day, North Africans the next and, no doubt, the wife everyday. The belief (and not the 'feeling') is the same in all three cases: the public will not call you to account for that.

The public means everyone from the neighbour who watches to the parliament that legislates, including the judge who passes sentence and the papers which indulgently, or scarcely, report the incident. They are all present, distributing prohibitions and permissions. But as their complicity is passive (they do not prevent), according to the received frameworks of thought it is not seen as collaboration with the criminal. To fail to recognize this is to condemn oneself to not understanding the related fact that a handful of wretched louts can, at any time, carry with them people who are not all positively hate-filled, nor set on doing the worst; who do not even have a reason to be angry about anything: comfortable people who are simply content to let things happen. I fear that, in our societies, there are thousands of people who are prepared to sign a blank cheque for the violence done by others to others and would adopt the position of bystanders, apparently as little involved as the Sunday walkers described above, but thus offering anyone who wants it a pledge not to help people who are already in danger. 'If you think that the persecution of people who are not the same as us might be useful, go ahead and try it; we shall let you do it and we shall imagine that you have your reasons.' In passive collaboration, there is a particularly frightening form of delegation: 'Go ahead, what you do costs me nothing.'

One then catches oneself expounding and spreading a morality of constant help to anyone in danger, wanting to restart 'civic instruction' courses in schools, getting children to sharpen their critical faculties by looking for the deficiencies of article 63 of the Penal Code on non-assistance to a person in danger. Children of twelve could find them, as long as they were not first given the idea that knowledge of the institutions and the law is a branch of apologetics. A future citizen should know the laws and be able to think of better ones; have we ever had the means to – has it ever been suggested that we should – provide this elementary civic training?

And yet, no sooner have we mentioned this wish, than we are obliged to withdraw it. Not so much because the idea of acting as the instructors of the people is pretentious (this objection is only aesthetic and only ever concerns decorum), but because it is presumptuous: it assumes that some people are capable of having a clear idea of what being a citizen is, in all its aspects. And who is capable of this? I have wearied my readers trying to convince them that the heads of the learned and scholarly are full of mud, at least when it comes to discussing a category of people who do not have equal rights with the standard citizen. And anyone who drops the principle of isonomy for any category of people has already entirely abandoned it. We cannot therefore look to scholars to provide us with the builders of a form of thought that can criticize the political and the social and formulate fairer principles in a creative way. If intellectuals are (at the least) passive collaborators, who will coin the words we need simply to describe this collaboration?

16   What are those great minds thinking of?

The notion of 'human rights' is giving new concern to present day philosophers. Some criticize its minimalist and thus derisory character: 'thank you for not killing me' is how Jankélévitch described it. According to him, the first effect of this concept is to make us forget that we want far more.[88] Others are trying to find a philosophical basis for these rights, which presupposes, to use the words of Luc Ferry and Alain Renaut, that the 'discourse of human rights' requires a philosophy.

For my part, I do not know about this, at least for the moment, and want to remain agnostic long enough to undertake a superficial, extrinsic and resolutely entomological enquiry. Let us see what the intellectuals (who may be bees or spiders, we do not know) are liable to say on this question, we shall always have time later to decide whether we should be working on webs or honey.

The March 1983 issue of the journal *Esprit* (meaning 'Mind') will be the object of our investigations. This issue was entitled: 'Thoughts on rights' with the subtitle: 'Sorel, Montesquieu, Constant and human rights'. The issue contained a very learned article by Ferry and Renaut, 'Thinking about human rights', which juggles with Heideg-

ger, Popper, Kant, Léo Strauss, Nietzsche, Hegel, Marcus Aurelius
Antoninus, Michel Villey, Marx, Lefort, *Ornicar* and so on. Having
advanced the view that 'thinking philosophically means thinking
about one's own thought', the two authors try to identify the philosophical place from which human rights can be considered philosophically, in other words to give them some basis. We have already
indicated our belief that 'thinking about one's own thought' is a
project doomed to failure, however hard one tries. This essay rests on
the assumption, which is never questioned, that human rights (whatever they may be and whatever the possibility of giving them a
philosophical foundation) are what is lacking in the countries of the
Eastern bloc. There are seven references to Poland in the first two
pages and one to the Soviet invasion of Afghanistan, a profusion of
terms classically used to refer to these regions of the world ('totalitar-
ianism', etc.), but no allusion to apartheid or to the civil rights
struggle of the American blacks in the 1960s. This surreptitiously
gives the concept of 'human rights' a particular shape, without that
concept ever being made clear. If, in a discussion of human rights, I
consider the American struggles or apartheid, for me this concept
contains the idea of isonomy (rights exist only when they are the
same for all) and that of convivence (I hope Robert Maggiori will
forgive me for using the word he created, giving it a slightly different
meaning), in other words non-segregation. The deep meaning of
isonomy is to enable everybody to 'live together'; let us recall that,
before civil rights were established, blacks and whites were separated
in the United States, even in buses.[89] But if one chooses to consider
the same subject by reference to the Eastern bloc countries, the sense
of the concept includes the idea of 'a defence of the individual or the
society against the state', which is what Ferry and Renaut's article
elliptically formulates.

Their essay is deliberately negative: the authors say that they will
confine themselves 'to outlining those theoretical frameworks in
which, unless we cultivate incoherence, there can be no place for an
understanding of human rights'. And it is certainly not unimportant
to show, as they do, how the current diffuse 'heideggerianization'
makes all juridical and political thinking impossible. Insofar as the
article shows that Heidegger's thought is totalitarian in nature and
thus insofar as the authors invite us to return to a kind of neokant-
ism, I have no objections to it. But I do have some questions
regarding what this thinking leaves out.

The first concerns how the sense of the concept of human rights is
to be understood: the different declarations of these rights take the

form of lists. If we want to give them a philosophical basis, should we not first ask ourselves whether that basis might not be different depending on the contents of the list? There is no reason why the procedure of finding a 'basis' should be the same when the list includes the 'right to resist oppression' as when it contains the 'right to property'. Can we understand the idea of 'human rights' in the abstract, in other words without first stating what those rights are? 'To give a philosophical basis to' has two meanings: either the thing which requires a basis exists, and we are retrospectively asking ourselves what makes it possible and gives it legitimacy (this is how the bases of mathematics were formerly established), or else it remains undefined until the establishment of a basis creates its existence and sketches its outlines. In the case of human rights, we could take a list proclaimed on this or that historical occasion and ask ourselves what metaphysics was required to judge it possible and legitimate, or we could choose the opposite procedure, considering that the basis will decide which articles should be on the list and which not, in other words it will give closure to the list; for lists are finite sets. In both cases, if we do not link the content with the formal principle of the basis (the quiddity and the quoddity) we shall be doing little more, when discussing the principle itself, than building cathedrals in the air.

In French the notion of 'human rights' is commonly expressed, as it sometimes still is in English, as 'the Rights of Man'. My second question thus explicitly concerns the reference of the term 'Man' used in the formulation 'the Rights of Man', although it is equally relevant to the use of the supposedly all-encompassing 'human'. In order that it should not be meaningless, the term 'Man' must refer to 'man in general', or to 'abstract man', expressions which reappear regularly in Rousseau's thought: to all 'featherless bipeds', if we are to be sure to exclude nobody. In itself this notion raises no philosophical problems and, logically speaking, does not contradict the notion that humans exist in concrete terms: Renaissance Italians, today's Russians, the Victorian English and so on. The particular is only a particularization of the universal, in other words its concretization; and if we have to choose between the abstract universal and the concrete particular, as though these were two incompatible ideas, we might as well stop thinking now. The universal may also relate to nothing observable and be so abstract that it is precisely nothing but the reference point for the right which we must assume everyone has, whatever they may be empirically.

But, while logic leads us to state that there is no theoretical problem here, experience tells us that logic is often flouted and that we must always ask what the term 'Man', and indeed 'human', covers. The American declaration of 1776 did not extend the principles of political liberty and equality to black slaves (nor to Indians or women): in France those of the Constituent (1789) and the Convention (1793) did not extend to women the 'natural imprescriptible and inalienable rights' of Man. This limitation certainly remains implicit in the declarations themselves; but each of them has served as the basis and preamble to constitutions which have then taken on the task of clarifying the point. If the lists which make up the Declarations of the Rights of Man do not themselves contain their exact meaning, and if they do not really define their field of application (what is covered by the concept of Man), this renders the project of giving a philosophical basis to these rights null and void, for to give something vague and meaningless a basis amounts to trying to give a plinth to a wisp of smoke.

Let me not be misunderstood here: I do not hold these Declarations in contempt. On the contrary I find some more promising than others and think that all in all that of 1793 makes for pleasanter reading than that of 1795.[90] However, since we must wait and see how they are put into operation to judge their meaning, we may be permitted not to take them entirely seriously. All the same, they can teach us something important about the notion of philosophical basis: they were designed to be founding texts, serving as bases for constitutions, and yet it is the constitutions themselves that really tell us something, not contained in the basis, about the crucial issue of knowing to whom the rights apply. Thus that which is given a basis is easier to understand than that on which it is based. Trying to find a philosophical basis for the rights of man means trying to give a basis to something which already acts as a basis. This procedure of establishing bases 'squared' (to the power of two) may very well be a 'jamming' operation or one of making important issues doubly vague. In all innocence, of course, and without our needing to read any malice into it.

In the case of the journal *Esprit*, it is not until page 117 that we see how the idea of the 'rights of Man' is put into operation. There we find an essay by Geneviève Jurgensen on clitoridectomy. This brief but staggering article comes into the category of apologies for torture. I chose Ferry and Renaut's article as an example of the philosophical 'jamming' of a principle which is already unclear in itself because this essay is not out of place when published next to another which proposes to 'find a meaning in horror' (sic). We have seen that the only idea one can glean from reading the two philosophers which is at all precise is that the 'rights of Man' (whatever they may be) are 'a defence of the individual or the society against the state', and this is because they focus on references to the Eastern bloc countries. Since 'Man' is an ambiguous term in French, it is always necessary to ask whether it is *vir* or *homo* who is being talked about, the male or the human being; but this is seen as a feminist tic. One must then seek out particularly gross examples and this issue of *Esprit* is one of them.

'A defence of the individual or the society against the state'. If we look at these words through the malacologist's lens, we realize that they contain very interesting presuppositions: for example, when the individual is threatened by other individuals or by society, the matter is unrelated to the 'rights of Man', since these only apply when the threat is from the state. If they are a defence of the society against the state, this implies that, in any conflict between 'society' and the 'state', the rights of Man lie on the side of the former. Let us imagine a country where 'the society' is traditionalist, indeed feudal, and the state is in the grip of progressivism, in imitation of its neighours or through too assiduous a frequentation of organizations like UNESCO or UNICEF. One day the state decides to send its little girls to school, and does so in a fairly authoritarian manner, since local traditions are absolutely opposed to it. The people rise up. In the name of the concept of the 'rights of Man' given by Ferry and Renaut, we must side with the people. But if we have in mind the 'right to education' proclaimed by the Declaration of 1793 (and if, naively, we forget that women are not covered by this Declaration), we shall side with the authoritarianism of the state, though without necessarily approving the appeal later sent by the Afghan government to their Soviet neighours.

More fundamentally, lack of definition can be seen as a non-negation. What is said today on the issue of 'human rights' is very ill defined, its only precise intention being reference to the Eastern bloc countries. As a result, no other polemic can be based upon it, and this is regrettable; for once one has said all the bad things one can about this notion, one realizes that it is still pertinent as a critical point of view. At the end of the eighteenth century it provided a response to the notion of 'monarchy by divine right'. It presented a challenge to the concentration of power in a single person, with the aim of increasing the number of those holding political power. I shall return to this question in the second volume, to try to show, in the light of the work of Mary Wollstonecraft, that the notion of 'the rights of Man' can be effective when used polemically, insofar as it protests against limitations or privileges. When this intention is lost, the notion may become vague and prove incapable of challenging scandalous phenomena. It loses its critical power. Geneviève Jurgensen's article was published in the same issue as Ferry and Renaut's essay; that the latter did not block the former is a judgement on the whole.

Jurgensen's article, '*Militer, c'est limiter*' ('It is limiting to be militant'), is a response to the televised discussion between Séverine Auffret, author of a book on clitoridectomy, and Françoise Dolto, author of one on feminine sexuality.[91] In the programme, Mme Dolto tried to give a 'human meaning' to the horror of clitoridectomy and in *Esprit* Jurgensen seeks to defend her point of view and further attack the limiting militant. Before opening the file, let us pause for a second. When do people look for a 'human meaning' to excuse horrifying things and when do they not? Political torture is a practice which is widespread across the surface of the globe and has long been so; moving people from their lands without their agreement, as though they were animals, goes back into the mists of time. Does this mean that we should start by looking for a 'human meaning' in these phenomena before and indeed instead of criticizing them? If we consider that any phenomenon which appears in the human context necessarily has a human meaning, since it pertains to humankind, then we can say nothing against anything.

In fact, as we indicated in the First Notebook, there is a kind of preliminary partition which outlines the areas of indifference. Metaphysical or in this case pseudo-psychoanalytic quibbling should be seen as a symptom of indifference seeking to maintain itself. When one begins to tackle the subject of clitoridectomy, there is no shortage of warnings such as, 'clitoridectomy is a delicate subject', 'be careful, you are bound to fall into ethnocentrism' 'and moralism'; these, too, are symptoms of resistance which, although it certainly appears in a more benign form than the one we are about to describe, still prevents people from grasping the urgent need for humanitarian action on the practice of clitoridectomy. As for me, I prefer to plunge straight in, following Renée Saurel and Séverine Auffret. Being called a 'moralist' is no great risk to run. As for 'ethnocentrism', we shall see on which side that lies.[92]

Let us have Françoise Dolto's point of view then, as reported and supported by Geneviève Jurgensen: 'In this practice, which today affects seventy million women, she seeks something more than chance or caprice, more than torture, more than slavery, more than a desire. She wants to find a human meaning in it [. . .] Dolto proposes an interpretation of this custom [. . .] As always, because Dolto's proposition comes from a truly psychoanalytic source, its effect is restorative.'

Who is restored in all this? If we wanted to illustrate what was said above, that many people are ready to let the violence done by others to others happen, here is a prime example. Dolto's proposition restores only Jurgensen, who is filled with anxiety at the idea that men can show cruelty to women, for example by having them undergo clitoridectomy and infibulation. The psychoanalyst's interpretation reassures her and it matters little that it does not restore, for example, those other women's unfortunate bodies. 'If a man has his future wife undergo clitoridectomy, if he has her infibulated, if millions of older women inflict this on the younger ones', we must not see this as cruelty: 'How can we refuse to seek greater complexity, greater richness, greater nobility in it? How can we regard so many people at once as fools?'

Séverine Auffret called no one a fool: the issue of torture requires quite a different register. Nor can we say for certain that this word is adequate to describe Dolto and Jurgensen and the 'use' they make of mutilations they have not personally suffered to settle problems related to their own fantasies. Mme Dolto's hypothesis, reported as having a 'restorative effect' by the journal *Esprit*, is this: the clitoris resembles a nipple; the adult man is thus afraid of the vulva, since it puts him in danger of regression to the maternal breast. 'In order that the woman can be an adult companion for him, he makes her in his own image. Where can he be penetrated? Through his anus. By clitoridectomy, infibulation and the removal of the labia the knives are trying to mould an anus. Not to kill a sex, but precisely to give it a sex.' The article does not fail to remind us after this that cultural imperialism is a shameful thing and concludes that 'respecting one's enemy is more than respecting oneself'.

When this type of argument appears in a special issue on 'the rights of Man', we may be permitted to abandon finesse; the crudest and most summary comments are justified. It is the macho's rights that are being defended here, and more precisely his right to shape other people's bodies in the image of his own fantasies. 'It is appalling that those people should talk about freedom of opinion and will not allow me mine' said Marat to the Assembly. He had just upheld the view that, for the sake of peace and quiet, two hundred and seventy thousand heads should roll and shouts from the Assembly had reduced him to silence.[93] But let us leave these gibes aside: one needs Flaubert's nerves of steel to deal epigrammatically with such serious subjects. Clitoridectomy kills a large number of girls every year, it makes sexual relations painful for millions of women and makes childbirth a more difficult ordeal than nature intended. Only a few rare women who have suffered clitoridectomy still feel sexual pleasure. Faced with this problem, the words 'thank you for not killing me' are nothing to laugh at.

And yet there is nothing in our stock of available intellectual models which enables us correctly to approach the problem and to back up the WHO in its modest attempts to combat it. We have just seen that a long dissertation on 'understanding human rights' does not prevent an apology for this practice from being published by the same editorial committee, who no doubt did not make the connection. Far from helping us get a grip on the problem, psychoanalysis, one of the great reference points of this century, legitimates it, thus moving from a position of 'passive collaboration' to one of almost active, although distant, collaboration. Indeed, Dolto's contribution does appear to have an 'active' sense, if we accept that 'mental excision' exists among European peoples. Even the category of 'cultural imperialism' is fallacious here, and perhaps always. Not that some facts which are usually placed in this category do not exist and are not deplorable. But the category in which they are placed is so poorly designed that it lumps together heterogeneous realities which have nothing to do with each other. When, on the same notices, the French Republic banned 'speaking Breton and spitting on the ground' in all public places, it displayed its odiousness; but must we turn to the notion of 'cultural colonialism' to criticize its action? This category, although apparently useful, is too large and floats far from the edges of reality. The ban on speaking Breton was partly related to a desire to control an oppressed and therefore dangerous minority and partly to a plan for the better use of Breton conscripts in the army: cannon fodder who could not speak French might not always be easy to manage and those who jabber incomprehensibly among themselves can also hatch plots. But had it been in any way useful to France for the Bretons to speak only Breton, I am sure the republic would have done its utmost to block their access to any other language. Should we then have gone into raptures at the respect shown for autochthonous culture, preserved from allogenic influences?

The notion of 'cultural imperialism' is again fallacious in that, while it seems to criticize ethnocentrism, it is itself twistedly ethnocentric. It presupposes that 'we' could (but, out of kindness, 'we' must not) change other cultures and make them fit with ours; thus that 'we' have the power to do this, if we want to. While it recommends respect for other cultures (or at least for those aspects of them which do not disrupt the exploitation of the Third World), this idea tends to fetishize them, *noli eas tangere*, while 'we' supposedly question our institutions, beliefs and customs constantly, and are very proud of doing so. A feeling of superiority then filters into our delicate abstention: the others are judged incapable of adopting a critical distance in relation to themselves, that marvellous critical distance which of course remains specific to, and moreover the great superiority of...we had better not say whom. For the capacity for reflective thought about oneself is certainly not the preserve of the 'modern West' which has, for some years, been performing routine episiotomies and increasing the numbers of unnecessary caesarians and cannot even arrive at a (collective) awareness of the fact that such surgery certainly does not reflect clinical necessity every time, thus revealing as much contempt for women's bodies as sexual mutilations do.[94]

The misunderstanding is still more serious inasmuch as Europeans describe clitoridectomy as an 'ancestral rite', which sets the seal on its fetishization. According to some African women, European scholarly language picks its concepts very badly, for that of 'measure' (as in the phrase 'to take measures against') would be better. Indeed, the aim of these mutilations is often expressed as: 'women must behave themselves', something seen as particularly necessary in the context of polygamy. A man may fear that he cannot satisfy four wives sexually; the wives might be tempted to be unfaithful if they had not undergone clitoridectomy. This concurs with the ethnographers' observation that the geographical region of clitoridectomy covers very different religious zones and thus does not reflect any particular faith: it is not a 'rite', and even less a rite whose origins are hidden from the understanding of those who practise it. It is a means of coercion. If African states took equally coercive measures to protect little girls and women from this tragic effect of a social structure, should human rights activists get upset and start shouting about ethnocide?[95]

17   What do we call symbolic, rite, taboo, etc.?

This issue now no longer involves some African states alone;[96] clitoridectomy is practised in France by families from some African regions, on babies or on school-age girls. The powerful trade union the Federation of National Education (FEN) decided to 'break the silence' and publish in the same volume both a 'scientific' enquiry carried out by an ethno-sociologist, Anne Raulin, and the minutes of a meeting which took place in December 1986 and in which many organizations besides the FEN participated. One of these was the Movement for the Defence of the Rights of Black Women (MODEFEN), which was represented by its president, Lydie Dooh Bunya.[97] She strongly attacks the ethno-sociologist's work, which she regards as 'luke-warm' and even 'indulgent' towards the practice of clitoridectomy and points out how dangerous it is to 'allow oneself to be seduced by the romanticism of the symbolic'. Are these the words of an activist opposed to scientific language? No: they represent a polite and pertinent epistemological objection to a study which bears the label 'scientific' but which has not thought through its concepts and methods.[98] The comparison between Anne Raulin's study and Lydie Dooh Bunya's contribution reveals how the former constantly uses the vocabulary of the 'rite' and the 'symbolic', while the latter simply talks about 'safeguards', explaining that in groups where clitoridectomy is practised, women are considered incapable of repressing their own drives and 'safeguards are needed for the greater peace of mind of the men'.[99]

In the same movement she sweeps away two ideas: firstly, the Pontius Pilate-like attitude that 'it is their culture, we must not meddle in it'; and, secondly, the thesis which sees clitoridectomy as one of the procedures establishing sexual difference: 'If somewhere in the world a people decided to institute, as a mark of their culture, the practice of blinding little boys in the right eye and cutting off their right ears, then blinding little girls in the left eye and cutting off their left ears', some people might at last decide to do something. Lydie Dooh Bunya is certainly right and her contribution can provide us with a kind of general theory: when something damaging exists which only causes harm to women and little girls, it is never considered serious; the phenomenon can easily be minimized in unquestioned ethnographic categories: it's their culture, and since women alone suffer from it, it is certainly a symbolic way of marking sexual difference.

We know, however, that the prime difficulty in ethnography is to describe a phenomenon. Our categories, which distinguish between 'the religious', 'the artistic', 'the political' or 'the functional', are often inadequate to understand a different society (or our own?). We also know that when ethnologists traditionally speak of Amazonian or African 'tribes', this is because the earliest explorers were great readers of the Bible and projected this concept from Genesis on what they saw. We also know that another generation of explorers were keen readers of Walter Scott; they thus called the subdivisions of the 'tribes' 'clans', after those in Scotland. Those not-like-us are all the same and anything we have read about one exotic country enables us to understand all the others. Captain Cook recorded the word *tapu* in Polynesia and wrote it as taboo; since then, where have taboos not been found? The notion of rite is Latin: a *ritus* is simply a custom, hence Cicero writes of a *peculum ritu* (in the manner of the beasts) and a *Latronum ritu* (in the manner of bandits); the adverb *rite* could mean 'according to form', 'in the proper way', 'rightly' or 'in accordance with religious custom'. Christianity later adopted the term to refer to a certain codification of ceremonies; then, in the work of some protestant authors, it took on a pejorative sense: the rite is an external thing, while faith implies the inner depths of the heart. More recently Marcel Mauss used the term rite to refer to the material or bodily aspects of religion. Thus the ethnographic concept of 'rite' is the endpoint of twenty centuries of European vagaries, combining three types of consideration. It is an element of religion, it concerns things or bodies (extended substances as Descartes would say) and it has a legal role (in the relation of religion to bodies), since it defines what should be done according to form ('in accordance with the rites'). There is no reason to regard this concept as any more 'scientific' than that of 'phlogistics' or any alchemical notion. In any case, we cannot be certain that it is valid for all cultural spheres and a fortiori for any bodily practice that we regard as strange and thus as quaintly outlandish.

The more neutral term of 'practice' used by Lydie Dooh Bunya and Sylvie Fainzang (a more sober ethnologist who was also present at the FEN meeting) seems in every way preferable to that of 'rite' for talking about clitoridectomy and preparing to fight against the phenomenon. And since Sylvie Fainzang reminds us that clitoridectomy is intended to 'enable women to submit to the regime of polygamous marriage', we realize at the same time that health information campaigns of the type that already exist in many of the African countries involved and also in France will not be enough. It is typical of educationalists to place all their hopes on information and education campaigns, so it is not surprising that a meeting organized by the FEN should put the accent on this project. In my tribe there is another ancestral belief which states that if one really wants to eliminate an effect, one has to eliminate the cause: if sexual mutilations are an effect of matrimonial structures, then it is likely that as long as these structures exist the mutilations will be carried out.

Bodily mutilations for young African women and mental excison and infibulation for a great many others.[100] Let us hope that the relation of 'cause and effect' is just one of my tribe's groundless beliefs. If we have to wait for monogamy-for-women-only to cease before we see the end of physical and mental clitoridectomy, then the personal wholeness of women is a long way off.

However, the matrimonial structure (which we shall describe as 'legal', for lack of a more all-encompassing word) affects adult women, while the mutilations are undergone by little girls in anticipation of their future status. If African families living in France regard the clitoridectomy of little girls as a sign of their hope of 'going home' one day and seeing their adult daughters integrated into the matrimonial and familial system their parents knew before they emigrated, then in spite of everything we must acknowledge that this matter does or could one day contain a symbolic element; however, at the same time we must define what is meant by 'symbolic', since this notion, even more than that of 'rite', is overloaded with confused values.

The most basic definition we can give of the symbol is that it represents something else; the symbolic is the mode through which one makes present something which is not, is no longer or is not yet there. It is thus notably the medium of the future. A marriage is anticipated which will take place in the context of a coercive structure (where the man completely appropriates the woman) and as a result the little girl is made to undergo a certain number of things which, fifteen or twenty years in advance, signify what is to come. A girl is brought up according to the known situation of adult women at the time when she is herself little. It has been said that the child is 'father to the man'; I do not know what to think of this old pedagogical credo, but what I am trying to articulate has the quite different consequence that all adult women, as they are known, are 'mother' to the girl–child. The legal and social contexts of a given time as they affect adult women are integrated into the educational context through representations and in the symbolic mode. When St Thomas says that a father must watch over his daughters' chastity and thus never smile at them, this recommended non-smile is a symbolic way of making the very young girl realize that later she will only encounter strict and pitiless authority. For subjectivity, a permanent non-smile must have almost the same weight as a clitoridectomy. But there are two things to note here: one is the social situation affecting adult women (in the Middle Ages those who broke the rules were often drowned), the other is the cultural 'medium' designed to mark the little girl in advance with a sign that anticipated her adult position and gave her a taste of punishment, also in advance. Or made her imagine her own incapacity, foresee her own exclusion, or know in advance how she would be made to suffer.[101]

18 Putting one's house in order and going round the world

If, on issues like these, the state does not defend people against 'society' with all the efficiency of which it is capable, we must ask it why not. But it would take thousands of us in the streets to make it answer, even with lies or prevarications. Esther Maronée's thesis on the question is already well advanced and soon Sorbford university will award its honours to this study, which is presented through personification: the state makes a sincere public confession. I do not know whether Esther, who is a true specialist on the question, will want to use the few fragments set out here, produced yet again by someone who is often wrong because she writes too soon or too late, at a time which is neither that of the 'heat of battle' nor that of olympian theories.

Clitoridectomy is practised in immigrant families in France. At the end of May 1988, a court in the Paris region had to pass sentence on parents (a man and his two wives) who had thus caused the death of their baby. Awa Thiam, author of *La Parole aux Négresses* and witness for the prosecution, made a clear and condemnatory statement on this practice. However, the verdict demonstrated the court's great 'understanding' and the sentence was lighter than that which a young bicycle thief could generally expect to get, whether immigrant or not. The penal code is designed to protect property and not people, as Inspector Maigret himself shows in an utterly convincing analysis.[102]

The life of a little black French girl is much less important than the daubs of the Versailles war museum. The Breton nationalists who tried to bomb France's ugliest museum (and, unfortunately, only managed to scratch a few battle scenes) were condemned to ten or twenty years in prison. The scratched bodies of women, whether black or not, do not arouse the same reaction from the law. But another aspect of this sad business of homicide by clitoridectomy should be noted: according to the newspapers, this baby was born in a hospital. It would seem that, at the time of the birth, no one took responsibility for telling the mother that clitoridectomy was forbidden in France. And yet when a woman who has herself undergone the practice gives birth in a state establishment, this is the perfect moment to convince her never to inflict on her daughters what she herself has suffered. The doctors, midwives, social workers, nurses and so on should be required by law to explain to her the unacceptable nature of this practice and the risk of prosecution run by anyone who carries it out. Since women having babies stay in hospital for about a week, there is always enough time to find an interpreter if necessary. It would not be so difficult to make a video in the five or six main vernaculars.

But if the woman giving birth had just undergone an episiotomy, would it be completely credible? She is cut, she is told not to cut, what kind of sense can she make of that? In her place I would be completely confused. And then who is going to force the medical teams to give this lesson? Can the Health Minister order them to do so directly? Would he have to negotiate with the councils of the different professional bodies involved? Would the measure have to be approved by Parliament? The ethnographical work that the issue of clitoridectomy demands should not be carried out only in the desolate streets of Bamako. The bizarre nature of the French system can be judged by the obstacles it is prone to erect against any WHO plan aimed at suppressing the practice here. There are already many africanists, but we need gallicists just as much.

So 'one should put one's own house in order first' is still a pertinent maxim, since from the point of view of the French legal system, a child's body belongs to its parents. I was twenty years and eight months old, had long been economically independent and had put six hundred kilometres between my parent's home and my own (incidentally, I also had a degree in philosophy), when acute appendicitis required my immediate hospitalization. At the time one was a minor until the age of twenty-one: I had to ask my family for permission to have an operation on what I had thought was my abdomen. For me, the business ended in this simple humiliation. The children of Jehovah's Witnesses are exposed to more serious consequences: since their parents' religion forbids blood transfusions, in an emergency the doctor must first ask a judge for a 'suspension of parental authority'. Before investigating African beliefs or 'superstitions', we should ask ourselves what twisted mind inspired French legislation. It was not Descartes in any case: he claimed not to be 'only the child of his parents'.

Every time that the issue of sexual mutilation is publicly discussed, because of a tragic case or a book, some newspaper always publishes a piece from someone saying, more or less: 'If you stop immigrant families from practising clitoridectomy on their daughters, what will happen when the girls go back to Africa? Will they be marriageable?' We shall keep to ourselves the view that not being marriageable is not the worst thing that can happen to a woman, as is demonstrated by clitoridectomy and its effects; we shall also keep to ourselves the hope that the migrants will stay of their own free will; let us take these comments literally. It then becomes obvious that we shall not get to the bottom of the phenomenon of mutilation in some immigrant families without help from their country of origin. We need at the least to get the various heads of state involved to agree to implement a plan of action against mutilation and to declare that they will definitely and completely eliminate these practices over the next fifteen years. They would be asked to say this, in front of a camera of course, and in the various languages of their country. The WHO and UNICEF could then show the film in the most far-flung villages of Africa. In France the Department of Social Affairs would not refuse a little funding to associations like MODEFEN so that they could carry out the same task in our depressing suburbs. What? the state may not have enough money for this? The Académie Française is already expensive enough? And the blessed Bicentennial of the Revolution? You are dreaming, Michèle, there is more to this problem. Go and ask a specialist on North–South relations. One cannot suggest this kind of thing to an African head of state, even one of the authoritarian sort who rules without consensus. Our trade relations with Central and West Africa are far too important to risk for something like that! Do you want to do without French beans, the very fine ones you see all nicely arranged in their crates on the market stalls every winter?[103] And there is more at stake than beans, but I chose an example that might affect you.

We can be sure that Esther Maronée's thesis will not be 'olympian'; when discussing this subject, she will also get worked up and will stick to eating potatoes. But, as she bears the name of the Thracian town where Hipparchia was born, she will be able to find the correct and caustic language which will allow her to get her teeth into the rough reality of the world like a true cynic. I am sure she will make her study into her spinning wheel: you pull at what looks like a bit of thread (the phenomenon of clitoridectomy, which is marginal in our part of the world) and everything unwinds with it: the penal code, strange standards of punishment, state power which leaves things be, the status of children here, 'modern' obstetric practices, imaginary representations of and about immigration ('when the Africans go back to their country'), public finances and North–South relations. Esther would do well to use Diogenes' words, 'I deny the value of marriage' as an epigraph to confer some scholarly legitimacy on her work. Naturally, the title of her thesis will be: 'On clitoridectomy, etc.', a form which has become standard at Sorbford university. Like Puck, she will put a girdle round about the earth, this time a girdle woven of critiques. Will she conclude, again paraphrasing Diogenes, that a fine law is all very well, as long as there is a city in which it applies?

19 *'You have many students, if you count the gods'*

If a social movement for the liberation of women were reborn tomorrow (some embers from the last one are not yet out), I should go and discuss all these ideas within it. While I wait, I continue to pull my thread, even though my personal demon is warning me that I may have only the Nine Muses for readers; he got that taunt from the Cynics too.[104]

To claim the role of 'instructor of the people' (and what else does an intellectual do?) is not simply an arrogant idea. It is lined on all sides with impasses of a different gravity from the aesthetics of the impasse in which philosophical academicism indulges. At least three difficulties can be identified. Firstly, since scholars currently appear unable to think, and one sometimes catches oneself in the act of getting things wrong, how can we find a way to be sure we are right? Secondly, since we no longer know whether we are addressing an audience of more than nine people (this is an allegory), there is nothing to guarantee – always supposing we find a valid idea – that a significant part of the city will hear it and establish it as a law of the city. Lastly, if there is no 'Movement', the problem does not even arise; and if there is one, the problems it reveals are usually quite different. I am taking things a bit far, but before I go on pulling my thread, I should like to point out that feminist educationalism in general needs to be, not rejected, but rethought.

For feminism has long been greatly concerned with the education given to girls, considering that the basic injustice they suffer comes during their childhood, thus providing a basis for more injustice. For, since it occurs at the time when the personality is being formed, anyone subjected to it becomes unable to resist further injustice. This idea is not wrong in itself and has inspired a whole literature in which women writers and readers rework their childhoods in their imaginations. One could even go so far as to say that *The Second Sex* was written more in favour of little and older girls than of women. In

more recent literature, Elena Belotti's book *Du côe des petites filles* gives
a perfect illustration of this point of view. From it we learn that, from
the earliest age, girls are treated brusquely and boys like princes, so
that 'the average length of time that a baby of two months is kept at
the breast is forty-five minutes for boys and twenty-five minutes for
girls'.[105] The feminism of equality finds something to be quantified
here. In the same way, it could be said that a particular little boy has
the right to make as much of a row as he likes, while his sister is
brought into line when she makes half the noise.

However, this approach presents several problems. The first is that
it is confined to an everyday reality of custom to which no reformer
has access, thus perpetuating the assumption that this reality has an
independent existence. I think that the anxiety with which more or
less everyone is filled at the thought of interference in domestic
privacy goes hand in hand with a belief in the independent existence
of that privacy, as though the great lines of force of society and the
public arena were not present everywhere, even when a mother gives
the breast to her baby of a given sex. Seen in this light, the idea that
'the personal is political' allows us to shift the classic feminism of
equality. Let us publicly debate as adults the means to create true
isonomy between men and women and let us hope that customary
forms of education will be changed as a result. It is hard to influence
the length of time a baby is kept at the breast, or the way that
parents of both sexes give their offspring the bottle, but we can ask
that there should be as many women as men sitting on the Council
of State; it is reasonable to demand that work done by women in a
family business (trade, craft, farming) should have proper legal
status;[106] it is always possible to boycott any political party which
fails to think that the people can be represented by women; lastly,
picking quarrels with the journal *Esprit* and some others is, as we
have seen, an ultimately delectable activity.

Whatever the practical difficulties inherent in this kind of idea
(who will do the asking, demanding, or boycotting, and how effective
will it be?), the fact of concerning ourselves primarily with the adult
world replaces educationalist pedagogy with pedagogy through politics. This idea is not so new and I do not even know of whose words
these are a pastiche: if you want your children to be just, to themselves and to everyone else, you must go and live in a just city. But if
we accept this wager, we must point out that the feminism of equality
should then add to the idea of equality that of community, and that
the latter would be even harder to establish than the ideal of equality.

The issue of *Esprit* will again show us where the problem lies. The main reason for their publishing a long dissertation on human rights, which the editor describes as seeking 'the restoration of transcendence', and then, a few pages further on, an apology for clitoridectomy, is that the editorial committee did not make the connection at all. This is a common phenomenon, which gets in the way of the feminism of equality. A little boy makes a row with impunity, his sister is scolded for less. But, in a sense, this inequality is not decided by the local legislators, here the parents. They permit in one case and forbid in the other, without necessarily 'making the connection', until the child's recriminations or a comment from someone else names this set of permits and prohibitions as a disparity of rights. Here too, the little scenes of daily life reflect the great stage of the law. Odile Dhavernas notes:

> the idea of discrimination exists only by reference to a principle of equality within a homogeneous legal category. There can be no discrimination between members of the nobility and those of the third estate, between brahman and untouchable or master and slave, for they are not covered by the same laws. Comparison, from which an observation of discrimination may result, can only take place between comparable elements; in other words, within a single category.[107]

In order for the feminism of equality to begin to implement its programme, it must at the same time construct a homogeneous category, without which no one will ever have to make the connection. On the one hand, the spectre of 'cultural imperialism' will be invoked when the issue is one of protecting little African girls; on the other people will express regret that 'Western Europe has been unable to devise a foreign policy which would make effective intervention possible' when the issue is one of the 'reconstruction of social independence' in the Eastern bloc countries.[108] A law on sexual balance within a community – *mixité* – should stress the full meaning of the term 'human being' and recall that the latter refers to any 'featherless biped', to use a very old definition. This would certainly not be enough to ensure the homogeneity of the category; the replacement of 'fraternity' by 'solidarity' in the Republic's motto would not be enough either. But they would be a beginning: the beginning of a prescriptive law which, to my mind, would be better than the prohibitive formulations of the anti-sexist law proposed in 1983 which gave rise to an enormous outcry.[109]

Yet here too, neither public opinion nor anyone else made the

connection: information and publicity on contraception are still prevented, but it is forbidden to prevent expressions of scorn or hatred
for women, or even incitement to 'jostle'. Indeed it is forbidden to use
appropriate graffiti to comment on the most shocking advertisement
posters, and this is true in all the industrialized countries. Take a
poster showing a car with a model lying across its roof and the
slogan: 'If this car were a lady it would get its bottom pinched'. By
night an illicit hand added, 'If this lady was a car she would run you
down.'[110] In 1983 some called the proposed anti-sexist law repressive,
saying that it would turn women into a 'protected species'. The
opposite is true: the pornocracy and the exploitation of the seductiveness of an unreal woman's body are totally 'protected', while an
improvement which might be of great interest for the daily, concrete
reality of the lives of women you mix with every day is strictly prohibited. Anyone who writes graffiti on a poster risks a fine, but thou
shalt not prosecute the most insulting statements or advertisements.

It is vital here to make the connection. So that only the exploitable
seductiveness of a woman–image can appear, there must be absolute
silence about the daily concrete reality of women who have committed the great sin of being real. The sirens spread across town walls,
bus shelters or television screens all have hidden bodies and, however
naked they may be, are masks: nothing that trembles or suffers
beneath the display of skin may show, just as the effort a ballet
dancer makes must not be seen on her face, although it is comparable
to that made by a market porter. An advertisement for the coil might
disturb such repression and force advertisers to rework the syntax of
their other productions, assuming it is true that a return of the
repressed demands a modification of the structure.

We are obliged to write about these issues in the mode of probability. Nothing can be known with certainty as long as the experiment
has not been carried out. I do not have a single element at my
disposal to support what I am saying, which is that the concealment
of various bodily misfortunes is a necessary condition for the advertisers' rhetoric in general. Even though it is now permitted by law in
France, the advertising of condoms (insofar as they are intended to
protect against AIDS) retains an indirect, discreet nature. The boxes
can be seen on chemists' counters, but local walls still say nothing
about them and continue to praise all sorts of other things with the
aid of womanly forms. It seems impossible to portray at the same
time both the glory of an artificial body and the possible misfortunes
of a real, living physiology.

20 The limits of my imagination

A prescriptive law on sexual balance, the lifting of the ban which still prevents direct advertising of contraceptives, the lifting of the ban on writing graffiti on the sacred posters of the advertisers and indeed the creation of an annual prize for the best popular response to a stupid advert, the replacement of the Académie Française with a Society for Humanist Research which would award these prizes and reward school textbooks which gave more prominence to the idea of 'living-with', in other words to the two sexes and the various communities which make up the France of today...[111] my political imagination does have limits. But it will have been observed that I have made no promises to be the individual Great Subject of a new reorientation of thought. Such a reorientation is necessary, but it cannot be brought about, even on the theoretical level, by some solitary utopian. All we can do is set our imaginations to work on devising some appropriate measures which might lead to a dynamic enabling the devising of yet more measures, which I cannot foresee.

Seventeenth-century English seafarers had a word to refer to the furthest visible point, corresponding to about twenty sea miles: the 'kenning'. There is a place for a unit of measure of this type in political philosophy. It would enable us to stop arguing always in terms of an infinitely distant point, where the overall solution lies, or in terms of a little-understood present, which makes a strange compound with the past: 'we have won the fight', 'enough laws have been passed' – it has all been settled. The kenning we need to give ourselves in politics is that of a generation: what should I be, do, demand, imagine today, so that those who are now being born will from their earliest years discover an adult world in which some questions are being settled, so that they can see different ones? If we could establish today that all authorities or decision-making bodies should be composed of equal numbers of men and women, sexism would very probably disappear from school textbooks. What a generation brought up in such a context could then think, what a truly mixed Parliament could concoct in the way of legislation are things that I cannot myself imagine because they go beyond my kenning. I am simply convinced that these would be moves in the right direction and that, in order that the next generation's political imagination should take flight, we must obtain the concrete realization of our aspirations and at the same time do as much as possible to sweep aside all the 'theories' which block everyone's view and prevent us from even knowing whether or not a particular aspiration might have the support of a consensus.

21 Living together despite Tocqueville

To end this notebook, I should like to stress that, in one sense, it has constantly argued against Tocquevillian doxa, which seems to be the dominant ideology of this century. From the point of view of imaginary representations or basic values, Tocquevillian thought plays on two apparently contradictory fears: a horror of mixing and isolation anxiety. (And also no doubt a third: the fear that equality will produce uniformity.) In combination, these two fears result in great value being placed on the closed local community, which is the object intended to ward them off. On the horror of mixing, one should consult the chapter entitled: 'The position of the black race in the United States; the dangers its presence constitutes for whites'.[112] The chapter begins thus:

> As soon as it is admitted that the whites and the emancipated blacks are placed upon the same territory in the situation of two foreign communities, it will readily be understood that there are but two chances for the future: the Negroes and the whites must either wholly part or wholly mingle. I have already expressed my conviction as to the latter event.[113] I do not think that the white and black races will ever live in any country upon an equal footing.

It then remains to think about separation (Tocqueville was in favour of the foundation of Liberia, although he thought it an insufficient measure) and to 'excuse the Southern Americans', who are 'obliged, to save their own race, to keep' the negroes in chains.

Signs of the opposite fear can be seen more or less everywhere, particularly in critiques of individualism as an effect of egalitarian despotism on the part of the state:

> 'What strength can even public opinion have retained, when no twenty persons are connected by a common tie? [...] When every citizen, being equally weak, equally poor, and equally isolated, has only his personal impotence to oppose to the organized force of the government?[114]

In *L'Ancien régime et la révolution*, he returns to this theme: when men are no longer 'bound together by any tie of caste, class, corporation or family', they are only too inclined to concern themselves entirely with their own interests, always too liable to think only of themselves and to retreat into a narrow individualism in which all public virtue is stifled. Far from combatting this tendency, despotism makes it irresistible, for it withdraws from citizens all opportunity to act together: it ripens them, so to speak, in private life. They already tended to keep themselves to themselves: it isolates them. They were becoming cold in relation to each other: it freezes them.[115]

Hence the idea that administrative decentralization, by which 'the special interests of some sections of the nation' can be run locally, is a guarantee of democracy. Let us make it clear that Tocqueville makes a distinction between the political and the administrative: he recommends political centralism (the model for this could be Louis XIV) and administrative decentralization, the ideal image of the latter being provided by 'communal enterprises' such as the American county or British local government.

Nostalgia for caste, class, corporation and family ties and praise of the communal enterprise lead to the idea that freedom is better assured when there are intermediary bodies between the individual and centralized power. Despotism on the other hand rules over an aggregate of atomized individuals. The contemporary apology for 'civil society' against what they call the 'all-ruling state' proceeds from the same idea, which is the complementary thesis of the one we described at the beginning of this Notebook according to which the will to reform (which may from time to time animate the state) fails because of this inert mass: the government does not govern it. Far be it from me to call the existence of local authorities into question or to deny that they are justified, pragmatically speaking at least. But it must be said that the groupings described by Tocqueville have two features. Membership of a caste, class, corporation or family, or citizenship of a borough are not matters of free choice. And one is no more free to be a non-member than a member. Moreover, there is no guarantee that these local authorities are independent of the state and, reciprocally, there is no guarantee that the state is independent of them. The existence and role of communes or guilds (like those governing the liberal professions) are determined by the state in the form of delegation of power. But, reciprocally, since the state exists as a mediation between these different collectivities (or bodies) and 'their' powers, dealing tactfully with what is dominant in local groups is obviously a part of elementary political skill. The consequence is that, far from being certain guarantors of everyone's freedom, 'local authorities' can be places of micropower, in other words where some individuals exercise power over others on a small scale.

The family is a good example of this, for it is a local collectivity which appears to have its basis in nature, membership of a particular family not being a matter of free choice. Its role is very precisely defined by the state and the law: it depended on the state to replace 'paternal authority' by 'parental authority'. Until 1970 in France, fathers were the only legally recognized decision-makers in relation to children (applying for passports for them, or not, enrolling them into a particular school or indeed placing them in a reform school). For twenty years or so, fathers and mothers have had the same degree of parental authority, which has moreover been somewhat restricted, but remains excessive to my mind.[116] This change came about a quarter of a century after women were granted the vote. It would have been impossible before, because no government would have run the risk of upsetting the 'heads of families', who were the only ones with a vote. In any case, in both 'liberal democracies' and 'totalitarian states', the state regulates the subordination of individuals to each other.

The only associations relatively independent of the state and which could be the guarantors of democracy or offer hope for freedom (even if limited) are those which one can join of one's own free will. When anyone can join but no one is forced to do so and when anyone can leave the grouping at any time, its internal structure reflects a different situation in relation to the state: the latter does not 'regulate' it.

The issue of the relationship between the state and local authorities recognized by the state, to which it delegates some of its power, is of very concrete importance to women, insofar as the alliance between the state and those who hold power locally often works against their interests. There is nothing like promising all the men of the country that the particular form of subjugation of women which the former prefer will be maintained to strengthen an unstable government. An African head of state who, despite the example of his neighbours or the projected interference of the WHO, pledges to do nothing against clitoridectomy is sure of strengthening his position if, in his country, most traditionally recognized leaders are in favour of this practice. An Iranian leader who has only recently come to power and seeks to build the widest possible consensus among those who count, thinks it opportune, as a measure of the highest priority, to make the wearing of the chador compulsory and to ban men and women from going to certain public places together. By acting as they did, the statesmen involved in these two cases set themselves up as arbiters and necessary mediators between the aspirations of husbands and fathers on the one hand and women's bodies and the attitudes of some of those women on the other. The simple fact that a form of arbitration exists establishes the idea of the importance of the state; when in addition this arbitration decides in favour of those whose consent matters, it anchors state power all the better. The Napoleonic Code, which made the husband the head of the family government, and the Revolution, which took a series of measures to exclude women from politics, practised similar strategies. When the state recognizes civic rights for all men and no women, this disparity does not really establish inequality: it creates a form of dependence within a defined space.

When it does not take such things into account, the feminism of equality remains a tenuous theoretical line or an inadequate approach. To take an example which affects me: of course I think it terrible that in the philosophical republic a women has to prove herself three times as much to get half as much intellectual recognition. But, apart from the fact that I do not know to whom we can address this kind of complaint, I am unable to establish who is getting what they deserve – what we deserve. Should we decide that men receive too much, or that women receive too little? The question of isonomy is always clear in fields regulated by the law whereas the register of simple comparison is not necessarily so. And constant comparisons between people present psychological difficulties. It is easier for me to want the panels who judge me always to be mixed; this means wanting them truly to represent the republic which employs me.

The feminism of equality also runs up against the objection that two things are entirely or qualitatively different. Having timed feeds, Elena Belotti expresses their different effects in two ways. When the mother hurries her daughter, she gives her to understand: 'I shall do the indispensable minimum for you; so hurry up and look after yourself.' But, by letting the little boy take his time, she transmits the idea: 'You can do as you like, that is your right; I am at your service and willing to remain so as long as possible.' Let us not ask ourselves which is worse, nor if all this does not store up misery for everyone. We shall first note that these two messages are of different natures, they are qualitatively different, and thus cannot be compared. The perception of this type of problem by feminists of my generation has led the egalitarian current to lose its language. However, I think they can be solved: inequality between male and female individuals is an effect of the relationships they have with a third party, that being one or several authorities, which we should always try to uncover. The fact that in the last analysis one always finds the state in its relationship to 'delegated administrations' enables us to politicise everything.

The Knesset provided an example of this in 1975. A Bill for a 'Fundamental Law' instituting equal rights for men and women was introduced. Before this there had been a 'revolutionary law' dating from 1951, which rivalled French legislation in its use of 'however' clauses: article 5 of this law exempted from the sphere of equality anything concerning the authorization or forbidding of marriage and divorce, bringing these into the exclusive jurisdiction of the rabbinical courts and religious law. If the law proposed in 1975 had been passed, this exemption clause would have been repealed and it would then have been necessary to create civil marriage and divorce. According to Nira Yuval-Davis, on whose words I am drawing here, this would have spared many women and children a lot of problems.[117] But Mr Rabin, the Prime Minister of the time, publicly promised the Minister for Religious Affairs that in no circumstances would this law be passed.

Let us not at once conclude from this that civil legislation on marriage and divorce would have gone against the interests of Israeli men in general, nor that the Prime Minister sided with men against women. What we are seeing in this case is rather a debate between institutions, between a section of the Knesset who wanted to construct a secular state and the rabbinical courts who were defending their prerogatives in a strictly corporatist way. Things that have a bad effect on women do not necessarily benefit men in general and a conflict may be decided in favour of a 'local authority' and not that of a unified 'class' of men; with the result, nevertheless – and we can see this in the 1951 law – that the declaration of equality between men and women is prevented, a sign that something which renders women the vassals of men has been maintained. Since it is the state which decides whether or not to allow a local authority to take over part of its power, it is the state which is totally responsible for what that authority might do, whether good or bad.

This should lead us to the idea that the 'cause' of a form of inequality, like that of a sexist mechanism, may be very distant; we shall stress this point in the second volume. We must also conclude that the aim of such mechanisms is not always directly to serve the interests of all men and, if every man nevertheless gets something out of it, we cannot know in advance whether this will be a piece of the cake or the crumbs that fall from the revellers' table. But we should also catch sight of the fact that a battle for power can be a struggle to be the sole agency determining relations between the sexes. It is important formally to be the decision-making power on this issue, which represents an enormous part of human existence. No power, be it religion, the state, a philosophy, or a political movement, has failed to show its strength by trying to impose a type (whether new or traditional) of relations between the sexes. And these 'authorities' seeking to be decision-making bodies have almost always consisted of men, either entirely or in a very strong majority. There has almost never been an arena where the sexes were balanced and where the issue of relations between men and women could be debated collectively and publicly between men and women. It is certainly high time that democracy saw its duty to become such an arena.

Tocquevillian ideology should also be challenged from another point of view. The groupings it regards as guarantors of the existence of a structured society in relation to the state (family, class, caste or corporation) are more or less 'natural' conglomerates. Hence a certain concept of 'natural barriers', or boundaries created by nature, underlies his thinking on 'races' as on sexes. On the other hand he seems very reserved on the subject of informal 'singular little societies'. While recognizing that these are inevitable in a democracy, he confines their legitimate area of activity to private life: people may gather in little groups of friends to entertain themselves, have fun and 'taste the delights of private life on their own'.

> In democracies [. . .] numerous artificial and arbitrary distinctions spring up, by means of which every man hopes to keep himself aloof lest he should be carried away against his will in the crowd [. . .] In aristocracies, men are separated from each other by lofty and stationary barriers; in democracies, they are divided by many small and almost invisible threads which are constantly broken and moved from place to place.

And it is a bad thing to move around like that.[118]

Of course, Tocqueville accepts the existence of groupings such as anti-alcohol leagues and currents of opinion structured by the newspapers, while 'confessing' (sic) that he had not even realized that such things could exist. This is because his heart lies elsewhere, with associations based on something other than an idea or project, based on something 'concrete': industrial commercial, communal or family groupings. Such a representation leads (I am not speaking here of Tocqueville himself, but of the Tocquevillian current) to approval of American-style unions, which are corporations, and to disdain for the situation we find in Europe where there are several unions for each profession and one always finds a fair number of individualists who do not belong to any of them. 'At any time' anyone can 'break off' with the union they belong to. From my point of view, this type of association is the true guarantor of democracy, while compulsory groupings based on 'concrete' factors are structures of oppression and exclusion.

In fact, I think that we must start with this underlying reference to 'natural groupings' to understand Tocqueville's thinking on blacks and women, which is far from libertarian, whatever his apparent goodwill.

> God forbid that I should seek to justify the principle of Negro slavery as has been done by some American writers! I say only that all the countries which formerly adopted that execrable principle are not equally able to abandon it at the present time. When I contemplate the condition of the South, I can discover only two modes of action for the white inhabitants of those states: namely, either to emancipate the Negroes and to intermingle with them, or, remaining isolated from them, to keep them in slavery as long as possible [. . .] Such is the view that the Americans of the South take of the question, and they act consistently with it. As they are determined not to mingle with the Negroes, they refuse to emancipate them.[119]

Without wanting to 'corner' Tocqueville by taking him at his word, we must recognize that the invocation which opens this argument is very apt: 'God forbid' indeed. For nothing in Tocqueville's theory would forbid anyone to be racist, nor would it provide any objections to the present regime in South Africa. 'Living together with our differences' is an unthinkable project in this system, where the group is based on similarity.

As for women, we need only quote: 'There are people in Europe' who would give men and women 'the same functions, impose on both the same duties, and grant to both the same rights; they would mix them in all things – their occupation, their pleasure, their business' and claim to make them 'not only equal, but alike'.[120] We can see here how the three concepts of 'equal rights', 'mixture' (also expressed as the 'crude mixture of nature's creations') and 'sameness' are strongly linked in Tocqueville's mind. This is as valid for men and women as it is for society as a whole:

> The Americans have applied to both sexes the great principle of political enconomy which governs the manufacturers of our age by carefully dividing the duties of man from those of woman in order that the great work of society may be the better carried on. In no country has such constant care been taken as in America to trace two clearly distinct lines of action for the two sexes [. . .] American women never

manage the outward concerns of the family, or conduct a business, or take part in political life [. . .] If, on the one hand, the American woman cannot escape from the quiet circle of domestic employment, she is never forced on the other to go beyond it. [. . .] Nor have the Americans ever supposed that one consequence of democratic principles is the subversion of the natural authorities in families. They hold that every association must have a head in order to accomplish its object, and that the natural head of the conjugal association is man.[121]

And so on. Let us note in passing the affirmative universal proposition, 'any association must have a head' and the concept of 'natural head' which naturally appears in what is said. What Tocqueville says of civil society in general probably finds its most accurate expression in the three short chapters dealing with women. Civil society is the decentralization of the despotism of some and the confinement of others.

Almost all men in democracies are engaged in public or professional life; and on the other hand the limited income obliges a wife to confine herself to the house in order to watch in person, and very closely, over the details of domestic economy. All these distinct and compulsory occupations are so many natural barriers which, by keeping the two sexes asunder. . .[122]

Democracy for men, domestic imprisonment for women; on the same page we find the idea that democracies produce 'a great number of courtesans and a great number of virtuous women'; prostitution certainly leads to 'lamentable cases of individual hardship', but the 'body of society', 'family ties' and 'morals of the nation' are ultimately served by it; a few pages further on, Tocqueville points out that the Americans punish rape with death, for they 'can conceive of nothing more precious than a woman's honour'. No feminist movement has ever praised the death penalty, not for rape or for anything else; but many feminists are touched by the 'individual miseries' of prostitutes and have tried to make people understand that the most widespread form of rape is that within marriage.[123] Two systems of thought can be contrasted here. The first is primarily concerned with 'family ties', recommends sexual apartheid, differentiates between 'virtuous women' and prostitutes, considers a woman's honour as part of the private property of her husband, and rape therefore as the act of a non-husband, and recommends extremely repressive legislation against that act. The second wants to see women integrated into democracy and hopes to see prostitution fall into obsolescence one day. Even if feminist movements are formed of good-willed women, these women refuse to be praised for being 'virtuous', for they know that such praise is uttered to the detriment of other women; yet, when they define rape as penetration without consent, juries ask for evidence which is often difficult to provide and feminist groups supporting the plaintiffs are often accused of being on the side of repression.

Tocqueville is still the bible of our various schools of politology. At Sorbford university, students will perform the collation of fragments, which is a speedier exercise than exegesis.

> It is true that Americans rarely lavish upon women those eager attentions which are commonly paid them in Europe; but their conduct towards women always implies that they suppose them to be virtuous and refined.
>
> The adventurers who migrate every year to people the Western wilds [...] take their wives along with them and make them share the countless perils and privations that always attend the commencement of these expeditions. I have often met, even on the verges of the wilderness, young women who, after having been brought up amid all the comforts of the large towns of New England, passed, almost without any intermediate stage, from the wealthy abode of their parents to a comfortless hovel in a forest. Fever, solitude and a tedious life of boredom had not broken the springs of their courage. Their features were impaired and faded, but their looks were firm. They appeared to be at once sad and resolute.
>
> As for myself, I do not hesitate to avow that although the women of the United States are confined within the narrow circle of domestic life and their situation is in some respects one of extreme dependence, I have nowhere seen woman occupying a loftier position.
>
> Adventurers take their wives along with them,
>
> American women are never forced to go beyond the quiet circle of domestic employments,
>
> which is why they always remain women.
>
> *Indicate with arrows the relations of discordant agreement between these words or ideas. The exercise will be marked giving one point per arrow.*

And I forgot, in my indictment, to mention what Tocqueville has to say about the Indians!

To reorientate myself in my thinking, not only do I not need Tocqueville, I must describe him as an epistemological screen or obstacle. This is not only because of what he says about women, black people or the Indians: in a more global sense, if we want to build an ethics of solidarity and the duty to help people in danger, we must reject the model of local groupings comprised of individuals whose interests are identical and thus based on membership which is or is generally considered concrete.

In practice, this model creates preferential circuits of solidarity which soon become closed, leaving non-members outside them, in the limbo of indifference, and maintaining intact within their microcosms structures of vassalage which are as undemocratic as possible. The fear Tocqueville points to (individuals could become so cold towards each other as to freeze) finds not a remedy but a cause in corporations, classes, families, religions or castes (and the American 'white race' comes into this latter category). This coldness – and we now have almost two centuries' distance across which to judge it – has constantly been manifested in relation to minorities in democracies, and on this point so-called liberal societies are no different from those of the Ancien Regime. The issue is thus one not of putting democracies on trial, but of recognizing that the promise of democracy has not, so far, been kept and will not be as long as the state does not take as its prime aim to create a space where all can live together with their differences, which will preferably be multiple and not planned by anyone. They should not even be intellectually (in other words phantasmagorically) managed by philosophy, or the philosopher, whether man or woman. Philosophy makes a claim to define and administrate differences. In rejecting this claim, I am aware that I am not losing much. But, by clearing away the twaddle, even in its tiny, trivial aspects, we can hope to be doing useful work. Assuming it is blocking our view, then overturning it means helping another generation to see further or to look elsewhere.

22 The charming and dumbfounding little girl: what should we hate and how can we tell?

At the start of this notebook, we described the youth of Marie du Deffand as recounted long afterwards and commented upon by M. de Lescure, who was so upset about women philosophers. Since he acknowledges that he took the anecdote from Chamfort, historical prudence demands that we go back to the source. In the work of the best of misanthropes, the tale is noticeably different. Obviously Lescure retouched it with a view to the comments he was going to make. He embroidered it. Chamfort says only this:

Mme du Deffant, when she was a little girl in the convent, preached irreligiousness to her little friends. The abbess asked the bishop Massillon to come and the little girl expounded her arguments to him. Massillon withdrew saying, 'She is charming.' The abbess, who thought all this most important, asked him what book she should make the child read. He thought for a minute and replied: 'A tuppenny catechism', nothing more could be got out of him.[124]

One could make a dozen comments on these few lines. For Chamfort, the anecdote is about Massillon and not Marie du Deffand. The preacher seems to have been disconcerted, or slightly dumbfounded, by the arguments which the girl was able to expound, but which the narrative of the time did not take the trouble to record; we are sorry not to have them. In the eighteenth century convents seem sometimes to have been hothouses of rebellion. Sophie de Grouchy, the future Mme de Condorcet, who entered the convent of Neuville-en-Bresse a very pious girl, left it twenty months later an atheist and reader of Voltaire and Rousseau.[125] But the intellectual pugnacity of these young ladies seems to have been extinguished later in the salons they held when they grew up. It seems that once they were freed of a yoke they found hard to bear, they reconciled themselves to the world they found, although Julie de Lespinasse and Marie du Deffand let it be understood how saddened they were by the emotional emptiness of their times. But to no group of 'little friends' did they preach independence of mind in relation to, for example, Rousseau, despite the fact that he too recommended that little girls should be given a simple catechism to read.

Understanding these women demands that we assume that when a group is heavily oppressed, individuals may rebel (and encourage others to share their revolt) against what most immediately weighs upon them – what is presented as obvious in their kenning – after which, with that particular burden gone, they hasten to live while they still have time. The convent may well have been a target (Gabrielle Suchon, while remaining a Catholic, also fought with all her might to escape its confinement) and a kind of object upon which rebellion was fixated. The problem is that, during that time, other chains were being prepared for us.

What stands out most clearly in Chamfort's short paragraph is that others were certainly needed, since in the eighteenth century the church had got to a point where a little girl could disconcert a famous prelate: 'Nothing more could be got out of him.' The truth behind this story is beyond it, of course, or ahead of it. It is the exclusion of women from the electorate, pronounced by the Constituent in December 1789; it is the prohibition against their presence at political meetings, in May 1795; it is the Napoleonic Code which systematized the legal exclusion of women from the social sphere. Since what could be got out of the church was not enough, the state took over control of the subjugation of women, shutting them away in the private sphere and thus indirectly restoring them to the church, since at the same time religion became a more private affair than it had formerly been.

This invites us to contemplate tempo. It takes informal and organized movements of or for women an incredibly long time to win their case on any given question: history drags its feet when the issue is one of liberating women from any form of alienation. But it acts like lightning when the problem is to invent, in a new historical situation, an ad hoc and lasting form of alientation which reflects that situation. And the kenning, because it is limited, may always focus on forms which are falling into disuse, so that one can never be absolutely sure where the danger, regression or new form of oppression is coming from. Today this danger may perhaps lie in the system of delegation set up by the state which, in the name of 'decentralization' is increasing the number of local authorities. As I am neither a prophetess nor a futurologist, I cannot make a statement on this, but I hope that a general obligation to ensure sexual balance in bodies that seem as irrelevant as the Académie Française or as specialized as the profession of midwifery might be a global answer. At least resistance to the principle of *mixité* might perhaps enable an early detection of emerging forms of resubjugation.

At the time of the Enlightenment, one would have needed second sight to guess that a Republic would soon come into being which would immediately take it upon itself to exclude women from the social sphere. Or else one would have needed to have read Rousseau very closely and to have taken those of Jean-Jacques' theses that Marmontel found so comical and worthy merely of a gibe for the serious threats they were.[126] As I am doubtful of my kenning from all points of view and in principle, I want to dive once more into the debate between twaddle and ideas, however thin and trivial the issues raised may seem. You never know: let us hasten at least to make their meanings apparent, just in case they contain the beginnings of some malevolent project, whose effects will weigh on our nieces.

'What about the abbess?'

'Abesses are of great interest and concern to me, as we shall see.'

Notes

First Notebook

1. Hegel, *The Phenomenology of Mind*, J. B. Baillie trans., 2nd edn, London, Allen & Unwin, 1936.
2. It was in 1925 that the first woman was (illegally) elected to public office in France. At Douarnenez in Brittany there had been a very solid strike by women canning factory workers. In the local elections the Communist Party, partly out of a desire to salute this strike, but much more out of opportunism because it knew that 'if women had voted [its] victory would have been all the greater', wanted to field 'at least one woman candidate, regardless of the law'. 'In fact, the problem was not so much one of getting her elected as of finding one woman citizen who would agree to act the suffragette like the ones in England! Not one household would accept this sacrifice. An attractive widow, Joséphine Pencalet, was the only one to give herself up to the task [. . .] All the Communist candidates were triumphantly successful. The Prefect was quick to declare the election of Joséphine Pencalet invalid. Women were not citizens.' This is how Charles Tillon, one of the other Communists elected at the time, tells the story long afterwards (*On chantait rouge*, Paris, Robert Laffont, 1977, p. 87). It was I who was generous enough to assume that the fine struggle put up by the sardine factory workers had something to do with the Communist Party's decision. Tillon only mentions their self-interested calculations. It can also be observed that, in French at least, to call someone a 'suffragette' was still pejorative, even in 1977!
3. For all important dates of the history of women, see Florence Montreynaud, *Le Vingtième siècle des femmes*, Paris, Nathan, 1989.
4. Although it was called anti-republican by some, this law banning abortion, contraception and any information about them was passed in Parliament by a massive majority. Insofar as it forbids information on contraception, it goes against the principle of freedom of expression, as was noted, in vain, by Vincent Auriol, Léon Blum, Marcel Cachin, etc.

On this law, which has not yet been repealed, see Roger-Henri Guerrand, *La Libre maternité*, Paris, Casterman, 1971. See also Fourth Notebook, section 6. Note added to the English edition: on 12 January 1991 during a European Symposium on the Right to Choose held in Paris, the French government announced that the lifting of the ban on the advertising of contraceptives was now under way. During the discussion I put forward the view that the scope of this change should be widened to include lifting the ban on information about establishments performing abortions, and indeed all other remnants of the 1920 law.

5. Reference provided by Richard Goulet, who is establishing an index of the philosophers of Antiquity, the *Clavis Philosophorum*. Some portraits of Greek women philosophers and a bibliography on them can be found in an article by Kathleen Wider, 'Women philosophers in the ancient Greek world', published in the journal *Hypatia*, Edwardsville, Illinois, 1986, no. 1.

6. Philosophy was not alone in being mistaken on this question: 'The Holy Spirit orders slaves to remain as they are and does not oblige their masters to free them' (Bossuet, *Avertissements aux protestants*); 'The traffic in slaves is contrary neither to humanity, nor to religion, nor to natural equity' (Mgr Bouvier, *Institutions théologiques*); these two phrases are quoted by Flaubert in Bouvard and Pecuchet's *sottisier*.

7. I should not like it to be thought that Beauvoir does not mention the abortion issue. She discusses it in detail in chapter VI of Book Two. I am seeking to emphasize a textual movement which begins philosophically and hesitates before recognizing the existence and nature of a 'problem'. Fortunately, however, the author lets herself be caught up in her subject and starts describing realities, as though she gradually began to notice them while writing her book, in other words through working.

8. *Twelfth Night*, Act III, scene 1.

9. All the same, there is one woman with a clown's inspiration in Shakespeare's work and that is Beatrice in *Much Ado about Nothing*. What she challenges is the touchy pride of the play's male protagonists and its effects on the position of women. We who have been involved in feminism are all Beatrices. But we had to experience feminism to identify with her and to see the importance of such a character. I had previously seen her merely as a piquant and infinitely reasonable woman, who was certainly excessive in calling Lord Benedick a 'fool', but is unjustly described by the latter as a 'fury'. I did not understand that each is paying the other a compliment and that each loves in the other what they wanted to be but could not: neither a lord nor a girl can let their 'gaiety' lead them to the point where they risk insults and blows.

10. Aristippus lived about 435-356 BC: Diogenes Laertius devoted a chapter to him in *Lives and Opinions of Eminent Philosophers*, R. D. Hicks

trans., London, Heinemann and Cambridge, Mass., Harvard University Press, 1925, vol. II, pp. 98–102.

11. In fact, it was distant and vague because it was censored. I know that the notion of 'purely verbal discourse' poses philosophical problems. But take a great novel dealing with passion or violent social conflict. Then tell a teacher to talk about it, in the context of a neutral and proper institution, to children who are supposed to go on knowing nothing of the violence of either love or social collisions. Does the notion of 'purely verbal discourse' still seem so problematic to you?

12. Kant, *The Critique of Pure Reason*, Norman Kemp Smith trans., London, Macmillan, 1929, pp. 597 and 598–9.

13. On 25 July 1985 the great 1972 law against incitement to racial hatred was modified: it was made to include the notion of incitement to sexist hatred. Moreover article 29 of the July 1881 law prohibits any 'attack on the honour of women and respect for them' and 'public insult to women'. It is regrettable that these texts are so little known. Sometimes one hears that an 'attack on honour' is a difficult thing to judge. If I manage to convince my reader that it is possible intellectually to determine that there is sexism in a given utterance, I shall have won a bet.

14. See, on this subject, Catherine Challier's book, *Figures du féminin*, Paris, La Nuit surveillée, 1982. I shall return to the question of the moral non-existence of the 'feminine' in the fourth notebook. By giving Lévinas' remark a sociological, historical and thus contingent meaning it is possible to justify it, but in a way which would not necessarily suit him.

15. Theodor W. Adorno, *Minima Moralia: reflections from damaged life*, E. F. N. Jephcott trans., London, NLB, 1970, and Verso, 1978, p. 45.

16. Mary Wollstonecraft, *Vindication of the Rights of Women*, 1972, Miriam Kramnick (ed.), Penguin Books, Harmondsworth, 1975.

17. It would be a sign of amazing progress if some men also looked into it.

18. The mention of Nizan would simply provide an easy reference point, although for my generation his *Chiens de garde* was indeed a reference point. We could incriminate the pre-postmodern generation of the 1906s, who vied with each other to demolish or deconstruct whatever came to hand, but we could also see self-criticism as an effect of exhaustion due to the demand for neutrality which can be imputed to the state take-over of philosophy teaching. The story could also be told as follows: state education is only allowed to use the critical or historical point of view and this leads to emptiness (or to the history of doctrines and sciences). Philosophical practice has thus become bloodless. Because philosophy also tends to think it controls its own destiny, it has claimed to be the origin of its own extinction and has thus produced self-criticism to justify its evanescence. This is my myth, to be taken as such. Or else see section 6 of the present notebook.

19. See, for example, the excellent *Sexisme et sciences humaines* by Claire

Michard-Marchal and Claudine Ribéry, Presses Universitaires de Lille, 1982.

20. On this subject, see *Les Femmes et la révolution*, 1789–1784, by Paule-Marie Duhet, Paris, Juillard, 1971.

21. In general I shall simply say 'the Movement' when referring to the French movement of the 1970s. I do this for many reasons. The women of this movement did not invent the name MLF (Mouvement de Libération des Femmes), that was done by the papers reporting the 'happening' of 26 August 1970, when a few women friends tried to place a wreath on the monument under the Arc de Triomphe 'for one more unknown than the soldier: his wife' (see *Histoires du MLF* by Annie de Pisan and Anne Tristan, Paris, Calmann-Lévy, 1977, p. 48). Besides, in November 1979, the 'Des Femmes' publishing company registered the acronym as a commercial brand name, thereby legally expropriating it from all other groups in a 'Movement' which had chosen to be non-centralized and plural (on this subject, see *Chroniques d'une imposture*, Paris, 1981, a collection of articles edited by the association 'Mouvement pour les Luttes Féministes'). A last reason is that mixed organizations, like Family Planning or the Movement for Free Contraception and Abortion (MLAC) remained distinct from the MLF, even between 1970 and 1979. These organizations, which challenged the concrete conditions of existence imposed on women, deserve to be included in something which, all things considered, we must none too precisely call 'the Movement'.

22. I shall often refer to this earlier essay, whose French title is 'Cheveux longs, idées courtes' and which was published in English-language journals in 1977 under the title 'Women in/and philosophy' and reprinted (in an amended translation) in Toril Moi, *French Feminist Thought*, Oxford, Basil Blackwell, 1987, and in my own collection of essays, *The Philosophical Imaginary* (London, Athlone, 1989) under the title 'Long hair, short on ideas'. As someone has no doubt already said, it is better to quote than to paraphrase oneself and to refer to another study rather than copying it out.

23. After all, the form of 'short essays' is not necessarily a bad one; it permits a kind of multiple approach to an issue which is hard to grasp. In philosophy, there is room for a genre of 'detached thoughts' which are longer than aphorisms, but less tightly linked than the various ideas in a treatise. Diderot illustrated this genre. My initial project was just that: to gather together my various scattered essays without linking them up, in order to leave at least fragmented thoughts which might serve as a point of departure or as material for someone else. Although these thoughts finally burst open like spring buds, requiring a different form of presentation, I am still convinced that this form is possible and also that someone else will manage to find a more simple philosophical language to take things further.

24. See *The German Ideology*, C. J. Arthew trans., London, Lawrence and Wishart, 1974.

25. '"Nothing is vanity, forward with science" says the modern Ecclesiastes, in other words everyone', wrote Rimbaud. Who better than poets or actors to reveal the state of a period or an author's intellectual mood? A few years ago Gérard Desarthe portrayed an unforgettable Rousseau on stage. It takes an artist to draw out the full meaning of Leibniz's words 'I scorn almost nothing' from a subjective point of view.

26. After the very scholarly seriousness of the preparation class for the Ecole Normale Supérieure, where they tried to teach us some philosophy and I felt I was acquiring a language, the modernity of Latin Quarter thought gave me a shock and affected me, as though I were being made to drink a potion to make me dumb. We can assume that many people had the same experience and concluded that traditional scholarly seriousness was infinitely preferable.

27. He remarked to the Athenians, who prided themselves on being autochtonous, that grasshoppers and snails were so too. And he recommended men only to have intercourse with women whom this would please.

28. This principle states that one cannot state something and deny it at the same time.

29. *Metaphysics*, book gamma, chapter IV, 1006a.

30. If I were to give examples here, I should write the whole book in terms of this set of problems.

31. Mathematicians and physicists are quite liable to say things of this order, but not in their work.

32. I shall talk about 'those who like us' in the second volume.

33. The 'status' Sartre gives to the Chinese will be outlined in this first volume. The 'status' given by Rousseau to the Caribs and Eskimos will be described in the second volume.

34. The reader should not be surprised that the present book contains comments on the injustice of contemporary philosophers towards the sciences. Structurally speaking, discrediting other people (women, Eskimos) amounts to the same thing as discrediting other forms of knowledge.

35. Plato, *Gorgias*, W. R. M. Lamb trans., London, Heinemann, and New York, G. P. Putnam's Sons, 1925, 508c.

36. *Vindication of the Rights of Women*, chapter II, p. 100 and 108.

37. *Paradise Lost*, book IV, 634 and 637–8.

38. *The Sceptical Feminist*, London, Routledge & Kegan Paul, 1980.

39. One of the main themes of the book is that freedom is neither self-evident nor a principle and that the right to a particular freedom must always be proved. With this idea, the author is able massively to justify her own existence: the philosopher is necessary to prove that which

needs proving so much, or to dismiss anything for which she refuses to grant her expert help. In this way she grants herself an apparently discretionary power over the subjects she discusses. Thus, on the question of whether or not it is acceptable that access to contraception should be forbidden or limited: 'It is not enough to answer, as though it were obvious, that every woman has the right to whatever number of children she wants: that is the question at issue, and if we want to maintain that it ought to be so, arguments must be found' (*The Sceptical Feminist*, p. 210.). Elsewhere Radcliffe Richards clearly says that women's right to control their bodies is not a simple idea. Denial of this right gradually leads her to substitute it with Malthusian arguments: 'there is a pretty high correlation between the groups of people who, for whatever reason, cannot be bothered with contraception and those most likely to produce children who are going to be very expensive to the state' (immigrants? the poor?); it is therefore 'one of the best investments of taxpayers' money there is' to pay for the non-procreative pleasure of others, although the idea itself is a problem; for if contraceptives were not free, those people would be only too pleased to use the excuse to cost the taxpayer even more (pp. 212–13). I hope my honourable readers will not be content simply to call this argument mean but will be so good as to ask themselves whether it is an example of philosophy gone astray or anti-philosophy.

40.   *The Sceptical Feminist*, p. 18.
41.   This conformism is made explicit at the end of the book: the author describes the chasm that exists between the ideas of feminists and those of 'people'; she states that, to 'set things going in the right direction', all feminists need do is to 'deal with problems which arise on their own side of the chasm created by feminism's inherent radicalism' (p. 268). This thesis betrays the anti-philosophical nature of her undertaking: a philosopher who denies the pertinence of divergence is committing suicide.
42.   I shall investigate this issue in the second volume, in the light of some of the ideas of Mary Wollstonecraft and Hannah Arendt.
43.   *The Sceptical Feminist*, p. 76.
44.   'As it happeneth to the fool, so it happeneth even to me; and why was I then more wise?' (Ecclesiastes 2,15, King James version).
45.   On occasion, I shall also refer to Jean Cau, Mgr Dupanloup or even more obscure people. They can help support an argument or produce a concept which is applicable to others. But above all, I do not want to let anyone think that sexist theories are the preserve of the most famous philosophers; they might then pride themselves on the fact and any misogynist might regard himself as the equal of these demi-gods simply by sharing their sexist theories.
46.   One of Jacques Le Goff's slips will be analysed in the second volume.
47.   To tell the truth, it is hard to believe that this is not a hoax. There is only one element which runs counter to this hypothesis: the book's

naivety. As a hoaxer I believe that hoaxes are more cunningly constructed. But there is a mystery here: the French philosophical milieu is not that big, nor is that of the feminists or feminophiles; yet not one of my colleagues, nor anyone in the bad company I keep has ever met Edmée Mottini-Coulon. Using my feminine intuition, I finally arrived at a horrible idea: I see a male academic philosopher who thinks deep down that women are bizarre animals, able to turn concepts sour just as they can wine or mayonnaise when they have their periods; I see a wife who for decades has heard her husband vituperating against the twisted minds of his women students and colleagues and gradually constructing a 'theory' about the way that women think 'philosophically', similar to the way Bachelard describes the functioning of the 'primitive soul' which survives deep inside scientific minds. I see this wife one day writing, under her husband's supervision, what her husband thinks about the way that women 'think', then publishing it under her maiden name.

48. See, for example, Gérard Simon's book, *Le Regard, l'être et l'apparence dans l'optique de l'antiquité*, Paris, Le Seuil, 'Des Travaux' series, 1988.

49. Let us clarify our concepts: throughout the present work I shall make a distinction between misogyny, phallocracy, masculinism, phallocentrism, machismo and so on. All these forms relate to a contempt for women, but they differ from each other. Misogyny is hatred for women, the fact of thinking bad things of them and wanting to keep them as far away as possible. Phallocracy is the affirmation of power over women in a master–slave relationship. I shall define the others when the need arises.

50. As Sorbford University has not yet been founded, I must confess that I know little about what happens in the other disciplines in other countries.

51. Matthew 28, 19–20.

52. To my knowledge, at least three collections of essays have been published in the United States: Carol C. Gould and Max W. Wartofsky (eds) *Women and Philosophy*, New York, G. P. Putnam's Sons, 1976; Mary Vetterling-Braggin, Frederic A. Elliston and Jane English (eds) *Feminism and Philosophy*, Totowa, New Jersey, 1978; and Sandra Harding and Meril Hintikka (eds) *Discovering Reality, Feminist Perspectives on Epistemology, Metaphysics, Methodology and Philosophy of Science*, Reidel, 1983.

53. See Dominique Vonoli, 'Les Ouvrières enfermées: les couvents soyeux', in *Révoltes logiques*, Paris, 1976, no. 2, a subject taken up by Claire Auzias and Annick Houel, *La Grève des ovalistes à Lyon*, Paris, Payot, 1980.

54. This is the subtitle of *La Formation de l'esprit scientifique*, Paris, 1938.

55. Ibid., chapter 1 in 1969 edn, p. 14.

56. Bergson, *The Creative Mind*, Mabelle L. Andison trans., New York, Philosophical Library, 1946, p. 177.

57. In book I of his *Opus Majus*, Roger Bacon advances the theory of
    offendicula, or the obstacles that hinder all forms of knowledge. These
    are: the fact that they are based on fragile or inadequate authority,
    inveterate habits, everyday opinions, lack of knowledge of one's own
    ignorance and the ostentation of apparent knowledge. At the beginning
    of the seventeenth century, Francis Bacon proposed a similar theory of
    'fallacies' or 'idols', which were structures of errors connected to,
    among other things, everday language.
58. Rousseau and Auguste Comte went in for a great deal of this; one can
    find many other examples. The *Summa Theologiae* offers them through-
    out and Saint Thomas Aquinas went so far as to say that a father
    should not smile at his daughters in case they saw it as an encourage-
    ment to sin against chastity (2a 2ae, Quaest. 114, art 1).
59. Francis Bacon in Spedding (ed.), London 1858, vol. I, p. 132. Placed
    by Kant as an epigraph to the second edition of the *Critique of Pure
    Reason*.
60. *The Order of Things*, London, Tavistock, 1970, preface, p. xxi.
61. Rousseau, *Emile*, Book 5.
62. A non-literal quotation from Kant, *Dreams of a Visionary*, Königsberg,
    1766.

SECOND NOTEBOOK

1. *Le Deuxième sexe* (1949). The quotations used in the present work have
    been retranslated and references given are to the most recent French
    paperback edition: Paris, Gallimard, 'Folio-Essais' series, 1986 vol. I,
    pp. 1–31.
2. See the interview with Luce Irigaray in the journal *Dialectiques* (1975,
    no. 8, particularly pp. 34 and 39.).
3. *Le Deuxième sexe*, vol. I, p. 21.
4. Ibid., p. 21.
5. Ibid., p. 17.
6. Ibid., p. 31.
7. See Plato, *Gorgias*, 524e–525a (see also 474c).
8. See Sandra Harding and Merril Hintikka (eds), *Discovering Reality*.
9. Toril Moi ('Vive la difference', *Women's Review*, 1986, no. 6) writes:,
    'There are some feminists who are Derridians, like Sarah Kofman,
    and others who are not, like Michèle Le Doeuff'. Long live that
    difference, certainly.
10. *L'Etre et le néant*, Paris Gallimard, 1943, 640. Quotations used here
    have been retranslated.
11. Ibid., p. 639.
12. Ibid., p. 642.
13. Ibid., p. 669.
14. Ibid., p. 560.

15. Late Antiquity and the early years of Chirstianity are an important time in relation to the mythico–philosophical definition of the sexes; see Peter Brown, *The Body and Society*, London, Faber & Faber, 1989. Documentation on this period can also be found in Raoul Mortley's book, *Womanhood, the Feminine in Ancient Hellenism, Gnosticism, Christianity and Islam*, Sydney, Delacroix Press, 1981.

16. *L'Etre et le néant*, p. 449.

17. Ibid., p. 434.

18. Ibid., p. 99.

19. I do not know if any linguistic philosopher has ever looked into this question, which deserves examination. Socrates openly uses reported speech, particularly when he wants to get out of an impasse; prophetesses, poets and oracles are then brought in, providing fragments of founding myths, supposedly the 'other' of the work of reason. In Sartre's writing the Viennese psychiatrist is a Diotimus. The philosopher makes him say what he wants and what he needs as dogma, while going on at the end of the book radically to criticize the validity of any form of psychiatry and psychoanalysis.

20. *L'Existentialism est un humanisme*, 1945. References given here are to *Existentialism and Humanism*, Philip Mairet trans., London, Methuen, 1973, pp. 38–9.

21. This book was not written in isolation. Various friends read drafts of it and some passages have been used as conference papers or even published as articles. The definitive editing owes much to feedback. Thus some pages from this notebook were first used in teaching at the Fontenay Ecole Normale Supérieure in 1978 and were then published in 1979 by Ideology and Consciousness. I wish to sieze this opportunity to tell my friends Colin Gordon and Graham Burtchell how important intellectual contact with them and the support they have given me have always been and still are.

22. *L'Etre et le néant*, p. 413.

23. Ibid., p. 395.

24. Ibid., p. 93.

25. *Existentialism and Humanism*, p. 51.

26. Ibid., p. 38.

27. *L'Etre et le néant*, p. 94.

28. In 1977 I was involved in the collective production of a play by Aquarium called *Shakespeare's Sister*, in which the position of women is the main issue. The group prepared for this show with a number of exercises, in particular the practice of 'invisible theatre', which makes it possible to study unadulterated social reactions to a given situation by setting up that situation. In one instance of this two actors, a man and a woman, get into a metro carriage, pretending that they do not know each other and in plain clothes, of course. The man discreetly puts his hand on the woman's bottom, upon which she slaps him and calls on the other passengers as witnesses. Most of the time she was

told she was imagining things, or accused of making a lot of fuss about nothing. Then the actors changed trains and swapped roles: the woman would discreetly put her hand on the man's bottom, he would slap her and call on the other passengers. In these cases, the actors got some very violent reactions and the poor girl was copiously and sharply insulted by both men and women, who were, literally, shocked. One person even burst into tears over it. What is true in a metro compartment must also be so of the readers of a philosophical work. As long as one remains within the stereotyped and established power relations one can be sure of invisibility and impunity; as soon as the roles are reversed, one encounters reactions that are, to say the least, unusual.

29. This book was first published in France in spring 1989. Some months later, an unpublished draft by Sartre, *Vérité et existence*, appeared. In it there is a simple statement which took me aback: 'each to thine own truth is an apt thought'. Now I know the nature of the 'tiny step' I thought lay between the two statements: it is simply the difference between a text Sartre thought fit for publication and one he preferred to keep to himself (note added to the English translation).

30. See the Fourth Notebook, section 10.

31. *Existentialism and Humanism*, pp. 46.

32. Ibid., pp. 46–7.

33. Elsewhere I have expounded the idea that we should not believe that historians are incapable of thinking about their own practice and discipline, we should not take artists for unconscious geniuses who cannot ask themselves questions about what they do, and so on. This idea is completed by those I am now developing. Philosophers must recognize the fact that specialists in every discipline theorize their own activities. However, the philosopher's role remains one of critically examining these specialist's theories and of understanding that other disciplines might also have a view of prime importance on the discipline concerned.

34. *L'Etre et le néant*, p. 666. We have kept the author's italics.

35. Ibid., p. 668.

36. Ibid., p. 667.

37. Ibid., p. 701.

38. Ibid., p. 701.

39. Ibid., p. 699.

40. Ibid., p. 700.

41. Ibid., p. 705.

42. Ibid., pp. 705–6.

43. 'Anyone who has never set foot in a brothel does not know woman and therefore understands nothing of politics because, in a democracy, politics is a female animal' (Jean Cau, *La Barbe et la rose*, quoted 'with tweezers' by Albert Lévy in his editorial, *Differences*, May 1982).

44. In fact no rhapsody of this type is really complete: each time one thinks

one has heard the full extent of the delusion, one finds another great fantasy somewhere else. Thus, to see that Sartre is not so exhaustive, one only has to glance at Auguste Comte, and so on.

45. To my knowledge, Margery Collins and Christine Pierce were the first to draw attention to part of this phantasmagoria (cf. C. Gould and M. Wartofsky, *Women and Philosophy*).

46. I have only limited experience of repression of the personal myth: when I translated and annotated Shakespeare's *Venus and Adonis*, the text was considered as being almost mine (!! – a great honour) and I was virtuously scolded by more than one person not known for prudery. The only part of the imaginary which a woman can legitimately reveal is that of motherhood and perhaps any maternal personal myth is acceptable. To lend one's tongue to Venus is not and links up with the experience described above, Second Notebook, note 28.

47. *Situations II*, Paris, Gallimard, 1975, pp. 134–5. I am very grateful to Jean Delaite for having pointed this passage out to me: I have only considered two works. Similarly, Luc Foisneau has indicated many most interesting elements in *The Roads to Freedom*. It is very likely that more still can be found.

48. Due to an interminable conflict at the National Centre for Scientific Research (CNRS), young researchers were obliged to have more contact than they might have wished with a particularly vulgar administrator. Although the group only ever sent delegations of men to see him, and deliberately so, his shameless sexism came out all the same, because the man was quite sure of dealing with subordinates: 'No, Mr S., I am not trying to screw you.' In pornocracy power is made into something obscene, no matter who is subjected to it.

49. Not many people are familiar with Marmontel and his *Apologie du théâtre*, which is a reply to M. Rousseau. *D'Alembert's Letter* said bad things about the theatre and about women. Marmontel undertakes to reply on both counts. This little work is amusing and sympathetic, displaying the author's desire to live in a mixed society, a community in which women and men exist together. With a great deal of humour, he makes the delusional elements of Rousseau's text explicit. Thus a man can perfectly well boycott masculinism. I shall allow myself to insist on this, for, like Marmontel, I want to live in a mixed community which is taking an extremely long time to come into being and would not be encouraged by any kind of feminocentrism.

50. *L'Etre et le néant*, p. 111.

51. Ibid., p. 717.

52. *Le Deuxième sexe*, vol. I, p. 15.

53. Let us clarify this point: according to Descartes, the 'I' of 'I think' is by rights knowable to all, but the 'I' alone is so. Certain knowledge of geometrical truths and material things depends on knowledge of the existence of God (*Fifth Meditation*), so that it could be said that an atheist could not be a geometer. This question is taken up again in the

Réponses aux secondes objections: 'I do not deny that an atheist can clearly know that the three angles of a triangle are equal to two right angles; I simply maintain that he does not know this by a true and certain science, because any knowledge that can be rendered doubtful cannot be called science.' Of course this is a kind of exclusion, which could be the basis for a *Berufsverbot*, or exclusion from professions. However, it is not as bad as it seems. First, because it appears along the way: the first point of the Cartesian journey, 'I think', is common to all and discrimination, if discrimination there be, only arises in the second place; moreover, it is not based on what people are, but on their theoretical decision to recognize or not that there is a God. Lastly, and above all, the other side to this is marvellous: not knowing a particular theorem of Euclidean geometry or a given mathematical proposition 'by a true and certain science' is far from being the worst way of knowing mathematics, and that was true even in the seventeenth century. Desargues and his disciple Blaise Pascal did not opt for the constitution of geometry into a 'true and certain science'. (On Desargues, see Gilles-Gaston Granger, *Essai de philosophie du style*, Paris, Colin, 1968, and Paris, Odile Jacob, 1988).

54. F. Bacon can be quoted as an example: in his metaphors, the 'fellow' of Solomon's house or any scientist is a man, and nature a woman. Although he is polite to Queen Elisabeth of Bohemia and sends her his works, in doing so he explicitly distinguishes her from other women (Bacon in Spedding (ed.), vol. XIV, p. 364). Elsewhere he interprets the adage 'Man is a god for man' as follows: science can give those who have it such superiority over those who do not, for example the Indians, that whoever has it is like a god in relation to whoever does not (*Novum Organum*, book I, 129 in Bacon in Spedding (ed.), vol. I, p. 222). Rousseau, whose phallocentrism is well-known, said that he tasted the pleasure of existing as God, in the *Rêveries d'un promeneur solitaire*. Sartre would clearly be a third example and there must be others.

55. *Le Deuxième sexe*, vol. I, p. 30. Earlier Beauvoir has shown how a description 'intended to be objective' is 'an assertion of masculine privilege', by noting a lack in a text by Lévinas: he says that 'Otherness reaches its full flowering in the feminine'. In this way he makes man the absolute point of reference and woman a relative being, thus manifesting an adherence to a particular differential distribution of values (see *Le Deuxième sexe*, p. 16, n.).

56. *L'Etre et le néant*, p. 711.

57. *Le Deuxième sexe*, vol. II, p. 258.

58. Ibid., p. 266.

59. Ibid., p. 266.

60. Ibid., vol. I, pp. 28–9.

61. However, there is an exception: one book is described as a 'monument to bad faith'. This is the work of a Dr Roy, published in 1943 and

dedicated to Marshal Pétain. Simone de Beauvoir attacks the author's argument, which says that abortion should continue to be prohibited, even when pregnancy puts the mother's life at risk: 'It is immoral to choose between one life and another, he declares, and, fortified by this argument, advises sacrificing the mother'(op. cit., vol. II, p. 637).

62. *Le Deuxième sexe*, p. 10 (Introduction).
63. We note, moreover, that the men who are given critical epithets in *The Second Sex* are, as a general rule, characters in novels and often in novels written by men. She is certainly wearing kid gloves! This reflects a historically specific 'experience of self'. The United Kingdom, which recognized women's right to own property and to vote thirty years before France, produced the more audacious Virginia Woolf: she explains that at the back of their heads, both sexes have a little dark place which can be criticized and that, at least since Juvenal, men have set to work describing this stain in women (for the latter's greater good, says Woolf ironically); it is time for women 'to go behind the other sex and tell us what [they] found there', in order to do them the same service (*A Room of One's Own*, London, Hogarth, 1929, and London, Granada, 1977, p. 86). Virginia Woolf was careful not to take her own suggestion seriously and carry it out. It is quite enough to make such a proposition in a humorous way; one points to the possibility of satire and hurries on to analyse institutions, thus the historical and political planes.
64. *Le Deuxième sexe*, vol. I, p. 28.
65. Gabrielle Suchon, *Traité de la morale et de la politique*, vol. 1 (1693) Séverine Auffret (ed.), Paris, Des Femmes, 1988, p. 145.
66. See Colette Guillaumin, 'Pratiques de pouvoir et idée de nature', *Questions Féministes*, May 1978, no. 3, pp. 14–15.
67. Quoted by Beauvoir in *La Force des choses*, Paris, Gallimard, 1963, vol. I, p. 261.
68. *Le Deuxième sexe*, vol. I, p. 21.
69. Ibid., p. 19.
70. Ibid., vol. II, p. 618.
71. I have deliberately chosen an example which gives a different image of Beauvoir from the usual one. It should not however be thought that the notion of a lack of 'concrete means' is only valid for 'typically feminine' issues; in the second volume we find the idea appearing in various forms on almost all possible questions, notably as the 'lack of serious training. . .'. This simple idea seems to me to have an application as wide as oppression as a whole. Beauvoir uses it in relation to American blacks and Africans in France. Others use it to describe the situation of working-class children at school. The idea of a social life which refuses describable concrete means to some people usually leads to demands. Philosophically speaking, it is interesting that lack of means is connected to the problem of freedom, for this changes the

concept of freedom itself, which then becomes qualified: it becomes the possibility of doing a particular thing, and is no longer seen as a not-suffering-about-decisions, but as an opening up to action.

72. The plane of Husserl's thought is not the same as that of Sartre's theory.

73. *The Crisis of European Sciences*, David Carr trans., Northwestern University Press, Evanston, 1970, p. 82, modified in the light of the interpretation given later (1976) by Gérard Granel in his French translation. The German text is in volume VI of the Husserliana. Sartre knew the ideas expressed there in the 1930s.

74. The way that Husserl treats Descartes makes us think. He regards him as both the Founding Father of modernity (thus of his own discourse) and someone who 'does not clearly realize' the true meaning of his own philosophy, so that he speaks of 'Descartes' misinterpretation of himself'. In this he combines two extremes of the history of philosophy, which I shall discuss in the next notebook. But he also sticks to the identifiable and habitual manner in which those who set themselves up as 'great philosophers' practise the history of philosophy: on the one hand one absolutely affirms the great value of a given philosophical system, thus its capacity to be a founding text; on the other, one shows that this same predecessor is deceptive, since he does not entirely know what he is saying. This legitimates the fact that the reinterpretation that 'I the great philosopher' gives is the real elucidation, thus it is I who am truly the Founder and the Father. Husserl thinks to make Descartes truly Cartesian in this way. One wonders what sort of oedipus complex it takes to think as he does.

75. *Le Deuxième sexe*, vol. II, p. 637.

76. Ibid., pp. 589–90.

77. She says the law banning abortion is ineffective: abortion has become part of people's way of life and only 'bourgeois hypocrisy' stops this from being said. She adds that the arguments used against legalization of the procedure are 'absurd'. She never imagined that it would take another quarter of a century before that legalization was obtained, and not without difficulty. Basically, she minimizes the importance of non-legalization and of the repressive legislation by saying abortion has become widespread. She has the same attitude towards contraception (which continued to be banned in France until 1967); furthermore a kind of repugnance at treating one's body 'as a thing' shows through when she discusses this latter question. But, because the techniques exist, she regards the problem as settled.

78. *Theaetetus*, H. N. Fowler trans., London, Heinemann, and New York, G. P. Putnam's Sons, 1928, 160b.

79. 'You, a woman? Surely not!' said an editor from *Elle* looking our friend Cathy Bernheim up and down during a memorable press conference organized by the magazine in 1970 (see *Perturbation, ma soeur* by Cathy Bernheim, Paris, Le Seuil, 1983, p. 101). These words

which were once explicitly addressed to Cathy are, in practice, said implicitly to all women every week: 'You, a woman? Surely not, as long as...'

80. Ibid., p. 82.

81. On the question of feminine desire and its prohibition, I should like to refer to 'Genèse d'une catastrophe', the postface to my translation of *Venus and Adonis* by Shakespeare, Paris, Alidades, 1986.

82. *Le Deuxième sexe*, vol. II, p. 636.

83. Hélène Védrine, *Les Ruses de la raison*, Paris, Payot, 1982, p. 5.

84. *Le Deuxième sexe*, vol. I, pp. 15–16.

85. On this subject see *Modern French Philosophy/Vincent Descombes*, L. Scott-Fox and J. M. Harding trans., Cambridge, Cambridge University Press, 1980.

86. *Le Deuxième sexe*, vol. I. p. 16 n.

87. Ibid., p. 17.

88. Ibid., p. 18.

89. According to F. Bacon, these simple relations of duality, opposition or symmetry are not the fundamental forms of thought, but rather primordial obstacles which hinder any effort to know. For, according to him, the great world to be discovered is more complicated than that. The question to ask of Kojève's heirs may be this: when you speak of the Same and the Other, are you using categories which enable us to think or which prevent us from thinking? Let anyone who tries to make us take the second for the first beware.

90. Here I am more or less using Bachelard's vocabulary in 'Le Monde comme caprice et comme miniature' in *Recherches philosophiques*, 1933–1934, reprinted in Etudes, Paris, Vrin, 1970.

91. Husserl, *The Crisis*, p. 8.

92. Ibid., p. 12.

93. In *La Philosophie silencieuse*, Desanti says that when Husserl talks about mathematics, it is not really mathematics he is talking about but a tame little object that is easy to handle and has taken their place. And when Sartre talks about women...?

94. Jankélévitch, *Le Je-ne-sais-quoi et le presque-rien*, Paris, Le Seuil, 1980.

95. Georges Canguilhem used to like to quote these words in his lectures. They well sum up his philosophical project. But I have never understood why what is foreign should be 'matter'. Does this mean that philosophy is form?

96. Hannah Arendt, *The Human Condition*, Chicago, Chicago University Press, 1958, and New York, Anchor Books, 1959, p. 169.

97. See 'Philosophie et politique', a conference paper given in 1954, the manuscript of which is kept in the Hannah Arendt Archives (Library of Congress, Washington) and which I only know through a partial translation published by Les Cahiers du Grif, Paris, Tierce, 1986, no. 33.

98. *Le Deuxième sexe*, vol. I, p. 24.

99. See, for example, ibid. vol. II, pp. 605–6.
100. Ibid. p. 254 and particularly p. 422.
101. Ibid., p. 263.
102. Ibid., p. 245 (author's italics).
103. Ti-Grace Atkinson, 'The institution of sexual relations' (November 1968), French translation in *L'Odyssée d'une amazone*, Paris, Des Femmes, 1975, p. 29.
104. I shall discuss Hélène Deutsch's ideas a little in the second volume.
105. The notion of theoretical failure does not mean that there are any successes in this field. 'To be an artist is to fail as none dare fail' says Beckett somewhere. To be a thinker too, probably.
106. Gabrielle Suchon, *Traité de la morale*, p. 35.
107. *Le Deuxième sexe*, pp. 95–6. By contrasting 'giving life' with 'risking one's life', Beauvoir contributes to the social silence in which death in childbirth was, so to speak, buried. In the nineteenth century one birth in six ended in the death of the mother. But social thinking maintained a barrier between discourses of motherhood and those of death.
108. 'Each consciousness seeks the death of the other' is a quotation from Hegel's *The Phenomenology of Mind*, which Simone de Beauvoir prefixed to her novel *She Came to Stay*. Whether she thought that Sartre's and Hegel's philosophies were similar or dissimilar is not quite clear. As we know from her letters, she read the then recently published French translation of the first volume of *The Phenomenology of Mind* in July 1940. In one letter to Sartre she says she wishes to expound Hegel's philosophy to him, because it is so close to his own ideas. In another letter she says that she would like to confront Hegel's problematics with that of Sartre, although both, she says, are true . . . (note added to the English translation).
109. Some women in the Movement have shown great hostility towards the figure of Simone de Beauvoir, that is towards both her work and her person at one and the same time. The same women have insisted on the idea of an essential feminine. To my way of thinking, these two points, taken together, should be seen as symptoms of the desire for ideological leadership.
110. *Le Deuxième sexe*, vol. II, p. 422.
111. Ibid., p. 577. This is an extract from a letter to Victor Hugo from Juliette Drouet.
112. There is, however, still at least one problem concerning language and identity. A male post office employee comes to your door saying, 'The postman with a registered letter!' A woman post office employee says, 'Registered letter!' because we do not yet use the word 'postwoman'. She abstracts herself from the situation, only mentioning the institution for whom she acts, while he identifies himself in and with his function.
113. We shall return to the question of 'genius' and the 'top of the pyra-

mid' in the Fourth Notebook of the present book and, perhaps, in the second volume, for it is a recurrent aspect of both classic feminist and anti-feminist works. All things considered, one might regard this as rather surprising, and such is my intention.

114. Apart from crèches, women who are mothers of children who are still children need evening childcare. Babysitting is not within everyone's reach. When people want to go to the cinema or to attend regular political or group meetings, often the father goes alone. This is not just a problem for couples: there are millions of divorced and single women who bring up children alone.

115. The University of B. has a programme of in-service training for local authority employees with places for twenty students. In the first year all of these were white men. There was a protest: 'In principle you have an equal opportunities policy, apply it!' The next year the University of B. took on ten white men and ten black women. Some battles keep your sense of humour alive.

116. In the last part of *The Second Sex*, Simone de Beauvoir says on several occasions 'the independent woman is split'. This is not at all what I am trying to say here. I am thinking of a contradiction set up by institutions, not a 'split' of the psychological type, and I think contradiction affects the lives of all women, not just those of the 'independent' ones. I shall return to this in the second volume.

117. *A Room of One's Own* is an extraordinary text from many points of view. It is presented as a fictitious conference paper, which begins thus: 'But, you may say, we asked you to speak about women and fiction.' Playing with this imaginary invitation, Virginia Woolf shifts the subject for consideration and asks: Why are women poor? Why do they never have a room in the house where they can work in peace? and many other things.

118. The pertinent answer came from the floor. A woman stated that we should be glad to have more children if their fathers did more of the resulting work and if there were more social provision for bringing them up. 'This remark is the most shocking of all', replied the gentleman. The psychodramas of a Royal Institute are most instructive. One can see how ideological praise of motherhood goes hand in hand with a refusal to give the baby even one bottle.

119. A question taken up later in the Fourth Notebook.

120. The idea that there is exploitation and not just alienation came to light in the various European and American movements of the 1970s, when feminists realized that the alienation of women is overlaid with benefits for others. Through housework, wives and mothers give their services to their families, either for nothing, if they also work outside the home, or for the simple fact of being kept. No servant would agree to work on this basis. When their consent is not sought, women are also exploited as reproducers, both by the husband who imposes more pregnancies upon them than they would like, and by the natalist state

which blocks their access to control of their fertility. Treated as living incubators, they are alienated; but insofar as pregnancy and motherhood are the forced production of tomorrow's workforce, they are also physically exploited.

121. Preface to *Avortement, une loi en procès*, collective work, Paris, Gallimard, 1973, reprinted in Claude Francis and Fernand Gontier's collection, *Les Ecrits de Simone de Beauvoir*, Paris, Gallimard, 1979, p. 508.
122. See the collection cited, p. 406, 'The feminine condition', an article published by *La Nef*, 1964, on the publication of Andrée Michel and Geneviève Texier's book, *La Condition de la Française d'aujourd'hui*, Paris, Denoël-Gonthier, 1964.
123. Beauvoir, *Les Ecrits*, p. 401.
124. Ibid., pp. 406–407.
125. Ibid., p. 587 (interview with Pierre Viansson-Ponté, 1978).
126. *Le Deuxième sexe*, vol. I, p. 35. However we still hear a personal voice in some articles: the one she wrote on Brigitte Bardot in 1959 in great praise of a 'dangerously sincere' B. B. is in the same vein as the end of *The Second Sex*.

THIRD NOTEBOOK

1. *La Force de l'âge*, Paris, Gallimard, 1960, 'Folio' series, vol. I, p. 9. Quotations have been retranslated for the present work.
2. *Memoires d'une jeune fille rangée*, Paris, Gallimard, 1958, 'Folio' series, pp. 403–1. Quotations have been retranslated for the present work.
3. Ibid., p. 480.
4. Ibid., p. 481.
5. Cf. *Les Présocratiques*, edited and translated by J.-P. Dumont, Paris, Gallimard, 'Bibliothèque de la Pléiade', 1988, pp. 753 and 873.
6. *La Force de l'âge*, vol. I, p. 18.
7. *Memoires d'une jeune fille rangée*, p. 473.
8. *La Force de l'âge*, vol. II, p. 493.
9. A slip of the ear: he thought I was asking for *Practical Reason*. Is this a coincidence? In the United States I heard colleagues distinguish between 'hard philosophy' (epistemology, theory of knowledge, some fields of the history of philosophy) and 'soft philosophy' (ethics and aesthetics) – with the 'hard' for young gentlemen only and the 'soft' occasionally accepting women.
10. Rousseau, *L'Emile*, Book V, p. 709.
11. *Mètis* is a common noun meaning sagacity, wisdom, prudence, cunning. It has the same root as *métron*, measure, and *mètio*, to think, to meditate. *Mètis* is also the name of a divinity, Zeus' first wife and Athena's mother, except that when she was pregnant, Zeus swallowed her then gave birth to the goddess. On the notion of *mètis*, see M. Detienne and J.-P. Vernant, *Les Ruses de l'intélligence*, Paris, Flamma-

rion, 1974 and the book already mentioned by Hélène Védrine, *Les Ruses de la raison*.

12. On Eumetis, alias Cleobulina, see Plutarch, *The Dinner of the Seven Wise Men*, 148c–155e; and Diogenes Laertius, *Lives and Opinions of Eminent Philosophers*, vol. II, pp. 98–102.

13. See Kepler, *Somnium, sive astronomia lunaris*, note 2, in the edition prepared by John Lear, translated by Patricia Fruch Kirkwood, University of California Press, 1965, p. 87.

14. Livy calls the war that Rome waged against its Italian allies who were demanding citizens' rights *sociale bellum*.

15. It should not be concluded from these remarks that I see coeducation as a regrettable thing. On the contrary, in the next notebook I shall plead in favour of the establishment of a balanced mix of the sexes as a generalized principle. I believe this to be the aim of women's struggles or the endpoint of feminism. But this ideal does not prevent us from seeing at least two difficulties. Firstly, the achievement of joint participation in institutions by women and men involves the effects described in the fable of the iron pot and the clay pot; after this point, things gradually re-establish themselves. Secondly, a distinction must be drawn between real 'mixity', that is to say, a community which has sexual balance as a principle, and a form that is slyly perverted. It is the latter that was set up and not the former. A simple point will make this clear: from now on, women compete with men, but the competitive exam selectors remain exclusively, or in the great majority, male. It is this kind of perverted mixed participation which makes women into clay pots.

16. Etienne Gilson, *Héloïse and Abelard*, L. K. Shook trans., New York, Ann Arbor, University of Michigan Press and Rexdale, Ambassador Books, 1960.

17. Ibid., p. 72.

18. The couple's folly of an immoderate desire for social recognition has a counterpart in Fulbert's equally mad desire to defend 'the family honour'.

19. See above, Third Notebook, note 5.

20. E. Benveniste. 'Catégories de pensée et catégories de langue', in *Les Etudes philosophiques*, no. 4, 1985 (PUF), reprinted in *Problèmes de linguistique générale* vol. 1, chapter VI, Paris, Gallimard, 1966.

21. Derrida, *Margins of Philosophy*, Alan Bass trans., Chicago, Chicago University Press, and Brighton, Harvester, 1982, p. 228.

22. Here I am freely drawing on p. 153 of *The Creative Mind*.

23. *The Advancement of Learning* in Spedding (ed.), vol. III, p. 365 and *De Augmentis*, ibid., vol. I, p. 563. See also *De Principiis.*, ibid., vol. III, p. 83; *Cogitata et Visa*, ibid., vol. III, p. 602; *Redargutio*, ibid., vol. III, p. 565; cf. the analogous idea in Filum Labyrinthi, ibid., vol. III, p. 502.

24. See First Notebook, section 6.

25. Husserl, *The Crisis*, p. 6.

26. Ibid., p. 12.
27. A random example: 'The liberation of women liberates them first of all from their femininity. "Operation-successful-patient-dead". The woman thus liberated is no longer a woman any more than a beast is a man', writes Georges Devereux, an 'ethnopsychoanalyst', in a work entitled *Femme et Mythe* (Paris, Flammarion, 'Champs' series, 1988, p. 5.). This familiar refrain is followed by a few fantasies involving snails, the praying mantis and the risk of humanity losing its human character. The big threats come at once: if you escape my domination, humanity will lose its soul. Even an ethnopsychoanalyst has the right to have fantasies about snails and praying mantises. However, when these fantasies are published, everyone is equally within their rights to wonder what relevance Flammarion saw in them. But this is not the real question. Has humankind particularly displayed its human character up till now? Hmm! And yet it has greatly insisted on the duality of the sexes which, according to Devereux, establishes the humanity of humankind. In 1928 Virginia Woolf (again) pointed out that no one proclaimed the importance of difference so much as Mussolini. For myself, I rally to Colette Guillaumin's statement: the difference that interests me is the difference between (real) women and the myths that some men continue to fabricate about us.
28. Shakespeare, *Twelfth Night*, Act III, scene iv: 'If this were play'd upon a stage now, I could condemn it as an improbable fiction.' Just after Jacques Chirac was elected in France, a newly appointed Minister did the villainous deed of cancelling an entrance exam for the CNRS when it was nearly over. The victims, of which I was one, got together to take the Minister to court and took advantage of this grouping to discuss scientific policy and the sciences in themselves. We won our appeal to the Council of State, then got Parliament to pass a law of retrospective reparation, and greatly benefited from the unusual contact between representatives of quite different fields.
29. Reprinted in *Essais critiques*, Paris, Le Seuil, 1964, p. 80.
30. *Memoires d'une jeune fille rangée*, p. 482.
31. *La Force de l'âge*, p. 29: Simone de Beauvoir was to contrive to stay in Paris for two years 'and we would spend them in the closest possible intimacy. After that, he advised me to take a job abroad. We would remain apart for two or three years, and then rejoin one another somewhere'.
32. A physics, chemistry and biology examination which students who had just taken the *baccalauréat* were preparing for. At the time, to enroll for the philosophy *agrégation* one had to have a scientific qualification.
33. *Lettres au Castor et à quelques autres*, Paris, Gallimard, 1983, vol. I, p. 79.
34. Ibid., vol. I, p. 81.
35. Ibid., vol. I, p. 57.
36. Ibid., vol. I, p. 37.
37. Ibid., vol. I, p. 110.

38. Ibid., vol. I, p. 43.
39. Ibid., vol. II, p. 88.
40. Ibid., vol. II, p. 106.
41. I am far from being the first feminist to regard the abstract ethics of universality and the law as a liberating point of view. For it enables us to see as morally neutral a great number of things which are required or forbidden by the social code. Thus I am drawing here on the tradition inaugurated by Mary Wollstonecraft. It is an important stage of the historical movement of the de-alienation of women to be able to put forward the idea that some things are morally indifferent, as much (to use the old example) as having an odd or even number of hairs on one's head. But the category of the neutral, or indifferent, can only be put forward by a procedure which is itself ethical, which, having located the law elsewhere, can declare that it is not here. It is thus not surprising that for two centuries feminism has been 'moralistic': this is the only way of unlearning the false values to which women are violently subjected.
42. *Lettres*, vol. II, p. 88.
43. Ibid., vol. II, p. 92.
44. Ibid., vol. I, p. 239.
45. It still is, in my opinion, now that Beauvoir's letters have been published. She seems not to react to what he does or says, but lets him have his monologue and does not interfere.
46. 'So overall, my letters are the equivalent of an account of my life', said Sartre in an interview in 1974. This phrase in itself indicates in a condensed form the problem I am trying to elucidate. To want to give an account of one's own life is to affirm that this life really is one's own; but if someone is absolutely the subject of her or his life, then there is no place left for relationships. Furthermore, in deciding after the event what may legitimately be regarded as evidence, one both reasserts control and places that evidence in the category of fiction.
47. *La Force de l'âge*, pp. 213–14.
48. *Lettres*, vol. I, p. 375 – *together* underlined by Sartre.
49. Ibid., vol. I, p. 469.
50. Ibid., vol. I, p. 470.
51. Ibid., vol. I, p. 379.
52. Ibid., vol. I, p. 470.
53. Genesis, 2, 29–20.
54. *Lettres*, vol. I, p. 336.
55. *The Portrait of a Lady*, London, Penguin, 1963, p. 286.
56. *Lettres*, vol. I, p. 429.
57. Claude Habib, 'Souvenirs du féminisme', *Esprit*, June 1988, no. 6.
58. *Protagoras*, W. K. C. Guthrie trans., London, Penguin, 1956, 328b.
59. Ibid., 329a.
60. Ibid., 342b.
61. 'While he was studying the stars and looking upwards, he fell into a pit, and a neat, witty Thracian servant girl jeered at him, they say,

because he was so eager to know the things in the sky that he could not see what was there before him at his very feet. The same jest applies to all who pass their lives in philosophy' when this leads them to know nothing of their fellows and even of their neighbours (*Theaetetus* 174ab).

62. 'Widely-held opinions' means commonly held by all those who have a little power over others. The importance of the comparison between the sophist and the tribune is that it enables us to distinguish doxa (at least that one) from the notion of 'popular ideas'. Doxa is the opinion not of the people, but of those who have some form of power over them. As regards sexism, if every man is potentially the 'head of family government', a plumber is in the same situation as the orator. There is thus, strictly speaking, no 'popular' sexism, only a doctrine which, from high to low and from low to high on the social scale, asserts the legitimacy of this government of women and children by men.

63. In brief, human life is like the games which brought all Greece together: the sportive ones go to win the victor's crown, others to do business, still others just to watch; the philosophers are like the latter. See Cicero, *Tusculan Disputations*, J. E. King trans., London, Heinemann, and New York, G. P. Putnam's Sons, 1927, book V, chapter III.

64. It must however be said that no one can teach philosophy only with what he or she is, one must also use what one knows and teach according to the particular educational and social conditions of the place where one teaches. But the fundamental point lies in the question: 'What do I want from these students?' Everyone has responsibility for that 'I want'.

65. See Third Notebook, note 63.

66. Cited by E. Lévinas, *Noms propres*, Paris, Fata Morgana, 1976, Chapter entitled 'Jeanne Delhomme, Pénélope ou la pensée modale'.

67. Seneca, 'On Tranquillity of Mind', in *The Stoic Philosophy of Seneca*, Moses Hadas trans., New York, Doubleday, 1958, p. 88.

68. Cicero, *On Moral Obligation*, J. Higginbotham trans., London, Faber & Faber, 1967, chapter 44, l. 158, p. 95.

69. These thoughts were inspired by Kant's article 'Was heiβt sich in Denken orientieren?', published in the journal *Berlinische Monatsschrift*, October 1786, pp. 304–30 and translated into French in 1959.

70. In the First Notebook I announced my intention not always to take questions to their extremes. This one of 'Why is there no unanimity?' ('why is it that not everyone agrees with me?') is one of those problems that it is better to leave hanging. When philosophers start to look for (and find) the terrible reasons why someone does not completely agree with them, thought falls back into the category we have called 'hegemony'. Of course, sometimes, there are sociological, political, or existential reasons for the disagreement which are immediately obvious; but that which is immediately obvious is not very important. We must establish as a principle that disagreement is always normal: it is agreement that is surprising.

71. See preceding note and First Notebook.
72. There are no known examples of philosophers who, however original or revolutionary or discontinuist, did not go fishing for words, models, examples of intellectual effort, warnings, lessons and so on in the great lake of the past of thought.
73. The anecdote and its reply are recorded by Diogenes Laertius in *Lives and Opinions*, p. 98.
74. Gabrielle Suchon, *Traité de la morale*, p. 33.
75. 'A girl can't go out at night like that!' 'That is a nasty thing for a little girl to say', 'Girls who are well brought up arrive at a dance late and leave early', 'Engineering is not a subject for girls', 'People will think you're a prostitute if you go on like that', 'A [thankless] job like that's not so bad for a woman', 'Anyway, you're only a woman' (said to me by a taxi driver who had just been asked to keep his racist sayings to himself; one hears the same words from the lips of Prof P. when his assistant says she would like to be given tenure), 'Oh! You're not married and he kissed your hand!', 'That's your job, you're a woman' (about hand-washing shirts during a lovers' trip), 'A classic, stable woman, you'll be able to give him all the tenderness he needs so much, weighed down with responsibilities as he is', 'Women must do philosophy in a feminine, in other words intuitive way; if you present us with arguments, you lose everything' (sic), 'Part-time work is a good balance for women', 'And the strangest thing is that she's not a blue-stocking at all!' (about a specialist in something), 'It would be better for Jean-Yves to read our protest motion; you'd come over as a harpy' [and the fact is...] 'On this question you should consult the work of Françoise F., who was, moreover, a formidable woman: she was a very good mother, despite being a member of the Academy' (how many male Academicians would have been reasonably present fathers? That is an irrelevant question). Little girl, young woman, decent woman (not a hussy), mother...an individual of the female sex is always seen in terms of first her sex, second the precise category she should occupy (girl or married woman), third the norms (being a mother and a good mother), fourth the fears which are always present, and so on. In the end this becomes tiring and burdensome.
76. H. Hamon and P. Rotman, *Génération*, Paris, Le Seuil, 1988, vol. II, p. 336.
77. FHAR (Homosexual Front for Revolutionary Action). This group was originally mixed, then the men expelled the women.

FOURTH NOTEBOOK

1. M. de Lescure, *Les Femmes philosophes*, Paris, 1881.
2. Recorded by Diogenes Laertius, *Lives and Opinions*, vol. I, book II, chapter V.

3. Seneca, 'On Tranquillity of Mind', IX, 4.
4. Gabrielle Suchon, *Traité de la morale.*
5. *Minima Moralia*, pp. 53 and 52.
6. Albert Jacquard, *Eloge de la Différence*, Paris, Le Seuil, 1978.
7. See Marie-Paule Duhet, *Les Femmes et la Révolution*, p. 223.
8. Ibid., p. 72.
9. The law on filiation has been slightly changed, but these improvements are not enough; the law distinguishes between registered name (the father's, if the child is recognized by both parents at the same time, or the mother's, to which the father's is later added if both parents agree to declare the child of 'unknown father' to start with and the father only comes forward later) and the usual name, which is used on the child's identity papers and in school. While the child is a minor the usual name can be formed of those of both father and mother. But the parents must have a photocopy of the law with which to confront the registrar and school heads. This legislation is unbalanced and extremely complex because it is not centred on the child's right to have the names of his or her father and mother and to choose, when he or she in turn becomes a parent, which half of the name to pass on.
10. Shakespeare, *Romeo and Juliet*, Act II, scene II.
11. Following Françoise Duroux's words in *L'Imaginaire de la différence sexuelle*, Colloque de Toulouse, 1983.
12. Cf. Claude Habib, 'Souvenirs du féminisme', Third Notebook, note 57.
13. However, the most active women in the Movement split into 'tendencies' along theoretical lines. The 'radical' tendency concerned itself with the issues of 'invisible work' – the unpaid work that the housewife does in the family – and men's appropriation of women's bodies. The journal *Questions féministes* reflected this tendency. Another was made up of women who had come from Trotskyist groups; this was particularly concerned with the additional problems of being a woman when one belongs to a group for whom life is already hard. *Les Cahiers du féminisme* continue this type of work. But, in every case, more was discussed than just theory. Observation of daily life, puns and biting or dazzling wit produced as much awareness of the position imposed on women as theories did.
14. Evelyne Le Garrec, *Les Messagères*, Paris, Des Femmes, 1976.
15. Attributed to Flo Kennedy, the first black American woman to become a lawyer.
16. Made up by Catherine Deudon.
17. Taken from Zoë Fairbairn's novel *Benefits*, London, Virago, 1980.
18. Made up by Liliane Kandel.
19. Hélène Védrine, *Les Ruses*, p. 234.
20. Luce Irigaray, 'Misère de la psychanalyse' in *Critique*, October 1977.
21. Letter to Alphonse Pollot, January 1641.

22. Virginia Woolf answered this question long before it was asked: 'sexual character', as she puts it, is manifested all the better and more pleasantly the less one thinks about it. Hyperawareness of one's own sex seems to her odious and false. She is writing in 1928 and thinking of Mussolini. I very much like the idea that one shows one is a man or woman inadvertently, without thinking. Such an idea never stopped anyone, and particularly not Woolf, from thinking about the social relations between women and men, which the feminism of difference leaves aside.

23. 'Seeing that ye have put off the old man with his deeds; and have put on the new man, which is renewed in knowledge after the image of him that created him: where there is neither Greek nor Jew, circumcision nor uncircumcision, Barbarian, Scythian, bond nor free: but Christ is all, and in all' (Paul's Letter to the Colossians, chapter 3, vs 9–11, King James version.) It is strange to note that, in this passage, only males are mentioned, although 'man', old or new, is meant in the generic sense of the word: it is *homo* in the Vulgate and *anthropos* in the Septuagint. This passage deserves comparison with the following: 'For as many of you as have been baptized into Christ have put on Christ. There is neither Jew nor Greek, there is neither bond nor free, there is neither male nor female: for ye are all one in Christ Jesus' (Paul's Letter to the Galatians, chapter 3, vs 27–28). When St Paul is thinking about going beyond differences, including sexual difference, he does not mention the 'new man'. Strange.

24. The Council of State's rulings bear the name of the person who brought the appeal.

25. A law setting out general civil service regulations.

26. One hears the junior doctors in Paris hospitals saying 'They're all women in paediatrics' – how many does 'all women' mean? Exactly 35 per cent! Weird arithmetic!

27. Every word in this sentence is admirable: the choice is between a 'high proportion of men' and a 'supplementary income'! In the current situation, primary teaching is a profession not for men, or for women, but for wives. As for the expression 'the simplest and most legal way', this merits lengthy discussion.

28. The very high academic level of women primary school teachers recruited over recent years is proof of this. A parallel can be drawn with a phenomenon pointed out by Huguette Bouchardeau: women workers are sometimes obliged to hide their skills in order to get a job. The state does not demand dissimulation, just the pure and simple renunciation of skills higher than those required at the level at which women are recruited.

29. My incredulity is particularly based on the following fact: the so-called burden of this legislation has never dissuaded an employer from taking on a woman when a typist's or cleaner's post needs filling.

30. Without risk of harming anyone, I can now acknowledge that this

event gave rise to the article and awakened my interest in these questions. One of the six failed women candidates was a former student of mine. Mireille Canals, another philosophy graduate who had gone into law and prepared for this exam, called to tell me that her friend, who was ill-prepared to be a victim of such discrimination and thus all the more in a state of shock, had laid siege to the Minister, demanding the names of the selectors. 'If she goes on, she'll get herself a bad name, which is disastrous if you want a career at the top of the civil service; but if we tell her to stop, she'll have a nervous breakdown. What can we do?' I suggested displacing this legitimate rage and avenging her friend by writing an article analysing such situations from a fairly general point of view. To help me in this, Mireille Canals gave her former tutor a remarkably clear lecture on public law. Philosophy and law studies produce wonderful brains.

31. See the second volume.

32. To complete the picture, we should need to propose a typology with three elements: jobs in which one sets other people's tasks, jobs with clearly defined tasks and jobs with infinite tasks. The job of secretary is the most appropriate paradigm of the third element insofar as the tasks a secretary can be given extend indefinitely: not just typing letters, answering the telephone and so on, but also watering the office plants, making the coffee, putting up with the boss's moods...*ad libitum*. It is not surprising that it is women who do this work, since it parallels the undefined and infinitely extensible nature of household–conjugal–maternal responsibilities.

33. Marcelle Marini pointed out to me that the 60 per cent of women among job applicants is an important indication of how attitudes are changing. Many women who were deprived of their jobs by the recession have registered as unemployed instead of going back into the home as many ideological powers are constantly inviting them to do. That 60 per cent of the unemployed are women is a phenomeon which once again proves the sexism of employers. But that there should be so many women among the registered unemployed is indeed a sign of women's realization that they have a right to paid work and that the role of housewife is neither natural nor desirable.

34. One particularly comical (or alarming) example of this in a 'republic' is provided by military schools. A quota of 80 per cent of the places (at the minimum) are reserved for boys, since girls are only accepted on condition that their numbers do not go beyond the 20 per cent threshold. Other quotas fix the proportion of children whose parents are soldiers and civil servants. France will never cease to amaze me. Moreover, these schools are quite shocking. They are barracks where adolescents are brought up according to military discipline, but get the best standards of education: very small classes and teachers hand picked from the best qualified. Thus generals' sons benefit from privileged education in a repressive context. It is not surprising that

many of them leave these establishments with attitudes which are, to say the least, anti-democractic. I do not understand why the so-called republic permits the creation of possible 'public enemies' of democracy.

35. I would not write this today: the nurses' revolt (October 1988) proves that something has changed and that a profession made up mainly of women can challenge pay that is so low that it has to be a 'supplementary' or 'temporary' income: for a long time nursing was a job for girls; today nurses still often leave after four or five years in the profession, often when they have a baby. It is a badly paid and very difficult job. The fact that nurses are striking for acceptable pay and working conditions, instead of leaving the job one by one to become housewives, proves that a remarkable change has come about.

36. She was born in 1824 and got her education from her family, who were of modest means but cultivated. In 1859 (before Victor Durury's establishment of secondary schooling for girls), she sought permission to sit for the *baccalauréat*. The Minister is said to have replied, 'Do you want to make my Ministry a laughing stock!' She finally obtained permission from the University of Lyon and passed in 1861. In 1866 she wrote a book, *La Femme pauvre au XIX-siècle*. The amount of fuss that institutions make when a woman pioneer asks for something new is horrifying. And then, it gets forgotten. Today the number of girls who pass the *baccalauréat* is slightly higher than the number of boys; but who would say that this has made the whole country a laughing stock?

37. This is only true if one looks at the figures for people who have *never* been married and no doubt I was too hasty over this. The drop in the number of unmarried people may be due to the reduction of two social categories: those of people in service on a permanent basis and church people, catholic priests and nuns. Some single lives were far from happy. To assess liberation in relation to marriage, it is more correct to take the statistics for children born out of wedlock and recognized by both parents. This number is rising.

38. Let it not be said that it is hard to find women with the necessary abilities. In 1979 the selectors for the *agrégation* in philosophy (and they do not come more masculine) disgracefully placed Thomas More's *Utopia* on the syllabus for the English oral, with no further details. When I went to ask them which English translation they wanted the candidates to retranslate, they did not understand what I meant and gave me a very bad reception. I had to insist, pointing out to them that I knew of several. These gentlemen had simply taken Robinson's version for More's original text. I swear that at the time it was impossible to find six women academics who were so incompetent that they did not know that dear old Morus wrote his *Utopia* in Latin. Those candidates who prepared for the exam in the isolation of some small town using Turner's excellent, modern translation and were

then unprepared for Robinson's fearsome Tudor English when it came to the oral would have been within their rights to challenge the exam in court.

39. The 7 May 1982 law affirms the principle of equal access for men and women to public service jobs and obliges the government to report to Parliament every two years on the measures taken to guarantee respect for this principle at every level of the hierarchy. To my knowledge, the popular press has never mentioned these governmental 'reports'. Have they even been drawn up? Other than in a laconic and sybilline form? How can a private citizen get information about this?

40. Yvette Roudy: Minister of Women's Rights in the Socialist government. Simone Iff: President of the Family Planning Association and policy adviser to the government.

41. To my knowledge as a private citizen, not much came out of it apart from (and it is something) a non-authorization of 'eros centres'. All the prostitutes' organizations had made it clear how much worse these factories make their already difficult conditions. Roudy did not find a way to improve their situation, she simply prevented the establishment of an even more appalling modern form of it.

42. It is not surprising that some covert appeals should be lost in the sands. But it was a bit much when, two years later, in 1983, our rulers had the cheek to complain about the silence of the intellectuals and to regret that they had put forward no proposals. A gracious offer had been made through the newspapers; what more did they want?

43. An example: in 1987, the Minister for Research and the Director of the CNRS clearly did not feel obliged to respect this circular when they had to set up the panels who would make appointments for the CNRS. On these panels, each of which has eleven members, there are no women selectors at all in some subjects and two for some others; on the interdisciplinary panel which appoints heads of research there is only one – but she is a member of the Academy of Sciences. I have no way of completely analysing the relationship between the 'masculinity' of the panels appointed by Chirac's government and the sudden noticeable drop in the proportion of women among the researchers. But is a complete analysis necessary?

44. The (real) thesis dedications which I have put together tend to show that few men became university teachers without setting their wives' noses to the grindstone. When she did not actually type their work, she often brought up the children as single-handedly as a single mother.

45. 27 October 1988: the 'event' of the withdrawal by the pharmaceutical group Roussel-Uclaf of the abortion pill RU 486 was an opportunity for the Catholic church to adopt a position which a section of the press dealt with very severely. Since this pill makes it possible to terminate a pregnancy without either anaesthetic or surgery, the bishops decided it made abortion too easy and showed their satisfac-

tion at Roussel-Uclaf's backtracking. Since, in any case, abortion is legal in France, their attitude came down to criticizing the greater comfort (or lesser discomfort) that this discovery could bring. We can rightly regard this as unpleasant. On 5 November 1988 there was a full page advertisement in *Le Monde* for 'the Church in the service of God and men' (God and men, perhaps, but not women!), which was in fact an appeal for money. This advertisement stated: Your gift is now tax-deductible for up to 5 per cent of your taxable income'. Ah ha. 'Now'? Which Minister made a ruling giving similar state approval to the church as that given to medical research establishments? What is happening to the separation of church and state if tax is no longer collected on sums going to the Catholic church and thus financing such appalling propaganda (and pressure) as that we have just described?

46. In families aspiring to old-fashioned forms of bourgeois respectability, it is a common thing to send sons to the nearest 'good' state school, for it is important for boys to get the best possible education, while girls are sent to a religious establishment for young ladies, where they chiefly learn good manners and good behaviour. Mary Wollstonecraft would add: a goodly dose of hypocrisy. One could do a whole microsociological study of sexual discrimination and private schools. Afterwards, one could think about the practices and attitudes to which education in a homosexed, or not-mixed, setting can give rise.

47. The various 'orders' of the medical profession were set up by the Vichy government, which already gives a good idea of their democratic worth. They are agencies with particular areas of jurisdiction, whose role is to seek to punish infringements of the professional code of ethics. They can go so far as to ban people from the profession. A detailed study of these principles and behaviour would be funny and very significant: for example, there is a Council of the Order of Midwives whose president is by law not a midwife but an obstetrician. Those women could not be left unsupervised! Chamfort said, 'Without the government, no one in France would laugh.' Nor without the administrative and legal systems!

48. From the beginning of the seventeenth century, scientists have shown their desire and need to work together and Bacon's idea that the state should fund collective scientific work has spread. Since its foundation, the Academy of Sciences in Paris has concerned itself with tracking down pseudo-scientific 'fakes' and so-called miraculous phenomena, it has made sure (as far as it could) that no branch of the sciences was neglected and lastly it has tried to defend scientists' freedom of thought everywhere, with a clear internationalist perspective. If it had been in existence when the Galileo affair erupted, it might have contributed to scientific solidarity in the unfortunate's favour. However, that is as far as its action goes: one cannot count on the Academy of Sciences to defend the idea of a humanistic control of

scientific research, even if some of its members adopt brave positions in a personal capacity.

49. To my knowledge, the first 'agnostic' to enter the Académie Française was Emile Littré, at the end of the nineteenth century. In his rage, Mgr Dupanloup resigned!

50. *Pourquoi des femmes à l'Académie?*, Paris, 1863, republished with other texts on the same subject in *Les Femmes et l'Académie Française*, Paris, Opale, 1980.

51. Marguerite Yourcenar is a first-rate writer in relation to other writers, but there is no reason to consider her a 'high-flying genius', to use the words of George Sand, who recalls that France has never produced forty all at once, and so can never fill the Academy's chairs with genius. As a priestess of the return to the old values of austerity, prayer and spelling, Marguerite Yourcenar had no reason to turn the Academy down. We already know her opinion on women's rights: she wrote of a woman forebear that she was 'the masterpiece of a society where woman has no need to vote or to demonstrate in the streets in order to rule' (*Archives du Nord*, Gallimard, p. 113). When she was received into the Academy, she sensibly made clear all the ill she thought of innovations, thus all the good there was to say of those who, resisting 'the fashion of the times', had voted against accepting a woman. She even expounded her ideas in Latin: *sint ut sunt*, may things remain as they are! Her speech was a well formulated moral statement, showing that she was ready to see eye to eye with the others on the exclusion of women, fine works in the French style and sentences so well-chiselled that they could at once be used as examples of grammar for schoolchildren. J. d'Ormesson's answering speech was crawling with unintentional jokes and contained one unforgivable sentence: 'Traditions, like women, are made to be both respected and jostled' (cf. *Le Monde*, 23 January 1981). This is a pure and simple incitement to violence; but at the time there was no law forbidding incitement to 'jostle', in practice, to rape and cause bodily harm (although there was already one to punish any 'attack on the morale of the army'); there are thus no legal grounds for us to take M. d'Ormesson to court for this barbarism. What a shame. Since 25 July 1985, it has become possible for conformists to contravene the 'laws of the kingdom', though we still do not have the right to take them to court. But, if there is such a gap between the Academy and good taste, what is the point of it, apart from writing its dictionary?

52. Richelieu was perfectly able to tell an excellent author from a no-hoper and he chose the no-hopers. Since there were less than forty of them, he added men of the world who had never written a line in their lives. I do not think he could have done it any differently. Could the political authorities permit the organization of a literary counter-authority or organize it themselves? Of course we must not overestimate what an Academy made up of the best minds from 1635

onwards could have done for good or ill: we cannot even be sure that people of this kind can get on together pleasantly for more than an hour. Anyway, Richelieu did not like any group to have the power to become a 'state within the state'. Even if to us the idea that a group of thinkers can constitute any kind of danger seems fantastical, at that time, people took such things seriously. In 1623 Paris was siezed by panic: the 'fine minds of the time', as a Jesuit contemporary put it, were said to have organized into a brotherhood, 'the Rosicrucian brotherhood', alias 'the invisible College', with the aim of restoring all knowledges and establishing protestantism and other devilish things throughout the country. Descartes, who regarded all this as eyewash, was accused by public opinion of being a member of the 'College'. The most extraordinary thing is that there were no grounds for this collective psychosis: it would seem that the thirty-six members of the invisible college were only ever the figment of an overheated imagination. This tells us yet more about the fear current at the time among 'fine minds' independent enough to think. The Academy could only accept them in tiny quantities. (On this question, see Baillet, *Vie de Monsieur Descartes*, Paris, 1961, and Frances Yates, *The Rosicrucian Enlightenment*, London, Routledge & Kegan Paul, 1972, and Paladin, 1974, chapter 8.

53. Cf. *La Justice*, January 1893.
54. Unless I am wrong, Mme Georgina Dufoix' ministerial position was not renewed because of her failure at the elections to the legislature in June 1988. But M. Thierry de Beaucé was appointed Secretary of State for International Cultural Relations despite a similar failure.
55. Plato, *The Republic*, A. D. Lindsay trans., London, J. M. Dent & Sons, 1976, book II, 368d.
56. *The Monadology of Leibniz*, H. W. Carr trans., London, Favil, 1930.
57. In J. Laplanche and J.-B. Pontalis' *Vocabulaire de psychanalyse*, all entries concerning the drives describe them as 'internal surges' or 'surges of the organism' or as having their source 'in a bodily excitation' and it is clear that they are talking about the body of the person concerned; this is even clearer when the same dictionary links a 'partial drive' to a 'particular erogenous zone': the baby's oral drive is an excitation of his or her mouth. No one wants to argue against these ideas, which are suficiently widespread among Freudians to structure a venture aiming to attain a certain consensus, which a dictionary must necessarily be. Indeed, they are sufficiently probable to meet with approval. However, I believe that this 'probability' partly springs from their congruence with culturally dominant models. If a model is probably true in what it asserts, but potentially false in what it denies (all models assert and deny), we must ask what this one 'drops'. All emotions or 'surges' whose origins are outside the body of the person concerned is the simplest answer. Of course, we can see that from time to time the psychoanalytic current seeks to reintroduce

this dimension. On the notion of affects, Freud mentions the hypothesis according to which these could be connected to pre-individual events, an archaic universal. Lacan, as we know, insists on a great Other, which brings law and language. To my mind, the best challenge to the Cartesian limitations of ordinary psychoanalysis are not directly to be found in Freud or in Lacan, but in a book by Maud Mannoni called *The Child, his 'illness' and the others* (New York, Random House, 1970, and London, Penguin, 1973.) This study shows how, in the fantasy (of the neurotic or psychotic child, in other words everybody), it is very difficult to tell other people's bodies and 'my' body apart, even though this distinction is the aim of treatment. We are no longer dealing here with a transcendental Other, but with concrete and present others and particularized drives which have effects in the child's body. While Lacan's Other can be taken into a Cartesian model (the God of the Meditations), Maud Mannoni's empirical 'others' are closer to Montaigne's characters, affected by the 'strong imaginations' around them.

58. I have invented this word by analogy with auto-suggestion, which assumes that a person's belief can have effects on that person's body. Even if the belief is prompted by other people, it is 'auto' to the extent that it is taken up by the person concerned. Allosuggestion does not require that the belief be adopted. Avicenna thought that the 'form' of health, as it was contained in the doctor's mind, in other words his knowledge, could have a direct influence on the patient's state. Ideas of this type were current until the beginning of the seventeenth century. In this tradition, Bacon wonders whether the hope of a cure among those close to patients might not have a beneficial effect, without its necessarily being shared by patients themselves. This would be a direct effect of one person's imagination on another person's body. On this question, I should like to refer the reader to my essay, 'Bacon chez Augias', *Les Etudes philosophiques*, 1985, no. 3, and to the postface to *Venus and Adonis*, p. 92.

59. See Virginia Woolf, *A Room of One's Own*, p. 84.

60. Ibid., p. 52.

61. David Hume, *An Enquiry Concerning the Principles of Morals*, reprinted from 1777 ed, Open Court Publishing Company, La Salle, 1953, pp. 23–4.

62. Belonging to the working class, being ill, very old, or an immigrant; it's hard for everyone, and even more so for women.

63. 'Women must keep dreaming of another poetic paradise away from this world, or else resolutely take on the problem of practical philosophy' (George Sand, *Pourquoi des femmes à l'Académie?*, p. 96.

64. At the time when the question of reimbursement for abortion was being discussed, it was said that a particular air display at Toulouse given in honour of the President of the Republic cost more than a year's worth of abortions. Was this merely conjecture? The army is

not in the habit of making the cost of its festivities public. Our dear Olympe de Gouges included as a citizens' right that of being able to 'observe' the distribution of public funds. This proposal is still revolutionary.

65. Paul Janiaud, Secretary of the National Union of Scientific Researchers, was good enough to calculate for me the budget the state devotes to research into contraception. There are no teams at the CNRS or at INSERM and no scientists appointed to work in this field. But some teams are working on subjects which could be related to it and may decide to spend a fraction of their time exploring the subject. Thus, at a very generous estimate and adding up the various 'fractions', one arrives at not more than twelve scientists' average salaries. It seems (at best) that the state employs twelve researchers to work on a matter which affects almost everybody sooner or later. It is time to bring the notion of 'science for the people' back into fashion.

66. *Libération*, 27 October 1988 and *Le Monde*, 28 October.

67. I am grateful to Nelly Trumel from Radio Libertaire for trusting me at a time when I had not yet had anything to do with her programme, 'Free Women'. The story of progress for women is often ironic. How is it that American laboratories carried out the research which ended in the contraceptive pill? Out of a concern for the freedom of American women? No way. Their concern was with the overpopulation of the Third World, perhaps even with an authoritarian policy of limiting births in countries controlled by the United States. (Let us recall in passing that a birth in a developed country 'promises' a consumption of energy, raw materials and water in a way that cannot be compared with that implied by a birth in a poor country, even if, for the Third World, its own overpopulation is one of many factors preventing it from escaping underdevelopment.) The irony of the affair is that women in the developed countries seized on this development which was not intended for them.

The other interesting point of the story is that when scientists work on pharmacological subjects or those connected to the physiology of reproduction, their work may not have a clear end from the outset. To start with, the potential applications of a basic discovery or technical find are vague. The subjectivity and ideology of the people involved then comes into play: If, in a corner of their minds, there is an idea that science should serve people's lives (women's well-being), they will think of certain potential applications and thus move their investigations in that direction. If they do not think in this way, they might completely ignore a use of this type, and think only, for example, of potential applications which will make a lot of money.

Lastly, the use of the molecule RU 486 for abortions was easier than the others to develop because in this case the medication is taken only once and it was established that the substance was rapidly eliminated by the organism. Any use requiring regular doses poses clinical problems which have not yet been completely explored and mastered.

68. Declaration by Mgr Julien, 'specialist in medical ethics', in *Le Monde*, 28 October 1988, p. 12.

69. Planned work in the field of contraception would be possible, even if one thinks (as I do) that research whose aims are strictly fixed at the start seldom comes to anything. For, in this case, we are not 'at the start'. If the physiological and pharmacological work carried out over the last ten years were closely examined, neglected trails would almost certainly be found and the research could then be taken in that direction. The molecule which nearly became a masculine contraceptive cannot be a unique example of work abandoned for ideological reasons.

70. An interesting trend has come to light over the last few years: there seems to be a lot of to-ing and fro-ing of intellectual interests between women and men. Tired of being shut away in 'typically feminine' subjects, many women have successfully become fascinated by trigonometry, the seed trade or prison administration. Some men who are aware of the difficulties of women's position are now proving able to devote their time and intelligence to this problem. However, the question of numbers still arises: when a decision-making body is made up of nineteen men and one woman, even if there are two or three men of the type I have just described, they will not be listened to. Decision-making bodies must be as sexually balanced as possible, by law, so that women and men who are concerned about women's lives can get a hearing. Furthermore, the idea of finding oneself in what one does is no worthless thing either.

71. Two examples will be enough. An adolescent girl was treated for minor problems by a gynaecologist who was medically conscientious (and had thus gained her trust), but also a fervent Catholic. One day she told him she had a lover and she wanted to go on the pill; he replied that her problems needed to be cured first and ended the conversation without suggesting any other contraceptive method. Three months later she was pregnant and furious. She blamed herself for having trusted this doctor to the point that it did not occur to her to go and see a different one.

A couple wanted an abortion which would be the woman's fifth. When they were asked 'why not use contraception?' the husband replied that he was against it: the pill would allow his wife to do as she pleased, 'but she knows I won't pay for the abortion unless I know it's mine'. The Académie Française is right: a novel of manners about the family would be far too depressing.

72. Every day women who became pregnant while using contraception decide to keep the baby, not without telling all those around them that there was a contraceptive failure. When one knows what one wants, one can also cheerfully change one's mind. Women who use

contraception feel in control of themselves and when one feels self-assured, one can easily choose to follow a different and unexpected path.

73. This sometimes has effects on the next generation: when the mother has experienced panic at the idea that a pregnancy was imposed on her without any possibility for her to choose, one sometimes finds a similar anxiety in her daughter(s), which stops them from asking themselves what they want.

74. Long live bad kings, etc., says Mentor, in other words Athena, to the people of Ithaca (*The Odyssey*, book II).

75. 'The bones that took the pains for me' (Shakespeare, *King John*, Act I, scene I). The context is that of a character who is not very sure who his father was. Stating that, in any case, he is better-looking than his brother or half-brother, he thanks his father, whoever he may be, for having taken the (physical) trouble to engender him. So what about the trouble his mother took?

76. One often hears conservative-minded people complaining that modern women have been made virile because they vote, or have an interesting job, or no longer wear clothes that hinder their movement and so on. Strangely enough, this great contemporary fantasy has not yet mentioned the (only) phenomenon in relation to which it might have some credibility. When a couple employ a 'surrogate mother', the wife is, strictly speaking, in a man's position: she provides a 'little seed' and leaves the burden of carrying the embryo to someone else. Marx says somewhere that money destroys the distinction between having and being: I am impotent, but rich enough to have a carriage and make my horses gallop, thus I am not impotent, I am ugly, but my money enables me to buy the most beautiful woman in the world, thus I am handsome, and so on. The new reproductive techniques have similar effects: they enable a couple's wealth to transform a sterile woman into a fertile man.

77. Albert Jacquard's book *Eloge de la différence*, already cited, discusses this point with greater precision than I can do here.

78. It is taboo to assume that a newborn has its own unpredictable temperament and this maintains belief in the child's ontological dependency on its parents. Indeed there are two ways of denying this 'specific temperament': either one assumes that any innate elements are atavistic (so the temperament is not specific to the child, it is inherited from an ancestor whom one seeks to identify while looking into the cradle), or one assumes that a baby is a *tabula rasa* and thus the education given by the parents will be everything to it. In both cases, the child is 'owned' by the family and not seen as a person in its own right. It seems people want to see in a child only what they have put there and nothing more or different.

79. In some family planning centres, people show a most laudable concern to ensure that an adolescent girl's request for an abortion comes

from her and not from her parents. However, the legislation in no way encourages consideration of a minor as a person in herself. In principle, she can only have an abortion with the consent of her parents (as is the case for any surgical operation) but the opposite is also true: a very young woman has very little chance of carrying a pregnancy to term without her parents' consent, unless she has extraordinary strength of character and arguments. However, it could simply be decided that when a minor becomes pregnant, parental authority is automatically suspended and responsibility for the very young woman passes to the social services, at least for a period that would permit her to decide for herself and to find some way of providing for an independent existence. But there I go again, dreaming of a state that would serve individual fantasies, which might just as well be never to have children as to give birth to the first one at the age of twelve. No utopian has ever gone that far. And yet this ultra-utopianism seems entirely in keeping with common sense and an elementary respect for individual decision-making.

80. Genesis, 2, 24.
81. Othello is the archetypal despot manipulated by another person's insinuations. Anyone who grants himself the power of life and death over his wife is a toy in the hands of others. The lesser-known Claudio of *Much Ado About Nothing* is caught in the same trap.
82. *Le Paradoxe de la morale*, Paris, Le Seuil, 1981, p. 161.
83. Ibid., p. 165.
84. In this sense and this sense alone can one justify Lévinas's thesis that 'the feminine does not have access to morality'. See the First Notebook, section 3.
85. For fifteen years Jankélvitch was my very kind supervisor and friend. My youth owes a great deal to his liberalism and benevolence. While officially guiding me, he gave me my head, which was the kindest thing to do. When *Le Paradoxe de la morale* was published, I put to him the questions set out here. With the good humour he was known for, he said, 'Oh! You're got reservations!' and nothing more. Like Simone de Beauvoir, he left me with my questions. I think that, all in all, I have been very lucky in my intellectual life.
86. 'We cannot ripen to this freedom if we are not first of all placed therein. [...] The first attempts will indeed be crude [...] yet we never ripen with respect to reason except through our own efforts' (Kant, *Religion within the Limits of Reason Alone*, Theodore M. Greene and Hoyt H. Hudson trans., New York, Harper and Row, 1960, IV, 2, 4, note 1.
87. Cf. *Le Monde*, 1 August, 1987.
88. See also Robert Maggiori, *De la convivance*, Paris, Fayard, 1985.
89. Angela Davis's autobiography provides a few staggering examples.
90. The idea that men are born and remain free and equal under the law no longer figures in that of 1795, which instead contains a fine list of duties, including respect for the authorities, property and the family.

When people talk about human rights, it is prudent to start by asking what they mean.

91. Séverine Auffret, *Des couteaux contre des femmes*, Paris, Des Femmes, 1982. The year before, Renée Saurel published a book on the same issue, *L'Enterrée vive (Essai sur les mutilations sexuelles féminines)*, with a preface by Simone de Beauvoir, Geneva-Paris, Slatkine, 1981.

92. Colonization destroyed those elements of custom which were a nuisance to it and left intact those which did not get in its way. Present-day neo-colonialism continues in the same way: in Mali the cultivation of green beans (for export) is now being substituted for that of food crops, without anyone making a fuss. However, when humanitarian organizations try to fight against clitoridectomy, this is considered scandalous interference. Men who are having everything taken away from them must at least be left their traditional form of domination over women, from whom everything is also being taken away.

93. Cited by Louis Blanc, *Révolution française*, vol. II and from there by Flaubert in Bouvard and Pécuchet's *sottisier*.

94. Episiotomy is an incision into the perineum, performed in the last stage of labour. It can be justified when there is a risk that the perineum will tear as the child passes through it. It is sometimes also recommended when the woman intends to give birth to several children, since in the long term the repeated passage of children can damage the pelvic region. In the case of a woman with standard anatomy who fits the statistics (liable to give birth two or three times in her life), it is pointless. It is more or less painful at the time and is always so in the weeks after the birth. However, in many maternity units it is performed routinely, in other words in 100 per cent of labours, because it saves time for the medical team and makes their work easier.

For a long time it has been known that caesarian section is an absolute necessity in some cases. But does this explain why there are many times more caesarians per thousand labours in the United States than in England? ('I read it in a book, but I can't remember which one', as Alice would say). This is because in the United States medicine is about profit and a caesarian makes money, while in England it is performed on the National Health Service and is practically free. Perhaps this means that in England they go too far the other way and leave women and babies to suffer for a long time, in order to save money and in the name of the puritan belief that the good body restores itself. Among people I know in France, I have seen a strange increase in the number of caesarians since use of the epidural has become widespread, in other words since the presence of an anaesthetist has become common anyway. We should like to be certain that this is always justified by the health and comfort of the woman and baby, and not by the interests of the medical team. To tell the truth, I am beginning to fear the worst.

95. To the best of my knowledge, there have until now been very few

campaigns aimed at influencing public opinion, such as that carried out by the government in Burkina Faso.

96. Let us clearly state that clitoridectomy is absolutely unknown in some regions of Africa.

97. The book is called *Femmes en cause* (Paris, 1987). I must strongly criticize the iconography of this book. The publication of shocking photographs when one is discussing clitoridectomy amounts to blocking the reader's intelligence; it is thus an anti-educational procedure to say the least, as the FEN should have known. Moreover, these photographs show us nothing of either causes or effects and are liable to generate an idea of 'barbarism' and thus a 'block' rejection, whereas it is important to know why some regions practise clitoridectomy while others do not and why so called enlightened minds cannot approach the humanitarian issue raised by sexual mutilations in a simple and effective way.

98. The chief methodological fault of Anne Raulin's work is that she interviewed (in Paris) only women who had undergone clitoridectomy and not African women from neighbouring groups where clitoridectomy is not practised. She thus recorded the former's criticisms of the latter (they are not real women), and not the explanations that some Senegalese women, for example, could have given her concerning their neighbours. The result is that one infers an 'African point of view' on the question which in no way reflects the experience and thinking of millions of Africans. Should future ethnologists be obliged to take a course in induction? In principle, a well carried out induction begins with 'negative cases', in other words it delimits the outside of a phenomenon by establishing in which 'cases' it does not exist, and them tries to define what differentiates the cases where it does exist from those where it does not. But this project for disciplinary imperialism of philosophy over ethnology is unnecessary: many ethnographers are perfectly well aware of the methodological precautions required by the use of induction.

99. *Femmes en cause*, p. 97.

100. Lydie Dooh Bunya mentions the fact that European women undergo clitoridectomy and infibulation in their heads. Her extension of the concept accords with the idea that this is not a religious matter, but a consequence of the obligation to be faithful which, as she says, 'all women know'.

101. News that comes to us from China should be considered as quite possibly mythical. However, in an article by Michelle Loi, I read that workers are paid according to 'work points'. For reasons which the article's author does not really make clear (and which I am afraid to guess at), the maximum available to a woman is eight work points, while a man can acquire as many as ten. The result is that when a birth is announced in a village, they say either 'poor things, they've had a little eight', or 'lucky them, they've had a big ten'. The econo-

mic difference between adults has given rise to a language in which to talk about newborns. See Michelle Loi, 'Les Femmes chinoises et la quatrième corde', in *Questions féministes*, 1979, no. 6, p. 38.

102. See Simenon, *Maigret and the Lazy Burglar*, D. Woodward and R. Eglesfield trans., New York, Harbrace, 1983.

103. See Fourth Notebook, note 92.

104. See Diogenes Laertius, *Lives and Opinions*, vol. II, p. 32. He is discussing the portraits of the muses decorating the walls of a school.

105. Elena Gianini Belotti, *Du côté des petites filles*, Milan, 1974, (French translation, Paris, *Des Femmes*, 1974, chapter I, p. 40).

106. This issue must be raised at both the European level and that of various European countries. Imagine a baker's shop; the baker has the status of 'head of the business' and, of course, his wife keeps the shop. What is her status? Sometimes she has none (she is then regarded as a housewife, even if she works ten hours a day selling bread), sometimes she has the status of an employee in the family business. In the latter case, she is a contributor to the various forms of social insurance in European countries. If the baker's shop closes, does she have a right to claim unemployment benefits? Not in all European countries; in France she recently gained this right. And what about her pension? If she was not declared? And even if she was?

107. Odile Dhavernas, 'Inscription des femmes dans le droit', in *Le Féminisme et ses enjeux*, a collection of articles published by the Centre Fédéral of the FEN, Paris, 1988, p. 316.

108. Paul Thibaud, issue of *Esprit* cited, p. 90.

109. Jill Posener has published two books of photographs of graffiti: *Spray It Loud* and *Louder Than Words*, London, Pandora Press; she dedicates the second to the 'brave graffiti artists' whom she advises to find a lawyer before they give free rein to their creativity.

110. I shall return to the question of advertising (and the use it makes of idealized women's bodies) in the second volume.

111. This problem is monotonous and interminable. From time to time, studies are published showing the stupidity of books for teaching children to read ('Mummy is washing the clothes, Daddy is smoking his pipe'), grammar books ('John was thinking he must stand for Parliament', 'Susan thought she would have three children and five dogs': analyse the tenses of the verbs), and even the illustrations of physics textbooks (a boy repairs a record player, a girl causes a short circuit while ironing). Some years later, the curriculum is changed and new textbooks appear, followed by new studies. This time, Daddy is drinking beer, Mummy is laying the table, and nine out of ten history textbooks discuss the period 1800–1950 without mentioning the reforms of the Civil Code (such as the one in 1907 which allowed married women to have their own salaries paid to them), and without noting the existence of Louise Michel, Irène-Joliot-Curie, Rosa Luxemburg, Florence Nightingale and so on. But these are not their only

faults. It is time that the reading books also showed us second-generation Arab–French children, children from the Antilles and children whose parents come from Asia.

112. Tocqueville, *Democracy in America*, Henry Reeve trans., New York, Alfred A. Knopf, 1948, vol. I, p. 375.

113. Tocqueville cites Jefferson in a footnote: 'Nothing is more clearly written in the book of destiny than the emancipation of the blacks; and it is equally certain, that the two races will never live in a state of equal freedom under the same government, so insurmountable are the barriers which nature, habit and opinion have established between them' (ibid., vol I, p. 373n.).

114. Ibid, vol. I, p. 328.

115. *L'Ancien régime at la révolution*, Paris, Gallimard, 1967, pp. 50–1.

116. As Dhavernas points out ('Inscription des femmes'), the right of correction no longer exists. But parental power continues to exist legally in areas where it could become abusive.

117. Nira Yuval-Davis, 'The bearers of the collective: women and religious legislation in Israel' in *Feminist Review*, London, 1980, no. 4.

118. *Democracy in America*, vol. II, p. 227.

119. Ibid., vol. I, p. 379. (my emphasis).

120. Ibid., vol. II, p. 222.

121. Ibid., vol. II, p. 223.

122. Ibid., vol. II, p. 218.

123. We shall perhaps never have any statistics on this question: marriage will disappear first. On non-conjugal rape, the Greater London Council Women's Committee published a figure in 1986 which should be publicized as widely as possible: 54 per cent of reported rapes were committed by a man who was well known to the victim. Women are more likely to suffer violence from someone they know, and in their own home, than from a stranger in the street. The same issue of the *London Women's Handbook* says that 25 per cent of assaults recorded by the Metropolitan Police are inflicted by husbands on their wives.

124. Chamfort, *Maximes, pensées, caractères*, Paris, Flammarion, 1968, p. 218 (741)

125. See E. and R. Badinter, *Condorcet*, Paris, Fayard, 1988, p. 210.

126. 'Apologie du théâtre, ou analyse de la lettre de M. Rousseau à M. d'Alembert', in new edition of *Contes moraux*, The Hague, 1766.

Index

Abelard, Peter   163–4, 196
abortion   8, 20, 101, 124, 268–78;
    and contraception   264, 267,
    277; French law on   4, 246–7,
    272; pills (RU 486)   268–71;
    Simone de Beauvoir on   130,
    131
Académie Française   251–2, 253,
    298, 303, 315
Academy of Sciences, Paris   251
action, theory of   110
Adam complex: in Sartre   191–2
Adorno, T.   13, 213–14
advertisement posters   302, 303
Aesop   150
AIDS (Acquired Immune
    Deficiency Syndrome)   264,
    265, 266, 302
Algren, Nelson   125
altruism, doctrine of absolute   280
antisemitism: and silence   161
Antisthenes   22
Anytos   147, 154
appearance of philosophers
    156–7, 159
Arendt, Hannah   110
Aristipus of Cyrene   10, 198
Aristotle   7, 22, 40, 65, 172–3,
    176, 196
Atkinson, Ti-Grace   114
Auffret, Séverine   289, 290
Augustine, Saint   213

authenticity, ethics of   111
authors, sex of   158–60
autrui, notion of   190–1
Avicenna   258
axiology in philosophy   11–13

Bachelard, Gaston   43–4, 63, 80,
    108–9, 122, 162; appearance
    156–7
Bachelier, Mademoiselle   238–40
Bacon, Francis   44, 76, 80, 143,
    171, 172–3, 176, 213, 221
Bacon, Roger   44
bad faith   60, 64, 69, 70–4, 92–3,
    95, 97, 118, 165, 181, 257
balance of the sexes *see* sexual
    balance
Barre, Raymond   240
Barthes, R.   178
*Bases of the Metaphysics of Custom,
    The* (Kant)   143
battered women   281, 282
Bauer, Bruno   17–18
Baulieu, Etienne   270, 271
Beauvoir, Simone de   7, 79, 84,
    88–94, 96–9, 120–33, 151, 165,
    231, 243, 264; on abortion   130,
    131; on adulthood   226–7;
    books by   16; and existentialist
    morality   89–91; Heloise
    complex of   162–3, 164–5;
    Memoirs of a Dutiful Daughter

135–7, 149, 179, 227; mother of 125; philosophy in work of 95–9, 100, 170–1, 175–6; *Prime of Life, The* 138, 179, 189; and Sartre 45–6, 125, 136–40, 141–2, 149, 151, 176–80, 191–2; *see also Lettres au Castor . . .* ; *Second Sex, The*

Being and Nothingness (Sartre) 45, 58, 60–74, 79–82, 84–5, 91, 92, 98, 165, 207, 208, 261

Belotti, Elena 300, 307

Benveniste, Emile 166

Bergson, Henri 43–4, 53, 63, 168–9

Berkeley, George 67

Bernheim, Cathy 104

biology 77, 80, 116, 168, 175, 206

Bobard, Mademoiselle 231–2

bodies of philosophers 156–7, 159

Bossuet, J. 212

Bourdin, Martine 183, 184–5, 186, 187–8, 189

boys: upbringing of 126, 233, 234, 265, 300, 301, 307

Breton, ban on speaking 291

Brontë, Emily 106

Brunschvicg, Léon 135–6, 156

Bunya, Lydie Dooh 293, 294

Callicles 30, 31

Canguilhem, Georges 110

Carneades 147

Catholic church: and contraception 256–7; Sartre's portrayal of Catholics 71–2; and sexual equality 313–15

Cato the Censor 147, 154

Cau, Jean 81

Chamfort, N. 37, 313–14

Charles VI, King of France 237

chemistry 80

children, rights of 217–18, 219, 297

choice 11–12, 36, 121, 194; and feelings of inferiority 60–1; notion of 20–1, 23

Christians, Sartre's portrayal of 71–2

church, the *see* Catholic church

Cicero 29, 171, 174, 198, 199, 201, 202, 294

citizens' rights for women 3, 75, 216, 229

civil society: and the state 230, 233, 305; Tocqueville on 311

Cixous, Helene 115

Clairvaux, Bernard de 164

Cleanthes 15, 196

Cleobulus 148, 149, 150, 152, 196, 198

Cleodorus 149–50

clitoridectomy (excision) 21, 104, 287, 289–99, 301, 306

Colbert, Jean Baptiste 251

collective thought 122–3

community: and philosophers 202, 204

Comte, Auguste 10, 12, 49, 53

concrete means, idea of 98, 99, 108, 111

condoms 265, 267

Condorcet, M. 25, 237

Conrart, Valentin 252

contraception 20, 23, 57, 75, 101, 114, 124, 266–78; and abortion 264, 267, 277; advertising ban 264–5, 267, 302, 303; and the Catholic church 256–7; French law on 4, 219, 246–7, 272, 275; Simone de Beauvoir on 131–2

Cordier, Marguerite 129

Critique of Pure Reason (Kant) 40, 144–5, 147

cultural imperialism 291–2, 301

culture 213–15

Curie, Marie 79–80, 129, 144, 259

Daubié, Julie 243

daughters *see* girls

de facto solipsism 62, 63

death penalty 311

Deffand, Marie du 211–12, 213, 313–14
Delacroix, F. 38
Deleuze, Gilles 168
Delhomme, Jeanne 202
della Mirandola, Pico 191
Delphy, Christine 40, 120
demand, notion of 21–2
democracy 309, 311, 313
Democritus 136, 164, 169
denial in philosophy 173
Denys of Syracuse 10
Derrida, J. 167
Desanti 108
Descartes, René 65, 89, 99, 141, 143, 167, 171, 172, 182, 221, 225–6, 257, 258, 297
despotism 305, 311
Deudon, Catherine 225
Deutsch, Hélène 114
Dhavernas, Odile 301
dialectics: Adorno's principle of 13
dialogues 33–4
difference, feminism of 193, 222, 224–9
Dinner of the Seven Wise Men, The 149–50
Diogenes the Cynic 10, 299
discourses, philosophical 30–1
disorientation 220–4
dissidence, political 35
divorce: law in Israel 308
Dolto, Françoise 115, 289–90, 291
dominance, relations of: in Sartre 93–4
Dream (Kepler) 50
Drouet, Juliette 121
Dumézil, Georges 107, 251

Eastern bloc countries: and human rights 285, 288
Ecole Normale Supérieure 140
education: of girls 129, 142–5, 260–1, 299; right to 21, 213, 288

ego, the: in Descartes 99–100
employment of women: in France 243; in public employment 231–41, 244–5
ENA (National School of Administration) 244–5
Engels, F. 17, 117
ENSPTT (National School of Posts, Telecommunications and Broadcasting) 235–7, 238, 240
Epictetus 10, 69
epistemology 37
equal opportunities 124
equality: feminism of 222, 225, 229–30, 300, 301, 307; and reciprocity 279; and the state 306–9
erotography 208
Esprit (journal) 284–5, 287–8, 289, 290, 300, 301
ethics see morality
ethnocentrism 289, 291–2
ethnography 293–4
ethnology 39, 77
Eumètis-Cleoulina 148, 149–51
existentialism: and creativity 106; in The Second Sex 56, 57, 59, 60, 131, 133
Existentialism and Humanism (Sartre) 67, 71, 73, 181
existentialist morality 73, 89–91, 111
expressive behaviour 68

Fainzang, Sylvie 294
family structure 217–20; and the state 305–6
fathers: and daughters 295; and French law 277–8, 306
feminism of difference 193, 222, 224–9
feminism of equality 222, 225, 229–30, 300, 301, 307
FEN (Federation of National Education) 292–3, 294
Ferry, Luc 284–5, 287–8, 289
fools 9–10

For-itself: in *Being and Nothingness*
80, 82, 86, 87, 88, 91, 92; in *The
Second Sex* 58
Foucault, Michel 19, 24, 48–9
freedom: Sartre on 71, 72, 73,
181; in *The Sceptical Feminist* 35,
36; Simone de Beauvoir on 99,
112, 113–16; and the state 305,
306
French Revolution 16, 216, 263
Freud, Sigmund 15, 265
frigid woman: in *Being and
Nothingness* 62, 64–8, 70, 71,
115

geometry 30
Gilson, Etienne 163, 164
girls: attitude of prohibition
towards 145–7; education
129, 142–5, 299; and
mathematics 260–1; mothers
and daughters 260–1, 265, 307;
upbringing of 126, 146–7, 233,
234, 299–300; *see also*
clitoridectomy
Gouges, Olympe de 216, 217,
218, 219
Greece, Ancient 17, 46, 148,
149–51, 205–7; philosophers
9–10; Seven Sages of 198–9;
women philosophers among 5
Grouchy, Sophie de 314
groups: understanding of other
groups 74
Guillaumin, Colette 40

Habib, Claude 194
happiness: Aristotle on 7; in *The
Sceptical Feminist* 35; in *The
Second Sex* 112–13, 115
Hegel, G. x, 2, 12, 197, 214
Heidegger, Martin 285
Heloise complex 59–60, 162–5
Hintikka, Jaakko 59
Hipparchia 205, 206, 213, 225,
298

historians 42–3
history of philosophy 166–8
Hobbes, Thomas 78–9
hole, image of: in *Being and
Nothingness* 81–2, 84
Homer 231
housewives as unemployed
people 242
housework 92, 101, 131
human rights 284–99, 301
humanism: in Sartre 190,
191–2
Hume, David 73, 135, 261–3,
279, 281
Husserl, E. 99, 100, 109, 173–4
Huygens, C. 251, 252

Iff, Simone 245, 246
imaginary view of oneself 154
In-itself: in *Being and Nothingness*
80, 81, 82, 86, 87, 88, 91, 165; in
The Second Sex 58
indifferentism 118–19, 122, 130
intersubjectivity 263, 278, 279,
281; and sexuality 186
Iran 306–7
Irigaray, Luce 56, 115, 224
isonomy 229, 230, 281, 284, 285,
300, 307
Israel, 308

Jacquard, Albert 215, 228
Jankélévitch, Vladimir 22, 37,
110, 280, 284
Jehovah's Witnesses 297
John of Salisbury 178
John-Paul II, Pope 256
Johnson, Samuel x
judgements, non-reciprocity of
75–6
Jurgensen, Geneviève 287,
289–90
justice, ethics of 279, 281

Kandel, Liliane 40, 120, 230–1
Kant, I. 12, 18, 40, 53, 135,

143–5, 170, 214; *Critique of Pure Reason* 40, 144–5, 147
Kepler, J. 50, 152–3
Kierkegaard, S. 60

La Fontaine, Jean de 61
La Rochefoucault, F. 37
Laertius, Diogenes 148
Le Pors, Anicet 231
Leclerc, Annie 227
legal rights of Frenchwomen 128–9
Leibniz, G. 135, 170, 244, 255, 256
Lenclos, Ninon de 211
Leon of Phlius 200–1
Lescure, M. de 211, 313
Lespinasse, Julie de 314
Lettres au Castor et à quelques autres (Sartre) 177–9, 180, 182–6, 187–9, 192, 193
Lévi-Strauss, Claude 107, 108, 251
Levinas, Emmanuel 13, 107
Lévy, Albert 81
liberal societies 35
liberalism: and social roles 123–4
liberation theology 119
'Liberty, Equality, Fraternity' 95
local authorities: and the state 305, 306, 308, 315
Locke, John 15
looks, non-reciprocity of 75–6
Louis XIV, King of France 305

magazines, women's 103
Maggiori, Robert 285
Man, rights of 218–19, 263, 286–9
Mansfield, Katherine 106
Marion, Jean-Luc 18
Marmontel, Jean 315
Maronée, Esther 296, 298–9
marriage: and clitoridectomy 295–6, 298; and fidelity 265–6;

law in Israel 308; and philosophers 163, 164; and pregnancy 273, 277–8; and rape 311; Simone de Beauvoir on 113; versus social contract between man and woman 217–18, 219
Marx, Karl 15, 17, 60, 107, 279
masculine community of philosophers 5
masculinism 42–4, 78–9, 96, 97, 139, 165
Massot, Jean 233, 239
mathematics 10, 206; and girls 260–1
Memoirs of a Dutiful Daughter (de Beauvoir) 135–7, 149, 179, 227
Merleau-Ponty 23, 183
meta-reflexivity 76
metaphorics, philosophical 167
metaphysics 37; existentialist 111
Michel, Andrée 40, 132
Michel, Louise 127, 253
Mill, John Stuart 25
Milton, John 31
mixité see sexual balance
MODEFEN (Movement for the Defence of the Rights of Black Women) 293, 298
Montaigne, M. de 113, 152
Montesquieu, C. 15, 198, 215
morality: choice of ethics 278–82; of constant help 283–4; existentialist 73, 89–91, 111; in Mottini-Coulon 39–40; sexual, and the upbringing of girls 146–7
More, Thomas 31
mothers: and children 39; and daughters 260–1, 265, 307; and sexual morality 146–7; Simone de Beauvoir on 99, 130; and sons 265, 307; surrogate 276
Mottini-Coulon, Edmée 38–40
murder 282–3

Naples, Sartre in   180–1
narcissism, philosophical   25
negation, philosophy's power of
    17–20
Negative Dialectic, The (Adorno)   13
Newton, Sir Isaac   174
Nietzsche, F.   15, 166, 184
Nightingale, Florence   127–8
Niol, Mademoiselle   238–40
novel, the   128

objectivism   100
objectivity, notion of: in Sartre
    67
optimism: in Simone de Beauvoir
    125, 126, 127
Order of Things, The (Foucault)   49
orgasm, vaginal   114–15
Other, the   108, 109, 132, 133

parapsychology   258
Paris Academy of Sciences   251
Pascal, Blaise   69, 197
passive collaboration   282–4, 291
Pelletier, Monique   232
Pericles   249
Perrot, Michèle   40
personal experience: in feminist
    writing   47–8
Peslikis, Irene   32–3
Phenomenology of Mind, The
    (Hegel)   2
philosophism   26
physics   10, 77, 80, 175
Plato   30, 76, 77, 102, 168, 195,
    255; dialogues   40, 41
Plotinus   168
Plutarch   149, 150
political dissidence   35
politics: and philosophy
    110–11; and sexual balance
    248–9
Pompidou, Georges   237
pornocracy   208–9, 302
Portrait of a Lady, The (James)
    192–3

positivism   100
Praise of Difference (Jacquard)   215
pregnancies   268; and fathers
    277–8; surrogate mothers   276;
    unwanted   8, 129, 264, 272–8;
    see also abortion
primary school teachers: sexual
    balance   233–4, 240–1, 254–5
Prime of Life, The (de Beauvoir)
    138, 179, 189
'pro-life' movement   22
professional organizations   250–3
property, right to   286
prostitution, law on   245–6
Protagoras   195, 196, 197
Proudhon, Pierre   49
public employment, women in
    231–41, 244–5
Pythagoras   11, 23, 141, 198, 199,
    200, 201, 203

racism   12, 215, 257, 281, 283;
    and silence   161; and
    Tocqueville   310
Radcliffe Richards, Janet   32–7,
    38, 216
Rambouillet, Madame de   252
rape   228–9, 311, 312
rationality   23, 51
Raulin, Anne   293
reciprocity, notion of   108
Reich, Wilhelm   115
religion   20; *see also* Catholic
    church
Renaut, Alain   284–5, 287–8, 289
reorientation   198–207, 213, 215
Republic, The (Plato)   224, 255
resistance, capacity for   261–3
Richelieu, Cardinal   251, 252
rights: of children   217–18, 219,
    297; human   284–99, 301; of
    Man   218–19, 263, 286–9;
    notion of   20–2, 23; woman's
    right to choose   20, 21–2
Rodano, Marisa   47
Rodis-Lewis, Geneviève   138

Room of One's Own, A (Woolf) 16, 128
Roudy, Yvette 231, 245, 246
Rousseau, Jean-Jacques 14, 31, 51, 116, 146, 182, 197, 218, 286, 314, 315
Royal Institute of Philosophy, London 129–30

Same, the 109
Sand, George 122, 252
Sartre, Jean-Paul 176–95; on Christians 71–2; *Existentialism and Humanism* 67, 71, 73, 181; on freedom 71, 72, 73, 181; on Marxism and revolutionaries 110; and the seizure of *Tout* 207; and Simone de Beauvoir 45–6, 125, 136–40, 141–2, 149, 151, 176–80, 191–2; writings on women 62–71, 72–4, 84–9, 115, 164–5; *see also Being and Nothingness*
Saurel, Renée 289
Sceptical Feminist, The (Radcliffe Richards) 32–7
scepticism 17
Scheherazade 159
Scheler, Max 69
Schopenhauer, A. 197
science: and philosophy 109–10, 173–5
scientific research: and philosophy 198–200
Second Sex, The (de Beauvoir) 4–5, 41, 45, 55–60, 93, 112–16, 117–18, 122, 130–3, 165, 299; and the idea of concrete means 98, 111; influence of 170, 171; Introduction to 88, 138; and personal experience 47–8; on puberty 227; on self-assertion 27; Steckel in 65–6; and the Women's Movement 100–2, 106–8, 120–1, 123, 124–5
self-assertion 27, 29, 140, 153

self-criticism of philosophy 25–6
Seneca 212
Senghor, Léopold 251
Seton-Woolf, Judith 261
sexism 257, 281, 303; anti-sexist laws 301–2; in philosophy 12–13, 14, 44–5, 64, 162; and silence 161
sexual balance 248–51, 259, 301, 303, 309, 315; of teachers 233–4, 240–1, 254–5
sexual difference 225, 226; fixity of 160–1
sexual morality: and the upbringing of girls 146–7
sexual mutilation *see* clitoridectomy
sexual pleasure: and freedom 113–16; objective signs of 66–9, 69, 70, 71
sexuality 264–78; in *Being and Nothingness* 61–70, 79–82, 84–5; fidelity or multiple relationships 186–7; vaginal orgasms 114–15
sexually transmitted diseases 265, 267
Seyrig, Delphine 120
Shakespeare, William 144, 266; characters in 9, 10
slavery 7, 15
Social Contract, The (Rousseau) 116
social movements 215–16
social sciences: contrast of women with men in 49; feminist studies in 42
sociology 42, 77
Socrates 9, 10, 22, 29, 33–4, 41, 147, 151, 195–6, 197, 198–9, 200, 203, 206, 207, 212, 221, 224, 256
Solon 150, 151, 198
sons *see* boys
Spinoza, B. 37, 184, 206, 214, 274
state, the: and sexual equality 306–9, 315; Tocqueville on 305
status of philosophers 162–5

Steckel 55, 64–5
Stendhal 123
Strachey, Lytton 128
subject disciplines: and
philosophy 76–8
subjects, women as 100–1
Suchon, Gabrielle 94, 116, 206,
213, 314
suffragettes 16, 222
surrogate mothers 276
'symbolic', meaning of 295

taboos 294
teachers: of philosophy 142–5;
sexual balance 233–4, 240–1,
254–5
Thales 150, 198, 200, 212
Theophrastus 163
Third World countries: and
Western culture 21
Thomas, St 295
Tocqueville, A. de x, 107, 230,
304–5, 309–13
torture 290
totalitarian societies 35
Tout, seizure of 207, 208
trade unions 309–10
tradition, identification with 102
trans-subjectivity 28, 256, 257,
264, 278
Trautmann, Catherine 264
tribes 292–3

unemployment, and housewives
242
unilinearity in thought 171–2
United States 240, 243; and the
Rights of Man 287;
Tocqueville on 304, 310–11,
312; Women's Liberation
Movement 193–4
universalism, philosophical 40–1
universality 279, 281
Utopia (More) 31

vaginal orgasm 114–15
Védrine, Helene 106, 224
Veil, Simone 259
venereal diseases 265, 267
Viansson-Ponté, Pierre 132
Victoria, Queen 127
Vindication of the Rights of Women
(Wollstonecraft) 41, 122
violence 281; and passive
collaboration 282–4
Virgil 221
virginity 84
Vivès, L. x
vote, right of women to 253

Waves, The (Woolf) 106, 242–3
we, concept of: in philosophical
writings 16–17
Weill-Hallé, Lagroua 132
Western culture: and Third
World countries 21
Wollstonecraft, Mary 14, 16, 17,
30, 31, 122, 288
women as philosophers 10–11,
24–9, 155, 204; access to
philosophy 5–6; attitudes to
130; writings of 16–17
Women's Movement 16, 101,
103, 104–5, 213, 216; and
disorientation 220–4; and
philosophy 31–2; and Simone
de Beauvoir 100–2, 106, 131;
in the United States 193–4
Woolf, Virginia 16, 106, 122, 127,
128, 214, 242–3, 261
words, negation of 19–20
world, use of word: by Simone de
Beauvoir 132–3

Yourcenar, Marguerite 251
Yuval-Davies, Nira 308

Zélinsky, Anne 120